Veritatis Amicitiaeque Causa

Essays in Honor of Anna Lydia Motto and John R. Clark

Veritatis Amicitiaeque Causa

Essays in Honor of Anna Lydia Motto and John R. Clark

Edited by
Shannon N. Byrne
and
Edmund P. Cueva

Bolchazy-Carducci Publishers, Inc.
Wauconda, Illinois

General Editor
Laurie K. Haight

Cover Design
Charlene M. Hernandez

Cover Illustration
Garden Mural from Primaporta, first century A.D.
Photograph by Raymond V. Schoder, S.J.
from *Masterpieces of Greek Art*
By permission of Ares Publishers, Inc., Chicago, Illinois

© 1999 Bolchazy-Carducci Publishers, Inc.

Bolchazy-Carducci Publishers, Inc.
1000 Brown St., Unit 101
Wauconda, IL 60084 USA

http://www.bolchazy.com

Printed in the United States of America
1999
by Trade Service Publications

ISBN 0-86516-454-1

Library of Congress Cataloging-in-Publication Data

Veritatis Amicitiaeque causa : essays in honor of Anna Lydia Motto and
John R. Clark / edited by Shannon N. Byrne and Edmund P. Cueva.
     p.   cm.
  Includes bibliographical references.
  ISBN 0-86516-454-1 (pbk. : alk. paper)
  1. Classical philology. 2. Seneca, Lucius Annaeus, ca. 4 B.C.-65
A.D.—Criticism and interpretation. I. Motto, Anna Lydia.
II. Clark, John R., 1930-   . III. Byrne, Shannon N., 1959-   .
IV. Cueva, Edmund P., 1964-   .
PA26.M69V47 1999
880'.09--dc21   98-54835
                                                            CIP

TABLE OF CONTENTS

Preface..vii

Acknowledgments..ix

Some Published Works of
   Anna Lydia Motto and John R. Clark.....................................x

Herbert W. Benario
Augustus, Rome, and the Romans..1

Shannon N. Byrne
Maecenas in Seneca and Other Post-Augustan Authors...............21

John Scott Campbell
Pisspots and Pumpkins:
   Three Notes To The *Apocolocyntosis*...................................41

Edmund P. Cueva
The Art and Myth of *Cupid and Psyche*....................................53

Linda W. Rutland Gillison
Tiberius' Roman Retirement:
   Antecedents and Implications..71

Linda Jones Hall
Latinitas in the Late Antique Greek East:
   Cultural Assimilation and Ethnic Distinctions.......................85

George W. Mallory Harrison
Claudian *Castores*:
   Seneca and Crispus..113

Alexander MacGregor
Wine, Women, and What? Some Vices in Seneca's *De Ira*.........129

Mark Morford
The Dual Citizenship of the Roman Stoics 147

Hans-Friedrich Mueller
Imperial Rome and the Habitations of Cruelty 165

J. D. Noonan
ΜΗ ΧΕΙΡΩΝ ΠΑΤΡΟΣ:
    The Rising Generation in Euripides' *Heracleidae* 197

Michele Valerie Ronnick
Concerning the Plane Trees in Seneca's Twelfth Epistle 219

Jo-Ann Shelton
Elephants, Pompey, and the Reports of
    Popular Displeasure in 55 BC 231

W. Jeffrey Tatum
Roman Religion: Fragments and Further Questions 273

Daniel R. White
Seneca and the Empire of Signs 293

William E. Wycislo
Seneca's Second Exile:
    Seneca and the Romantics 321

PREFACE

Students and colleagues of Anna Lydia Motto have fond memories of her throughout her distinguished professional career, whether they recall time spent together at the American Academy of Rome, her tenure as President of the Classical Association of the Middle West and South, or have simply enjoyed the pleasure of her classroom presentations. Students of classical antiquity in general acknowledge the debt which our field owes to the learned and enlightening scholarship produced by both Anna and her husband, John R. Clark, whose passing deeply touched all who knew him. The essays gathered here provide a few of their students, colleagues, and admirers the opportunity to express gratitude for all that they have given to the teaching profession, to the formation of new scholars, and to scholarship. We are representative of a host of well-wishers, all of whom have benefited over the years from the contributions of this outstanding scholarly team.

John R. Clark, whose area of expertise is English literature, received his BA from Pennsylvania State University, MA from Columbia University, and PhD from the University of Michigan. Anna Lydia Motto received her BA from Queens College, MA from New York University, and PhD in Classics from the University of North Carolina, Chapel Hill. Anna has been Assistant Professor at Washington College and Alfred University, Associate Professor at Muhlenberg College and St. John's University, and Professor at Drew University, where she served as Chair of the Department of Classics. John has been Assistant Professor at Alfred University, Muhlenberg College, and City College of CUNY, and Associate Professor at Fordham University, Drew University, the University of Michigan, and New York University. Both John and Anna went to teach as Professors at the University of South Florida beginning in 1973, where John was Chair of the Department of English (1973-

1978), and Anna was Chair of the Department of Foreign Languages (1974-1978), and of the Department of Classics (1985-1992).

Both have been awarded numerous scholarships and fellowships throughout their careers, with Anna receiving one of the highest honors that Classics can bestow, the CAMWS Annual Award for Scholarship 1987-1988, complete with Ovatio (1989). One of the many talents to their credit is a knack for poetic translation of such poets as Horace, Catullus, and Martial. Their translations have appeared in scholarly journals over the years and greatly amused readers. In addition to scholarly articles, John has also published extensively in satiric fiction.

As the list of their joint publications shows, the bulk of their collective efforts focuses on Seneca, but, as the list also shows, the breadth of their knowledge extends into all areas of classical studies. Indeed, John's many publications on Swift, modern fiction, and teaching (to name a few) gain for him recognition as a true Renaissance man. Neither he nor Anna limited their research to Seneca, so the essays that appear here run the gamut of classical studies and range in time from the fifth century BC to Late Antiquity. Our indebtedness to the insight and inspiration of Anna and John is immeasurable, and we hope that this modest collection of essays begins to convey our appreciation for all that they have done and shared.

Shannon N. Byrne
Edmund P. Cueva

ACKNOWLEDGMENTS

If our table of thanks for financial contributions seems small, it is because of the generous support given by the University of South Florida. When George R. Newkome, Vice President of Research and Distinguished Research Professor, learned that we were putting together a collection of essays in honor of Anna Lydia Motto and John R. Clark, he immediately offered to furnish the funds necessary for bringing this project to publication. We therefore thank George R. Newkome and the Office of Research at the University of South Florida, and hope that other universities will wish to emulate such generosity and be as quick to honor their own.

At the University of South Florida we would also like to thank Sara M. Deats, Chair of the Department of English, C. Eugene Scruggs, Director of the Division of Languages and Linguistics, Christine Probes, Linda Hayes, and J. D. Noonan for their swift responses to our questions and inquiries. Thanks to Jean Alvares, Francis Dunn, George Harrison, Alexander MacGregor, Robert Murray, and Susan Shapiro for their help, and a very special thanks to John Rettig, whose tireless and cheerful efforts deserve their own recognition. We thank Herbert W. Benario for supplying the title of this volume. Thanks to Lou Bolchazy for his support, and to all the editors at Bolchazy-Carducci Publishers for their patience and advice, especially Laurie Haight, Allan Kershaw and Charlene Hernandez. Lastly, we thank Martin C. J. Miller at Ares Publishing for the cover photo.

SOME PUBLISHED WORKS OF ANNA LYDIA MOTTO AND JOHN R. CLARK

This brief survey of the scholarly works of Anna Lydia Motto and John R. Clark is by no mean exhaustive, but rather a sampling of their efforts throughout their long and productive careers. While all books published jointly or individually are given, only a selection of articles that they published together are presented. In addition to the articles listed below, each has published numerous articles alone, and these too have done much to further Classical and English Studies. A complete list of all their articles, however, would increase the number of pages five-fold. In the spirit of this collection, therefore, which is dedicated to both Anna and John, we list only articles that they published together.

Books by John R. Clark

Form and Frenzy in Swift's 'Tale of a Tub.' Ithaca, New York. 1970.
Satire. Special issue of *Seventeenth-Century News*. 1975.
Satire. Special issue of *Thalia*. 1982.
The Modern Satiric Grotesque. Lexington, Kentucky. 1991.

Books by Anna Lydia Motto

Seneca Sourcebook: Guide to the Thought of Lucius Annaeus Seneca. Amsterdam. 1970.
Seneca. New York. 1973.
Seneca: Moral Epistles. Chico, California. 1985.

Books by Anna Lydia Motto and John R. Clark

Satire—That Blasted Art. Anthology of World Satire. New York. 1973.
Senecan Tragedy. Amsterdam. 1988.
Seneca: A Critical Bibliography. Amsterdam. 1989.

Essays on Seneca. Frankfurt and New York. 1993.

Articles

1965

"*Per Iter Tenebricosum*: The Mythos of Juvenal 3." *Transactions of the American Philological Association* 96 (1965) 267–276.

1968

"*Paradoxum Senecae*: The Epicurean Stoic." *Classical World* 62 (1968) 37–42.
"Senecan Irony." *Classical Bulletin* 45 (1968) 611.

1969

"The Classics in Revolt." *Classical World* 62 (1969) 109–112.
"*Ise Dais*: The Honor of Achilles." *Arethusa* (1969) 109–125.

1970

"Ancients vs. Moderns: An End to the *Querelle* at Michigan." *Classical World* 64 (1970) 5–6, 9–10.
"*Epistle* 56: Seneca's Ironic Art." *Classical Philology* 65 (1970) 102–105.

1971

"*Et Terris Jactatus et Alto*: The Art of Seneca's *Epistle* 53." *American Journal of Philology* 92 (1971) 217–225.
"Idyllic Slumming 'Midst Urban Hordes: The Satiric Epos in Theocritus and Swift." *Classical Bulletin* 47 (1971) 39–44.

1972

"Senecan Tragedy: Patterns of Irony and Art." *Classical Bulletin* 48 (1972) 69–77.

1973

"*Descensus Averno* in Seneca's *Epistle* 55." *Classical Journal* 68 (1972–1973) 193–198.
"Dramatic Art and Irony in Seneca's *De Providentia*." *L'Antiquité Classique* 42 (1973) 28–35.
"Seneca's *Epistle* 57: A Journey to Wisdom." *Classical Bulletin* 49 (1973) 33–36.
"Seneca's Last Years." *Classical Outlook* 50 (1973) 76–79.
"Senecan Tragedy: A Critique of Scholarly Trends." *Renaissance Drama* 6 (1973) 219–235.

1974

"*Violenta Fata*: The Tenor of Seneca's *Oedipus*." *Classical Bulletin* 50 (1974) 81–87.

1975

"The Development of the Classical Tradition of Exile to Seneca." *Mosaic* 8 (1975) 109–115.
"*Ingenium Facile et Copiosum*: Point and Counterpoint in Senecan Style." *Classical Bulletin* 52 (1975) 1–4.

1978

"Gasps, Guffaws, and Tears: A Modest Defense of Sentimentality, Bathos, and Melodrama." *Thalia* 1 (1978) 61–70.
"Philosophy and Poetry: Seneca and Vergil." *Classical Outlook* 56 (1978) 3–5.
"Seneca's *Thyestes* as Melodrama." *Rivista di Studi Classici* 26

(1978) 363-378.
"'There's Something Wrong with the Sun': Seneca's *Oedipus* and the Modern Grotesque." *Classical Bulletin* 54 (1978) 41-44.

1979

"Anthologies of Satire in Print (1979), A Critical Bibliography." *Studies in Contemporary Satire* 6 (1979) 35-52.
"*Hic Situs Est*: Seneca on the Deadliness of Idleness." *Classical World* 72 (1978-1979) 207-215.

1980

"A Bevy of Negations Invades the Popular Arts." *Studies in Popular Culture* 3 (1980) 20-34.
"The Death of the Humanities and Other Atrocities." *Humanities In the South* 52 (1980) 1-4.
"Menippeans & Their Satire: Concerning Monstrous Learned Old Dogs and Hippocentaurs." *Scholia Satyrica* 6 (1980) 35-46.
"Moderns & Mordants, Revilements & Revivals." *Renaissance & Renascences in Western Literature* (1980) 6.

1981

"Cynical Hercules and the Contemporary Hero." *Classical Bulletin* 17 (1981) 65-69.
"*Maxima Virtus* in Seneca's *Hercules Furens*." *Classical Philology* 76 (1981) 101-117.

1982

"Art and Ethics in the Drama: Senecan 'Pseudotragedy' Reconsidered." *Illinois Classical Studies* 7 (1982) 125-40.
"Miming One's Way to Urbanity." *Notes on Teaching English* 10 (1982) 7-10.
"Skeleton in the Closet of Hades: Seneca's *Agamemnon* 766-768."

Classical Bulletin 58 (1982) 45–49.

1983

"Running Down and Dropping Out: Entropy in Modern Literature." *Studies in Contemporary Satire* 10 (1983) 9–22.
"Satiric Plotting in Seneca's *Apocolocyntosis.*" *Emerita* 51.I (1983) 29–40.
"Scholarship on Seneca's Prose: 1968-1978." *Classical World* (1983) 69-123.
"The Senselessness of an Ending: Comic Intrusions upon the 'Higher Seriousness.'" West Virginia University *Philological Papers* 29 (1983) 62–66.
"Volunteers to Necessity: Character in Seneca's *Agamemnon.*" In *From Pen to Performance: Drama as Conceived and Performed*, University of Florida Comparative Drama Conference Papers, ed. Karelisa V. Hartigan (Lanham, Md.: New York: University Press of America, 1983), 80–90.

1984

"Grotesquerie Ancient and Modern: Seneca and Ted Hughes." *Classical and Modern Literature* 5 (1984) 13–22.
"*Nefas*: The Way of the World in Seneca's *Troades.*" *Maia* 36.2 (1984) 157–163.
"The Progress of Cannibalism in Satire." *Midwest Quarterly* 25 (1984) 174–186.
"Seneca's *Troades*: Hecuba's Progress of Tribulation." *Estudios Clasicos* 26.2 (1984) 273–281. ("Apophoreta Philologica E. Fernandes-Galieno a Sodalibus Oblata")

1985

"*Fata Se Vertunt Retro*: Seneca's *Agamemnon.*" *Classical Bulletin* 61 (1985) 1–5.
"Mayhem and Corruption in Seneca's *Troades.*" *Classical*

Bulletin 61 (1985) 62–66.
"Seneca e il Paradosso dell'Aversitá." *Atene e Roma* 30 (1985) 137–153.
"Seneca's *Agamemnon* Tragedy Without a Hero." *Athenaeum* 63 (1985) 136–144.
"We're Entitled to a Title." *Arizona English Bulletin* 28 (1985) 61–64.

1986

"Intrusion, Obstruction, & The Self-Reflexive Narrator in So-Called Post Modern Literature." *Classical and Modern Literature* (1986) 31–37.
"Lucius Annaeus Seneca." In *Research Guide to Biography and Criticism Drama*, ed. Walton Beacham (Washington, D.C.: Research Publishing 1986), 558-563.
"Modern Gothic: The Satiric Grotesque." *Studies in Contemporary Satire* 13 (1986) 5–15.
"Paradox: Shocks and Jolts for Readers and Writers." *English Teaching Forum* 24 (1986) 44–45.
"Seneca." In *Critical Survey of Drama* (Foreign Language Series), ed. F. N. Magill (Pasadena, Calif.: Salem Press, 1986) vol 5, 685–694.
"The Uses of Parody and Excess in Composition." *Exercise Exchange* 31 (1986) 11–13.
"Write-and-Think to Write A-Right." *North Carolina English Teacher* 44 (1986) 30–32.

1987

"At War With Our Roots; Karel Capek Revisited." *Studies in Contemporary Satire* 14 (1987) 1–15.
"*Fluctus Varii*: Imagery In the Senecan *Agamemnon*." *Classical Bulletin* 63 (1987) 113–118.
"Funny Bones: The Deadly Laughter of the Grotesque." *Thalia* 9.2 (1987) 24–31.

"Irony in Senecan Tragedy." *West Virginia University Philological Papers* 33 (1987) 1–9.
"Paradox, Reversal & Mental Disorder in the Senecan *Troades*." *Classical Bulletin* 63 (1987) 99.
"Time in Seneca: Past, Present, Future." *Emerita* 55 (1987) 31–41.

1988

"Heraclitus and the Ambivalence of Greek Tragic Idealism." *Classical Bulletin* 64 (1988) 3–5.
"*Tenebrae* and the Wandering Spouses: Irony in Seneca's *Medea* 114–115." *Rheinisches Museum für Philologie* 131.iii–iv (1988) 338–342.
"*Tempus Omnia Rapit*: Seneca on the Rapacity of Time." *Cuadernos de Filologia Clasica* 21 (1988) 129–138.

1989

"Knaves and Fools in Senecan Drama." *Illinois Classical Studies* 14 (1989) 119–134.
"Writing to Climax in an Essay's Finale." *Statement* 25 (1989) 15.

1990

"The Art of Paradox in Seneca's *Epistle* 60." *Maia* 42 (1990) 47–50.

1991

"Gluttony & The Erosion of Heroic Ideals." *Classical and Modern Literature* (1991) 155–167.
"The Artistry of Seneca's *Epistle* 62." *Athenaeum* 79 (1991) 583–588.

Veritatis Amicitiaeque Causa

*Essays in Honor
of Anna Lydia Motto
and John R. Clark*

Augustus, Rome, and the Romans

Herbert W. Benario
Emory University

Annae Lydiae Motto, feminae philosophi Senecae peritissimae, hunc libellum de primo principe scriptum d. d. auctor.

More than two thousand years ago, on September 2, 31 BC, Octavian and Mark Antony met at Actium in one of the most decisive battles in the history of the world. When Antony fled, in company with the Egyptian queen Cleopatra, the century-long Roman revolution came to an end. Now, for the first time since Tiberius Gracchus challenged the hegemony of the senatorial aristocracy in government of the empire, there were no competing factions. Octavian stood alone, acknowledged master of the Roman world, with more than sixty legions and nine hundred warships under his command. His response to his opportunities is still a subject that evokes lively debate, but all will surely agree that the form of government that evolved during his many years of primacy was one of the most significant achievements of antiquity.

Survival had not been easy. Octavian's public life between the fateful Ides of March when Julius Caesar was murdered and the final triumph over Antony was full of hazard, marked by rivalries in which his own position was the seemingly less favorable one. When, in the spring of 44 BC, he returned to Rome from Apollonia in Illyricum to claim his inheritance, the fortune as well as the name of Caesar, his chances of successfully challenging Antony must have seemed slim indeed to all but his most sanguine supporters. Rejection of Caesar's son by Caesar's closest associate produced an unnatural tension among the late dictator's followers and veterans, and threw the young Octavian into the camp of the *optimates*, whose leading figures had slain Caesar or had rejoiced in the deed. Cicero obviously thought that he could use Octavian at least until Antony was destroyed and then routinely cast him aside: the young man was to be praised, honored, elevated or eliminated: *laudandum adulescentem, ornandum, tollendum* (*Fam.* 11.20.1). But Octavian was not to be so used; his political acumen was greater than his seniors had given him credit for, and the march on Rome, the demand for the consulate, reconciliation with Antony, and the triumvirate for the reestablishment of orderly government followed in rapid succession. Now realistic battle lines were drawn, those for Caesar on the one side, his assassins and enemies on the other. Octavian was just twenty years old.

Yet Antony proved almost more dangerous as an ally than he had been as an opponent. Major credit for the victory over the "liberators" Brutus and Cassius in October 42 at Philippi accrued to Antony, and the subsequent division of responsibilities took him to the east for operations against Parthia, while Octavian was left in Italy with the thankless tasks of confiscation of property and settlements of veterans, violent opposition by Antony's brother and wife, and the constant threat of Sextus Pompey's band of republicans, or band of pirates. No matter what he did, Octavian could not fail to offend someone.

But his personal *felicitas* did not fail him. Himself physically frail and militarily a novice, he had attracted to his cause men whose talents supported and complemented his own, Maecenas, Agrippa, Statilius Taurus, and, until blinded by ambition or misjudgment, Salvidienus Rufus. His first test came when Antony's brother and wife rose against him at Perugia; he suppressed their revolt in February 40. This first breach between Antony and Octavian was healed (so it was thought) by the agreement reached at Brundisium the following autumn. The threat posed by the young Pompey was temporarily removed by the pact of Misenum in mid 39. Neither settlement endured long, and at Tarentum in spring 37 the two dynasts strengthened their own forces for the elimination of Sextus Pompey as well as for the defeat of Parthia. Octavian would obtain greater safety from the former, Antony greater glory from the latter, and, if all had gone as planned, Antony's prestige would have risen enormously, as the avenger of Crassus' disaster and death at Carrhae in 53.

Again, expectations were baffled. Antony's relationship from 41 on with Cleopatra, whom he had known since she was a teenager in the 50s, and his own disastrous venture against Parthia in 35, which almost brought a repetition of Crassus' debacle, caused his popularity and *auctoritas* to wane. In the meantime, Octavian, less glamorously perhaps but more effectively, consolidated his position. The defeat of Sextus Pompey in 36 by a fleet built and commanded by Agrippa freed Italy of the constant danger of famine. Octavian's newly-won military renown was confirmed by campaigns in Illyria from 35 to 33; the picture of the Roman general of old, successful in the field, gradually swung favor to him. The pendulum shifted; by skillful management of public opinion, Octavian made himself appear as the champion of the civilization of the west against the perils rising from the degenerate east and a renegade Roman. Although he had been consul in 43 and 33, he held no office in 32. Nevertheless, he maintained his position in the state without triumviral powers or any magistracy, relying on the enthusiasm which culminated in the *coniuratio Italiae*, the oath of all Italy to him as its patron. It was as leader of *tota Italia* and the western provinces that he sailed against Antony in late summer of 31. As Vergil was later to write:

hinc Augustus agens Italos in proelia Caesar
cum patribus populoque, penatibus et magnis dis.
(Aen. 8.678–679)

On this side is Augustus Caesar, leading the Italians into battle, with the senate and the people, the household gods and the great ones.

The victory at Actium has been equated with the end of freedom at Rome. Such a statement must, of course, indicate what freedom actually was, and must recognize that different periods and different circumstances altered the definition of *libertas*. But, even in the narrowest sense, it is surely too strong a statement to argue that the triumph of Actium sounded the death knell for individual liberty. Was it not more precisely the reverse?

Tacitus, in the prooemium of his *Historiae*, divides the 820 years of Roman history through the year AD 68 into two periods separated by the battle of Actium, but he does not state that the end of freedom of speech coincided with the battle. Literary talent did not disappear after 31; on the contrary, there followed a renaissance of achievement that is rightly called a golden age. Tacitus says as much in the beginning of the *Annales*, when he states *temporibusque Augusti dicendis non defuere decora ingenia* (1.1.2). Freedom had ceased much earlier, perhaps in the dictatorship of Caesar, perhaps in the entire period of the successive *dominationes* beginning with Marius. *Libertas* is not easily equated with the five successive consulates of that great man. This was the view of Cassius Dio, writing some two and a half centuries after the events, who divided Roman history down to 29 BC into three periods, the kings, the republic, and the δυναστεῖαι. Octavian did not destroy the freedom of the Roman state; rather, over a period of years, he rebuilt much of the traditional and revered fabric of that state. In this enterprise, he was assisted not only by the general weariness of the Roman people and their yearning for peace, by astute associates like Agrippa and Maecenas, by literary giants such as Vergil and Horace who were not paid to propagandize but expressed, in heartfelt tones, their appreciation of a new day, but also by his own perceptive insight into human nature, his respect for tradition, and a peculiar kind of genius for compromise, which permitted him to succeed where men of far greater natural gifts, Sulla and Caesar, had failed.

The impact at Rome and in Italy of the triumph over the forces of barbarism and the east was somewhat muted by the fact that Octavian did not return to Rome for almost two years. The ultimate conclusion of the republic's last civil war was signified by the grand triple triumph that he celebrated in mid-August 29, commemorating his achievements in Illyricum, at Actium, and in Egypt. Vergil recorded the event, giving it place of high import on the shield of Aeneas in book eight of the *Aeneid* (714–723):

> at Caesar, triplici invectus Romana triumpho
> moenia, dis Italis votum immortale sacrabat,
> maxima ter centum totam delubra per urbem.
> Laetitia ludisque viae plausuque fremebant;
> omnibus in templis matrum chorus, omnibus arae;
> ante aras terram caesi stravere iuvenci.
> Ipse sedens niveo candentis limine Phoebi
> dona recognoscit populorum aptatque superbis
> postibus; incedunt victae longo ordine gentes,
> quam variae linguis, habitu tam vestis et armis.

> But Caesar, having entered the walls of Rome in triple triumph, dedicated his vow to the Italian gods, a vow which would endure forever, three hundred very great shrines throughout the whole city. The streets echoes with joy and games and cheering; in all the temples were choruses of mothers, in all were altars; before the altars slain bullocks covered the ground. He himself, sitting on the snow-white threshold of gleaming Phoebus, reviews the gifts of the peoples and attaches them to the haughty doorposts; the conquered races pass by in a long column, as varied in their languages as they are in the appearance of their dress and in their weapons.

Many significant monuments in Rome and Italy underscored the launching of a new era. One of the most revealing was the arch, now known as the Actian arch, constructed just northeast of the Temple of Castor and adjacent to the Temple of the Deified Julius, similarly dedicated in this year, that helped transform the eastern end of the Forum into an area evoking the greatness of the *gens Iulia*. The only previous arch in the Forum had been the modest Fornix Fabianus, built in 121 BC by Q. Fabius Maximus to commemorate his victory over the Allobroges. Spanning the Via Sacra at the eastern end of the Regia, it was now obliterated from view for those in the main part of the Forum by the impressive, almost theatrical appearance of Caesar's temple and the young Caesar's arch. The divine ancestry of the ruler of the world and his *virtus* in public life were irrevocably suggested by these two monuments.

Whether this arch had an inscription on its attic is uncertain. A dedication, found nearby, is generally assigned to it; the date fits, and the reason for the building of the monument, *re publica conservata*, justly expresses the emotions of the time and parallels coin slogans. But no inscription was really necessary, for the mere fact of its existence told a large story. Part of this story may well have been to suggest that, unlike many of the dynasts who had preceded him, Octavian was content with an honor that was republican in the best sense of the word without seeking legal prerogatives such as had accrued to Sulla and Caesar. He did not desire the title of *dictator*; he rather wished to be respected because of who he was and what he did, and in this sense one may find a certain antecedent for his aspirations in the careers of the two Africani. Did Livy have Augustus in mind (and Caesar too, perhaps, in contrast?) when he wrote, not too many years after the battle of Actium, of the first Africanus' rejection of the title of king when it was offered him by the Spaniards? These words have a remarkable relevance to the political climate of the thirties and twenties: *regium nomen alibi magnum, Romae intolerabile esse; regalem animum in se esse, si id in hominis ingenio amplissimum ducerent, tacite iudicarent, vocis usurpatione abstinerent* (27.19.4–5).

After the battle of Naulochus in 36 BC, which brought the career of Sextus Pompey to an end, Octavian was, for the first time, free to show his real character. "By temperament he was moderate, conservative, and prudent. Whether he was calculating, or whether for the first time he was following his natural inclination, certain it is that from this time on Octavian maintained his position of patriotic citizen devoted to the best interests of his country. He was aware of the prejudices against him, of his own lack of personal magnetism for the multitude of men. His instinct for power was not military but distinctly civil, and he believed that in devoted attention to the restoration and preservation of the republic lay his only chance for real service to the state or for making and preserving for himself a position of dignity and influence among his fellow men."[1] The very existence of the arch gave witness to the efficacy of his wielding of *imperium*, to his overriding *dignitas*, to the extent of his *auctoritas*.

In the last years of the decade of the thirties, Octavian was subjected to vitriolic abuse by Antony and his partisans. But Antony's actions in the east made him a ready target for more meaningful criticism. The construction of the huge mausoleum in the northern reaches of the Campus Martius in the late thirties was surely not begun in anticipation of an early death, but rather as a Roman answer to Antony. The latter had laid himself open to charges of *externi mores* and *vitia non Romana* chiefly because of his expressed desire to be buried in Alexandria, in the company of the Egyptian queen. Octavian chose a final resting place for himself which recalled, not the great tumuli of the Troad, but the burial mounds of the Etruscans, who had played such an important role in the early history of Rome and had helped mold her political and social institutions. The immense structure would remind everyone that, unlike Antony, Octavian and his family would be buried in Rome, between the river Tiber and the Via Flaminia. As early as 28 BC, further, he opened the area around it as a public park; its wooded regions and walkways were now consigned to the people's enjoyment.

Almost a score of years later, Augustus had the opportunity to expand "his" complex in the Campus Martius, and his response to it was unparalleled in the urban history of the city. In 13 BC, he returned to Rome after an absence of three years in Spain and Gaul; the senate decreed the consecration of an altar of peace, of the Augustan peace. The famous *ara pacis Augustae* was dedicated in

[1]Slaughter 111.

9 BC. But simultaneously with its construction there was laid out the largest solarium the ancient world ever saw. This enormous undertaking, along with the altar and the mausoleum, made the entire northern part of the Campus uniquely Augustan.

For this monument, which would continually benefit the *populus Romanus*, he imported an obelisk from Heliopolis in Egypt to serve as the *gnomon*. The inscription on the pedestal shows that it was set up in 10 BC; it is of red granite, stands some seventy feet high, and is covered with hieroglyphics. The sun dial was formed by laying an extensive pavement of white marble on the north side of the obelisk; on the pavement the lines were indicated by strips of gilt metal inlaid in the marble. Figures of animals represented the signs of the Zodiac. The marble pavement extended about 120 yards in an east-west direction and a bit more than half that distance north and south.

Portions of the pavement were found at various times in the fifteenth and sixteenth centuries but were again covered over. The obelisk, which had been toppled, was discovered in pieces in 1512, but not excavated until 1750 nor set up once again until 1792, when it was given place of honor in the Piazza Montecitorio, where today it still stands, in front of the Palazzo which houses the Chamber of Deputies of the Italian Republic.

A small segment of this huge solarium, about half the size of St. Peter's Square, was rediscovered in recent years by the extraordinary archaeological sleuthing on the part of Edmund Buchner of the German Archaeological Institute in Rome, who, under extremely difficult conditions, was able to bring a very small portion to light and then to explain the significance of the monument in relation to the others which commemorated Augustus. The solarium was so laid out that, on September 23, the birthday of the *princeps*, the shadow produced by the obelisk passed precisely through the central opening of the west facade, the front of the *ara pacis*. With the mausoleum to the north, altar and sundial produced a triangle of Augustan monuments. The enormous park, about twice the size of St. Peter's Square, of which they were a part, had everywhere specific links with the emperor. The Roman people enjoyed this *rus in urbe* because of his almost divine achievements, because of the stability promised by the dynastic nature of the mausoleum, and because of the peace for which he had been responsible.

When Antony and Cleopatra were dead, Octavian must surely have begun to think, in the years 30 and 29, of the nature of the political settlement that he would institute, so that the state could be freed of the last vestiges of triumviral rule and be returned to orderly government. With the conclusion of the triumphal festivities of 29, serious work went on apace, with the result that the year 28 and the month of January 27 were perhaps the most significant thirteen months of his long reign. For in that period the pattern of the principate was established, his overriding position in the commonwealth put into a new and different focus, and his relation to his fellow citizens underscored.

In the *Res Gestae*, written near the end of his life, the emperor claimed that, in his sixth and seventh consulates, the years just mentioned, after he had become master of the state following the termination of civil war, he transferred the commonwealth from his own power to the jurisdiction of the senate and people: *in consulatu sexto et septimo, postquam bella civilia exstinxeram, per consensum universorum potitus rerum omnium, rem publicam ex mea potestate in senatus populique Romani arbitrium transtuli* (34.1). Whatever interpretation *res publica* and *arbitrium* bear here, I certainly think that his claim was an accurate one and that the great majority of the people and the ruling class believed him. Velleius Paterculus, the soldier-historian who served under Tiberius, called Augustus *conditor conservatorque Romani nominis* and spoke of the return of the old type of government, *prisca illa et antiqua rei publicae forma revocata* (2.60.1; 2.89.4). But a return to the chaos of the late republic—*non mos, non ius*—was unthinkable; anarchy was now finished, and lawful government took its place.

For this truly significant renunciation of power, on January 13, 27 BC, Octavian received rewards as indications of trust and gratitude, both tangible and intangible. Three days later, he was honored with the name Augustus, an appellation that set him apart from the rest of mankind. He received an extended *provincia* to govern which comprehended most of the armed might of the empire and which put at his disposal a large portion of its revenues. The door posts of his home were decked with laurel; the *corona civica*, Rome's highest military distinction *ob civis servatos*, was affixed above his doorway; a shield was placed in the senate house, which announced to all the world that it had been presented to him *virtutis clementiaeque et iustitiae et pietatis caussa*. This is the well known *clupeus virtutis*, which was to play an important role in the history of imperial virtues. Where was the prime emphasis in the first years of the *princeps* Augustus?

It has long been recognized that these four virtues have their origin in the cardinal virtues of the Greeks, wisdom, justice, fortitude, and moderation. But they are different, a Roman statement for a particular occasion. The general belief is that *pietas* is the most important of the Augustan virtues, because it is the final one in the listing. But I should like to argue that in the political and emotional climate of 27 BC, *virtus* is the dominating excellence, which allows the emperor to display the others. These virtues, having rescued Rome from the foreign enemy, were requisite to preserve the empire in the days of peace.

A replica of the shield, dedicated at Arles in southern France the following year,[2] lists the virtues without connectives and expands *pietatis* by the addition of the phrase *erga deos patriamque*. Yet, in the *Res Gestae* (34.2), Augustus links the last three with the word *et* but joins *virtus* to the group that follows with *-que*. Is this only for stylistic variation, or does the emperor underscore the importance of *virtus* by making it the first member in what is substantially a pair? *Clementia* and *iustitia* are clearly subordinate and tend to be absorbed by *virtus* and *pietas* respectively, so that the prime qualities throughout the first two centuries of the empire are *virtus* and *pietas*.

---

[2]Pictured in Kähler, pl. 119, bottom.

The recitation of the *virtutes* on the replica should not affect interpretation of Augustus' own words. In Arles, emphasis is consciously placed upon *pietas*, with the additional words *erga deos patriamque*. Important as *pietas* always was, it most appropriately receives prime emphasis in a statement of allegiance and devotion on the part of the provincials in a year when the *princeps* is in Spain and may, indeed, have visited Arles on his journey thither the year before.

In 27, however, *virtus* must have overshadowed *pietas*, for it underlies all Augustus' services to Rome. It had been through *virtus* as displayed in the field of battle that he had reached his present preeminence; it was by *virtus* that he could hold out to the empire the hope and expectation that the current peace would long endure. Without *bellica virtus* and its attendant *victoria*, there would not be, to quote the elder Pliny (*NH* 27.1.3), the *immensa Romanae pacis maiestas*. Surely it was not merely coincidental that the shield was placed in the Curia Iulia—the very name of the building recalled Augustus' unique ancestry and position—where, only two years before, he had placed a statue and altar of the goddess Victoria, a statue that came to symbolize the immortality of the empire. Further, *Victoria* and *Virtus* are the most prominent among the "Virtues" of the Emperor, both closely associated with Jupiter and therefore especially applicable to his viceregent on earth.

Numismatic evidence supports this view. It is *virtus* that has primary importance on coins, with representations of the shield designated, in a kind of shorthand, as CL V. *Virtus* is the quality before the public eye. *Victoria* was a conception which had been no stranger to republican coinage; *Pax* was something of a newcomer—an ironical reflection upon later republican history. From the beginning of the principate onwards they were to become strictly complementary conceptions. Only victory could precede peace, and no peace could endure without the future guarantee of victory. Thus they had achieved a primary status among the "virtues" inherent in and operating through a *princeps*: without them no government could stand firm and no empire survive.

Cassius Dio was well aware of the relationship between *pax Augusti* and *victoria Augusti* when he wrote of the ceremonial honors of 27 being conferred upon Augustus as "perpetual victor over his enemies and savior of his citizens." Victory, Mars Ultor, and the *clupeus virtutis* appear together as the symbols of successful foreign policy.

These honors looked backward and forward, like the two-faced god Janus. Augustus was to have great success and joy in his dealings with other peoples, as well as disaster and sorrow. In the *Res Gestae* (26.1–4), he rightly trumpeted his achievements:

> Omnium provinciarum populi Romani quibus finitimae fuerunt gentes quae non parerent imperio nostro fines auxi. Gallias et Hispanias provincias, item Germaniam, qua includit Oceanus a Gadibus ad ostium Albis fluminis pacavi. Alpes a regione ea quae proxima est Hadriano mari ad Tuscum pacificavi nulli genti bello per iniuriam inlato. Classis mea per Oceanum ab ostio Rheni ad solis orientis regionem usque ad fines Cimbrorum navigavit, quo neque terra neque mari quisquam Romanus ante id tempus adit, Cimbrique et Charydes et Semnones et eiusdem tractus alii Germanorum populi per legatos amicitiam meam et populi Romani petierunt.

> I extended the boundaries of all provinces of the Roman people which had neighboring tribes who were not subject to our empire. I made peaceful the provinces of the Gauls and Spains, and likewise Germany, a territory which stretches from Cadiz to the mouth of the river Elbe. I made peaceful the Alps from the Adriatic coast to the Tuscan Sea, bringing war against no people unjustly. My fleet sailed through the Ocean from the mouth of the Rhine to the east as far as the territory of the Cimbri, whither no Roman had penetrated before this time, neither by land or by sea, and the Cimbri and Charydes and Semnones and

other Germanic peoples of that region requested my friendship and that of the Roman people through legates.

There is much else, dealing with other parts of the empire, which I pass over here, save to mention the recovery from the Parthians, in the year 20 BC, of the legionary standards lost by Crassus, an event of high political import which was commemorated as the central scene on the cuirass of the great statue of Augustus as *imperator* from Prima Porta and which was celebrated by a new arch in the Forum. We focus now upon the western provinces and the northern border of Italy. With his conquests in Spain, in the Alpine region, and along the entire Danube frontier, he added more territory to Rome's empire than either Pompey the Great or Julius Caesar before him.

Spain had become Roman after the second Punic War against Hannibal, and two provinces had been formed as early as 197 BC. But to establish peace and dominion among these recalcitrant tribesmen proved a long and difficult task, which had required the talents, among many commanders, of Scipio Aemilianus, Pompey, and Caesar. In the mid twenties Augustus campaigned against the Cantabri, but these obstinate foes were not finally broken until Agrippa defeated them in 19 BC.

Gaul remained peaceful, with few exceptions, in the generations following Caesar's conquest, but communication between Italy and Gaul remained difficult and hazardous because Rome did not control the passes of the Alps. Bitter warfare joined with diplomacy to pacify this forbidding territory, with the establishment of a colony called Augusta Praetoria, now Aosta, the conquest of forty-four tribes, and the visible declaration of mastery in the arches of Aosta and Susa and the extraordinary Alpine trophy, the *tropaeum Alpinum*, high above the sea on the heights near Monaco.

Similar success in Germany proved elusive. Augustus had planned to conquer the territory between Rhine and Elbe, which would have produced a much more defensible border against the tribes of *Germania libera*. But initial success could not be consolidated, and in the year AD 9 the aged emperor's hopes were dashed, when three legions were led into an ambush in the Teutoburg Forest by the inept Publius Quinctilius Varus and destroyed. The numbers of these legions, XVII, XVIII, and XIX, were never again employed, and the name of their conqueror, Arminius, joined those of Hannibal and Cleopatra in the pantheon of Rome's greatest and most fearsome opponents. But his victory was more devastating than even Hannibal's had been, for Arminius fundamentally changed Roman policy, causing the emperor and his successors to be content with what was essentially a Rhine frontier. In his despair, Augustus wandered around his residence, banged his head against the walls, and cried out repeatedly, *Quintili Vari, legiones redde* (Suet. *Aug.* 23.2).

But this misfortune came late in life, long after his reputation had been secured. His life and achievements exemplified *virtus*, and *virtus* is a subject foremost in the minds of Vergil and Horace. The latter emphasizes it frequently throughout the Odes, particularly in the "Roman Odes" and the fourth book. Vergil gives at least as much emphasis to the warrior Aeneas as to the symbol of *pietas*, to the extent that some discern an unsatisfactory tension between the claims of *pietas* and the requirements of *ferocia* in war. Yet if, as seems fair, Aeneas does represent Augustus, he must display both, *virtus* primarily in his relations with men, *pietas* especially in his relations with the gods, his father, and Pallas. The two qualities support each other, they do not contradict each other. Anchises puts it very plainly to Aeneas, after describing the future birth of *Augustus Caesar, divi genus* (*Aen.* 6.792):

> et dubitamus adhuc virtutem extendere factis,
> aut metus Ausonia prohibet consistere terra?
> (Aen. 6.806–807)

and do we hesitate to extend our valor by our deeds, or does fear prevent our settling in the Ausonian land?

It is by *bellica virtus* that Rome will bring war to an end, establish peace, and rule an empire. To Vergil, and to the Roman people, that moment in time had at last come with Augustus:

> tu regere imperio populos, Romane, memento
> (hae tibi erunt artes), pacique imponere morem,
> parcere subiectis et debellare superbos.
> (*Aen.* 6.851–853)

> You, Roman, remember to rule the peoples with thy sway
> (these will be your arts), to impose civilization upon peace,
> to spare the humbled and to crush the proud.

The great monuments of Augustus' reign display this tension between war and peace; *virtus* won the former and protected the latter. The *fasti* on the second arch in the Forum, the so-called Parthian arch of 19 BC, recorded the names of the consuls and *triumphatores* of the past, legendary and historical, and the statues present in the Forum of Augustus, with their *elogia*, emphasized the martial greatness of the Roman people. Apollo received his sumptuous home on the Palatine in large part because of his active support at Actium in the ultimate struggle against Antony. Mars, god of war, standard bearer of *virtus*, in the role of *Ultor*, representative of *pietas*, was housed in a magnificent temple in the new imperial forum. Yet perhaps the most Augustan achievement of the entire principate was the Ara Pacis, an altar not only of peace but of the Augustan peace. Mars and Pax must live together, each at the service of the other. Peace's finest memorial was located on the Field of Mars, in a form which recalled the *ara Martis*, itself located nearby, and completed the Augustan complex of parkland and monuments which produced an almost mystic sense of Augustus' remarkable person and achievements.

Octavian had differed from his predecessors and contemporaries in the long period of internal strife because he was able to gain the support of the people as the one last hope for the establishment of an enduring peace. Personal honors accrued as his ability to bring this about became ever more evident. *Auctoritas* was his because he possessed the *virtutes* mentioned on the shield; *imperium* enabled him to win and maintain peace. In the last analysis, one could not exist without the other, as Augustus himself implied in the *Res Gestae* 34.3:

> post id tempus auctoritate omnibus praestiti, potestatis autem nihil amplius habui quam ceteri, qui mihi quoque in magistratu conlegae fuerunt.
>
> After this time I excelled all in influence, but I had no more power than others who were my colleagues in each magistracy.

The gradual development of the principate continued for another quarter century after the settlement, and culminated, in 2 BC, with the honorary title of *pater patriae*. Granted that some members of the aristocracy remained recalcitrant in their acceptance of the primacy of one man, the *populus Romanus* and the provincials embraced the new form of government with alacrity. Augustus was able to win the all-important battle for men's minds, and he also had the extraordinary luck, after a sickly youth and young manhood, to outlive most of his contemporaries. As Tacitus put it, in AD 14:

> iuniores post Actiacam victoriam, etiam senes plerique inter bella civium nati: quotus quisque reliquus, qui rem publicam vidisset? (*Ann.* 1.3.7)
>
> The younger men had been born after the victory at Actium, even most of the older men had been born in the times of the civil wars: how few were left, who had seen the free republic?

The triumph of Octavian led to the establishment of the principate of Augustus. The latter did not destroy individual *libertas*; it changed the focus of that freedom. *Principatus* could protect liberty equally as much as *consulatus* had done in the heyday of the free commonwealth. Tacitus put it to the great credit of Nerva that he had brought together two concepts once incompatible, *principatus ac libertas* (*Agr.* 1.3.1); the same claim can be made for Augustus. Stability of government had been totally absent in the chaos of the late republic; Augustus hoped that his great achievement would prove to have been precisely this stability:

> Ita mihi salvam ac sospitem rem p. sistere in sua sede liceat atque eius rei fructum percipere, quem peto, ut optimi status auctor dicar et moriens ut feram mecum spem, mansura in vestigio suo fundamenta rei p. quae iecero. (Suet. *Aug.* 28.2)

> Thus it may be permitted me to establish the state, safe and sound, on its own foundation and to reap from this thing the fruits, which I seek, so that I may be called the founder of the best form of government and that I carry with me, when I am dying, the hope that the foundations of the republic will remain on the footings which I shall have laid.

This indeed he succeeded in doing; the new principate survived for many generations of men before it underwent significant change. He accomplished this, further, with the affection and approval of almost all the empire, as exemplified by the tribute of the Alexandrian sailors whom he passed in the gulf of Puteoli at the very end of his life, *per illum se vivere, per illum navigare, libertate atque fortunis per illum frui* (Suet. *Aug.* 98.2).

Think what one will of the activities of the young Octavian and the power politics that were employed against Antony and afterwards, the tribute of one of this century's greatest Roman historians, Sir Ronald Syme, must carry the day: "For power he had sacrificed everything; he had achieved the height of all mortal ambition and in his ambition he had saved and regenerated the

Roman People."[3] Augustus was without doubt the foremost man, the *princeps*, of all Roman history up to his day; his achievement has not lost its greatness in the centuries since.

BIBLIOGRAPHY

Benario, H. W. 1975. "Augustus Princeps." *ANRW* II.2:75–85.
—. 1975. "Octavian's Status in 32 B.C." *Chiron* 5:301–9.
Benario, J. M. 1960. "Book 4 of Horace's *Odes*: Augustan Propaganda." *TAPA* 91:339–52.
Buchner, E. 1982. *Die Sonnenuhr des Augustus*. Mainz.
Carter, J. M.1970. *The Battle of Actium. The Rise & Triumph of Augustus Caesar*. London.
Chilver, G. E. F. 1950. "Augustus and the Roman Constitution 1939–1950." *Historia* 1:408–35
Earl, D. 1968. *The Age of Augustus*. New York.
Hammond, M. 1968. *The Augustan Principate in Theory and Practice during the Julio-Claudian Period*. (with Appendix *The Augustan Principate 1933–1967*, 335–386). New York.
—. 1965. "The Sincerity of Augustus." *HSCP* 69:139–62.
Kähler, H. 1958. *Rom und seine Welt*. Munich.
Kaiser Augustus und die verlorene Republik. 1988. Berlin.
Kienast, D. 1982. *Augustus. Prinzeps und Monarch*. Darmstadt.
Kraft, K. 1967. "Der Sinn des Mausoleums des Augustus." *Historia* 16:189–206.
Millar, F. and E. Segal. 1984. *Caesar Augustus. Seven Aspects*. Oxford.
Petzold, K.-E. 1969. "Die Bedeutung des Jahres 32 für die Entstehung des Prinzipats." *Historia* 18:334–51.
Raaflaub, K. A. and M. Toher, eds. 1990. *Between Republic and Empire. Interpretations of Augustus and His Principate*. Berkeley and Los Angeles.

[3] Syme 524.

Richardson, L., Jr. 1992. *A New Topographical Dictionary of Ancient Rome.* Baltimore.
Rowell, H. T. 1962. *Rome in the Augustan Age.* Norman, OK.
Ryberg, I. S. 1966. "*Clupeus Virtutis.*" In *The Classical Tradition. Literary and Historical Studies in Honor of Harry Caplan*, edited by L. Wallach, 232–38. Ithaca, NY.
Salmon, E. T. 1956. "The Evolution of Augustus' Principate." *Historia* 5:456–78.
Simon, E. 1986. *Augustus. Kunst und Leben in Rom um die Zeitenwende.* Munich.
Slaughter, M. S. 1925. "The Character of Augustus." In *Idem, Roman Portraits*, 103–28. New Haven.
Starr, C. G. 1969. "Horace and Augustus." *AJP* 90:58–64 = *Idem*, 1979. *Essays on Ancient History*, 241–47. Leiden.
—. 1956/57. "How Did Augustus Stop the Roman Revolution?" *CJ* 52:107–12 = *Idem*, 1979. *Essays on Ancient History*, 222–27. Leiden.
—. 1955. "Virgil's Acceptance of Octavian." *AJP* 76:34–46 = *Idem*, 1979. *Essays on Ancient History*, 228–40. Leiden.
Sutherland, C. H. V. 1951. *Coinage in Roman Imperial Policy 31 B.C.-A.D. 68.* London.
Syme, R. 1958. "*Imperator Caesar*: A Study in Nomenclature." *Historia* 7:172–88 = *RP* 1:361–77. 1979. Oxford.
—. 1939. *The Roman Revolution.* Oxford.
Timpe, D. 1962. *Untersuchungen zur Kontinuität des frühen Prinzipats. Historia Einzelschriften* 5. Wiesbaden.
Wallace-Hadrill, A. 1981. "The Emperor and his Virtues." *Historia* 30:298–323.
Wells, C. M. 1972. *The German Policy of Augustus. An Examination of the Archaeological Evidence.* Oxford.
Wickert, L. 1974. "Neue Forschungen zum römischen Principat." *ANRW* II.1:3–76.
Witte, B. 1963. *Tacitus über Augustus.* Münster.
Zanker, P. 1987. *Augustus und die Macht der Bilder.* Munich.

Maecenas in Seneca and Other Post-Augustan Authors

Shannon N. Byrne
Ball State University

There is no ancient biography on Maecenas. Information about his life, political career, and literary activities is found scattered throughout the works of ancient authors, usually in contexts that have nothing to do with Maecenas himself. No comprehensive biography can be obtained from these sources, though an analysis of them can elucidate certain aspects of his life. One interesting fact emerges: the majority of ancient authors record information about Maecenas without criticism. Only his prose writings receive unanimous criticism, and rightly so, judging from the few surviving fragments. Ancient historians in particular discuss Maecenas' service to Augustus during the civil wars and his role as an adviser, often in connection with Agrippa and often with praise. Matters pertaining to his private conduct, when they are raised at all, are stated as fact. Velleius Paterculus' single and brief mention of Maecenas, which occurs within the context of Lepidus' conspiracy against Octavian, represents the type of information about Maecenas most often related by ancient historians, and the chance manner in which that information is presented:

> Erat tunc urbis custodiis praepositus C. Maecenas equestri, sed splendido genere natus, vir, ubi res vigiliam exigeret, sane exsomnis, providens atque agendi sciens, simul vero aliquid ex negotio remitti posset, otio ac mollitiis paene ultra feminam fluens, non minus Agrippa Caesari carus, sed minus honoratus—quippe vixit angusti clavi plene contentus—nec minora consequi potuit, sed non tam concupivit. (2.88.2)

There was then in charge of the city guards C. Maecenas, born of an equestrian but illustrious family, a man who, when circumstances demanded vigilance, was most alert, foreseeing and capable of action, but as soon as he could relax from business he would fall into leisure and effeminacies almost more than a woman; he was no less dear to Augustus than Agrippa, but did not hold high office—for in fact he lived fully content within the narrow stripe [of the equestrian order]— he could have achieved as many honors, but he did not so desire them.

The salient points of this description are that Maecenas performed his duties as Octavian's representative admirably, remained a knight though he could have pursued a senatorial career, and spent off-hours indulging in pleasure. The first and second points are well attested in ancient literature.[1] The third point was no secret, though it does not preoccupy the narratives of ancient authors. Apparent signs of Maecenas' notorious decadence, such as his passion for his freedman Bathyllus, his innovative and short-lived fad of eating young donkey meat at banquets, his supposed love of gems, and his warm-water swimming pool, do not seem to have provoked outrage or much notice in antiquity. Seneca is the only ancient author to make an issue of Maecenas the voluptuary, and his relentless vituperation is responsible for most of the unsavory information taken for granted about Maecenas today. In the absence of supporting evidence, readers should exercise caution before accepting Seneca's criticism at face value. Seneca's comments on Maecenas had no influence on later ancient authors

---

[1]Ancient sources on Maecenas' efforts on behalf of Augustus include Plin. *NH* 37.10; Tac. *Ann.* 3.30.2–3, 6.11, 14.53; Plut. *Ant.* 35; App. *BC* 4.52, 5.51, 5.92, 5.99; Dio 49.13, 51.3, 54.30, 55.7; see also Watson 98–104. On Maecenas' decision to remain an *eques*, see Tac. *Ann.* 3.30.2–3; Dio 49.16.2, 55.7.4; Porphyrio on Hor. *Sat.* 1.6.98, *Od.* 1.20.5; Ps. Acro on Hor. *Od.* 1.20.6; 3.16.20; see also Cresci 169–76. All translations that appear in this essay are my own.

except for Martial and Juvenal, who found Seneca's Maecenas ripe for satire, and Tacitus, who used Seneca's Maecenas to enhance his own damaging portrait of the principate.

Few references to Maecenas occur in post-Augustan literature before the time of Nero, perhaps not surprisingly as so little literature survives from these years. Velleius and the elder Seneca mention him, and though neither has much to say, the few details furnished in their accounts form a respectable impression. Velleius' brief description of Maecenas cited above suggests the topos of a man of action who wins approval for his keen political command in public as well as for private excesses. The first of this kind to impress the imagination of writers was Alcibiades, and the type quickly became a popular subject of literature. Maecenas himself may have been aware of this type and purposely tried to flaunt the image.[2] In any case a tendency towards private indulgence was not the main focus of Velleius' attention, but rather the swiftness (*mira celeritate*) and discreet action (*nullaque cum perturbatione aut rerum aut hominum*) with which Maecenas thwarted Lepidus' conspiracy (2.88.3).

The elder Seneca mentions Maecenas five times in his *Controversiae* and *Suasoriae*, and, unlike his son, he nowhere indicates that Maecenas was distasteful or morally lacking. On the contrary, the elder Seneca finds Maecenas' wit amusing and records several of his *bon mots*, such as the use of Homer's description of Diomedes on a rampage to describe a man who declaimed in both Latin and Greek: "you could not know which side the son of Tydeus was on."[3] Several references show Maecenas quoting from and defending Virgil's poetry (*Suas.* 1.12; 2.20). On one occasion the elder Seneca suggests that Maecenas had mischief in mind when the orator Latro was delivering a speech against *nobiles* who adopted children born of obscure parents (*Contr.* 2.4.12–13). Augustus at the time was preparing to adopt Agrippa's children by Julia.

---

[2] Griffin (1977) 21–22 and (1985) 39–40.
[3] Sen. *Contr.* 9.3.14: Τυδείδην δ' οὐκ ἂν γνοίης, ποτέροισι μετείη (*Il.* 5.85).

Maecenas, Agrippa, and Augustus were in attendance at Latro's declamation, and Maecenas gave a signal to Latro to cut his speech short. Some believed that Maecenas did this as an insult to call attention to Agrippa's obscure parentage. Whatever Maecenas' motives, Seneca's point was that the quality of free speech in the days of Augustus was remarkable, since Latro suffered no repercussions for his *faux pas*.

Despite the fact that the favorable comments of Velleius Paterculus and the elder Seneca are the only references to Maecenas until the time of Nero, certain scholars nevertheless argue that slanderous material against Maecenas was in constant circulation both before and after his death.[4] The main reason for this belief is the elaborate defense of Maecenas' reputation and character found in the *Elegiae in Maecenatem*. The *Elegiae in Maecenatem* are two poems of anonymous authorship and unknown date joined together as if one continuous poem and included in the *Appendix Vergiliana*. The scope of this paper does not allow for a discussion on when and why the *Elegiae in Maecenatem* might have been composed, and even if it did the matter would remain unresolved. I am convinced by the arguments put forth by Schoonhoven and others that the poems were products of the rhetorical schools, date to the late Neronian or Flavian period, and were written specifically in response to Seneca's attacks on Maecenas,[5] which, as we shall see, also caught the attention of Martial, Juvenal, and Tacitus. They contain no information that cannot be gleaned from the Augustan poets, and the points chosen for defense match Seneca's attacks too closely to be coincidental. The *Elegiae in Maecenatem* certainly do

---

[4]For example, the younger Seneca cites a work of Maecenas that an interpolator entitled *De cultu suo* (Lunderstedt 85–86). Because of the title the work has been explained as Maecenas' attempt to defend himself against critics of his lifestyle, just as Antony's *De ebrietate sua* was written to counter accusations of excessive drinking (André 105 n. 5; Bardon 17; Courbaud 62–63). We are not sure, however, that the title *De cultu suo* is correct, and the lines quoted by Seneca in no way suggest a theme of defense. Given the style and tone of the fragments, it has been suggested that the work was a Menippean satire; see Hirzel 6.

[5]Schoonhoven 39–68; see also Axelson 23–24; Steele 3–5.

not provide proof that hostile attacks on Maecenas had always existed. On the contrary, if historical or rhetorical sources of a critical nature were in circulation before Seneca, they leave no trace.[6]

Seneca's attacks on Maecenas are among his worst character assassinations, including those against Mamercus Scaurus and Hostius Quadra.[7] The criticism, which starts around 62,[8] is consistent: Maecenas was ruined by his own good fortune. In most instances Seneca links weaknesses and faults of Maecenas' character to those found in his writing style, as in *Ep.* 19.9, where

---

[6] Nicastri (296–98) sees proof of on-going slander against Maecenas in Labienus' declamation against Bathyllus (Sen. *Contr.* pf. 10.8), an actor whose fame endured long after his death and a freedman of Maecenas. If Maecenas was an object of slander through Bathyllus, the elder Seneca, Tacitus, and Dio, all of whom mention Bathyllus in connection with Maecenas, are strangely silent on the matter. Nicastri also cites an obscure quote of Cassius Severus supplied by the grammarian Charisius: *Cassius Severus ad Maecenatem "gausapo purpureo salutatus"* (Gr. L. I, 104 K). One of Maecenas' many faults, according to the younger Seneca, was his bizarre fashion sense, and Nicastri interprets Severus' comment as part of a long-standing polemic against Maecenas' style of dress. Charges of effeminate attire were commonplace attacks in Rome, if in fact Severus' words constitute an attack. The word describes a cloth of heavy wool (Lucil. 598; Hor. *Sat.* 2.8.11); cloaks of this material began to appear towards the end of the first century BC and were practical protection against the cold, which is probably why Augustus himself made use of the garments (Char. Gr. L. I, 104 K; see also Sebesta and Bonfante 69–70). By the mid-first century AD, garments of this heavy wool can be lavish (see Pers. 6.46; Petr. 21.2; 28.4), but even Seneca wore them (*Ep.* 53.3). The quote that Charisius cites may in fact be from Severus' insolent books (*procacibus scriptis*), which maligned distinguished men and women and caused Severus to be exiled c. AD 12 (Tac. *Ann.* 1.72.3), but Severus was a prolific orator and writer (Sen. *Contr.* 3 pf.), and without a context it is rash to assume the quote is an attack or refers to Maecenas' own style of dress.

[7] According to Seneca, Mamercus Scaurus became consul despite the fact that he drank menstrual blood (*ancillarum illum suarum menstruum ore hiante exceptare, Ben.* 4.31.3). The story about Hostius Quadra and the magnifying mirrors in his bedroom is found in *NQ* 1.16.

[8] Seneca mentions Maecenas on two separate occasions before 62 without a hint of criticism in *Ben.* 4.36.2 and 6.32.2–4. *De Beneficiis* dates to c. 58/59; see Motto 10.

Seneca exhorts Lucilius to withdraw from the business of politics or risk ending up with a writing style as poor as that of Maecenas: "that man was talented and would have provided a great example of eloquence, if good fortune had not enervated, or rather castrated him" (*ingeniosus ille vir fuit, magnum exemplum eloquentiae daturus, nisi illum enervasset felicitas, immo castrasset*).

Seneca cites a poem of Maecenas in *Ep.* 101.11 that appears to be a plea for life regardless of the worst physical ailments:

> Debilem facito manu, debilem pede coxo,
> tuber adstrue gibberum, lubricos quate dentes:
> vita dum superest, bene est; hanc mihi, vel acuta
> si sedeam cruce, sustine.

> Make me weak in hand, weak in twisted foot,
> throw a hump upon my back, shake loose my teeth:
> while life exists, it is well; sustain this for me,
> even if I should sit upon the sharp cross.

An analysis of these verses would require more space than can be allotted here.[9] What is important is the vehement attack that this poem inspires in Seneca, who chastises Maecenas for having a temperament so weak that he would choose to live under appalling circumstances rather than face death. A good Stoic, Seneca often expresses admiration for men who bravely choose death when life becomes too burdensome, and scorn for those who fear death.[10] For example, Seneca denounces Junius Brutus' cowardly pleas for life as an assassin prepared to slit his throat: "'I will offer my throat,' he said, 'thus let me live.' What madness is it to flee, when you cannot go back? 'I will offer my throat,' he said, 'thus let me live.' He almost added, 'even under Antony.' O man worthy of being

---

[9] West provides an especially keen and witty discussion of this poem.
[10] See *Ep.* 70.10; 77.8.

surrendered to life!"[11] Seneca's contempt for Maecenas' supposed fear of death is harsher and longer than any of its kind, as each line is paraphrased and faulted along with its author's character.

> Quod miserrimum erat, si incidisset, optatur et tamquam vita petitur suplicii mora. Contemptissimum putarem, si vivere vellet usque ad crucem: "tu vero" inquit "me debilites licet, dum spiritus in corpore fracto et inutili maneat; depraves licet, dum monstroso et distorto temporis aliquid accedat; suffigas licet et acutam sessuro crucem subdas." (*Ep.* 101.11)

> He desires a thing that would be most wretched, if it had happened, and a delay of suffering as if it were life. I would think him most contemptible if he wished to live to the point of crucifixion. "You indeed," he says, "can cripple me, provided breath remains in my broken and useless body; you can contort me, provided a little time is granted to me in my unnatural and twisted state; you can nail me on a cross and put under me a sharp cross to sit upon."

The tirade continues with a string of rhetorical questions indicating outrage and disbelief, one of which asks what such effeminate verses can possibly mean (*quid sibi vult ista carminis effeminati turpitudo?*). The intensity of this criticism is startling.

The main theme of *Ep.* 114 is that a man's *oratio* is a reflection of his *vita*, and in this case Seneca resumes his invective against Maecenas' lifestyle and writing style (4–8, 20–22). Everything about Maecenas' *vita* can be inferred from his *oratio*, including how he walked (*ambulaverit*), his effeminacy (*delicatus*), and his exhibitionism (*vitia sua latere noluerit*). "He would have been a

---

[11]Sen. *Ep.* 82.12: "*praebebo,*" *inquit,* "*ita vivam.*" *quae dementia est fugere, cum retro ire non possis?* "*Praebebo,*" *inquit,* "*ita vivam.*" *paene adiecit:* "*vel sub Antonio.*" *o hominem dignum, qui vitae dederetur!*

man of great talent if he had kept to a more upright path, if he had not avoided being understood, if he had also not been diffuse in his speech" (*Ep.* 114.4). Seneca quotes examples of Maecenas' prose, then continues his scathing critique of Maecenas' character:

> Non statim, cum haec legeris, hoc tibi occurret, hunc esse, qui solutis tunicis in urbe semper incesserit? Nam etiam cum absentis Caesaris partibus fungeretur, signum a discincto petebatur. Hunc esse, qui in tribunali, in rostris, in omni publico coetu sic apparuerit, ut pallio velaretur caput exclusis utrimque auribus, non aliter quam in mimo fugitivi divitis solent? Hunc esse, cui tunc maxime civilibus bellis strepentibus et sollicita urbe et armata comitatus hic fuerit in publico spadones duo, magis tamen viri quam ipse? Hunc esse, qui uxorem milliens duxit, cum unam habuerit. Haec verba tam improbe structa, tam neglegenter abiecta, tam contra consuetudinem omnium posita ostendunt mores quoque non minus novos et pravos et singulares fuisse. Maxima laus illi tribuitur mansuetudinis: pepercit gladio, sanguine abstinuit nec ulla alia re, quid posset, quam licentia ostendit. Hanc ipsam laudem suam corrupit istis orationis portentosissimae deliciis: apparet enim mollem fuisse, non mitem. Hoc istae ambages compositionis, hoc verba transversa, hoc sensus miri, magni quidem saepe, sed enervati dum exeunt, cuivis manifestum facient: motum illi felicitate nimia caput. (*Ep.* 114.6–8)

Does it not at once strike you when you read these words that this was a man who always marched around the city in loose-fitting tunics? For even when he was performing the duties of Caesar in the latter's absence he gave his seal in a state of undress. Does it not strike you that this was a man who appeared on the bench, the rostra, and at every public meeting with his head concealed by a Greek cloak that left his ears sticking out on both sides just like a rich man's runaway slave in mime? That this was a man who, at a time when civil war was raging and the city was anxious and in arms, was attended in public by two eunuchs, both more manly than he was? That this was a man who married a thousand times, though he only had one wife? These words, arranged so perversely, cast down so negligently, set up so contrary to custom, show that his character likewise was no less strange, depraved, and singular. The greatest praise is given to him for gentleness: he spared the sword, abstained from bloodshed and he did not display his power in any matter other than his wantonness. He ruined this praise with his unnatural sports of style: for he appears to have been soft, not mild. This fact is proved by those windings of composition, transferred words, and strange meanings which often seem great but end up weak: his head was turned by too much good fortune.

The wearing of loose-fitting tunics or Greek attire, an act of sheer effeminacy, was a common slander against one's enemies among Romans.[12] However, this is the first time in extant sources that a penchant for strange dress is attributed to Maecenas, and the only time it is mentioned in prose, though, as we shall see, the image is twice picked up by later poets. More important, this is the first and only time in extant sources that Maecenas' management of Rome during the civil wars is directly criticized, the first and only mention of his fondness for eunuchs, the only time he is faulted for marital problems, and the only time the genuineness of his clemency is questioned, a quality which Dio (55.7.3–4) found particularly praiseworthy, but which Seneca here attributes to effeminacy. All of these faults are betrayed in Maecenas' literary style, and both his unsavory habits and writing style, according to Seneca, are due to the fact that "his head was moved by too much good fortune" (*motum illi felicitate nimia caput*). Seneca next talks about faulty

---

[12]See Richlin 92–93.

styles and how they spread, and touches upon a few other authors by name whose faults lie mainly in carrying imitation of predecessors too far (*Ep.* 114.9–19). He then returns to his thesis that style is the man, and that affectations such as oddly shaved beards, perversely colored cloaks, and see-through togas are faults characteristic of men desperate for attention, a class for which Maecenas serves as paradigm: "Such is the style of Maecenas and of all the others (*talis est oratio Maecenatis omniumque aliorum*), who err not by accident but knowingly and willingly" (*Ep.* 114.20).

The idea that Maecenas was overwhelmed by good fortune appears also in *Prov.* 3.9–11, though this time writing style is not an issue. Seneca explains to Lucilius that real evils do not befall the good man, but only things that seem to be evil, and Fortune purposely seeks out the brave to see if she can break the most resolute. Seneca lists six men, Mucius, Fabricius, Rutilius, Regulus, Socrates, and Cato among those who successfully resisted the evils of Fortune (*Prov.* 3.4–9).[13] Fortune was unable to harm Regulus the Punic War hero because he submitted willingly to his sufferings, and thereby became an example of faith and patience. Maecenas, on the other hand, was so withered by pleasure and so busy struggling with good fortune (*voluptatibus marcidum et felicitate nimia laborantem*) that he could not endure the daily repudiations of his wife, Terentia. He had to search for sleep by means of symphonies, wine, and running water (*Prov.* 3.10). Seneca is comforted by the thought that most men would still prefer to be born a Regulus than a Maecenas, and adds that anyone who admits that he would rather be born a Maecenas really admits that he would rather be born a Terentia (*Prov.* 3.11).

Of the six men in *Prov.* 3.4–9 whom Seneca holds up as great resisters of Fortune, only Regulus and Rutilius are matched with opposites. Rutilius is paired with L. Cornelius Sulla Felix, who recalled Rutilius from exile. Rutilius, however, did not heed the

[13]Many of these men appear together elsewhere in Seneca's works in recognition of their endurance to trials and tribulations and their impervious resolve against the attacks of Fortune; see *Ad Marc.* 22.3; *De Beata Vita* 18.3; *De Tranq.* 16.1 and 4; *Ep.* 67.7.

summons because he could not condone Sulla's slaughter. In this case the antithesis is between contemporaries, and the contrast between the seemingly *felix* Sulla and the not at all *infelix* Rutilius results in a meaningful pun. Less effective is his pairing of Regulus, a senator, military leader, and war hero with Maecenas, an *eques* who spent most of the 30s and 20s BC managing Rome while the civil wars were being waged. Admittedly the two are opposites in terms of character, but the differences in the times they lived, their ranks, and political pursuits do not make for as clever a contrast as in the case of Rutilius and Sulla. The same criticism against Maecenas that appears three times in the *Epistles* is raised: his head was turned by too much good fortune (*nimia felicitate*). Whatever caused Seneca to pair Maecenas with Regulus, he seemed eager to remind the reader that Maecenas' character was flawed, and that in particular he could not deal with good fortune.

Proof that Seneca had come to detest Maecenas is again evident in *Ep.* 92.35. Here Seneca portrays the Soul personified as discoursing eloquently on the uselessness of man's concern for the body after death. He then writes "Maecenas eloquently says 'I care nothing for a tomb. Nature buries those left behind'" (*diserte Maecenas ait: nec tumulum curo. sepelit natura relictos*). As if to correct himself, Seneca quickly adds, "You would suppose that a man of principles had said this. Indeed he did have strong and manly natural talent, except he became lax with good fortune" (*alte cinctum putes dixisse. habuit enim ingenium et grande et virile, nisi secundis discinxisset*). Seneca cannot allow himself a kind word for Maecenas. Works written in the last three years of his life show that Seneca's contempt for Augustus' minister became second nature, as seen in the discussion on the evils of inconsistency in *Ep.* 120.19–20, where Seneca gives Maecenas a passing slight in the observation that some men vie with Licinus in wealth, Apicius in dining, and Maecenas in pleasures (*Licinum divitiis, Apicium cenis, Maecenatem deliciis*).

Around the time that Seneca's criticism intensified, praise for Maecenas as a patron of literature—a role prose authors never discuss—was becoming a common theme among poets. The principate of Nero is marked by a revival of interest in Augustan literature, and for poets in need of support Maecenas at this time comes to symbolize the ideal patron.[14] For example, the author of the *Laus Pisonis* ends his lengthy plea for patronage with the poignant and suggestive observation that Virgil, Horace, and Varius might never have become famous had Maecenas not opened his door to them and protected them from poverty in their old age (230–245). The poet prays that Piso will be his Maecenas (*tu mihi Maecenas*) and provide support in exchange for verses (246–248).[15] Calpurnius Siculus alludes to Maecenas in *Ecl.* 4.152–163, where the poet Corydon hopes Meliboeus will pass his poetry along to the emperor, and so be to Corydon what Maecenas was to Virgil.[16]

According to Martial, there are no contemporary poets of the quality and genius of Virgil, Horace, and Varius because there are no generous patrons like Maecenas (see 1.107; 8.56; 11.3). When Martial retires to Spain in the last years of his life, he finds his Maecenas, whom he praises with sentiments made famous by Augustan poets.[17] Just once does Martial allude to Maecenas' less seemly side: he describes a toga that he received as a gift as being so lavish it would have pleased Maecenas (10.73.4). At first glance this reference to Maecenas' extravagant taste is in keeping with the sort of unmanly indulgence Velleius attributed to Maecenas. In fact, however, it is noteworthy that Martial chooses to portray Maecenas

---

[14]See Momigliano 96–100; Mayer 305–18.

[15]The debate over the authorship and date of the *Laus Pisonis* remains unresolved. For a summary of opinions and bibliography, see Bellandi 84 n. 14.

[16]*Ecl.* 4.160–163: *tum mihi talis eris, qualis qui dulce sonantem / Tityron e silvis dominam deduxit in urbem / ostenditque deos et "spreto" dixit, "ovili, / Tityre, rura prius, sed post cantabimus arma."* Calpurnius Siculus is as much a debated figure as the author of the *Laus Pisonis*; some scholars believe they are the same person; see Bellandi 84 n. 14.

[17]Mart. 12.4.1–3: *Quod Flacco Varioque fuit summoque Maroni / Maecenas, atavis regibus ortus eques, / gentibus et populis hoc te mihi, Prisce Terenti, / fama fuisse loquax chartaque dicet anus.* Cf. Hor. *Od.* 1.1.1: *Maecenas atavis edite regibus*; Prop. 3.9.1: *Maecenas, eques Etrusco de sanguine regum.*

as a proverbial literary type representing lavish luxury, especially as the poet links Maecenas with M. Apicius, a notable glutton of the time of Tiberius and the same Apicius who is linked with Maecenas in Seneca *Ep.* 1.120.19–20 (*Apicium cenis, Maecenatem deliciis*). By mentioning Maecenas with Apicius, Martial demonstrates to his readers knowledge of Senecan imagery. Thanks to Seneca, Maecenas has become a literary type.

Familiarity with Senecan themes also explains the two instances in which Juvenal names Maecenas as a literary type for luxury. In *Sat.* 12.37–38 Juvenal describes purple clothing as being suitable enough even for soft Maecenases (*vestem / purpuream teneris quoque Maecenatibus aptam*), an image which recalls Martial's remark on the toga Maecenas would have appreciated. More important is the forger of wills (*signator falsi*) in *Sat.* 1.63–68, a worthless character whom Juvenal describes as being carried about in an oversized litter while lounging on his back like Maecenas (*et multum referens de Maecenate supino*). The image recalls Seneca's description in *Ep.* 114.6 of a self-indulgent Maecenas who gave his *signum* in a state of undress (*signum a discincto petebatur*). These comments are fitting for the genre of satire, but they appear to be modeled on criticisms first uttered by Seneca. It is unlikely that Maecenas would have been targeted for satire if Seneca had not held him up to constant reproach.[18]

Later prose authors for the most part are unaffected by Seneca's harsh opinions. Pliny lists Maecenas in the indices of authors in his *Historiae Naturales*, and mentions him seven times in the books that have survived. Some of the information is intriguing, such as that Maecenas had a seal with the stamp of a frog for collecting taxes (*NH* 37.10), and related a story about a boy's friendship with a dolphin in some literary work (*NH* 9.25). On no occasion does Pliny criticize Maecenas, not even when he relates that Maecenas introduced the innovation of dining on the young of

---

[18]The one remaining mention of Maecenas in Juvenal echoes Martial's lamentations that good patrons like Maecenas no longer exist (*Sat.* 7.93).

she-asses (*mulae*) at banquets, which were preferred to wild asses (*praelatos onagris*) at that time.[19] The whole of Book 8 concerns animals, and Pliny inserts this note on Maecenas in a section concerning donkeys, stating the fad as a fact without adding personal comment. Despite Pliny's neutrality, this passage has become an example of Maecenas' affectation and lavish living, as though he were notorious among Romans of his own time and after for strange culinary appetites.[20] Pliny does not say that Maecenas was prone to introduce unusual delicacies to the Roman table on a regular basis, but merely observes one occasion on which Maecenas did. The incident perhaps should not be exaggerated.

Plutarch likewise supplies disconnected and at times bizarre pieces of information about Maecenas, such as that each year in celebration of the *princeps*' birthday Maecenas would send Augustus a drinking cup (*Mor.* 207 C 6).[21] Like Pliny and others, Plutarch relates points about Maecenas without personal comment. One incident concerns a host who pretended to be asleep at a dinner party so that Maecenas could make off with his wife without fear of reproach (*Mor.* 759–760 F). Numerous references place Maecenas at various celebrations in Augustan poetry, and there is every reason to believe that he, like many Romans before and after,

---

[19]Plin. *NH* 8.170. The habit went out of fashion soon after Maecenas' death: *post eum interiit auctoritas saporis asino.*

[20]For example, Syme (342) writes that Agrippa "despised the vile epicure [Maecenas] who sought to introduce a novel delicacy to the banquets of Rome, the flesh of young donkeys." On the other hand, Griffin has recently questioned whether Maecenas lived much differently than his poets except inasmuch as his wealth could afford more luxury. Nevertheless, included among Maecenas' "luxurious tastes" Griffin lists a notoriety for "affected epicurism at table" (1976) 94; (1986) 13.

[21]Gardthausen (1.2:767–68) suggests that these drinking cups were inscribed with verses, and explains the gesture in terms of slaves who, upon manumission, offered the gods an offering of drink and made a gift of the bowl. Augustus restored freedom to everyone, and therefore Maecenas was thanking the *princeps* for his own personal freedom.

enjoyed giving and attending banquets.²² On the other hand, the story about a host feigning sleep to allow his wife freedom to practice adultery is found as early as Lucilius and seems to have been a fairly well-known yarn among Romans.²³ In a letter Augustus humorously hails Maecenas as padding or a mattress for adultresses (μάλαγμα *moecharum*) (Macrob. *Sat.* 2.4.12), and Maecenas is known to have defended an adulterer on trial for the crime (Dio 54.30.4). Perhaps adultery was one of Maecenas' faults.²⁴ One can be an adulterer, however, without being decadent or effeminate, as Augustus' own adulterous affairs attest,²⁵ and this behavior cannot be attributed to the character defects cited by Seneca.

Tacitus presents a unique case in the transmission of information about Maecenas. He does not find Maecenas personally objectionable, as Seneca did, but he takes advantage of the exaggerated image of Maecenas that Seneca had promoted not long before. Such imagery suited Tacitus' intent to project an unsavory image of individual emperors and cast doubt on the nature of the principate as a whole, which he achieves through innuendo and

---

²²Maecenas' fondness for banquets may be seen in Horace, who depicts himself and his patron dining and drinking together (*Epod.* 3 and 9), Maecenas attending banquets (*Sat.* 2.8) or preparing to throw dinner parties (*Sat.* 2.7.32–37).

²³Lucil. 251 "*non omnibus dormio*," according to Festus, seems to be a reference to a proverb that arose when a certain Cipius feigned sleep so his wife could could freely commit adultery. Cicero twice uses the proverb about Cipius in his letters (*Fam.* 7.24.1; *Att.* 13.49.2). In Plutarch, the host while feigning sleep sees a slave stealing wine, and cries out "Don't you know I sleep only for Maecenas?" (οὐκ οἶσθ' ὅτι μόνῳ Μαικήνᾳ καθεύδω;).

²⁴Stein (*RE* 214) lists adultery as one of Maecenas' many faults (which include, not surprisingly, strange dress and the eating of donkey flesh), and adds that such behavior is expected from a man raised and spoiled in luxury all his life. See also Griffin (1976) 96; (1986) 13.

²⁵For instances of Augustus' adultery, see Suet. *Aug.* 69, and for his affair with Maecenas' wife, Terentia, see Dio 54.19.1–6.

stylistic sleight of hand.[26] His skillful blending of non-factual material almost imperceptively raises doubts in the reader's mind as to the propriety of imperial deed and function.

One of the ways Tacitus incorporates non-factual material is by introducing into his narrative tangential incidents and characters of a questionable nature that reflect poorly on the larger issue at hand.[27] When a dubious incident or character is discussed in connection with an emperor or imperial practice, the questionable qualities of the former taint the latter by implication. An example of Tacitus' use of Maecenas to cast suspicion on imperial motives occurs when the historian writes that newly inaugurated *Ludi Augustales* of AD 14 were disrupted by a quarrel among the actors (*Ann.* 1.54.2). Rather than discussing this particular quarrel, Tacitus digresses and recalls that Augustus used to tolerate theatrical performances to "comply with Maecenas, who was passionately in love with Bathyllus" (*Maecenati obtemperat effuso in amorem Bathylli*), and because Augustus thought it good politics to mingle in the pleasures of the common people. The obvious reason that Tacitus brings up Maecenas and his freedman Bathyllus at this point is because of a quarrel c. 18 BC involving Bathyllus and fellow actor Pylades. The event is related by Dio (54.17.5), who notes the closeness between patron and freedman (Βαθύλλῳ ὁμοτέχνῳ τέ οἱ ὄντι καὶ τῷ Μαικήνᾳ προσήκοντι διεστασίαζεν) but without implying that the relationship had a bearing on Augustus' policy regarding popular theater. Tacitus never mentions the quarrel between Bathyllus and Pylades, which is the only real connection between the *Ludi Augustales* of AD 14 and the *ludicrum* of c. 18 BC. Instead he focuses on the distasteful

---

[26]For Tacitus' less than objective approach to his material and further bibliography see Sullivan; Vogt; Ryberg. Historical facts for the most part are the same in Tacitus as in other sources, but his interpretation and manipulation of those facts are often startlingly different; see von Fritz.

[27]This technique is what Walker (66–67) defines as Tacitean "allusiveness," and occurs when "an event or person is not described directly, or not only directly, but in connection with another set of circumstances, or persons, or ideas, which make us see the immediate subject in a new light."

qualities of *histriones* and insinuates that a homosexual passion between a friend of the *princeps* and his freedman actor determined imperial policy. Augustus is at least partially redeemed because he was not averse to such spectacles and felt he should mingle with the people. Tacitus ends this passage by noting that Tiberius, despite his loathing of theatrical performances, allowed them to take place because he did not yet have the nerve (*nondum audebat*) to anger the common crowd by removing their base pleasures. Neither *princeps* was movitated purely by public interest.

Most of Tacitus' references to Maecenas manage to disparage the deeds of Julio-Claudian emperors and belittle the nature of the principate without directly criticizing Maecenas himself.[28] It is unlikely that Maecenas would have served Tacitus in this manner if Seneca had not made him famous for decadence. Such ulterior motives in the presentation of facts concerning Maecenas are lacking in other ancient writers, whose comments on Maecenas are unaffected by Seneca's negative commentary on Augustus' minister. Suetonius' ancedotal observations contain no criticism of Maecenas for public or private extravagances. For example, he tells that Maecenas at times was unable to keep a secret (*Aug.* 66.3) and that Augustus made fun of his writing style (*Aug.* 86.2), calling his prose "ringlets drenched with perfume" (*myrobrechis cincinnos*), but there is no added commentary to suggest that Suetonius took exception with Maecenas. Suetonius presents Maecenas as a friend of poets in an entirely favorable light.

---

[28] Two other examples of Tacitus' use of Maecenas to denigrate the principate may be found in Byrne (1999 forthcoming). The first involves the appearance of the name "Cilnius Maecenas" at *Annals* 6.11.2, in a digression on the history of the office of *praefectus urbi*. Maecenas' official name was "Gaius Maecenas," and the extra nomen "Cilnius" occurs only in this passage. Maecenas may have been related to the powerful Cilnian *gens* on his mother's side, but in any case the name "Cilnius" denoted vast foreign and monarchical power, with grim implications for Augustus' choice in his first *praefectus urbi*. At *Annals* 3.30, Tacitus likens the sinister Sallustius Crispus' relationship with Tiberius to that of Maecenas' with Augustus, thereby implying that behind-the-scenes power existed at the very beginning of the principate.

Appian treats Maecenas' activities during the late 40s and triumviral period without a hint of scandal, and by his account Maecenas was a capable man of state. In particular Appian focuses on Maecenas' diplomatic role and shows him as being instrumental in soothing tempers between Octavian and Antony (*BC* 5.7.64; 5.10.93). He also describes the circumstances in which Octavian first placed Maecenas in control of Rome (*BC* 5.10.92; 5.11.99). Thanks to this historian we learn more about Maecenas' role in the suppression of Lepidus' conspiracy (*BC* 4.6.50), and discover that Maecenas played a crucial role in arranging Octavian's short-lived marriage to Scribonia (*BC* 5.6. 53).

Dio, who mentions Maecenas more than any historian, never alludes to the unpalatable character promulgated by Seneca. He observes Maecenas' activities during the civil wars and casts him as an advocate of monarchy with visionary advice for the future operations of the principate, to which all of Book 52 is dedicated. Dio composed an exceptionally positive obituary for Maecenas (55.7) in which he mentions Maecenas' loyal service to Augustus, his wide popularity, his influence in furthering the careers of others, and his ability to calm Augustus' quick temper. In the same passage Dio credits Maecenas with the installation of the first warm-water swimming pool in Rome and the creation of a system of shorthand. If a warm-water swimming pool was considered a sign of his decadence in his own day, it elicited no criticism from Dio some two centuries later.

Descriptions of a loose-living, dissolute Maecenas found in modern works derive from Seneca's criticism, consciously or not. Without Seneca's exaggerated vituperations, the common image of Maecenas the hopeless decadent becomes untenable. On the contrary, Maecenas' excesses are no worse than those of his contemporaries, while his services to Augustus, which often go unnoticed, are equal to those of Agrippa through the mid 20s BC. Unfortunately, this brief overview of ancient sources on Maecenas does not allow for a discussion on why Seneca held Maecenas in contempt. I can say, however, that unless we are prepared to believe that Seneca truly harbored a grudge against Augustus' long-dead minister, an idea that hardly makes sense, then the source of this hatred must be sought elsewhere. Seneca's criticism and contempt, in my opinion, makes sense if we imagine that it was not meant for Maecenas at all, but rather was aimed at a contemporary who was an imperial adviser and a man of questionable character, someone who likely became Nero's adviser when Seneca himself lost favor. Maecenas just happened to embody the qualities and social position of this person whom Seneca knew and whose real name he refused to entrust to posterity.[29]

BIBLIOGRAPHY

André, Jean-Marie. 1967. *Mécène: Essai de biographie spirituelle.* Paris.

Axelson, B. 1930. "*De aetate Consolationis ad Liviam et Elegiarum in Maecenatem.*" *Eranos* 28:1–33.

Bardon, Henry. 1956. *La littérature latine inconnue.* Vol. 2. Paris.

Bellandi, Franco. 1995. "L'immagine di Mecenate protettore delle lettere nella poesia fra I e II sec. D.C." *A&R* 40:78–101.

Byrne, Shannon. 1999. Forthcoming. "Pointed Allusions: Maecenas and Sallustius in the *Annals* of Tacitus." *RhM*.

—. Forthcoming. "Seneca, Maecenas, and Petronius."

Courbaud, Edmond. 1914. *Horace: Sa vie et sa pensée à l'époque des epîtres.* Paris.

Cresci, Giovannella. 1995. "*Maecenas, Equitum Decus.*" *RSA* 25:169–76.

Fritz, K. von. 1957. "Tacitus, Agricola, Domitian, and the Problem of the Principate." *CP* 52:73–97.

Gardthausen, Viktor. 1896. *Augustus und seine Zeit.* 6 vols. Leipzig.

Griffin, Jasper. 1986. *Latin Poets and Roman Life.* Chapel Hill.

—. 1977. "Propertius and Antony." *JRS* 67:17–26.

---

[29]See Byrne (forthcoming).

—. 1976. "Augustan Poetry and the Life of Luxury." *JRS* 66:88–105.
Hirzel, Rudolf. 1895. *Der Dialog*. Vol. 2. Leipzig.
Lunderstedt, Paul. 1911. *De C. Maecenatis fragmentis*. Leipzig.
Mayer, Roland. 1982. "Neronian Classicism." *AJP* 103:305–18.
Momigliano, Arnaldo. 1944. "Literary Chronology of the Neronian Age." *CQ* 38:96–100.
Motto, Anna Lydia. 1973. *Seneca*. New York.
Nicastri, Luciano. 1980. "Sul Maecenas pseudovirgiliano." *Vichiana* 9:258–98.
Richlin, Amy. 1992. *The Garden of Priapus: Sexuality and Aggression in Roman Humor*. Revised edition. New York.
Ryberg, I. 1942. "Tacitus' Art of Innuendo." *TAPA* 73:383–404.
Schoonhoven, H. 1980. *Elegiae in Maecenatem: Prolegomena, Text and Commentary*. Groningen.
Steele, R. B. 1933. *The Nux, Maecenas and Consolatio ad Liviam*. Nashville.
Stein, Arthur. 1927. *Paulys Real-Encyclopädie*. Vol. 27. Cols. 207–218.
Sullivan, D. 1976. "Innuendo and the 'Weighted Alternative' in Tacitus." *CJ* 71:312–26.
Syme, Ronald. 1939. *The Roman Revolution*. Oxford.
West, David. 1991. "*Cur me Querelis* (Horace, *Odes* 2.17)." *AJP* 112:45–52.
Vogt, J. 1969. "Tacitus und die Unparteilichkeit des Historikers." In *Tacitus*, edited by V. Pöschl, 39-59. Darmstadt.
Walker, B. 1952. *The Annals of Tacitus: A Study in the Writing of History*. Manchester.
Watson, A. J. M. 1994. "Maecenas' Administration of Rome and Italy." *Akroterion* 39:98–104.

Pisspots and Pumpkins: Three Notes To The Apocolocyntosis

John Scott Campbell
University of South Florida

"Pumpkinification" was coined in English solely to translate *Apocolocyntosis*, the title ascribed by Dio Cassius to a work of Seneca, which purported to describe the deification of Claudius.[1] The title has long since been identified with a surviving text, which satirizes Claudius' reception by the gods after his death. The "pumpkin" of the English title suggests to the English-speaking reader a largish orange squash, undoubtedly conjuring for Americans, consciously or unconsciously, the image of a jack o' lantern with its ghoulish face, which would surely accommodate the vision and intent of a satirist determined to lampoon a cruel and foolish despot. But such a squash is a product of the new world and unknown to Seneca and his contemporaries.[2] After discounting the modern image of the pumpkin, the obvious question is to what then in fact does the title refer. An answer here immediately yields a second question: how does this picture relate, if at all, to the surviving text? But before discussing the sense of the title, since the

---

[1] According to the *OED*, the first appearance of "pumpkinification" in English was in 1856 in reference to Seneca's satire in Charles Merivale's *History of the Roman Empire*.

[2] Bailey 31: "The field pumpkin and the bush summer squashes are not known in a native state. At present we assume they have developed in the course of time from a small hard-shelled gourd. Such a gourd, belonging to this species, is now wild and apparently indigenous in river valleys in southern Texas; probably it occurs also in Mexico. It has been known in the literature of botany for eighty-six years as *cucurbita texana*. . . . American Indians grew pumpkins for food at the time of the discovery of the country; it is supposed their fruits had been developed from something like the Texan gourd."

accuracy of the title itself is suspect, the source of the title deserves a serious look. In this paper, therefore, we shall seek the answers to these three questions: 1. What was in fact the title of Seneca's satire? 2. What would the κολοκύντη of that title mean to a Roman audience? 3. And finally, how does the title in Dio Cassius relate to the content of the extant satire?

1. The reference to the *Apocolocyntosis* was made in the *Bibliotheca* of Dio Cassius. It survived in an anecdote preserved in an epitome of Xiphilinus, a twelfth century monk, commissioned by the Byzantine emperor, Michael Ducas (1064–1075), to abridge from Dio Cassius a history of the Caesars. The text makes mention of the pretended grief of Nero and Agrippina for the dead Claudius, whom they had murdered and nevertheless deified. In this context, the explication of a satirical remark about Claudius' death by Lucius Junius Gallio, the brother of Seneca, prompts a reference to a work of Seneca, satirizing the deification of Claudius.

> Ἀγριππῖνα δὲ καὶ ὁ Νέρων πενθεῖν προσεποιοῦντο ὃν ἀπεκτόνεσαν, ἔς τε τὸν οὐρανὸν ἀνήγαγον ὃν ἐκ τοῦ συμποσίου φοράδην ἐξενηνόχεσαν. ὅθενπερ Λούκιος Ἰούνιος Γαλλίων ὁ τοῦ Σενέκα ἀδελφὸς ἀστειότατόν τι ἀπεφθέγξατο. συνέθηκε μὲν γὰρ καὶ ὁ Σενέκας σύγγραμμα, ἀποκολοκύντωσιν αὐτὸ ὥσπερ τινὰ ἀθανάτισιν ὀνομάσας· ἐκεῖνος δ' ἐν βραχυτάτῳ πολλὰ εἰπὼν ἀπομνημονεύεται. ἐπειδὴ γὰρ τοὺς ἐν τῷ δεσμωτηρίῳ θανατουμένους ἀγκίστροις τισὶ μεγάλοις οἱ δήμιοι ἔς τε τὴν ἀγορὰν ἀνεῖλκον κἀντεῦθεν ἐς τὸν ποταμὸν ἔσυρον, ἔφη τὸν Κλαύδιον ἀγκίστρῳ ἐς τὸν οὐρανὸν ἀνενεχθῆναι. (60.35.2–4)

Agrippina and Nero pretended to grieve for the man they had murdered and elevated to heaven after they had carried him from a banquet on a stretcher. This inspired Lucius Junius Gallio, Seneca's brother, to utter a very witty remark. Seneca himself composed a work which he entitled

"Pumpkinification" as though it were some kind of deification. But his brother was remembered for saying a great deal in a few words. For since the public executioners were accustomed to drag those put to death in prison to the Forum with large hooks, and from there to haul them to the river, he remarked: "Claudius has been elevated to heaven on a hook."[3]

Since the sixteenth century commentators[4] have generally presumed that the Ἀποκολοκύντωσις of Dio Cassius' title refers to the extant satire and that the title is a wordplay on ἀποθέωσις. The wordplay works because ἀποθέωσις shares with the neologism a common prefix and suffix, which play on the sound of the words, while contrasting θεός and κολοκύντη.[5] The action noun, ἀποθέωσις, however, is not common in either Greek or Latin, although formed on ἀπο-θεόω, and undoubtedly clear to any Greek speaker, especially with the honorific θεῖος applied to the deified emperor. In the text of Xiphilinus there are three references to deification, none of which are ἀποθέωσις: the first and third, ἐς οὐρανὸν ἀνήγαγον and ἐς τὸν οὐρανὸν ἀνενεχθῆναι, suggest a formula, comparable to the Latin *inter deos referre*, while the second, ἀθανάτισιν,[6] is formed on the adjective ἀθάνατοι, answering the Latin *immortales*. Ἀποθέωσις is found in the title of the extant satire in the earliest manuscript (Sangallensis 469, 9/10th cent.): *Divi Claudii* ΑΠΟΘΗΟΣΙΣ *Annaei Senecae per saturam*. The other manuscripts are variously titled *Ludus de morte Claudii Caesaris*. Contrary to what appears

---

[3]All translations are by the author.
[4]For a discussion of the bibliography, see Coffey (1961) and Bringmann; for more recent bibliography, see Focardi 57–65.
[5]For a recent discussion of the variant reading ἀποκολοκέντωσις, see Stagni.
[6]ἀθανάτισιν is the reading of the best manuscripts (Vaticanus 145 and Coislinianus 320) and in context with ἀποκολοκύντωσις more likely to have been corrected to ἀπαθανάτισιν.

to be common usage, however, ἀποθέωσις appears four times in Cicero's letters where the connotations seem to vary. In three of the letters, Cicero refers ἀποθέωσις to Tullia, his deceased daughter:

> Insula Arpinas habere potest germanam ἀποθέωσιν, sed vereor ne minorem τιμὴν habere videatur ἐκτοπισμός. (*Att.* 12.12.1)

> The island of Arpinas can handle a second shrine, but I'm afraid being out of the way it may appear to have less honor.

> Fanum fieri volo, neque hoc mihi dissuaderi potest. Sepulcri similitudinem effugere non tam propter poenam legis studeo quam ut maxime adsequar ἀποθέωσιν. (*Att.* 12.36.1)

> I wish the shrine built, nor can I be dissuaded from this. I would like to avoid the appearance of a tomb, not so much for fear of the law as that I am determined to create a memorial.

> Quod me a maestitia avocas, multum levaris si locum fano dederis. Multa mihi εἰς ἀποθέωσιν in mentem veniunt, sed loco valde opus est. (*Att.* 12.37.4)

> Since you would alleviate my grief, it would be extremely helpful if you could find a place for the shrine. I have many things on my mind about the memorial, but there is a pressing need for a location.

The meaning of ἀποθέωσις in the letters seems to be broadly "the passage of the dead from this life into eternal life," and despite its etymology was not subsequently adopted in the empire as a formula indicating public deification (ἐς οὐρανὸν ἀνήγαγον). Cicero's usage seems to encompass a spectrum of meaning extending from "glorification" and "memorialization" to the actual memorial, *fanum*. In the fourth letter, Cicero laments that the election of Afranius will make his consulship, which a certain Curio once called an ἀποθέωσις, a *fabam mimum*, "a joke":

> Sed heus tu, videsne consulatum illum nostrum, quem Curio antea ἀποθέωσιν vocabat, si hic factus erit, fabam mimum futurum? (*Att*. 1.16.13)

> But come now! Do you realize that my consulship, which Curio once called a "glory," if he is elected, will be a "farce."

This text in turn shows a remarkable similarity to a line in the satire:

> Multa dixit (Janus) de magnitudine deorum: non debere hunc uulgo dari honorem. "olim," inquit, "magna res erat deum fieri: iam Fabam mimum fecisti(s)." (*Apoc*.9.3)

> (Janus) spoke a great deal about the greatness of the gods, that this honor ought not to be vulgarized. "Once," he said, "to be made a god was serious business; now you have made it a "farce."

The ἀποθέωσις of Cicero's administration as well as the honor of deification have become a *faba mimus*. Although the exact meaning of *faba mimus* is the subject of some discussion,[7] the contexts of Cicero and Seneca suggest something approaching the English sense of "joke" or "farce." The juxtaposition in the two texts of "deification" (*deum fieri* in the text of Seneca, ἀποθέωσις in the manuscript title) and *faba mimus* is an extraordinary coincidence. Undoubtedly Seneca and his contemporaries knew their Cicero, and a conspiracy of literary cognoscenti is certainly conceivable. Nevertheless, it is still difficult to believe that Seneca was alluding

---

[7] For a discussion of *faba mimus*, see Eden 109.

to a letter of Cicero. The coincidence, in any case, draws attention to the link between deification and farce in the text.

What follows here from what little we think we know is a skein of speculation argued more from probability than from the limited information available to us. The text of Dio Cassius, which mentions the title of Seneca's satire, is an abridgment. The title itself was probably abbreviated since a title should reasonably give some indication of its subject, but ἀποκολοκύντωσις is essentially nonsense in need of clarification, "a subtitle."[8] Seneca needed ἀποθέωσις to drive the wordplay in ἀποκολοκύντωσις, whose κολοκύντη he presumed would be self-evident to his Latin audience from their knowledge of Greek. If we follow the precedents of Varro for Menippean Satire,[9] or the sometime practice of comedy,[10] Seneca's title had a subtitle which was in all likelihood ᾿Αποκολοκύντωσις ἢ ἀποθέωσις τοῦ θείου Κλαυδίου. Since the juxtaposition of the two nouns in the nominative case was important for the wordplay, ᾿Αποκολοκύντωσις περὶ ἀποθεώσεως τοῦ θείου Κλαυδίου, closely modeled on Varro, was probably not Seneca's title. The title was doubtless cited complete in Dio Cassius' history. Since it is unlikely the epitomizer would add words, Dio Cassius added the gloss, ὥσπερ τινὰ ἀθανάτισιν, because ἀποθέωσις with a broader meaning than senatorial deification (εἰς οὐρανὸν ἀνήγαγον) might somehow be inappropriate or even confusing, while ἀθανάτισιν is unambiguous, the creation of an ἀθάνατος, an immortal, a member of the pantheon. The τινὰ glossed the ἀθανάτισιν and indicated the perversion intended in the title and fulfilled in the satire of Claudius' deification. The epitomizer a thousand years later found ἀποθέωσις and ἀθανάτισιν redundant and eliminated ἀποθέωσις. An early copyist lifted ἀποθέωσις from the original title of a manuscript now lost to us

---

[8]Eden (2) disagrees: "That a work's title must be descriptive of its contents is manifestly false."

[9]For a brief discussion of double titles, see Coffey (1976) 260 n.6; for a list of titles, see Astbury xxi–xxv.

[10]For a list of titles, see the appendices of Edmonds.

and preserved it in a Latin title. Subsequent cataloguers found ἀποθέωσις less than helpful and reduced the title to a description of the work's content, *Ludus de morte Claudii Caesaris*, "a satire on the death of the Emperor Claudius." These conclusions join irrevocably the work mentioned in Dio Cassius and the extant satire by confirming the long assumed wordplay of ἀποκολοκύντωσις on ἀποθέωσις, which emphasizes the intent of the work in the contrast between θεός and κολοκύντη, between *deum fieri* and *faba mimus*, which looks to the Olympic debate at the heart of the satire which concerned itself with the abuse of deification and the crimes of Claudius.

2. Since κολοκύντη gives meaning to ἀποκολοκύντωσις, we might reasonably ask, what is a κολοκύντη, or rather what would κολοκύντη mean to the Roman audience for which the satire was intended?[11] Ἀπο-κολοκύντ-ωσις is a regular Greek formation for a noun denoting action.[12] It is formed upon a factitive verb, which understandably is not extant: ἀπο-κολοκυντόω or κολοκυντόω, "to make into a gourd," or "to gourdify."[13] The Greek prefix ἀπο provides here a sense of completion to the action denoted in the verb.[14] The κολοκύντη of ἀποκολοκύντωσις is a variation of κολοκύνθη, both of which are alternatives to the later κολοκύντα and κολοκύνθα. A fifth form, κολοκύνθις, is identical to the Latin *colocynthis*, an undomesticated gourd (Plin. *NH* 20.8.14–17), and distinct from the κολοκύντη. In English we distinguish among cucumbers, melons, squash, and gourds, where gourds are essentially ornamental, while the others are table vegetables. The Greeks and Romans distinguished between "gourds" and "melons" according to the texture of their skin, that is, between κολοκύντη

---

[11]*LSJ* defines the κολοκύνθ-η as a "round gourd, Cucurbita maxima"; the *RE* under *Kürbis* comments: "Der von den Alten angebaute K. ist nach der Ansicht neuerer Schriftsteller nicht Cucurbita Pepo L., als dessen Heimat Mexiko und der Südwesten Nordamerikas angenommen wird, sondern der in heissen Gegenden aller Erdteile wildwachsende Flaschen-K" *(Cucurbita Lagenaria L.)*.
[12]Smyth 230.840.a.2.
[13]Sihler 522.468.3.
[14]Smyth 371.1680.

(*cucurbita*) and σίκυος (*cucumis*),[15] all of which modern botanists catalogue in the family *cucurbitaceae*. Some Greeks distinguished the σικύα from the κολοκύντη. Theophrastus treats the σικύα as if distinct from the κολοκύντη and σίκυος.[16] The Hellespontians according to Athenaeus (59a) considered the σικύα oblong and the κολοκύντη spherical, while the Athenians made no distinction between the κολοκύντη and σικύα (59b). The wild varieties of the gourd were used for herbal medicine,[17] while the domestic gourd, properly prepared, could be eaten[18] or dried for use as a jug.[19] The modern botanist distinguishes among the many varieties of gourds the *cucurbita maxima* and the *lagenaria* as well as the *cucurbita pepo*, the "pumpkin," which again is new-world.[20] Although gourds hybridize so quickly that it is very difficult to relate absolutely the

---

[15]Plin. *NH* 19.22.61: *Cucumis cartilagine et carne constat, cucurbita cortice et cartilagine; cortex huic uni maturitate transit in lignum,* "the cucumber consists of fiber and flesh, the gourd of fiber and rind; the rind of the gourd becomes wooden when ripe"; cf. Thphr. *HP* 1.10.10: ἐκ σαρκὸς μὲν καὶ ἰνὸς ὁ τῶν κοκκυμήλων καὶ σικύων, ἐξ ἰνὸς δὲ καὶ δέρματος ὁ τῶν συκαμίνων καὶ τῆς ῥόας, "the plum and the cucumber consist of flesh and fiber, the mulberry and the pomegranate of fiber and rind."

[16]Thphr. *HP* 7.2.9: ἁπλῶς δὴ πάντα τὰ θερινὰ βραχύρριζα· καὶ γὰρ ὁ σίκυος καὶ ἡ κολοκύντη καὶ ἡ σικύα καὶ διὰ τὴν ὥραν καὶ ἴσως ἔτι μᾶλλον διὰ τὴν φύσιν, ἥπερ συνηκολούθηκε τῇ ὥρᾳ, "in general all summer plants have short roots; for example, the cucumber, the gourd, and the calabash because of the season and perhaps still more because of their nature, which accommodates the season."

[17]Plin. *NH* 19.24.74: *Sunt et silvestres in utroque genere et omnibus fere hortensiis; sed et his medica tantum natura est,* "in both species there are wild varieties as in almost all domesticated plants; but their use is solely medicinal"; see also Dioscorides Medicus 2.162 and 4.178.

[18]Ath. 59a: καὶ ἡ μὲν Ἰνδικὴ (σικύα) κατὰ τὸ πλεῖστον ἕψεται, ἡ δὲ κολοκύντη καὶ ὀπτᾶται, "the Indain bottle gourd is for the most part boiled, while the gourd is also baked"; see also Apicius, *De re coquinaria,* esp. 3.4.

[19]Plin. *NH* 19.24.71: *Cucurbitarum numerosior usus . . . nuper in balnearum usum venere urceolorum vice, iam pridem vero etiam cadorum ad vina condenda,* "numerous are the uses for gourds . . . recently they have found use in latrines in place of chamber pots; for a long time now indeed they have been used as jugs to store wine."

[20]See Bailey 2–24.

modern with the ancient,[21] the *cucurbita maxima* is spherical and suggests the κολοκύντη, while the *lagenaria* is the bottle gourd, the calabash, and suggests the σικύα. The κολοκύντη of the title was probably a *cucurbita maxima*, at the very least spherical, possibly hollow, and consequently fit for use as a bowl. But we must keep in mind that 'Αποκολοκύντωσις is a Greek title for a Latin work meant for a Roman audience, however bilingual. Although Roman botany and horticulture were much influenced by the Greeks, nevertheless, in Latin both the κολοκύντη and the σικύα are simply *cucurbita*.[22] If the κολοκύντη was understood to be more or less identical with the *cucurbita*, as will be presumed later, the title could still suggest a calabash as well as a pot.

3. The context of Seneca's satire was the court of Nero, which punctuated its Latin with Greek,[23] and presumably saw little or no difference between κολοκύντη and *cucurbita*. The obvious interpretation of *Apocolocyntosis* is a pun on ἀποθέωσις,[24] suggesting the nonsensical "gourdification," which most scholars argue, beyond simple ridicule of Claudius' *consecratio*, conjured in the mind of the reader his "foolification."[25] But the obvious

---

[21]"Many varieties of Cucurbita are under cultivation in tropical and temperate climates, especially in southern Asia; but it is extremely difficult to refer them to definite specific groups, on account of the facility with which they hybridize; while it is very doubtful whether any of the original forms now exist in the wild state" (*Enc. Brit.* 11th ed. 286).

[22]Even Theophrastus (*HP* 7.4.6) mentions the lack of real differences among the gourds, which Athenaeus cites in 2.58f: σικύου δὲ καὶ κολοκύντης τοῦ μὲν εἶναί φασι γένη τῆς δ' οὐκ εἶναι, καθάπερ τῆς ῥαφανῖδος καὶ τῆς γογγυλίδος, ἀλλ' ἐν τῷ αὐτῷ γένει τὰς μὲν βελτίους τὰς δὲ χείρους, "of the cucumber and the gourd, the former they say has distinct varieties, the latter does not, like the radish and the turnip, but all are in the same family, where some are better, while others are inferior."

[23]See, for example, Suet. *Nero* 20; 33; 38; 49.

[24]The substance of the argument presented here first appeared in Campbell.

[25]See Eisenberger 270: "Bei einer ἀποκολοκύντωσις würde Claudius die Gestalt der *cucurbita* erhalten, deren Name ihm wegen seiner Torheit schon vorher zukam—eine durchaus angemessene Metamorphose. Das war die Pointe des Titels."

sometimes sits uneasily. There is little proof beyond modern usage that κολοκύντη or *cucurbita* might suggest a fool to Seneca's audience. The analogy between a gourd and an "empty head," which suggests the Italian *zucca vuota* or the English "numskull" or "blockhead," is unattested in contemporary Greek and Latin. The text of Seneca, moreover, does not in fact describe the "foolification" of Claudius, but rather his enslavement in the afterlife: the presumption of the text is that he was already a fool in life. The κολοκύντη (or *cucurbita*) of the wordplay in *Apocolocyntosis* is a metaphor, involving a colloquialism: "So and so is a pumpkin!" Since relatively few colloquialisms survive in either Latin or Greek, any interpretation of *Apocolocyntosis*, and the following is no exception, necessitates again a web of speculation.

Pliny the Elder, a contemporary of Seneca, remarks that one of the more recent uses of gourds was as a chamber pot: *[cucurbitae] nuper in balnearum usum venere urceolorum vice* (*NH* 19.24.71): a *cucurbita* was in fact a cheap "pisspot." Trimalchio at his dinner party interprets the signs of the zodiac pictured on an elaborate offering at his banquet: *in aquario [nascuntur] copones et cucurbitae* (Petr. 39.13). The context demands a person. Alongside the water carrier, *cucurbitae* could mean "chamber pot carriers," λασανοφόροι, whose responsibilities are evident in the *Satyricon*[26] and whose status was a commonplace for degradation.[27] Petronius' use of *matella* to describe an unfaithful

---

[26]Petr. 27.3–6: *nam duo spadones in diversa parte circuli stabant, quorum alter matellam tenebat argenteam, alter numerabat pilas . . . cum Trimalchio digitos concrepuit, ad quod signum matellam spado ludenti subiecit*, "for two eunuchs stood on opposite sides of the circle, one held a silver chamber pot, while the other counted balls . . . when Trimalchio snapped his fingers, the eunuch set his basin under the player."

[27]Mart. 10.11.1–4: *Nil aliud loqueris, quam Thesea Pirithoumque, / Teque putas Pyladi, Calliodore, parem. / Dispeream, si tu Pyladi praestare matellam / Dignus es aut porcos pascere Pirithoi*, "You speak of nothing but Theseus and Pirithous, and you consider yourself the equal of Pylades, Calliodorus, I'll be damned if you're fit to offer Pylades his chamber pot or to serve Pirithous his sausages."

and lascivious wife[28] indicates a distinction between *matella*, a "pisspot," and *cucurbita*, a "pisspot carrier." Scholars have long argued the meaning of the *cucurbita* in *Apocolocyntosis* from a bit of dialogue in Apuleius' *Golden Ass*, a century or so later, where the porter of an inn refused to open the doors too early for fear of bandits: *nos cucurbitae caput non habemus, ut pro te moriamur* (*Met.* 1.15.2). But the porter feels the need to gloss *cucurbita* with *caput*, since *cucurbita* without it may make no sense; the meaning of *cucurbitae caput*, "a head like a gourd," seems self-evident, while the κολοκύντη in *Apocolocyntosis* is a person and a metaphor and different from *cucurbitae caput*.

At the center of Seneca's satire, Claudius' deification became the subject of a debate that amounted to a trial for his crimes. He is banished to Hell where he is finally adjudged a slave of Caligula, who in turn presents him to Aeacus, who passes him on to his freedman: *Menandro liberto suo tradidit, ut a cognitionibus esset* (*Apoc.* 15). Claudius, who had been judge and lord of all the world, is in the end a law clerk to a freedman, his λασανοφόρος, his "pisspot carrier." For Seneca and company, Claudius was a fool and didn't need death to make him one. The point was humiliation and vengeance: instead of becoming a god, a θεός, the Divine Claudius became a slave, a κολοκύντη (a *cucurbita*).

BIBLIOGRAPHY

Astbury, Raymond, ed. 1985. *M. Terentii Varronis Saturarum Menippearum Fragmenta*. Leipzig.

Bailey, L. H. 1958. *The Garden of Gourds*. Boston.

Bringmann, Klaus. 1985. "Seneca's 'Apocolocyntosis': Ein Forschungsbericht 1959–1982." *ANRW* 32.2:889–92.

---

[28]Petr. 45.8: *quid servus peccavit, qui coactus est facere? magis illa matella digna fuit quam taurus iactaret,* "Why was the slave at fault when she forced him? That "pisspot" deserved even more to be tossed by a bull."

Campbell, John Scott. 1995. "Pisspots and Gourds: A Footnote to Apolocolocyntosis." *LCM* 20:9–10.
Coffey, Michael. 1976. *Roman Satire*. New York.
—. 1961. "Seneca, Apocolocyntosis 1922–1958." *Lustrum* 6:239–71.
Eden, P. T, ed. 1984. *Seneca: Apocolocyntosis*. Cambridge.
Edmonds, John Maxwell, ed. 1957–1961. *The Fragments Of Attic Comedy*. Leiden.
Eisenberger, H. 1978. "Bedeutung and Zweck des Titels von Senecas 'Apocolocyntosis.'" *HSPh* 82:265–70.
Focardi, Gabriella, ed. 1995. *Apokolokyntosis: la deificazione della zucca*. Firenze.
Sihler, Andrew L. 1995. *New Comparative Grammar of Greek and Latin*. Oxford.
Smyth, H. W. 1972. *Greek Grammar*. Cambridge.
Stagni, Ernesto. 1996. "Apokolokuntosis: Apunti sulla tradizione di Dione Cassio-Xiphilino." *RFIC* 108:298–339.

The Art and Myth of *Cupid and Psyche*

Edmund P. Cueva
Xavier University

In the introduction to his commentary, Louis C. Purser notes that the story of Cupid and Psyche is of considerable antiquity and assumes various forms at various times and places until Apuleius gave it its final form by giving the heroine the name Psyche.[1] Carl C. Schlam, however, firmly believes that no literary evidence exists for the story.[2] Although there may be no single text that serves as the source, there exists an abundance of pre-Apuleian art depicting Cupid (Eros),[3] some with Psyche and some without her.[4] These works of art have not been interpreted as representing any one moment of the Apuleian narrative.[5] Ludwig Friedländer suggests that Eros and Psyche, as lovers, are found in numerous works of

---

[1] Purser li and liv.
[2] Schlam (1976) 2. On the genre and origin of the Cupid and Psyche story see Schlam (1992) 85 and (1993) 63–73, esp. 68. See also Lang 64, 79; Boberg 213; Hooker 28–30; Swahn; Merkelbach; Weitzmann 109–10; Arnott 233–47, esp. 241 n. 24; Perry 248; Nethercut; Walsh 191, 195, 218; Wright 281; Stabryla 261–72, esp. 261–64; Penwill 59; Fehling; Griffiths 151; Tatum 51, 53 n. 46; Dowden 352; Hägg 182, 183–90; Scobie (1969) 37 and (1983) 39; von Franz; Purser 132–33; Anderson 198; James 119; Kenney 9. On its relationship to the rest of the novel see Stabryla 271, Fredouille 27 and Scobie (1978) 43–61. The collection of essays edited by Binder and Merkelbach contains the essential theories on these problems.
[3] See Wlosok for a discussion on these names.
[4] See the following examples from *LIMC* 7.2, *Psyche*: 87, 91, 99, 105, 106, 107, 111, 112, 115, 121a, 122, 124, 135, 138b, 141a, 147a.
[5] An attempt to identify the man with the ass in 6.18–20 with the mythological figure of Ocnus was soundly rejected by Arnott. The three characters that appear in Psyche's last labor have always puzzled scholars, and there seems to be no resolution or identification of these people in sight.

art,[6] and E. J. Kenney argues that Apuleius drew on iconographical tradition.[7] A re-examination of some of the myths in this novel and their artistic depictions is needed in order to ascertain whether pre-Apuleian artistic representations of the Cupid and Psyche story do exist. I shall first examine some of the myths found in the non-Psyche-Cupid passages and their artistic representations in order to show that most of the mythological references in Apuleius were known well enough to have been depicted on vases and rings. I shall then match passages from the Cupid and Psyche tale with pre-Apuleian art.

In 1.10 Aristomenes relates to Socrates that the woman who has brought him to his sorry state was like Medea.[8] The story continues with the witches then entering the sleeping quarters of Aristomenes and Socrates, whom they describe thus: *Hic est . . . carus Endymion, hic Catamitus meus* (1.12). Endymion is known for the eternal sleep into which Selene made him fall in order to embrace him without waking him (Paus. 5.1; *Sch.* Apoll. Rh. 4.57). This, of course, is what Psyche would have wanted to be able to do in her voyeuristic escapade. Ganymede is difficult to explain: perhaps it is a slur at sexual preference or Ganymede is the soul reaching the absolute.[9] I have not been able to find a work of art showing Ganymede and Endymion together. This lack of depiction may be explained by a suggestion of H. J. Mason, who found in this scene "a close parallel in the description of Aesop by his owner's wife as Ἀπόλλωνα ὄψει ἢ Ἐνδυμίωνα ἢ Γανυμήδην, *Vita Aes.* (G)

---

[6]Friedländer 99. Tatum (56–57) somewhat disagrees with this idea: "Although we cannot have a direct connection between any ancient artistic monument and the events of Apuleius' novel, a certain antagonism is often apparent between Cupid and Psyche. They are not always embracing; sometimes she is shown advancing upon the sleeping god, and sometimes she is depicted applying a torch to his body."

[7]Kenney 20; for a different opinion, see James 160 n. 2.

[8]A good example of a vase painting of the Medea myth is the Lucanian red-figure calyx-krater in the Kimbel Art Museum in Fort Worth (57), *c.* 400 BC.

[9]Schlam (1976, 4) writes that the figures of Ganymede and the eagle can be interpreted as "figures which can be related allegorically to the transition of the soul to the eternal care of the divine."

29."[10] The teaming of the two figures, therefore, may be a literary creation. In the same passage Meroe sees herself as Calypso, and Socrates as Ulysses.[11]

In 2.23 Telephron says that like Lynceus and Argus he will be alert in his duty. The allusion to Argus is understandable, and Lynceus was know for his keen eyesight (Pind. *Nem.* 10).[12] Examples of depictions of Argus can be found on an Attic black-figure amphora from Bomarzo (London, British Museum B 164, *c.* 530 BC) and on an Attic red-figure amphora by the Eucharides Painter (Hamburg, Museum für Kunst und Gewerb 1966.34, *c.* 480 BC).

In the courtyard of Byrrhaena's house (2.4) a statue of Victory hints at the two winged deities in the Cupid and Psyche story, and the mythological motif of the courtyard foreshadows the well-known story of Diana and Actaeon and portends the transformation of Lucius.[13] There are also two other important architectural passages that hint at the labors of Psyche.[14] In 6.1 Ceres' temple is described with the proper accouterments.[15] This description of the temple and the narrative describing the house cleaning of Psyche portends one of the trials of Psyche; after all, the girl has to repeat this action in her first labor.[16] Perhaps it is Ceres, in gratitude for

---

[10]Mason 10.

[11]See the Lucanian red-figure hydria, Naples, Museo Nazionale 81839 (H 2899), *c.* 390–380 BC, for Calypso; for more examples see *LIMC* 5.1 and 5.2.

[12]For an artistic representation of Lynceus see Apulian red-figure lekythos, *c.* 340–330 BC; Richmond, Virginia Museum 8.162.

[13]For a depiction of Actaeon, see Nestoris by the Dolon Painter (British Museum F 176). Mason (10–11) suggests that the myth of Actaeon may have been treated in a mime. On this passage Kenney (11) writes: "Lucius is warned against inopportune curiosity by coming across a group of statuary depicting Actaeon spying on Diana, a warning that is then reinforced both implicitly and explicitly by his kinswoman Byrrhena." See also Nethercut 110–19 and Tatum 38.

[14]For an interpretation of Psyche's task see, von Franz 97–109.

[15]For an artistic representation of Ceres see the Attic red-figure bell-krater, which dates to *c.* 440 BC, New York, Metropolitan Museum 28.57.23.

[16]See James 184.

Psyche's unsolicited house cleaning, who sends the ants to help Psyche. This trial of separating a heap of mixed grains may have its depiction in a cut gem that shows an unidentified, wingless girl holding ears of grain and sitting by an ant.[17] The second reference is found in 6.3, a description of the temple of Juno. This passage may hint at the golden wool that Psyche will have to collect as one of Venus' trials. I refer below to works of art that, in my opinion, capture moments of the Apuleian narrative and that depict a wingless Psyche; she is not described as having wings in the novel.

In 6.16 the myth of the realm of Orcus and of Proserpina is related:

> Protinusque ad inferos et ipsius Orci ferales penates te derige. Tunc conferens pyxidem Proserpinae, "Petit de te Venus," dicito, "Modicum de tua mittas ei formositate, vel ad unam saltem dieculam sufficiens."

> Straightaway take yourself to the underworld and to the house of Orcus himself. Then taking this box to Proserpina say, "Venus seeks that you send a bit of your beauty, enough for one day."

Nothing is wrong here, and the underworld is often depicted in art. While in the underworld (6.18–20) Psyche is told about and sees:[18]

> ipsam Orci regiam . . . Charon . . . Canis namque praegrandis, teriugo et satis amplo capite praeditus, immanis et formidabilis, tonantibus oblatrans faucibus mortuos, quibus iam nil mali potest facere, frustra territando ante ipsum limen et atra atria Proserpinae semper excubans servat vacuam Ditis domum.

---

[17]Schlam (1976) 33.
[18]On the literary models of Psyche's underworld trip see Tatum 60.

> The very palace of Orcus ... Charon ... a huge dog endowed with three heads, great and terrible, barking at the dead with thundering jaws, to whom no harm is able to be done, in vain terrifying them, always lying down before the threshold and the dark gate of Proserpina it keeps safe the desolate house of Pluto.

There is no problem with the allusions to the palace of Orcus and to Charon. The reference to Cerberus presents a problem: he is reduced to what can be best described by a cliché: his bark is worse than his bite.[19]

Employing an underworld theme,[20] the novelist has a reanimated corpse say that it has already tasted the waters of Lethe (2.29), which prompts a prophet to threaten the wrath of the Furies to get the corpse to speak. In art work the Furies appear binding the dead.[21] This peculiar reference to the Furies is further emphasized in 5.12, where Apuleius compares Psyche's sisters to the Furies. Since the Furies are connected with the underworld, Psyche may be in a metaphorical death. She was, after all, supposed to have been put to death.

After the murder of the three wine skins, Apuleius compares Lucius to Hercules when he mentions Geryon (2.32). The mythological allusion is correct in detail, and may foreshadow 3.19, where Lucius mocks his own deed:

---

[19] Apollodorus (2.5.12) tells us that said dog had three heads, and Homer (*Il.* 8.368) mentions a dog of Hades; Hesiod's (*Theog.* 311) dog has fifty heads.

[20] For other underworld allusions see 3.9 and 6.13.

[21] For example, the late fourth century Apulian red-figure volute-krater catalogued as Ruvo, Jatta, 1094.

> Igitur iam et ipse possum . . . mihi primam istam virtutis adoriam ad exemplum duodeni laboris Herculei numerare, vel trigemino corpori Geryonis vel triplici formae Cerberi.

> Therefore now I am able . . . to reckon that first glory of virtue as an example of Hercules' twelve works, such as that of Geryon with the three bodies or Cerberus with three heads.

Geryon and Cerberus are depicted on an Attic red-figure cup by Euphronios (Munich, Antikensammlungen 2620, *c*. 510 BC).

Lucius also likens himself to Cupid after he sees Pamphile turn herself into a bird. He wishes to do the same so that he may stand like Cupid next to a Venus (3.22): *ac iam perfice ut meae Veneri Cupido pinnatus adsistam tibi*. This wish of Lucius perhaps may be a reference to the numerous works of art that have Cupid and Venus together (e.g., the fourth century BC gold finger ring in the British Museum [65.7–12.59]). The possible use of art as a source for a mythological allusion is also found in 4.8, where the meal of the robbers resembles that of the Lapiths and Centaurs (see the Attic red-figure volute-krater from Italy in the Metropolitan Museum, New York [07.286.84]; *c*. 450 BC). This indeed is an interesting observation, since one of the most famous temples in the ancient world, the Parthenon, has such a depiction on it. The motif of a disturbed wedding re-occurs in 4.26, where the marriage of Charite resembles that of Attis or Protesilaus.[22]

A very detailed myth of Venus is supplied in 4.2, where Apuleius associates Venus with the Graces, and in 4.30 the judgment of Paris is recalled.[23] Finally, in what appears to be an artistically inspired passage, he supplies a list of the Venus'

---

[22]On representations of Attis see *LIMC* 3.1 (22–44) and 3.2 (15–45).

[23]Penwill (77 n. 22) says this passage "looks forward to the Judgement of Paris mime in Book 10." For a depiction of the Judgement of Paris see: Attic black-figure hydria from Vulci, *c*. 540, Munich, Antikensammlungen 1722.

servants (4.32).[24] A stool-pigeon reveals the name of the girl with whom Cupid has fallen in love (5.28). Mention is also made of Vulcan as Venus' husband (6.6).[25] Apuleius tells his reader that these allusions to myth are found in literature, that is, in the works of the Muses: *Dei conscripti Musarum albo*, "Gods registered in the book of the Muses" (6.23).

Pan and Echo also make an appearance: when Cupid leaves Psyche, she encounters these two who had also suffered in their own amorous adventures (5.25).[26] It is odd that Pan is attempting to teach Echo how to speak, as she is just an echo according to myth. More importantly, this scene involving Pan and Echo reflects what happened to Cupid and Psyche: a love affair gone awry.[27]

In 6.30 Apuleius compares Lucius in ass form to Pegasus, and does the same again in 7.26, when the unnamed stranger who found the ass is accused of murdering the boy killed by the bear. If the

---

[24]*Adsunt Nerei filiae chorum canentes, et Portunus caerulis barbis hispidus, et gravis piscoso sinu Salacia, et auriga parvulus delphini Palaemon; iam passim maria persultantes Tritonum catervae; hic concha sonaci leniter buccinat, ille serico tegmine flagrantiae solis obsistit inimici, alius sub oculis dominae speculum progerit, curru biiuges alii subnatant. Talis ad Oceanum pergentem Venerem comitatur exercitus.* Nereus is known well enough, and Portunus is the Italian god of ports and havens. He is, however, identified with Palaemon of the Greeks. Palaemon was originally Melicertes, the son of Ino, who was transformed into a god when his mother jumped into the sea (see *Od.* 5.333). Keightley (484 n. 6) notes that Salacia was the wife or sister of Neptune (see Varr. *LL* 5.72, Aul. Gell. 13.22), and was "considered identical with Amphitrite or even Tethys." All the allusions seem to be correct, except the problematic references to Portunus and Palaemon, who were one and the same to the Romans.

[25]See the Attic black-figure dinos signed by Sophilos, London, British Museum 1971.11–1.1, *c.* 580 BC.

[26]See *LIMC* 3.1, 683 (Corinthian lamp, late 2nd-early 3rd cent. AD, Berlin, Staatliche Museum TC 5022) for an artistic representation of Pan and Echo. This is the one of the few examples depicting Pan and Echo together. Although the lamp may be contemporary to or later than Apuleius, nevertheless the joining of the two figures is found in Hellenistic and Roman literature.

[27]Friedländer (106) calls this scene "totally unnecessary"; for a different opinion see James 153–59.

stranger is Bellerophon, the author must be assimilating the ass to Pegasus. This allusion to the story of Bellerophon emerges once again in 10.2, where Cupid makes the stepmother fall in love with her stepson. This reference echoes many myths, for example, Joseph and Potiphar's wife, Bellerophon and Stheneboea, and Hippolytus and Phaedra.[28]

In 7.16 reference is made to Diomedes, king of Thrace, when the ass is maltreated by the horses:

> Sic apud historiam de rege Thracio legeram, qui miseros hospites ferinis equis suis lacerandos devorandosque porrigebat.

> Thus I had read in a history about the king of Thrace, who used to throw his wretched guests to his wild horses to be torn apart and eaten.[29]

A somewhat fitting parallel to the boy, who was supposed to be treating the ass with honor. In 10.14–15 the two brothers who accuse each other of stealing food state that they do not want to resemble Eteocles and Polyneices.[30] The final example of a myth depicted in art is in 10.19–22, when the woman who falls in love with the ass is compared to Pasiphae.[31]

I have shown that most of the numerous mythological references appear in pre-Apuleian art. It is warranted therefore to ask whether the mythological references in the story of Cupid and

---

[28]For one of many artistic representations of Pegasus and Bellerophon see the Apulian red-figure stamnos in the Museum of Fine Arts, Boston (00.349), c. 400 BC. In 11.8–9 the final mythological allusion to Pegasus occurs.

[29]For a depiction of Diomedes see the Attis black-figure (on coral red ground) cup by Psiax in Hermitage, Leningrad, c. 510 BC.

[30]For examples of these two figures see *LIMC* 7.1.730–748, and 7.2.539–46; the examples are listed under *Septem*.

[31]See Pasiphae with the infant Minotaur on her lap. Paris, Cabinet des Médailles, 1066.

Psyche are depicted in art. I now list some examples that may capture some of the narrative dealing with the adventures of Psyche.

1) The first work of art has Aphrodite on a *biga* drawn by Eros and Psyche; Hermes is also shown (terracotta relief, Locri, *c*. 470–460 BC, Taranto, Museo Nazionale).[32] The winged figure in the foreground is Cupid; the figure next to him has caused much speculation as to her identity, but I concur that it is Psyche.[33] I base this identification on the alabastron carried by Psyche, which represents the box that held a piece of Prosperina's beauty. Further support for this suggestion is found in the inclusion of Hermes in this relief (as Venus' agent and perhaps as psychopomp); the scene refers to the *Scheintod* of Psyche.

2) A fourth century BC, banded onyx scarab depicting a winged Psyche in front of whom is a bow.[34]

3) A fourth century BC gem with a woman seated on rocks in a bent position. An oinoche and an ant are before her; behind her there are ears of grain and above her a crow with wreath.[35]

4) A fourth century BC gem with a woman seated on the ground. In front of her there are ears of grain and a basket with fruit; behind her there is a plant.[36]

5) A fourth century BC gem with a woman seated on rocks holding an oinoche in right hand; before her are ants, above her there is a crow holding a wreath and behind her there are ears of grain.[37]

---

[32]Langlotz (pl. 9) identifies the draped woman as Psyche.

[33]For a thorough analysis of the problematic identification see Prückner 22–27. See also Schlam (1976) 44–45, 45 n. 16.

[34]Walters fig. 657. Schlam (1976, 4) identifies this woman as Psyche. See also Maaskant-Kleibrink 23–25.

[35]Walters fig. 1032. For the problems with the association of the woman in figs. 1032–1035 with Psyche see Walters 120. The major obstacle to the identification is that the woman is wingless, but Psyche in the *Metamorphoses* is also wingless.

[36]Walters fig. 1033.

[37]Walters fig. 1034.

6) A gem with a woman seated on the ground. There are ears of grain and an ant before her and behind her there is a plant.[38]

7) A first century AD gem depicting Aphrodite and Adonis in car, which is led by Psyche, Hermes, Pan, and Eros. Psyche is playing pan-pipes.[39]

8) A second century AD papyrus fragment (Florence, Mus. Arch. Pap. 919) depicting Cupid "lying on a couch while Psyche, characterized by her butterfly wings, stands behind and offers an object which can no longer be identified."[40]

9) The column-krater (shown at the end of this essay) depicting a "woman with situla, thyrsus (?), cista and tambourine... looking back at... Eros holding torch and pomegranate."[41]

The vase dates to around 330 BC (British Museum F 294) and belongs to the Trieste Owl Group and may pertain to the workshop of the Patera Painter.[42] It has never been associated with the *Metamorphoses* narrative, but I believe that it may reflect a synoptic view of the labors of Psyche.

In her first labor Venus orders Psyche:

> discerne seminum istorum passivam congeriem singulisque granis rite dispositis atque seiugatis ante istam vesperam opus expeditum approbato mihi. (6.10)

> Sort out this random pile of seeds, and with each grain rightly sorted and arranged, before this evening offer for my approval the disentangled work.

On the right side of the woman there is a stalk of grain.

In the second task Venus orders Psyche to obtain some golden wool:

---

[38]Walters fig. 1035.
[39]Walters fig. 3856.
[40]Weitzmann 110.
[41]Trendall and Cambitoglou 748.
[42]*Ibid.*, 747.

oves ibi nitentis auri vero decore florentes incustodito pastu vagantur. inde de coma pretiosi velleris floccum mihi confestim quoque modo quaesitum afferas censeo. (6.11)

There sheep shining with the beauty of real gold wander on the unguarded field. I decree that you go there and from the hair of the precious fleece immediately bring me, in one way or another, a required tuft.

Over the left arm of the woman hangs a fillet, or as I interpret it, a piece of wool.
The third labor of Psyche is to bring to Venus some water from the river Styx:

indidem mihi de summi fontis penita scaturrigne rorem rigentem hauritum ista confestim defer urnula. (6.13)

From that very place, from deep within the spring of bubbling water of the very summit bring to me in that vessel the freezing water.

In the right hand of the woman is a situla, a vessel used to carry liquids.
The last labor, as mentioned above, is Venus' request to have a piece of Proserpina's beauty:

Protinusque ad inferos et ipsius Orci ferales penates te derige. Tunc conferens pyxidem Proserpinae, "Petit de te Venus," dicito, "Modicum de tua mittas ei formositate, vel ad unam saltem dieculam sufficiens. (6.16)

Straightaway take yourself to the underworld and to the house of Orcus himself. Then taking this box to Proserpina say, "Venus seeks that you send a bit of your beauty, enough for one day."

The woman on the vase carries a cista in her left hand.

It can be argued that this vase painting has nothing to do with the story of Cupid and Psyche. Indeed the accouterments (cista, situla, stalks of grain, fillets) of the woman I would like to identify as Psyche are found on the other vases associated with the Trieste Owl Group. For example: Bologna 572 Group, column-krater, Glasgow 1690, ex Burrell coll. 19/46; Painter of the Ruvo 1092, stemmed plate, Once London Market, Charles Ede Ltd.; Group of New York 17.120.240, volute-krater, Dresden 519; Seated Woman Group, volute-krater, Leningrad inv. 581; Stanford-Conversano Group, amphora, Taranto 61498, from Ruvo; Berkeley 8/61 Group, hydria, Leiden K 1948/12.1; Fragmentary Vases from Altamura, amphora, Taranto.

It has also been noted that the "stock subjects" of southern Italian and Apulian vases have Eros surrounded by women with "perfunctory draped youths . . . on the backs of bell-kraters."[43] Indeed R. M. Cook, limits the depictions to "Dionysiac groups," "women at their toilet (some-times attended by Eros)," and "on the back familiar young men in cloaks."[44] Cook, however, does point out that on "more ambitious pieces mythology is illustrated."[45] This vase, in my opinion, is one of those ambitious pieces.

In the above examples numbered one through seven, Cupid is not included or as clearly delineated as in the Trieste Owl krater. Nor is Cupid depicted in any of vases in the above groups as having a pomegranate in his hand. This pomegranate can be interpreted in two ways. The first interpretation derives from the type of vase: the column-krater is a funerary artifact and therefore the pomegranate can be understood as denoting the underworld, as in the "Bride of Hades" motif. The second interpretation, and the one I prefer, also views the pomegranate as having underworld undertones: the pomegranate symbolizes the *Scheintod* of Psyche and her adventure to the underworld. Thus I argue that the vase painting on Trieste

---

[43]Cook 185.
[44]*Ibid.*, 187.
[45]*Ibid.*, 185.

Owl B. M. F. 294 offers the viewer a synoptic depiction of the labors of Psyche.

I have shown that Apuleius employs mythological stories in his novel that occur in works of art, and that all of these myths, with the exception of the Ganymede-Endymion combination, appear in art work created before the composition of the *Metamorphoses*. I have included in this selection of art gems upon which are depictions of a wingless woman surrounded by insects, grains, birds, and shown close to water. This woman was thought perhaps to have been a depiction of Psyche, but the lack of wings precluded the identification with the heroine of Apuleius' novel. But, as I have mentioned above, Apuleius does not describe Psyche as having wings. The woman on these gems, therefore, can be said to be Psyche.

Since the wingless woman is Psyche, I am of the opinion that Psyche need not be depicted as winged in other artistic media. This concept leads me to a process of identifying the woman of Trieste Owl Group B. M. F. 294 as Psyche. I am not basing the identification on the fact that she is wingless and with Cupid, but rather I argue that the painter presents synoptically the four labors of Psyche, and reinforces the narrative moment by including Cupid holding a pomegranate.[46]

BIBLIOGRAPHY

Anderson, Graham. 1984. *Ancient Fiction: The Novel in the Graeco-Roman World*. London and Sydney.
Arnott, W. G. 1962. "Ocnus, with Reference to a Passage of Apuleius and to a Black-Figure Lekythos in Palermo." *C&M* 23:233-47.
Beazley, J. D. 1976. *Etruscan Vase Painting*. New York.

---

[46]See Trendall (1989) 12-13, who states that the Trieste Owl Group belongs to those Late Apulian red-figured vases that tend to have on them depictions of lesser known myths.

Binder, Gerhard and Reinhold Merkelbach, eds. 1968. *Amor Und Psyche*. Darmstadt.
Boberg, Inger Margrethe. 1938. "The Tale of Cupid and Psyche." *C&M* 1:177–216.
Carpenter, Thomas H. 1991. *Art and Myth in Ancient Greece: A Handbook*. London.
Cook, R. M. 1997. *Greek Painted Pottery*. 3rd edition. London and New York.
de Vries, J. 1954. *Betrachtungen zum Märchen besonders in seinem Verhältnis zu Heldensage und Mythos*. Helsinki.
Dowden, Ken. 1982. "Psyche on the Rock." *Latomus* 41:336–52.
Fehling, D. 1977. *Amor und Psyche: Die Schöpfung des Apuleius und ihre Einwirkung auf das Märchen, eine Kritik der romantischen Märchentheorie*. Wiesbaden.
Franz, Marie-Louis von. 1980. *A Psychological Interpretation of the Golden Ass of Apuleius*. Irving, Texas.
Fredouille, J.-C. 1975. *Apulei Metamorphoseon Liber XI*. Paris.
Friedländer, Ludwig. 1913. *Roman Life and Manners Under the Early Empire. Vol. 4. Appendices and Notes*, translated by A. B. Gough. London.
Griffiths, J. Gwynn. 1978. "Isis in the *Metamorphoses* of Apuleius." In *Aspects of Apuleius' Golden Ass*, edited by B. L. Hijmans Jr. and R. Th. van der Paardt, 141–66. Groningen.
Hägg, Tomas. 1983. *The Novel in Antiquity*. Berkeley and Los Angeles.
Hooker, Ward. 1955. "Apuleius's 'Cupid and Psyche' As a Platonic Myth." *BR* 5.3:24–38.
James, Paula. 1987. *Unity in Diversity: A Study of Apuleius' Metamorphoses*. Hildesheim, Zurich, and New York.
Keightley, Thomas. 1976. *Classical Mythology: The Myths of Ancient Greece and Ancient Italy*. 2nd edition. Chicago.
Kenney, E. J., ed. 1990. *Apuleius: Cupid & Psyche*. Cambridge.
Lang, Andrew. 1884. *Custom and Myth*. London.
Langlotz, Ernst. 1954. *Ancient Greek Sculpture of South Italy and Sicily*. New York.
Lexicon Iconographicum Mythologiae Classicae.

Maaskant-Kleibrink, Marianne. 1990. "Psyche's Birth." In *GCN III*, edited by H. Hoffmann, 13-33. Groningen.
Mason, H. J. 1978. "Fabula Graecanica: Apuleius and his Greek Sources." In *Aspects of Apulieus' Golden Ass*, edited by B. L. Hijmans Jr. and R. Th. van der Paardt, 1-15. Groningen.
Merkelbach, Reinhold. 1958. "Eros und Psyche." *Philologus* 102:103-16.
Nethercut, W. R. 1968. "Apuleius' Literary Art: Resonance and Depth in the *Metamorphoses*." *CJ* 64:110-19.
Neumann, Erich. 1962. *Amor and Psyche: The Psychic Development of the Feminine: A Commentary on the Tale by Apuleius*, translated by Ralph Manheim. New York.
Penwill, J. L. 1975. "Slavish Pleasures and Profitless Curiosity: Fall and Redemption in Apuleius' *Metamorphoses*." *Ramus* 4:49-82.
Perry, Ben Edwin. 1967. *The Ancient Romances: A Literary-Historical Account of their Origins*. Berkeley and Los Angeles.
Prückner, Helmut. 1968. *Die Lokrischen Tonreliefs: Beitrag zur Kultgeschichte von Lokroi Epizephyrioi*. Mainz am Rhein.
Purser, Louis C. 1983. *The Story of Cupid and Psyche as Related by Apuleius*. 2nd edition. New Rochelle, New York.
Robertson, D. S. and Paul Vallette. 1940. *Apulée: Les Métamorphoses*. Paris.
Schlam, Carl C. 1993. "Cupid and Psyche: Folktale and Literary Narrative." In *GCN* V, edited by H. Hofmann, 63-73. Groningen.
—. 1992. *The Metamorphoses of Apuleius: On Making an Ass of Oneself*. Chapel Hill and London.
—. 1976. *Cupid and Psyche: Apuleius and the Monuments*. Ephrata, Pennsylvania.
Scobie, Alex. 1983. *Apuleius and Folklore: Toward a History of ML3045, AaTh567, 449A*. London.
—. 1978. "The Structure of Apuleius' *Metamorphoses*." In *Aspects of Apuleius' Golden Ass*, edited by B. L. Hijmans Jr. and R. Th. van der Paardt, 43-61. Groningen.

—. 1969. *Aspects of the Ancient Romance and its Heritage: Essays on Apuleius, Petronius and the Greek Romances.* Meisenheim am Glan.

Stabryla, Stanislaw. 1973. "The Functions of the Tale of Cupid and Psyche in the Structure of the *Metamorphoses* of Apuleius." *Eos* 61:261–72.

Steiner, Grundy. 1969. "The Graphic Analogue from Myth in Greek Romance." In *Classical Studies Presented to B. E. Perry*, 123–37. Urbana, Illinois.

Swahn, J.-Ö. 1955. *The Tale of Cupid and Psyche.* Lund.

Tatum, James. 1979. *Apuleius and the "The Golden Ass."* Ithaca and London.

Trendall, A. D. 1989. *Red Figure Vases of South Italy and Sicily: A Handbook.* London.

—. 1967. *The Red-Figured Vases of Lucania Campania and Sicily: I Text.* Oxford.

—. 1967. *The Red-Figured Vases of Lucania Campania and Sicily: II Indexes and Plates.* Oxford.

Trendall, A. D. and Alexander Cambitoglou. 1982. *The Red-Figured Vases of Apulia. Vol. 2.* Oxford.

Walsh, P. G. 1970. *The Roman Novel.* Cambridge.

Walters, H. B. 1926. *Catalogue of the Engraved Gems and Cameos, Greek, Etruscan, and Roman in the British Museum.* London.

Weinreich, Otto. 1930. "Eros und Psyche bei den Kabylen." *Archiv für Religionswissenschaft* 28:88–94.

Weitzmann, Kurt. 1959. *Ancient Book Illumination.* Cambridge, Massachusetts.

Wlosok, Antoine. 1975. "Amor and Cupid." *HSCP* 79:165–79.

Wright, James R. G. 1971. "Folk-Tale and Literary Technique in *Cupid and Psyche.*" *CQ* 21:273–84.

Tiberius' Roman Retirement: Antecedents and Implications

Linda W. Rutland Gillison
University of Montana

Suetonius (*Tib*. 15) relates that, upon his return from Rhodes, Tiberius moved from his house in the Carinae, which had formerly belonged to Pompey and then to Antony,[1] and took up his abode in the *horti Maecenatiani*, there dedicating himself completely to private business. Because we know so little of Tiberius' activities and attitudes during the period, the report assumes a particular interest. Within a short time, Augustus' beloved grandsons were dead and with them, apparently, the *princeps'* plans for a peaceful transferral of power at his death. At that time, Augustus adopted Tiberius, and from then until the *princeps'* death Tiberius was occupied with important military commands. As many honors accrued to him, it became increasingly clear that Augustus intended him as his successor. Suetonius (*Tib*. 14) assures his readers that Tiberius had returned to Rome "with the same great and secure expectation of a glorious future that he had conceived in his mind since childhood" (*rediit . . . magna nec incerta spe futurorum, quam et ostentis et praedictionibus ab initio aetatis conceperat*). That "secure expectation" may, however, have been a construct after the fact. Certainly for several months after his return to Rome, Tiberius' situation vis-à-vis Augustus continued uncomfortable and his future doubtful. Examination of the move recorded by Suetonius and of its significance will repay the trouble, if it can cast light on Tiberius' intents and hopes.

---

[1]Decorated with the rostra taken from pirate ships, the house was also called the *domus rostrata* (Cic. *Phil*. 2.68; SHA *Gordiani* 3); for Mark Antony as later owner, see Dio 48.38, Flor. 2.18.4, [Aur. Vict.] *De Vir*. 84.3.

Suetonius describes the increasing concern with which Tiberius had tried to reassure Augustus of his loyalty during his absence in Rhodes (*Tib.* 12). He knew that it was in his interest to appear unthreatening to Augustus, and his behavior upon his return to Rome was certainly designed to that very purpose. Possibly that return took place only under terms of an agreement with the young Gaius, prohibiting Tiberius' participation in public affairs. And the occasion of the return may actually have been the introduction of Tiberius' son Drusus to public life.[2] Whatever the occasion and the conditions, Tiberius did go into relative seclusion, engaging only in the private duties which fell to him as head of the Claudian family. He had just introduced his son Drusus to public life. Thenceforth he contented himself with the making of private gifts, the freeing of slaves, the accepting of inheritances and legacies in the role of *pater familias*.

And he left his old residence for a new one.[3] In fact, not only his refusal to participate in public life but even his choice of residence begged Augustus to see in him a loyal son and citizen and a threat neither to the security of the Principate nor to the peace of Rome. Tiberius' change of residence was significant not because of the distance involved, but because of the way Romans and especially Augustus would perceive it. To them certain "addresses" suggested potentially dangerous ambition on the part of their residents, while others did not.

The Carinae, lying just to the north of the Forum Romanum in the area of the present-day Via Cavour and Via degli Annibaldi and Piazza S. Pietro in Vincoli, was a perfect neighborhood for politically ambitious Romans, and such inhabitants appear in the

---

[2]Dio (55.10a.10) and Suetonius (*Tib.* 13.2) report that the decision about Tiberius' return fell to Gaius Caesar. Seager (32) concludes that an agreement was struck at the time, banning Tiberius from political life. Levick (46) considers Drusus' public introduction as the occasion of the return.

[3]Seager (35) writes "significantly" he moved.

sources for early and late Republican times as well as the Principate.[4]

The young and energetic Spurius Cassius, for instance, whose story lends excitement to Livy's early narrative (2.41.11), had a house in the neighborhood. When his obvious ambition frightened everyone, he was condemned for *perduellio* and destruction of his residence followed. Referring to the incident and the later construction of the temple of Tellus on the site, Valerius Maximus (6.3.1b) comments: *itaque quod prius domicilium inpotentis viri fuerat, nunc religiosae severitatis monumentum est*, "and so that which was earlier the residence of a man without sense of limit now is a monument of strict religious observance."

Another active republican who resided in the Carinae was L. Marcius Philippus, the renowned orator and step-grandfather of Octavian. According to Horace, Philippus once complained, as he made his way home from public duties in mid-afternoon, that the Carinae was simply too far from the Forum.[5] His complaint, however, must be understood in context. The Carinae was by no stretch of the imagination a peripheral or suburban area: at the time of his comment, long after his tribunate of 104 BCE and his consulate of 91 BCE, Lucius was already an old man (*grandis natu*), and clearly the neighborhood had served his political needs for many years.

Q. Cicero also owned a house *in Carinis*, which he rented during his absence to members of the Lamia family—"smart renters," (*mundi habitatores*), as Marcus dubs them and known both for their taste and for their political abilities.[6] The most famous residence in the neighborhood, though, had belonged to the great Pompey. Suetonius specifies its location *in Carinis* at the

---

[4]See Richardson, "*Carinae*," and Fridh 133–34.
[5]See *Ep.* 1.7.46–51, esp. 48–49: *dum redit atque Foro nimium distare Carinas / iam grandis natu queritur.*
[6]*QFr.* 2.3.7: (*domum*) *tuam in Carinis mundi habitatores Lamiae conduxerunt.*

temple of Tellus,⁷ and it was certainly known in his day. It passed to Antony after Pompey's defeat at Pharsalus—a transfer to which Sextus Pompey referred in a sardonic joke in 39 BCE, when he met with the triumvirs on his ship: "he said he was hosting the banquet 'in his Carinae'—referring his comment to the name of the place where Antony was now in possession of his paternal residence."⁸ Subsequently, the residence passed to Tiberius' hands, while, over two-hundred years later, the Gordians, emperors of Rome, still resided there and counted it among their most noble possessions.⁹ One of their neighbors was Balbinus, whose brief reign took place during that same confused period. His house must have been very special, since the biographer mentions that it was still pointed out to travelers and other curious types at the end of the fourth century.¹⁰

In short, it was probably not due merely to geographical proximity that Vergil recalled how Evander and Aeneas "saw the herds as they lowed here and there in the Roman forum and the smart Carinae." The Roman Forum was the hub of political life

---

⁷*Gramm.* 15: *Lenaeus, magni Pompei libertus . . . schola se sustentavit docuitque in Carinis ad Telluris in qua regione Pompeiorum domus fuerat.*

⁸Velleius 2.77.1: *dixit in Carinis suis cenam dare, referens hoc dictum ad loci nomen, in quo paterna domus ab Antonio possidebatur.* Dio 48.38 relates the same quip: πρὸς τὸν Ἀντώνιον, ἐπειδὴ τὴν οἰκίαν αὐτοῦ τὴν πατρῴαν τὴν ἐν ταῖς Καρίναις κατεῖχε (τόπος γάρ τις τῆς τῶν Ῥωμαίων πόλεως οὕτω καλούμενός ἐστιν), ἀποσκώψας τρόπον τινὰ ἥδιστον (ταῖς γὰρ τροπίσι ταῖς τῶν νεῶν τῆς αὐτῆς ὀνομασίας οὔσης, ἐν ταῖς Καρίναις αὐτοὺς ἑστιᾶν ἔφη).

⁹SHA *Gordiani* 3.6: *exstat silva eius memorabilis, quae picta est in domo rostrata Cn. Pompei, quae ipsius et patris eius et proavi fuit;* 17.2 cites ownership of the property as evidence of the family's high quality: *quod domum Pompeianam in urbe habuit.*

¹⁰SHA *Maximus et Balbinus* 16.1: *domus Balbini etiam nunc Romae ostenditur in Carinis, magna et potens et ab eius familia huc usque possessa.*

during the Republic and the nearby Carinae was the home of many of Rome's politically active elite.[11]

At a date not recorded in the sources, Augustus' friend Gaius Maecenas acquired land on the Esquiline hill and laid out his park.[12] This acquisition and utilization of the property may well have been at the instigation of Augustus, who is known to have encouraged his loyal supporters in building projects beneficial to the entire city.[13] Clearly the plot along the *agger*, having long served as a burial ground for paupers, was an unhealthy eyesore, and Horace's satire (1.8.14–16) gives the most concise testimony to the important urbanistic effect which the park had on the area: "now you can

---

[11]*Aen.* 8.360–361: *passim . . . armenta videbant Romanoque foro et lautis mugire Carinis.* Servius, at *Aen.* 8.360–61, notes that Augustus was reared in the neighborhood.

[12]See Richardson, "*Horti Maecenatiani*," and Grimal 143–45.

[13]Only the most trusted adherents were allowed to finance and dedicate buildings which would be of public utility. Marcius Philippus restored the Temple of Hercules and the Muses. Munatius Plancus' contribution, after his governorship and subsequent triumph *ex Gallia*, was a restored Temple of Saturn. L. Cornificius was proconsul of Africa and triumphed in 32. After his triumph and the decision at Actium, he restored the Temple of Diana on the Aventine. Statilius Taurus triumphed in 34 after securing Africa and dedicated his amphitheater in 30—again, when Actium had given relative "leisure" to Octavian and his military supporters. After his Illyrian triumph in 39, Asinius Pollio had repaired the Atrium of Liberty and installed in it Rome's first public library. When the departure for Actium was imminent, he was to decline Octavian's invitation. Nonetheless, his complete retirement from politics and dedication to leisure and studies revealed that he was no threat to the plans of the latter. The younger Balbus dedicated a theater in 13, having celebrated in 19 his African triumph, the last granted to a senator. The vast contributions of Octavian's strong right-hand man, Marcus Agrippa, hardly need mention: aqueducts, baths, a bridge, the Pantheon. All of these were men whom Augustus was sure he could trust not to take hostile advantage of the popular favor garnered by such new constructions in order to rival or threaten the new order which he was attempting to establish. Harris (159) detects a certain hesitation on the part of the first-century senate to authorize gifting of the *populus Romanus* by outstanding individuals of the kind who might, in earlier days, have contributed bridges, roads, temples, or aqueducts as a public service and in advancement of their own reputations.

promenade on the healthy Esquiline and on the sunny *agger*, where only recently sad visitors used to observe a field ugly with whitened bones." The old burial site had, by law, been outside the city limits, and the gardens now replaced it in that peripheral location.[14]

By objective measurement, the park of Maecenas was not far from the Carinae. One simply proceeded up the Esquiline to reach the Porta Esquilina and the neighborhood of the garden estate. Although in his later days L. Philippus might have complained of the added distance, it was not great. The location, however, was somewhat less central, and the Servian *agger* still had symbolic significance as the city's far edge. Most importantly, such *horti* had, from their first appearance at the city's walls, served as places of retreat for wealthy Romans, and as such they were perceived. They neither necessarily invited nor announced political activity.

Urban *horti* began to appear around Rome during the first half of the first century BCE. The earliest were the properties of military men like Lucullus and Pompey, who found them useful for several

---

[14]Hor. *Sat.* 1.8.14–16: *nunc licet Esquiliis habitare salubribus atque / aggere in aprico spatiari, quo modo tristes / albis informem spectabant ossibus agrum.* The ancient sources record further features on the Esquiline near the *horti Maecenatiani*, and they were probably located there just because of the proximity of Maecenas' property. Suetonius (fr. 298) records that [*Horatius*] *humatus et conditus est extremis Esquiliis iuxta Maecenatis tumulum.* The neighborhood clearly had not lost its attraction as a location for burials. But these burial sites will have been quite different from the earlier paupers' graves. *Horti* were favored as sites for tombs. Donatus (*Vita Vergilii* 13) relates that the poet had a home *Romae Esquiliis iuxta hortos Maecenatianos.* In the gardens was the *turris*, from which, according to Suetonius (*Nero* 38.2), Nero watched the great fire, *incendium e turre Maecenatiana prospectans.* Whether or not that structure is the same as the *domus Maecenatis* whither Augustus was accustomed to retreat during illness (Suet. *Aug.* 72) may be debated. The same is the case of the lofty construction—*fastidiosam copiam, molem propinquam nubibus arduis*—from which Horace (*Carm.* 3.29.9–12) tries to entice his friend. Dio (55.7.6) reports that Maecenas was the first Roman to install a warm swimming pool on his property (πρῶτός τε κολυμβήθραν θερμοῦ ὕδατος ἐν τῇ πόλει κατεσκεύασε), but he fails to specify the exact location of the pool.

reasons, and the examples of some of those early owners are instructive.

Such was L. Licinius Lucullus. After the loss of his Asian command to Pompey, Lucullus returned to Rome.[15] His political star was on the decline and retirement seemed in order. But Lucullus had not lost all, and he still had goals to accomplish. Since it was of extreme importance that he be available for quick political action when such action could further his cause, his numerous splendid villas at Baiae and elsewhere in Italy simply would not serve. Instead, he withdrew to his garden establishment on the Pincian—the earliest urban *horti* of which we have any definite information—and thus initiated a trend which was to change the face of Rome and the life of Rome's governing class.

He did not retire completely nor for good and all. His final retirement came only when his ally Cato was sent away to Cyprus and Cicero exiled. Meanwhile he continued, as Plutarch says (*Luc.* 42), to intervene on his friends' behalf in the senate and forum, "when occasion offered to humble the ambition and pride of Pompey." The park which he had laid out on the Pincian served him well as a headquarters during his campaign against senatorial approval of Pompey's eastern settlement and payment for his veterans. In 58, it merely became a deeper retreat than the politically active Lucullus had earlier required. And from then until his death, Lucullus enjoyed in his gardens a retirement which became legendary or notorious for its luxurious elegance.[16]

The usefulness of an estate on the very edge of the city and overlooking the Campus Martius to such a man as Pompey is clear. Of course it offered a luxurious retreat for him, when he had leisure to absent himself completely from business. When affairs were

---

[15]Recently, on the career of Lucullus, see Keaveney, and Antonelli.
[16]On the "softness" of this phase of Lucullus' life, see Plutarch *Luc.* 39: εἰς παιδιὰν γὰρ ἔγωγε τίθεμαι καὶ οἰκοδομὰς πολυτελεῖς καὶ κατασκευὰς περιπάτων . . . , and *Mor.* 792b. At *Luc.* 41.6 and 42.1, however, Plutarch hints at a deeper, more political understanding of Lucullus' retirement expenditures. Keaveney (142) refines the picture. On the park, see Richardson, "*Horti Lucullani.*"

more pressing and complex, however, he could exert tremendous pressure on Rome's political life as he sat in his Pincian park, carefully observing the behavior of various groups and individuals without being, himself, embroiled in the political storms.

Pompey owned at least one house in the city, the famous *domus Pompeiana* in the Carinae. There he could stay when it was comfortable for him and when his bodily presence within the city was necessary. Plutarch, however, complains (*Pomp.* 48) that Pompey's love for his young wife Julia caused him to retreat from a serious political life and take refuge in gardens and luxury. The tradition of a deep affection between the partners is strong, but it is quite possible that the complexities of Pompey's political life during the years of his marriage (59–54), rather than simple devotion to his young wife, were the cause of numerous retreats to his private garden holdings during that time. Like Tiberius later, he seems to have found it expedient to absent himself from the political center.

The sources preserve numerous explicit references to Pompey's use of his park, and there are several additional instances when such a retreat would have been useful to him. In 61, when he had just returned from the East and wished to advance the consular campaign of Afranius, he distributed bribes among the tribes, "and people came and received [them] in his own gardens."[17] Clodius' insulting attacks in 58 drove Pompey to withdraw from sight for several months and neglect public life (Plut. *Pomp.* 49), nor was he

---

[17]Plut. *Pomp.* 44: καὶ τοῦτο κατιόντες εἰς τοὺς Πομπηίου κήπους ἐλάμβανον. Pompey must certainly have begun the work on his gardens during his absence and through some agent. Plutarch (*Pomp.* 40.5) reports that a pampered freedman of Pompey named Demetrius, while still absent from the city with Magnus, had "purchased the most pleasant suburban retreats of Rome" and that very expensive gardens were called "Demetrian" after him. Plutarch next asserts that Pompey himself, up to the time of his third triumph, contented himself with a simple dwelling, and the park, which he certainly owned by 61, must have represented a striking change. We know of no park called Demetrian. Perhaps Demetrius was Pompey's agent, purchasing the properties in his own name during Pompey's absence. Kaster (110) speculates on the meaning of the Demetrian reference.

present on the occasion of Cicero's recall from exile (App. *BC* 2.16). At least part of that time may have been passed in the *horti Pompeiani*. Certainly, in April of 56, when the triumvirate which had been so delicate was just being reaffirmed, Cicero (*QFr.* 2.5.3) found Pompey in his park and requested the quick return of his brother Quintus from Sardinia, where he was in Pompey's service: "After dinner," he reported to Quintus, "I was conveyed to Pompey in his park. During the day I had not been able to meet him, since he had been away. I really wanted to see him, though, because I was leaving Rome on the next day and he was intending to journey to Sardinia." Although we do not know how lengthy Pompey's garden stay was on this occasion, one attraction of the *horti* was that retreat thither needed not be a long-term matter. In 54, he avoided the provinces but also the city (Plut. *Pomp.* 53), and, when in 53 he received the grain commission with the great power and repute consequent upon it (App. *BC* 2.18), he drew out his sojourn beyond the city walls. The Pincian *horti* would have offered a perfect headquarters for Pompey in that year, as he watched the deterioration of the urban predicament and awaited the senate's plea for his help and offer of the sole consulship. Asconius, in his commentary on Cicero's *pro Milone*, remarks that for a time Pompey refused to reside at his townhouse, fearing or pretending to fear Milo. Rather, he took to spending most of his time in the *horti*.[18] When the crowds (*illa Clodiana multitudo*), enraged at the death of the favorite Clodius, sought leadership, they found Pompey in his park (Asc. *Mil.* 33).

---

[18] Asc. *Mil.* 37: *timebat autem Pompeius Milonem, seu timere se simulabat, plerumque non domi suae sed in hortis manebat, idque ipsum in superioribus circa quos etiam magna manus militum excubabat. Senatum quoque semel in porticu sua habuerat Pompeius quod diceret timere se adventum Milonis;* 25: *sed in hortis superioribus ante iudicium mansisse, ita ut villam quoque praesidio militum circumdaret;* 52: *ob has suspiciones Pompeius in superioribus hortis se continuerat.* In the commentary on *Pro Milone* 67, Asconius notes Cicero's reference *in contione* to a time (January 24, 52) *cum Milo ... venire ad Pompeium in hortos eius voluisset.*

Finally, as the motion to have both Caesar and Pompey lay down their commands was being debated, Pompey hung on the outskirts, since it was unlawful for a commanding general to enter the *pomerium*. There he could oversee (and influence) affairs in the city and yet not subject himself to the buffetings so characteristic of "civic" life at the time. Caesar saw the contradiction and understood its implications: that "commands of a new kind were being established against him, with the result that one individual presided *ad portas* over city matters and retained for so many years the *imperium* over two warlike provinces *in absentia*" (*Civ.* 1.85).

For wealthy political Romans as a group, fully involved in the Republic's vicissitudes, the parks on the city limits offered the same general advantage as the *horti Pompeiani* offered to the city's potential savior. The *horti* allowed their owners to be absent from the everyday maelstrom of Roman politics and yet to keep watch on the political scene and intervene if necessary or expedient. In this respect they were preferable to the *villae suburbanae* which lay several miles distant from the city and had not the possibilities for instant communication offered by the urban *horti*.

Maecenas' situation, of course, was quite different from that of Pompey and Lucullus. Content with the status of an *eques*, he never ran for public office in Rome, but still surpassed in wealth and power many senators who involved themselves in political life via the *cursus honorum*. His influence and power depended not on public office, but on the patronage of Augustus, who trusted him well and relied on him in many a critical situation.[19] Maecenas' political needs were of a different sort from those of Pompey and Lucullus and other Romans who held public office. In crisis, his

---

[19] Only a few instances need note. Maecenas represented Octavian before Sextus Pompey and Mark Antony on the occasion of the treaty of Brundisium in 40. In 38, he applied, on Octavian's behalf, for help from Antony, after his disastrous confrontation with Pompey. While Octavian campaigned against Pompey in Sicily, Maecenas looked after things in Rome. And when Octavian departed for Actium, where he was to eliminate his last looming republican enemy, Maecenas was left to manage Rome and Italy.

considerable abilities were required not in the forum or the Campus Martius, but wherever Augustus needed him.

Maecenas was accustomed to a life of elegance and luxury which led some to charge him with sloth and softness.[20] But even in times of retreat he needed to be available to Augustus at a moment's notice. From the *horti Maecenatiani* on the city's edge he could set out instantly for the scene of the action to serve his friend in the appropriate fashion. And so he did. Though relations between them may have cooled somewhat during later years, Maecenas named

---

[20]Certainly, Maecenas owned property in Rome in addition to the *horti*. Suetonius (*Aug.* 72) mentions a *domus Maecenatis*, which Augustus used as a retreat during illness. Horace (*Epod.* 9.3) begs Maecenas to come down from his *alta domo*, and the same building may be the reference in *Carm.* 3.29 (*molem propinquam nubibus arduis*). The *turris Maecenatiana* (Suet. *Nero* 38.2) is famous as the vantage point from which Nero allegedly observed the great fire of 64. (Tacitus maintains at *Ann.* 15.39 that Nero sang his firelight aria *in domestica scaena*.) Whether the *domus* of *Aug.* 72 is the same as the garden dwelling mentioned in *Nero* 38 and which, if either, is the *alta domus* of the *Epodes* is debatable. The two towers, at least, are likely to be one. The semi-underground building (in Via Merulana at Largo Leopardi) called by excavators the *auditorio di Mecenate* is nowhere mentioned in the ancient sources.

Maecenas' park must certainly have been impressive. If the continued use of it as an imperial retreat did not alert us to that fact, additional evidence would come from the dedication by Sabinius Tiro of his book *Peri Kepourikon* to their owner (Plin. *NH* 19.177; Dio 55.7.6).

Concerning his effeminacy, see Juv. 1.66: *hinc atque inde patens ac nuda paene cathedra / et multum referens de Maecenate supino / signator falsi;* Tac. *Ann.* 1.54: *dum Maecenati [Augustus] obtemperat effuso in amorem Bathylli;* Vell. Pat. 2.88.2: *otio ac mollitiis paene ultra feminam fluens*. Seneca (*Ep.* 114.4) uses him as an example of the point that *talis hominibus fuit oratio qualis vita*, and a telling phrase in Suetonius (*Aug.* 86) reports that Augustus, a man of straightforward oratorical style, "parodied mercilessly" Maecenas' phrase "myrrh-distilling ringlets" (*myrobrechis . . . cincinnos*). Pliny (*NH* 8.170) reports that he wanted to introduce the flesh of young donkeys as a taste treat at Roman banquets.

Augustus his chief heir, and in 8 BCE all of his vast properties, including the urban park, came into the *princeps'* possession.[21]

In view of what was said earlier about the non-threatening associations of the *horti Maecenatiani*, it may seem paradoxical that a chief advantage of these gardens was a political one. The paradox, however, inheres in the nature of the urban *horti*. And it was precisely this consideration which led a man in Tiberius' position to retire to such a park. Those estates just beyond the city boundaries were neutral ground in an important sense—perfect retreats for a Roman with no urgent political agenda. But this retirement to an urban park needed not be either long-term or even temporarily deep. It did not distance a man intolerably from the political scene, nor did it cut him off from sources of valuable political information.

Tiberius had very specific needs upon his return to Rome. He needed, first of all, to reassure Augustus of his loyalty. In addition, he needed to stay informed concerning developments in the household of Augustus. In both respects, his choice of Maecenas' park as a retirement residence was an eminently happy one.

The multiplication of rumors during his absence in Rhodes had clearly indicated the wisdom of his residence in Rome, close under the eye of Augustus. And yet not every domicile in Rome was of a sort to reassure the *princeps*. Since Tiberius needed to abstract himself from any threatening associations, a move was necessary. He left his home in a neighborhood which had strong and continuing connotations of political activity and ambition and moved into the garden estate whose first owner had been one of Augustus' most trusted advisors—a man who had determinedly refused to seek public office and had relied instead, to the end, on the patronage of Augustus. Never had a hostile sally from those gardens threatened Augustus or the order which he was working to establish. Those

---

[21] Dio 55.7.5. The park remained a unit and was still known as such under Nero, who had joined it with the Palatine residence, and in Tacitus' day (*Ann.* 15.39). Cf. Dio 54.23.2 on Vedius Pollio's will and its intent versus Augustus' subsequent use of the legacy. Maecenas was, with Agrippa, a dedicatee of Augustus' autobiography.

gardens were tarnished by no challenging associations from the republican period. The park had for years now been in Augustus' possession, so in one sense Tiberius was moving in under Augustus' own roof.

Dedicating himself to the personal concerns of a private citizen, he undertook no public duties. Augustus could only be reassured. Throughout the next months, however, Tiberius could carefully observe—from his garden retreat—occurrences in the household of Augustus. When cruel Fortune had played her last trick on the old *princeps* and his plans for the succession, he was immediately available as a support. In Maecenas' gardens, Tiberius was only as isolated as he chose to be.

The beauty of the urban *horti* had always been that they allowed the wealthy Roman to mediate between two desirable opposites: absence from the pressures and threats of political life and presence on the scene when such presence was useful. For diverse reasons and on specific occasions, the centrally-located and elegant *domus in Carinis* came to serve the needs of both Pompey and Tiberius less effectively than it had previously, and on each occasion the astute owner vacated the townhouse for an urban park. By residence in his *horti*, Pompey had contrived for himself absences which he shrewdly utilized to his political advantage. Certainly the inscrutable Tiberius, in his highly delicate position, appreciated and utilized fully the ambiguous state of retirement offered uniquely by the *horti Maecenatiani* as he awaited developments in Augustus' plans for the succession.

BIBLIOGRAPHY

Antonelli, G. 1989. *Lucullo*. Roma.
Fridh, A. 1987. "Three Notes on Roman Toponymy and Topography." *Eranos* 85:115–33.
Grimal, Pierre. 1969. *Les jardins romains*. 2nd edition. Paris.
Harris, W. V. 1979. *War and Imperialism in Republican Rome, 327–70 B.C.* Oxford.

Kaster, Gert. 1974. "'Die Gärten des Lucullus.' Entwicklung und Bedeutung der Bebauung des Pincio-Hügels in Rom." Diss. Munich.
Keaveney, A. 1992. *Lucullus. A Life*. New York.
Levick, B. 1976. *Tiberius the Politician*. London.
Richardson, L., Jr. 1992. *A New Topographical Dictionary of Ancient Rome*. Baltimore.
Seager, R. 1972. *Tiberius*. London.

Latinitas in the Late Antique Greek East: Cultural Assimilation and Ethnic Distinctions[1]

Linda Jones Hall
St. Mary's College of Maryland

In the Late Antique Greek East, the study of Latin, especially the works of Cicero and Virgil, was seen as a way to advance in the legal profession or in a bureaucratic career.[2] As many students came to claim the privilege of identifying themselves as "Roman," they also accepted societal definitions of themselves as "Phoenicians," "Syrians," or other ethnic groups as depicted in these writers. Ironically, education in the imperial language initially fostered assimilation but came in time to provide an intellectual and social vocabulary for ethnic distinctions and imperial dissolution.[3]

Although the teaching of Latin (as well as Greek) in the Roman Near East is usually perceived as fostering assimilation to the Roman rule centered in Constantinople, modern imperial situations

---

[1]Grateful acknowledgment is made to Profs. Timothy E. Gregory and Michael J. Zwettler of the Ohio State University, to Prof. J. H. W. G. Liebeschuetz of the University of Nottingham, and to Dr. Fred W. Jenkins of the University of Dayton for their willingness to discuss and critique the ideas in this essay. Thanks also to Prof. N. David Cook and Drs. Sumita Chatterjee and Patricia Lorcin of Florida International University for stimulating conversations about the formation of ethnic identity. Appreciation is expressed to the editors and anonymous readers for their careful suggestions. Any errors that remain are my own.

[2]For the popularity of these two Latin authors in the Greek East, see Gaebel (1968) 8 and (1970) 284–325, and Colt. For social mobility in this period, see MacMullen (1964).

[3]See Laurence, Hall (1997), and Morgan for important studies of ancient Roman and Greek ethnicity.

suggest that another, unintended outcome may have been produced. Just as the Francophone schools in Algeria and Anglophone schools in India enhanced the production of loyal literate bureaucrats,[4] so centers of learning in the cities of the Levant (Berytus, Antioch, Gaza, and Alexandria)[5] trained many ambitious provincials in the languages of imperial administration.

Modern events in India, Algeria, and other post-colonial countries suggest that although there is an initial acceptance of the values of the dominant imperial power through the study of the language and literature thereof, eventually the portrait of the conquered peoples in the imperial literature holds great appeal for the indigenous student.[6] Furthermore, the evidence suggests that imperially constructed definitions of ethnic distinctions can become internalized and lead to separatist movements in the name of categories that the conqueror constructed.[7] These categories of separateness may not even have existed until the arrival of the "superior" outsiders who re-interpreted the world for the insiders.

In this paper I will suggest that "Phoenician" ethnicity became "heroized" by a study of Greek and Latin (especially the *Aeneid*) from the first to the sixth centuries AD and that this "reclaimed" ethnicity had far-reaching consequences for the creation of distinctive provincial and ethnic identities in the Late Antique era and beyond.[8] Although the evidence for this argument comes from the case-study of Late Antique Berytus in the province of Phoenicia, the conclusions may have wider applicability.

---

[4]See Kaye and Zoubir for French North Africa, and Metcalfe for British India.
[5]See Hall (1996) 241–66, Liebeschuetz 242–55, Downey (1961) 314, 384 and 395, and (1963) 99–116, and Haas 154–56.
[6]See Hall (1997) 143–81, and Gruen for the relation between literature and ethnic or cultural identity.
[7]Anderson 163–85.
[8]The concept of Phoenicia as a center of learning continued into the Byzantine era. Psellus, in the eleventh century, bemoaned the closure of centers of classical learning in Athens, Nicomedia, Alexandria, Phoenicia, and the two Romes; see Sewter 177.

The formation of neo-Phoenician identity in the Roman era. Berytus, a Hellenized Phoenician settlement of little importance, became a Roman colony in the time of Augustus and was endowed with buildings by the Herodian dynasty.[9] From the time of Pompey's settlement of the East until Septimius Severus' redrawing of provincial divisions, the city was part of the province of Syria.[10] Yet the powerful story of *Phoenissa Dido* must have resonated with special emotional affect in not only Tyre and Sidon but also in nearby Berytus.[11] Such a story undoubtedly attracted many students in a city populated by the descendants of the veterans of the battle of Actium.[12]

One of these Berytian readers of Virgil, M. Valerius Probus, became a respected commentator on the *Aeneid*. Suetonius tells us:

> Marcus Valerius Probus, of Berytus, long sought the centurionate but finally gave up in disgust and devoted himself to scholarship. For he had previously read certain old books with a *grammatista* in the province, where the memory of the ancient authors was still alive and had not yet passed entirely away as it had at Rome . . . he left behind an abundant trove of observations on ancient usage.[13]

Although Probus produced his work at Rome, it seems likely that he was descended from one of the original Berytian veteran colonists

---

[9] See Roller 47, 90, 94, 220–22, 249, and 255; see also Millar (1983) 54–71 and (1990) 10–23 and 39–46.

[10] See Millar (1993) 279–85 and 523–28. For reports on the recent archeological excavations in Beirut which are refining our knowledge of these various settlements, see Butcher and Thorpe 291–306, Williams, et al., Seeden.

[11] For local identification with the Dido legend, see Hexter. For the emotional affect on a reader such as Augustine, see MacCormack 89–100 and Desmond 74–98. The influence of Virgil has even been detected in the *Geoponika*, an agricultural handbook attributed ultimately to Vindanios Anatolius of fourth-century Berytus; see Rodgers.

[12] See Baldwin (1976) 361–68; (1982) 81–92; and (1985) 237–41 for the study of the *Aeneid* in the Greek East.

[13] Kaster 28–29.

from whom he may have inherited not only an interest in Roman military service and classical texts but also his knowledge of the ancient forms of Latin.[14] Probus's reputation for erudition was such that Jerome later described him as "the most learned of the scholars at Rome."[15]

Severan construction of imperial identity by means of the *Aeneid*. In the early third century Septimius Severus and his successors used imperial propaganda which glorified the author and characters of the *Aeneid*. Such conscious archaizing enhanced the nobility of Severan rule through identification with both the greatest opponents the Romans had ever faced and the victorious Romans themselves.[16] For example, coins of Tyre in the Severan period show Dido supervising the foundation of Carthage.[17] Millar has collected additional evidence from Severan coins and inscriptions which link Lepcis Magna in North Africa with the metropolis of Tyre.[18]

The Severan structures still survive in the Libyan desert, but evidence for other building programs must come from literary references. A lengthy poem of the fifth century AD in the *Greek Anthology* describes the life-like statues of characters unique to the *Aeneid* and of the author Virgil himself, which were to be found in a public museum in Constantinople called the Zeuxippon.[19] Malalas reported that Septimius Severus began the construction of this building which Constantine subsequently completed and dedicated, perhaps as a restoration of the Severan project.[20] Similar

[14] Kaster 242–69; Millar (1990) 16.
[15] Kaster 243.
[16] Millar (1990) 31.
[17] *Ibid.*, 36.
[18] Millar (1990) 31–46. For example, note the inscription from Lepcis Magna to Geta which honored *SEPTIMIA TYROS COLONIA METROPOLIS PHOENICES ET ALIARUM CIVITATUM,* "Tyre the Septimian colony, mother-city of Phoenicia and of other cities."
[19] See Christodorus of Thebes of Egypt in Paton, vol. 1, 57–91; see "Zeuxippos, Baths of," *ODB* 2226, for information on this structure; see Baldwin (1976) 367 for this poet.
[20] Malalas, *PG* 97.441 and 97.481.

propaganda purposes may have been served by a Severan building program in Berytus itself. Certainly, the family took an interest in the city, as the three inscriptions to the "Phoenician" empress Julia Domna discovered so far attest.[21]

Berytus as the "most Roman" city: the teaching of Latin and imperial advancement. Berytus was known pre-eminently as a center of legal studies and training in Latin language and literature from the third through the sixth century.[22] The city developed a reputation as the *locus* of various jurists who were in the circuit of the Severan dynasty. Berytus, known as the "most Roman city" of the Greek cities of the East, attracted students who wished to master Roman law from world-renowned professors.[23] Such a period of immersion in the language and the laws of Rome must not only have enhanced the students' scholarly knowledge, but must also have shaped their view of who they were as individuals.[24]

Although most educated residents of the Greek East spoke Greek, no matter what other language they spoke as a regional language, Latin was an entree to promotion in the Later Roman Empire. It remained an elite language whose use was almost entirely

---

[21] See Lauffray (1944–1945) 60–62 and (1978) 149, and Butcher 212–14 for these inscriptions. Although Julia Domna is usually described as Syrian, it should be noted that Caracalla designated her birthplace Emesa as part of Phoenicia: *Sed et Emisenae civitati Phoenices imperator noster ius coloniae dedit iurisque Italici eam fecit*, "But our emperor gave the right of a colony to the city of Emesa in Phoenicia and awarded her the Italian right" (*Dig.* 50.15.1.4). Other references to Emesa as part of Phoenicia, cited in Millar (1987) 158–59 include: Hdn. 5.3.2–7; Hld. *Aeth.* 10.41.4; and Malalas 296–97.

[22] See Marrou, and Lemerle 53 and 94–96 for the legal curriculum.

[23] See Honoré (1982) 1–46 for the relation of the Severans and the jurists. *Polis romaikotera* is the description of Berytus given by Gregory Thaumaturgus, *Panegyricus in Originem* 5.58–59 (239) in *PG* 10, 1065–66. These law professors were called by such terms as "heroes," "the most illustrious teachers," and "teachers of the whole world." See McNamee 399–414 citing the *Basilicorum libri LX*, excerpts of 6th century commentaries on the fifth century teachers of law at Berytus. Bischoff 70–73 suggests that law books in Latin were produced in the city.

[24] Young 312–28, and Trombley 1–53 discuss the struggle for self-realization by the law students in fifth-century Berytus.

confined in the East to the courtroom, the army, and the court. It was not corrupted by provincial developments that one notes in the Latin of Europe. It was a taught language, somewhat fossilized, which had to be conscientiously studied and mastered by ambitious young men who saw what such knowledge could do for their careers.[25]

Latin thus became a means to an end. Libanius' letters indicate that such an education cost a significant amount of money which was spent with the intention of realizing some return for the learner.[26] John Chrysostom pinpointed the political and social advancement that would come to young men who gained competence in Latin and the law. Although Chrysostom may have been referring to the training available in Antioch or Constantinople as well as Berytus, clearly such benefits would have persuaded ambitious young men to attend the law schools in Berytus. "Again, another person says such and such a one having learnt the language of the Italians [Latin] has a brilliant position in the imperial service and conducts and administers all internal matters."[27] Clearly, social and political advancement motivated the students who came to Berytus from various regions in the Greek East.[28] Gregory Thaumaturgus and his brother set forth from Neocaesarea in Pontus with the intention of studying law at Berytus in the AD 230s.[29] A papyrus verse epitaph (of perhaps the 4th century) commemorates a student from Cilicia who traveled to Berytus for "the sake of the Roman muse and the laws."[30] Two

---

[25]See Vidén 151–57, Brandsma 1–40, and Honoré (1978) 70–123 for analyses of legal Latin as written by these lawyers and bureaucrats.

[26]See Petit for a detailed study of Libanius' students.

[27]John Chrysostom *Adversus oppugn. vitae monasticae*, 3.5, *PG* 47.357.

[28]Note the careers of these lawyers who studied or taught in Berytus: from *PLRE I*, Apringius, Anatolius 3, Celsinus 3, Fl. Domitius Leontius 20, Lupercus 1, Scylacius 2, Severinus 1, and Theodorus 11; from *PLRE II*, Zacharias 4, Severus 12, Patricius 10, Leontius 20, and Leontius 23; from *PLRE III*, Anatolius.

[29]Gregory Thaumaturgus, "*Panegyricus in Origenem*," *PG* 10, 1065–66.

[30]Gilliam 147–50, and *SEG* 26, 1456.

brothers Arcadius and John, of a senatorial family of Constantinople in the time of Constantine, journeyed to Berytus to study law there.[31] Named or addressed in the fourth-century correspondence of Libanius were these law students at Berytus: Hilarinus of Euboea, Artemon of Antioch, and Peregrinus of Tarsus in Cilicia.[32] Later in the fifth century, in the "Life of Severus" by Zacharias of Mytilene, there are references to other law students from Armenia, Asia Minor, Egypt, Illyricum, and Lycia.[33]

In a speech to the *curia* of Antioch, Libanius explicitly linked the study of Latin to the schools in Phoenician Berytus (or Rome) and the training in Greek rhetoric to the schools of Syrian Antioch. Such a recognition of this division in linguistic acquisition may reflect other cultural distinctions as well.

> Every spring you see the sons of present, or past, members of the council sailing off to Berytus or to Rome. . . . It is out of no concern for justice or to avoid any inadvertent breach of the laws that they set sail for Phoenicia, nor do they sail to the other place so as to assist the council by their proficiency in both languages; their concern is to have their legal or linguistic qualifications as a means of getting out of membership of council. Nor have they been deceived in their ambition.[34]

Libanius was, in fact, bemoaning a period of transition in societal certainties. He made it clear that the students who endeavored to master Latin would not be disappointed in their goal of improving their lives, both financially and socially.

---

[31]*Vita et Res Gestae Sancti Xenophontis et filiorum eius Joannis et Arcadii. Acta Sanctorum Januarius* III (1863) 338–45.
[32]Libanius *Ep.* 533, 652, 1539 in Foerster.
[33]Kugener 55–57.
[34]Libanius *Oratio* 48.22 in Foerster; Norman (1969–1977) vol. 2, 438–41.

Moreover, as regards my studies, they had now lost ground to Latin even more than before, so that I am afraid that they may, through the agency of law, become completely superseded. Yet it is not law or edicts that have brought this about, but the honour and power reserved for those acquainted with Latin.[35]

The level of opportunity is revealed most clearly in the following passage in which Libanius contrasts the working-class students studying in Berytus with the upper-class students staying in Antioch. The orator thereby affirms that the law schools were open to young men from poorer backgrounds.

But indeed, on the one hand, formerly one could see the youths from the workshops [artisans] who are concerned about a barely sufficient livelihood, going to Phoenicia to study the laws. On the other hand, those young men of the wealthy houses who have distinguished lineage, property, and fathers who have carried out their curial duties remained in our studies.[36]

Corroboration of the advantages of acquiring bilingual competency is provided from the account of Ammianus Marcellinus, whose own successes demonstrated the advantages of knowing Latin well:[37] "Musonianus governed the East with the rank of praetorian prefect, a man famed for his mastery of both

---

[35]Libanius *Autobiography* 234 in Norman (1992) vol. 1, 291.
[36]My translation, based on the text from Libanius *Oratio* 62.21 in Foerster.
[37]For Ammianus' knowledge of classical Latin literature, see Jenkins 148–86, and Matthews 71 and 261–66.

languages, from which he won higher distinction than was expected."³⁸

Governmental and geographical expression of "Phoenician" identity. Geographical designations serve to create and sustain concepts of ethnicity. One may note the diligence of modern cartographers in redrawing territories and renaming regions in the wake of recent ethnic conflicts. Thus, we should view the carving up and renaming of Roman provinces in the Late Roman period with some attention to the implications for ethnic identity. Since the time of Septimius Severus, Berytus had been part of the province of Phoenicia. The demarcation of this area as Phoenicia persisted throughout the Later Roman Empire.³⁹ Early fourth century sources, such as the minutes of the Council of Nicea (AD 325), the Council of Sardica (AD 343–344), and the Council of Constantinople (AD 381), refer to Phoenice. Ammianus Marcellinus (14.8) also referred to the area as Phoenice, and there are references in the *Papyrus Rylands*⁴⁰ and in the *Codex Justinianus* (2.57.1) to the governing officials of Phoenice. The *Verona List* distinguished between Phoenice and Augusta Libanensis while the *Notitia Dignitatum* distinguished between Phoenice and Phoenice Libanensis. It is noteworthy that only Polemius, living in fifth century Gaul, used the term Syria Phoenice,⁴¹ and this suggests that western writers preserved the designation of Syria long after the eastern authorities routinely used the name Phoenicia.⁴²

---

³⁸*facundia sermonis utriusque clarus* is usually taken to imply Greek and Latin. Although Drijvers 532–37 suggests that Aramaic was the second or third language of this translator, the context makes it more likely that Latin was the second language. Ammianus Marcellinus 15.13.1–2; Rolfe vol.2, 198–99.
³⁹Matthew of Edessa, writing in the twelfth century about the victory of John I Tzimskes in AD 975–6, refers to Beirut, Sidon, and Baalbek as part of Phoenicia; Ostrogorsky 297; Dulaurier 22.
⁴⁰Jones (1954) 88–94.
⁴¹Jones (1964) vol.3, 390.
⁴²Jerome, *In Ezech.* 27.15–16 in *PL* 25, 267C, characterizes Tyrians as Syrians.

Governmental arrangements in Late Antique Berytus are reflected in an inscription of the fourth century AD which honored Leontius, the Praetorian Prefect and *consul ordinarius*.

> LEONTI
> PRAETORIO ADQVE OrdINARIO CONSVLI
> PROVOCANTIBVS EIVS MERITIS QVAE PER
> SINGVLOS HONORVM GRADOS AD HOS
> eVM DIGNITATVM APICES PROVEXERVNT
> DECRETIS PROVINCIAE PHOENICES SENTEN/
> TIA DIVINA FIRMATIS DD NN CONSTANTI ET
> CONSTANTIS AETERNORUM PRINCI/
> PVM ORDO BERYTIORVM STATVAM
> SVMPTIBVS SVIS *Ex* AERE LOCATAM
> CIVILI HABITO DEDICAVIT

> To [Flavius Domitius] Leontius,[43]
> praetorian [prefect][44] and ordinary consul,
> by the urging of his prominent merits
> which have carried him through
> the individual grades of offices to these
> summits of distinction,
> by the decrees of the province of Phoenice
> which have been confirmed by the divine opinion
> of our lords, Constantius
> and Constans, eternal princes,
> the [curial] order of the Berytians dedicate
> this statue of bronze,

[43]Editor's note from *ILS* 1234: Leontius was praetorian prefect in AD 338 (*Cod. Theod.* 9.4.7) and in AD 342 to 344 (*Cod.Theod.*1.5.4; 7.9.2; 9.21.5; 11.36.6; 12.1.35; 13.4.3), and ordinary consul in AD 344. The name Flavius is shown in *C. X. 478* [*sic*] and the name Domitius is shown in *Cod. Theod.* 9.1.7. This inscription was also seen by Waddington [no citation given], according to the editor of *CIL* 3.167.

[44]The editor of the *ILS* 1234 text inserts *vc* [*vir clarissimus*], "of consular rank," and *praefecto* before *praetorio*.

set up at their own expense,
on account of his civil bearing.⁴⁵

This inscription is interesting in several respects. Although the phrasing follows that for a seemingly traditional *cursus honorum*, the honoree is praised for holding imperial offices rather than for local civic achievements. It is important to notice that the province of Phoenicia precedes the *ordo Berytiorum* (the city council, *boule* or *curia*) and the names of the rulers in the list of those who have commissioned the inscription. This emphasis on the province may suggest that more and more decisions were being made at that level, and that identity as a provincial (Phoenician, in this case) was beginning to rival allegiance to a particular city or to the empire.

Furthermore, the use of Latin at this late date suggests that Berytians continued to see themselves as speakers of the authentic Roman language and affirmed their establishment as a Roman colonial foundation and their connection with Roman legal training.⁴⁶ The preservation of this historical distinctiveness may have enabled the Berytians to maintain a sense of non-Syrian, non-Greek ethnic heritage as well.

In the late fourth century AD, the designation of the province was further refined as Phoenicia Maritima which extended from Arados in the north and to Tyre (the capital) in the south. According to Malalas, it was Theodosius I (AD 379–395) who separated Phoenicia Maritima (literally Phoenicia Paralia) from Phoenicia Libanensis which included the Biqa'a Valley near Baalbek, the

---

⁴⁵*CIL* 3.167 = *ILS* 1234, dated to AD 344 by Isaac 319. For this last difficult phrase, several readings have been offered. Peter Brown, in a private letter of August 18, 1996, noted: "*civili habito* may simply mean that he was polite to everyone, an important virtue, with rarity value among high officials; cf. Aur. Victor on Julian—*civilis in cunctos.*" Liebeschuetz, in personal correspondence of October 31, 1996, suggested that the reading perhaps should be *civili ob habitu*, an interpretation that would justify the proposed translation above. The *CIL* text seems to suggest that the last line was broken or difficult to read.

⁴⁶Berytus produced more Latin epigraphy than any other city of the Greek East; see Isaac 319–21; MacAdam 103–15; Millar (1993) 279–80.

Anti-Lebanon mountains and the steppe areas near the Syrian desert, and the major city of Damascus.[47]

The city of Berytus, as part of the province of Phoenicia Maritima, was subordinate to Tyre, the civil capital and ecclesiastical metropolis.[48] The governor of Phoenicia Maritima very likely presided over a provincial assembly at Tyre (*Cod. Theod.* 12.12.12). In the mid-fifth century Berytus was also given the title of *metropolis* by a rescript of Theodosius II and Valentinian III (*Cod. Just.* 11.22.1). Although this shared status of *metropolis* of the province grew out of the religious controversies of AD 449, Berytus retained the title even after AD 451.[49] The desire for leadership in the province may spring not only from Berytus' pre-eminence in legal studies and traditional competitiveness with Tyre, but also from a growing realization of the importance of decision-making at that level of administration.

By AD 533, an edict of the emperor Justinian reflected the organization and administration of the city of Berytus. Clearly the city enjoyed a certain imperial tolerance and was expected to manage its affairs in a manner dissimilar to that of the city of Constantinople.

> Next we make a necessary order, with a very strong threat, that none of those who are engaged in legal studies, either in this most revered *civitas* [Constantinople] or in the excellent town of Berytus, is to perpetrate unworthy and most harmful—or rather servile—jokes (the commission of which is a wrongful act) and other crimes, against either the professors themselves or their colleagues, and especially against those who are coming to study law without experience. . . . In this most generous *civitas*

---

[47]Malalas 345, *PG* 97, 513–15; Devreesse 193–201; Kennedy 168–69.
[48]See Jones (1964) 373–74, and (1971) 540–47, tables XXVIII–XLI.
[49]The fourth canon of the Council of Chalcedon, Mansi vol. 7, 79–98; Schaff and Wace, vol. 14, 276–77.

[Constantinople], the eminent man who is prefect of this generous city must take care both to observe and to enforce all these ordinances . . . but in the *civitas* of Berytus this task falls to the *vir clarissimus* who is governor of the Phoenician coast[50] and to the most blessed bishop of the same *civitas* and the professors of law. (*Dig. Constitutio Omnis* 9–10)

In Constantinople, the urban prefect was expected to deal with civil misbehavior. In Berytus, however, civic administration had come to rest on a triangle of leadership—the governor of Phoenicia Maritima, the local bishop,[51] and the highly respected law professors. Simply put, the emperor laid the responsibility for keeping order in this particular sixth-century city on the imperially appointed governor who may have had some troops to command, the ecclesiastical appointee who undoubtedly attracted local allegiance, and the leading interpreters of law who seem to have dominated the social structure of the city.[52] Again, as the fourth-century inscription to a government official revealed, there is evidence that provincial and imperial organization take precedence over the local leadership which is now constituted of the bishop and the law professors.

It should be noted that the emperor did not appear to be pre-empting the authority of either the province or the city.[53] Lawyers and imperial officials who were "Roman" in every respect—speaking the Latin language, trained in Roman law,

---

[50]*Poenica maritima* is probably the name of the province, not a geographical description of the coast.

[51]Fowden 55–58.

[52]Whittow (12) postulates a triangle of leadership in the Late Antique city of "bishop and clergy, the major landowners (of whatever rank), and certain lay officials with financial and judicial responsibility." In Berytus, there seems to have been an influential merchant class rather than a dominant curial class; see Hall (1996) 34–46 and 117–21.

[53]Contrast the respect towards Berytus with the closing of the schools at Athens; Blumenthal 375–83, and Cameron (1969) 7–12.

devoted to Christianity, loyal to the Roman empire—now dominated the sixth-century power structure of Berytus in the province of Phoenicia. Yet, although Roman identity was richly rewarded by access to positions of influence in the wider empire, increasingly the sense of local Phoenician identity appears to have been underscored by the assignment of administrative responsibilities on the level of a province bearing an historic ethnonym.

Perpetuation of ethnic distinctions in imperial languages. Because the Punic language is not attested as surviving by inscriptional evidence past the second century AD in this area,[54] it might seem at first that the loss of the language might represent a decline in "Phoenician" identification. However, as Mitchell has demonstrated in his study of the preservation of Lydian ethnicity in Asia Minor, loan words and provincial divisions can maintain a sense of indigenous distinctiveness although the local language has ceased to be used.[55] Similarly, it seems clear also that the Phoenicians perpetuated a unique cultural identity, particularly by the continued knowledge of Semitic terms, as revealed in even Latin or Greek texts.[56] There may well be corrollaries between the methods of maintaining Phoenician and Hebrew identity in the Late Roman period.[57]

The ancient interest in ethnic distinctiveness is reflected in the writings of numerous writers, from Herodotus to Stephen of

---

[54] See Hill 264 for late Phoenician coins, issued by Tyre (from AD 80–131) and Sidon (in AD 75). Berytus issued coins inscribed with archaizing Phoenician script to mean "Laodoceia of Phoenicia," an ancient name for Berytus, according to Harris (1936) 7–8.

[55] Mitchell 172–73.

[56] Compare this situation to North Africa where Punic words were preserved to a later date in the texts of Augustine and Procopius; Harris (1936) 7–8, and Millar (1968) 126.

[57] Lucian, *Alexander* 13 refers to Hebrew and Punic as "outlandish" languages. Origen distinguished between Hebrew and Punic in *Contra Celsum* 3.6. See Cameron (1996), and Schwartz for Jewish identity in the Late Roman era, and Millar (1987) for a comparative treatment of Jewish and Syrian cultural identity.

Byzantium.⁵⁸ From an epigram of Meleager who grew up in Tyre, the near neighbor of Berytus, comes evidence that during the first century BC distinctions were maintained between Syrians, Phoenicians, and Greeks: "If you are a Syrian, Salam! if you are a Phoenician, Naidius!" "If you are a Greek, Chaire! (Hail!) and say the same yourself." ⁵⁹

The use of these local languages may have persisted even into the time of Ulpian in the third century AD if Millar is correct in his interpretation that *alium (sermonem), Poenum forte vel Assyrium* may mean "some other language, Phoenician perhaps or Syriac" and may be used in the formation of contracts.⁶⁰

Certainly local ethnicity was also maintained by naming practices. Porphyry, who was born in Tyre in AD 234, indicated that his personal name was from his native language and was understood by its Greek equivalent by his colleague:

> He [Amelius] dedicated it [a book] to me under the name of Basileus [King]. Basileus was in fact my name, for in my native language I was called Malkus (Μάλκος) (my father's name), and if one translates Malkus into Greek it is interpreted as Basileus.⁶¹

The perpetuation of ethnic distinctions by pagan and Christian writers. In Late Antiquity Christian writers sometimes preserved ancient indigenous pagan texts in order to refute them. Eusebius, in the fourth century AD text of the *Praeparatio Evangelica*, incorporated portions of *The Phoenician History* by Philo of Byblos, dated to the late first or early second century AD, which, in turn, reputedly preserved the works of Sanchuniathon, a

---

⁵⁸See Jones (1996) for the linguistic shading of the term *ethnos* in the writings of Herodotus. See Diller on the *Ethnika* by Stephen of Byzantium.
⁵⁹Meleager (7.419) in Paton, vol. 2, 227.
⁶⁰Ulpian, *Dig.* 45.1.1.16; Millar (1983) 66.
⁶¹Porphyry, *V. Plot.* 17 in Armstrong, vol. 1, 46–47.

Phoenician priest who had lived in Berytus during the eleventh century BC.[62]

Although Eusebius was preserving the account of Philo as a means of discrediting pagan religion, he echoed the traditional viewpoint that Phoenician (and Egyptian) religious texts predated such Greek versions as the *Theogony* of Hesiod.[63] Eusebius thus linked Phoenician ethnicity and pagan identity together so effectively that any future readers of his work would be inclined to accept the thesis that Phoenicians had distinctive religious beliefs and practices. Of particular interest here is the equating or merging of Zeus with local deities:

> Then he [Philo] says that from the wind Kolpia and his wife Baau (and that he renders "Night") there were born Aion and Protogonos, mortal men called by these names. Aion discovered the food obtained from trees. The children born of them were called Genos and Genea and they settled Phoenicia. And when there were droughts, they stretched out their hands to heaven, towards the sun. For (he says) they considered him to be the sole god, the ruler of heaven, calling him Beelsamen (θεὸν ἐνόμιζον μόνον οὐρανοῦ κύριον Βεελσάμην), which means to the Phoenicians "Ruler of Heaven," but to the Greeks "Zeus."[64]

The following reference to Hephaistos, or Zeus Meilichius, reveals more of this tendency to blend both Greek and Phoenician divine names and attributes:[65]

> One of these [brothers named] Chousor, composed [magical] formulas and incantations and prophecies; and he was Hephaistos. He also discovered the fishhook and

---

[62] See the excellent text and commentary in Baumgarten. Porphyry *de abstinentia* 2.56 in Attridge and Oden 16–21.
[63] Baumgarten 93.
[64] Baumgarten 141; *FGH* 807.19–26.
[65] Baumgarten 142–43; *FGH* 808.2–23.

bait and the fishing line and the raft, and was the first of all men to sail. Therefore they also revered him after his death. And he was called Zeus Meilichius (καλεῖσθαι δὲ αὐτὸν καὶ Δία Μειλίχιον).⁶⁶

The importance of these Phoenician legends lies not in tracing the various elements back to their most ancient parallels, but in the meaning to the listeners. The stories reinforced the Phoenician self-identity of artisans, craftsmen, sailors, and merchants who were favored by specific gods.

The stories told by the Phoenicians were seen as distinctive, even by other Mediterranean peoples. Pausanias, for example, cites the "Phoenician" version of a myth told at a Greek site:

> In this sanctuary of Asklepios a man of Sidon entered upon an argument with me. He declared that the Phoenicians had better notions about the gods than the Greeks [Hellenes], giving as an instance that to Asklepios they assign Apollo as father, but no mortal woman as his mother. Asklepios, he went on, is air, bringing health to mankind and to all animals likewise; Apollo is the sun, and most rightly is he named father of Asklepios, because the sun, by adapting his course to the seasons, imparts to the air its healthfulness.⁶⁷

Julian and the construction of Late Antique ethnicity. Julian sought to restore paganism by availing himself of every weapon at his disposal. Pagan practice was encouraged by imperial legislation, restoration of temples, and re-institution of public sacrifice.⁶⁸ Furthermore, the emperor sought to discredit

---

⁶⁶Baumgarten 143 and 14; *FGH* 808.21–28.
⁶⁷Pausanias 7.23.7–8; Jones (1918–1935), vol. 3, 309.
⁶⁸There are many useful details in the following: Libanius' funeral oration for Julian, Ammianus Marcellinus' encomium, and laws bearing Julian's name; see Bowersock (1978), and Liebeschuetz 43.

Christianity as a mixed religion that lacked the strength and purity of an ethno-centric religion. In *Contra Galileos* Julian set forth the idea that nations must honor their own indigenous deities who foster native character traits.

> Therefore, as I said, unless for every nation separately some presiding national god (καθ' ἕκαστον ἔθνος ἐθνάρχης τις θεός), and under him an angel, a demon, a hero, and a peculiar order of spirits which obey and work for the higher powers, established the differences in our laws and characters, you must demonstrate to me how these differences arose by some other agency.[69]

Julian then provides examples of specific strengths and weaknesses of the various "nations":

> Come, tell me why it is that the Celts and the Germans are fierce, while the Hellenes and Romans are, generally speaking, inclined to political life and humane, though at the same time unyielding and warlike? Why the Egyptians are more intelligent and given to crafts, and the Syrians unwarlike and effeminate, but at the same time intelligent, hot-tempered, vain and quick to learn?[70]

Julian then attributes native abilities by *ethnos* and describes the specific talents of various Semitic peoples in stereotypical terms. Although he feels that a non-Semitic people, the Greeks, brought all these discoveries to full development, he grants honor to the path-finders in these "nations."

> For the theory of the heavenly bodies was perfected among the Hellenes, after the first observations had been made

---

[69] Julian, *Contra Galileos* 143A in Wright, vol. 3, 355. See also Athanassiadi 162.
[70] Julian, *Contra Galileos* 116B in Wright, vol. 3, 347.

among the barbarians in Babylon. And the study of geometry took its rise in the measurement of the land in Egypt, and from this grew to its present importance. Arithmetic began with the Phoenician merchants, and among the Hellenes in course of time acquired the aspect of a regular science.[71]

In Julian's view the essence of greatness for a nation or people arose from the worship of the traditional gods of that *ethnos*. His followers well may have been influenced to re-establish the worship of indigenous deities. Although paganism has sometimes been described as Hellenism because of its linkage with Greek *paideia*,[72] veneration of pagan gods in their local or indigenous aspects persisted, as various narratives, both pagan and Christian make clear (Pausanias, Philo, Achilles Tatius, Nonnus, the *Life of Severus*, and the *Life of Matrona*). Indeed, Julian's theory of "national gods" probably reflects a widespread view that gods had local *personae* which might be designated by names in any language, imperial or native.[73]

Continuities and discontinuities in acquired identities. Although students continued to come to Berytus to study both Latin and the law well into the sixth century, there was an increase in the use of both Greek and indigenous languages.[74] Ironically, when John Lydus complained about the declining use of Latin, he wrote in Greek for his intended audience in Constantinople.[75]

By way of contrast, Syriac, the language of the Aramaean population, was rising in status.[76] Particularly, once the hymns of

---

[71] Julian, *Contra Galileos* 178B in Wright, vol. 3, 369.
[72] Bowersock (1990) 7–13.
[73] Even Christians might appeal to a number of divine helpers by multilingual names, as seen in Jordan. See Servais-Soyez, and Milik (1972) 411–23 for religious syncretism in the environs of Berytus.
[74] Hopkins 13.
[75] John Lydus, *On Powers* 2.12 in Bandy 100–3.
[76] Millar (1987) 161–64.

Ephrem revealed the artistry possible in Syriac, one sees an increased usage of the language, both qualitatively and quantitatively. Scriptures were translated into Syriac as were many of the saints' lives.[77] Furthermore, even the rules of legal practice were recorded in the Syriac text of the *Syro-Roman Lawbook*.[78] Although the precise nature of this text, dated to the fifth century or earlier, is unclear, the laws deal with such problems as family relations, slave ownership, and rules of succession. Perhaps the book is a student's notes from lectures at Berytus or perhaps it contains operational guidelines for an ecclesiastical court. The key issue is the improved status of an indigenous Semitic language: this esteem for a local language appears to represent a profound shift in the Greek East.[79]

Phoenician identity appears to have gained superior status to Syrian identity in some perceptible way in this period. Moreover, the long-existing definition of Berytus and the neighboring cities as "Phoenician" cities rested not only on geographical divisions but also on a reputation enhanced by schools which trained an intellectual elite and by shops that produced luxury textiles and expensive dyes.[80] The actions of the populace in various religious and political crises confirm that the people of Berytus regarded themselves as separate from the people of Alexandria in Egypt, Antioch in Syria, and Gaza in Palestine. Just as modern scholars of ethnicity have learned that Hispanics or Arabs or Blacks see hierarchical differences within their own groups, so it seems that ancient peoples assigned hierarchical differences to their distinctive *ethnos*. The difficulty of translating this term should not blind us to the realization that in antiquity, differing strengths and weaknesses were assigned to various divisions, or "nations," of humanity.

---

[77]Brock, especially articles printed as II, III and IV.
[78]See Vööbus (1982) for the text and translation and (1973) 156–60 for his theories about the nature of the text itself.
[79]MacMullen (1989) indicates that local Semitic languages were regarded as lower class in the fourth century.
[80]Hall (1996) 323–32 presents this evidence with full documentation.

Although the idea of Phoenician identity had been revived for purposes of imperial propaganda by the Severan dynasty, the definition, once in place, remained entrenched up through the sixth century and beyond, as the literary, geographical, and legal evidence shows. Although this sense of provincial identity or ethnic separateness has sometimes been obscured by our tendency either to focus on the Greco-Roman nature of these cities or to conflate Syria with Phoenicia, it is clear that real societal forces were at work which would lead to a final detachment of this area from the Roman empire.[81]

BIBLIOGRAPHY

Anderson, B. 1991. *Imagined Communities*. London.
Armstrong, A. H. 1966–1988. *Plotinus*. 7 vols. Cambridge.
Athanassiadi, P. 1992. *Julian and Hellenism*. London.
Attridge, H. W., and Oden, R. A., eds. and trans. 1981. *Philo of Byblos: The Phoenician History*, Washington, D.C.
Baldwin, B. 1985. "Latin in Byzantium." In *From Late Antiquity to Early Byzantium*, edited by V. Varrinek, 237–41. Prague.
—. 1982. "Vergil in Byzantium." *A&A* 28:81–92.
—. 1976. "*Vergilius Graecus*." *AJP* 97:361–68.
Bandy, A. C., ed. and trans. 1983. *Ioannes Lydus On Powers or the Magistracies of the Roman State*. Philadelphia.
Baumgarten, A. I., trans. and ed. 1981. *The Phoenician History of Philo of Byblos: A Commentary*. Leiden.
Bischoff, B. 1990. *Latin Paleography*, translated by D. Ó Cróinín and D. Ganz. Cambridge.
Blumenthal, H. J. 1978. "529 and its Sequel: What Happened to the Academy?" *Byzantion* 48:369–85.
Bowersock. G. W. 1990. *Hellenism in Late Antiquity*. Ann Arbor.
—. 1978. *Julian the Apostate*. Cambridge.

---

[81]See Pentz for the transition to the rule of Islam.

Brandsma, F. 1996. *Dorotheus and His Digest Translation*. Groningen.
Brock, S. 1984. *Syriac Perspectives on Late Antiquity*. London.
Butcher, K. 1996. "A New Dedication to Julia Domna from Berytus (BEY 006)." *BAAL* 1:212–14.
Butcher, K. and R. Thorpe. 1997. "A Note on Excavations in Central Beirut 1994–96." *JRA* 10:291–306.
Cameron, Alan. 1969. "The Last Days of the Academy at Athens." *PCPS* 15:7–29.
Cameron, Averil. 1996. "Byzantines and Jews: Some Recent Work on Early Byzantium." *BMGS* 20:249–74.
Collinet, P. 1925. *Histoire de l'École de Droit de Beyrouth*. Paris.
Colt, H. D. 1946. "Who Studied Latin in Zin?" *CJ* 42:313–23.
Desmond, Marilynn. 1994. *Reading Dido*. Minneapolis.
Devreesse, R. 1945. *Le Patriarcat d'Antioche*. Paris.
Diller, A. 1938. "The Tradition of Stephanus Byzantinus." *TAPA* 69:333–48.
Downey, G. 1963. *Gaza in the Early Sixth Century*. Norman.
—. 1961. *A History of Antioch in Syria*. Princeton.
Drijvers. J. W. 1996. "Ammianus Marcellinus 15.13.1–2." *CQ* 46:532–37.
Dulaurier, E., ed. and trans. 1858. *Chronique de Matthieu d'Edessa*. Paris.
Fears, J. R. 1977. *Princeps a diis electus: The Divine Election of the Emperor as a Political Concept at Rome*. Rome.
Foerster, R., ed. 1903–1927. *Libanius: Opera Omnia*. Leipzig. Repr. Hildesheim 1963.
Fowden, G. 1978. "Bishops and Temples in the Eastern Roman Empire A.D. 320–435." *JTS* n.s. 29:53–78.
Gaebel, R. E. 1970. "The Greek Word Lists to Cicero and Virgil." *BRL* 52:284–325.
—. 1968. "A Study of the Greek Word-Lists to Vergil's *Aeneid* Appearing in Late Latin Papyri." Diss. University of Cincinnati.
Gilliam, J. F. 1974. "A Student at Berytus in an Inscription from Pamphylia." *ZPE* 13:147–50.

Gregory, T. E. 1986. "The Survival of Paganism in Christian Greece: A Critical Essay." *AJP* 107:229–42.
Gruen, E. 1993. "Cultural Fictions and Cultural Identity." *TAPA* 123:1–14.
Haas, C. 1997. *Alexandria in Late Antiquity.* Baltimore.
Hall, J. M. 1997. *Ethnic Identity in Greek Antiquity.* Cambridge.
Hall, L. J. 1996. "Berytus, 'Mother of Laws': Studies in the Social History of Beirut from the Third to Sixth Centuries A.D." Diss. Ohio State U.
Harris, W. V. 1989. *Ancient Literacy.* Cambridge, Mass.
Harris, Z. S. 1936. *A Grammar of the Phoenician Language.* New Haven.
Hexter, R. 1992. "Sidonian Dido." In *Innovations of Antiquity,* edited by R. Hexter and D. Selden, 332–90. New York.
Hill, G. F. 1910. *Catalogue of the Greek Coins of Phoenicia.* London.
Honoré, T. 1982. *Ulpian.* London.
—. 1978. *Tribonian.* London.
Hopkins, K. 1991. "Conquest by Book." In *Literacy in the Roman World,* edited by M. Beard, 133–58. Ann Arbor.
Isaac, B. 1992. *The Limits of Empire.* Rev. ed. Oxford.
Ivison, E. A. 1996. "Burial and Urbanism at Late Antique and Early Byzantine Corinth (c. AD 400–700)." In *Towns in Transition,* edited by N. Christie and S. T. Loseby, 99–125. Brookfield, VT.
Jeffreys, E., M. Jeffreys, and R. Scott, trans. 1986. *The Chronicle of John Malalas.* Melbourne.
Jenkins, F. W. 1985. "Ammianus Marcellinus' Knowledge and Use of Republican Latin Literature." Diss. University of Illinois.
Jidejian, N. 1975. *Baalbek: Heliopolis, City of the Sun.* Beirut.
—. 1973. *Beirut through the Ages.* Beirut.
—. 1969. *Tyre through the Ages.* Beirut.
Jones, A. H. M. 1971. *The Cities of the Eastern Roman Provinces,* revised by Michael Avi-Yonah *et al.* 2nd ed. Oxford.
—. 1964. *The Later Roman Empire: 284–602.* 3 vols. Oxford.
—. 1954. "The Date and Value of the Verona List." *JRS* 44:88–94.

Jones, C. P. 1996. "*Ethnos* and *genos* in Herodotus." *CQ* 46:315–20.
Jones, H. L., ed. and trans. 1917–1932. *Strabo*. 8 vols. London.
Jones, W. H. S., ed. and trans. 1918–1935. *Pausanias*. 5 vols. London.
Jordan, D. R. 1991. "A New Reading of a Phylactery from Beirut." *ZPE* 88: 61–69.
Kaster, R. A. 1995. *C. Suetonius Tranquillus, De Grammaticis et Rhetoribus*. Oxford.
Kaye, J., and A. Zoubir. 1990. *The Ambiguous Compromise: Language, Literature, and National Identity in Algeria and Morocco*. London.
Kennedy, H. 1985. "The Last Century of Byzantine Syria." *ByzF* 10:141–83.
Kent, J. H. 1966. *Corinth* 8.3. *The Inscriptions 1926–1950*. Princeton.
Kugener, M.-A., ed. and trans. 1903. *Vie de Sévère par Zacharie le Scholastique. Patrologia Orientalis* 2.1, 7–115. Paris.
Lauffray, J. 1978. "Beyrouth. Archéologie et Histoire." *ANRW* II.8:135–63.
—. 1944–45. "Forums et monuments de Béryte." *BMB* 7:13–80.
Laurence, R. 1998. "Territory, Ethnonyms and Geography." In *Cultural Identity in the Roman Empire*, edited by R. Laurence and J. Berry, 95–110. London.
Lemerle, P. 1986. *Byzantine Humanism*. Canberra.
Liebeschuetz, J. H. W. G. 1972. *Antioch: City and Imperial Administration in the Later Roman Empire*. Oxford.
Maas, M. 1992. *John Lydus and the Roman Past: Antiquarianism and Politics in the Age of Justinian*. London.
MacAdam, H. I. 1983. "Epigraphy and Village Life in Southern Syria During the Roman and Early Byzantine Periods." *Berytus* 31:103–15.
MacCormack, S. 1998. *The Shadows of Poetry: Vergil in the Mind of Augustine*. Berkeley.
MacMullen, R. 1989. "The Preacher's Audience (AD 350–400)." *JTS* 40:503–11.

—. 1964. "Social Mobility and the Theodosian Code." *JRS* 54:49–53.
Mansi, J. D. 1759–1798. *Sacrorum conciliorum nova et amplissima collectio*. Florence.
Matthews, J. F. 1989. *The Roman Empire of Ammianus*. Baltimore.
Marrou, H. I. 1956. *A History of Education in Antiquity*, trans. George Lamb. New York.
McNamee, K. 1995. "Missing Links in the Development of Scholia." *GRBS* 36:399–414.
Metcalfe, T. 1994. *Ideologies of the Raj*. Cambridge.
Migne, J.-P., ed. 1844–1880. *Patrologiae cursus completus, Series Latina*. 221 vols. in 222 parts. Paris.
Migne, J.-P., ed. 1857–1860. *Patrologiae cursus completus, Series Graeca*. 161 vols. in 166 parts. Paris.
Milik, J. T. 1972. *Dédicaces faites par des dieux*. Paris.
Millar, F. 1993. *The Roman Near East 31 B.C. to A.D. 337*. Cambridge.
—. 1990. "The Roman *Coloniae* of the Near East. A Study of Cultural Relations." In *Roman Eastern Policy and Other Studies*, edited by H. Solin and M. Kajava, 7–58. Helsinki.
—. 1987. "Empire, Community and Culture in the Roman Near East: Greeks, Syrians, Jews and Arabs." *JJS* 38:143–67.
—. 1983. "The Phoenician Cities: a Case Study of Hellenization." *PCPS* 29:55–71.
—. 1968. "Local Cultures in the Roman Empire: Libyan, Punic, and Latin in Roman Africa." *JRS* 58:126–34.
Mitchell, S. 1993. *Anatolia: Land, Men, and Gods in Asia Minor*. Oxford.
Mommsen, T., and P. M. Meyer, eds. 1905. *Codex Theodosianus*. Berlin.
Mommsen, T., P. Krueger and A. Watson, eds. 1985. *The Digest of Justinian*. Philadelphia.
Morgan, C. 1991. "Ethnicity and Early Greek States: Historical and Material Perspectives." *PCPS* 37:131–63.

Norman, A.F., ed. and trans. 1992. *Libanius: Autobiography and Selected Letters*. 2 vols. London.
—. 1969–1977. *Libanius: Selected Works*. 2 vols. London.
Ostrogorsky, G. 1969. *History of the Byzantine State*. New Brunswick.
Paton, W. R., trans. and ed. 1916–1918. *Anthologia Graeca: The Greek Anthology*. 5 vols. New York.
Pentz, P. 1992. *The Invisible Conquest*. Copenhagen.
Petit, P. 1956. *Les Étudiants de Libanius*. Paris.
Pharr, C. et al., eds. and trans. 1952. *The Theodosian Code*. Princeton.
Rey-Coquais, J.-P. 1977. *Inscriptions grecques et latines découvertes dans les fouilles de Tyr (1963–1974)*. BMB 29.
Richardson, E. C., ed. 1896. *Hieronymus Liber De Viris Inlustribus*. TU 14. Leipzig.
Rodgers, R. H. 1978. "Varro and Vergil in the *Geoponica*." *GRBS* 19:277–85.
Rolfe, J. C., trans. and ed. 1952–1956. *Ammianus Marcellinus*. 3 vols. Cambridge.
Roller, D. W. 1998. *The Building Program of Herod the Great*. Berkeley.
Rouse, W. H. D., trans. 1940–1942. *Nonnus*. 3 vols. London.
Schaff, P. and H. Wace, eds. and trans. *The Seven Ecumenical Councils*. *NPNF* Vol. 14.
Schwartz, S. 1995. "Language, Power, and Identity in Ancient Palestine." *P&P* 148:3–47.
Seeden, H. 1998. "William A. Ward and Beirut: Archaeological News from the Capital of his Choice." In *Ancient Egyptian and Mediterranean Studies in Memory of William A. Ward*, edited by L. H. Lesko, 215–27. Providence.
Servais-Soyez, B. 1986. "La 'triade' phénicienne aux époques hellénistique et romaine." In *Studia Phoenicia IV, Religio Phoenicia*, edited by C. Bonnet, E. Lipinski, and P. Marchetti, 347–60. Namur.
Sewter, E. R. A., trans. 1966. *Fourteen Byzantine Rulers: The Chronographia of Michael Psellus*. New York.

Trahman, C. R. 1942. "The Latin Language and Literature in the Greek World." Diss. U. of Cincinnati.
Trombley, F. R. 1993. *Hellenic Religion and Christianization c. 370–529*. 2 vols. Leiden.
Vidén, G. 1984. *The Roman Chancery Tradition*. Göteborg.
Vööbus, A. 1982. *The Syro-Roman Lawbook*. Stockholm.
—. 1973. "New Light on the Textual History of the Syro-Roman Lawbook." *Labeo* 19:156–60.
Ward-Perkins, J.B. 1993. *The Severan Buildings of Lepcis Magna*, edited by P. N. Kenrick. London.
Whittow, M. 1990. "Ruling the Late Roman and Early Byzantine City." *P&P* 129:3–29.
Williams, T., et al. 1996. "Archaeological Excavations in the Souks Area of Downtown Beirut 1994–1995: Interim Report." http://www.aub.ac.lb/aub-online/faculties/arts_and_sciences/archaeology/index.html.
Wright, W. C., ed. and trans. 1913–23. *Julian*. 3 vols. Cambridge.
Young, R. A. D. 1990. "Zacharias: *The Life of Severus*." In *Ascetic Behavior in Greco-Roman Antiquity*, edited by V. Wambush, 312–28. Minneapolis.

Claudian *Castores*: Seneca and Crispus

George W. Mallory Harrison
Xavier University

During late antiquity, the middle ages, and into the Renaissance, a *corpus* of seventy-two poems, largely composed in elegiac couplets and early imperial in style, preserved in the *Anthologia Latina*, had come to be attributed to Seneca.[1] The *Codex salmasianus* (Paris lat.10318; *saec.* VIII) and the *Codex thuanaeus* (Paris lat. 8071; *saec.* IX–X) attribute three of the poems to Seneca in the *lemma* to each poem, while the *Codex vossianus* (Lat. Q. 86; *saec.* IX) gathered the *corpus* together without attribution or comment. The supplement to Haase's 1852 Teubner was the first to accept nine of these poems as genuine, the first three of which are the ones attributed to Seneca in the two oldest surviving manuscripts. Subsequent scholars have, with one exception, been more critical, although everyone has taken Haase's judgment as his or her starting point.[2] The only full text and commentary to all of the poems is that of Prato, whose 1964 second edition to the *Epigrams* is in many senses less bold and sanguine

---

[1] An oral version of this paper was presented at the 1994 Annual Meetings of the American Philological Association at Atlanta. It was primarily written while I was a visiting professor at the Rome Center of Loyola University Chicago. I am deeply indebted to my colleagues both in Atlanta and in Rome for their help and suggestions as also to my two anonymous readers. Gratitude is also owed to my research assistant, Mr. Steven Noga. I would like to note that the debt of all readers of Seneca to Anna Lydia Motto is enormous and her long-term collaboration with John R. Clark is one of the most gracious and resonant features of an extraordinary career.

[2] Prato (2 esp. n. 7) has gone so far as to admit unease over even the poems which have manuscript authority because of lack of verbal parallels in the plays. Estefanía (124–27) adduces several instances in which the *Codex salmasianus* incorrectly attributes poems to well-known writers.

than his original 1955 publication. His text is largely that of Riese's 1894 Teubner edition of the *Anthologia Latina* while further advances in the text have been made more recently by D. R. Shackleton Bailey in his 1982 edition of the first volume of the Teubner *Anthologia Latina*.

Although some doubts persist, a consensus favoring authenticity has formed around these poems, making them an appropriate place to start:

Haase 7, Riese 232, Shackleton Bailey 224, Prato 1

Omnia tempus edax depascitur, omnia carpit,
    omnia sede movet, nil sinit esse diu.
flumina deficiunt, profugum mare litora siccat,
    subsidunt montes et iuga celsa ruunt.
quid tam parva loquor? moles pulcherrima caeli   5
    ardebit flammis tota repente suis.
omnia mors poscit: lex est, non poena, perire;
    hic aliquo mundus tempore nullus erit.

Haase 1, Riese 236, Shackleton Bailey 228, Prato 2

Corsica Phocaico tellus habitata colono,
    Corsica, quae patrio nomine Cyrnus eras,
Corsica, Sardinia brevior, porrectior Ilva,
    Corsica, piscosis pervia fluminibus,
Corsica terribilis, cum primum incanduit aestas   5
    saevior, ostendit cum ferus ora Canis.
parce relegatis, hoc est, iam parce sepultis:
    vivorum cineri sit tua terra levis.

Haase 2, Riese 237, Shackleton Bailey 229, Prato 3

Barbara praeruptis inclusa est Corsica saxis,
    horrida, desertis undique vasta locis.
non poma autumnus, segestes non educat aestas,

>   canaque Palladio munere bruma caret.
>   umbrarum nullo ver est laetabile foetu   5
>   nullaque in infausto nascitur herba solo.
>   non panis, non haustus aquae, non ultimus ignis;
>   hic sola haec duo sunt: exsul et exsilium.

Although much of the language is conventional, these three poems by repetitive cadence and word choice nevertheless convey the despair, the anger and the anguish[3] of Seneca's relegation to Corsica from AD 41 to AD 48, putatively on a charge of adultery with Julia Livilla, one of the sisters of Caligula and niece to the newly enthroned Claudius. No one has ever challenged the assumption that any of the other poems accepted by Haase or in the *Codex vossianus*, if composed by Seneca, should belong to this period, and thus stylistic and other affinities to these three must form the first level of evidence on which arguments for or against authenticity of these poems and the two about Crispus must be based.

Another level of evidence is literary reminiscence: echoes from Ovid are only to be expected and are not hard to find. Such influence is hardly remarkable since Ovid's poems, the *Metamorphoses* in particular, were rich veins continuously mined by almost all of the early imperial writers. For Seneca's epigrams, however, echoes seem to come principally from the *Tristia* and *Epistulae ex Ponto*, and the echoes are intelligent ones, appropriate to their context. Further, Seneca seems to have been one of a discrete number of admirers of Catullus and Tibullus among the later Julio-Claudian and early Flavian writers.[4]

---

[3]One might conveniently compare the less charged language of Seneca's *consolationes* to his mother and to Polybius; parallels in tone and emotional color are more readily to hand in Catullus' farewell to his brother or Ovid's brief in *Tr.* 2.

[4]The evidence here, however, may be skewed since most of the literary remains of the reigns from Tiberius through Titus are in prose. The poets drawn to the court of Nero form the only exception.

A more weighty kind of evidence is afforded by the verbal echoes and reminiscences, and the similarity of language, diction, and rhetoric which one notices between the *Codex vossianus* epigrams and Seneca's plays. The themes of the nine poems accepted by Haase and the plays are remarkably similar: violence, treachery, injustice, ingratitude, and desolation. Although these themes animate all of his work of all periods, there are definable differences in tone and language between his plays and poems and the philosophical essays. Even so, one is struck by the continuity of thought and style among the plays and poems and earliest philosophical works, such as *De Ira*, generally dated to the beginning years of his exile.

Comparisons are complicated, however, by the apparent lack of consensus among scholars on the absolute dating of the plays, even though some general areas of agreement exist. Tarrant's surmise that the *Thyestes* and *Phoenissae* belong to Seneca's years of retirement from court has found approval and been seconded by Fantham's credible reconstruction of the *Phoenissae*.[5] The relative chronology established by Fitch in 1981 has been met with almost universal agreement.[6] The majority of the plays must thus belong to the period of exile or to the years of his restoration to court up to the death of Claudius. Few have been as assured as Costa in dating the plays specifically to the period of exile,[7] although no one is willing to dismiss the possibility.[8] At the very least if the epigrams are not contemporary with the plays, they are very nearly so.

One poem among the nine Haase considered genuine stands out for its tenderness:

[5]Tarrant (1985) 12; Fantham (1983) 61–76.
[6]Fantham (1982) 14 is the exception.
[7]Costa 7.
[8]Scholars are united in preferring the death of Claudius as the *terminus ante quem* for the plays other than *Thyestes* and the *Phoenissae*. The disagreement is on a *terminus post quem*; see, for example, Ahl 14, Coffey and Mayer 3, and Pratt 12–13.

Haase 6, Shackleton Bailey 401, Prato 14

Crispe, meae vires lassarumque ancora rerum,
    Crispe, vel antiquo conspiciende foro,
Crispe potens numquam nisi cum prodesse volebas,
    naufragio litus tutaque terra meo,
solus honor nobis arx et tutissima nobis   5
    et nunc afflicto sola quies animo.
Crispe, fides dulcis, placideque acerrima virtus
    cuius Cecropio pectora melle madent,
maxima facundo vel avo vel gloria patri,
    quo solo careat si quis, in exsilio est: 10
an tua, qui iaceo saxis telluris adhaerens,
    mens mecum est, nulla quae cohibetur humo?

Its repetitions and sequence of phrases in apposition immediately associate this poem with the ones which have manuscript authority. Among many other kinds of similarities, it shares with the first poem rhetorical questions and a much more limited use of superlatives than is generally observable in the works of other Late Augustan and in Silver Latin poets; with the second it shares a need to establish identity through ancestry; and with the third it shares the images of rocks and of exile. Allusions cannot be expected to be as numerous or obvious as one might like or should expect, since the tone of this poem is markedly different from the other three.[9] The echoes from the *Aeneid* and from the *Tristia* and *Epistulae ex*

---

[9] Even here one would expect a poet of the first rank to be able to invert the same language in diametrically opposite contexts, such as Martial, who used *notam, superbam, nobilem, locupletem* to describe Erotion (5.37.22) in the longest of his *epitaphia* but sarcastically styled Fabullus (5.37.6) than whom *numquam nequior fuit clavis* as an *equiti superbo, nobili, locupleti*.

Ponto assure an early imperial date and at the very least point to Seneca.[10]

If so, the addressee most probably is C. Sallustius Passienus Crispus,[11] namesake of the historian, Seneca's close friend,[12] and perhaps most importantly husband of Agrippina during the AD 40s.[13] The allusion to Crispus' death in the closing phrase of line 12 and the conceit of death-as-exile in line 10, itself an inversion of the conceit of death-as-exile so familiar from Ovid's *Tristia* and *Epistulae ex Ponto* and Seneca's epigrams, would assign this poem and the following one to the closing months of AD 47 or the first half of AD 48. In addition to its formal structure as a lament, it almost certainly also was written out of gratitude for attempts to effect Seneca's recall. It adds to the *pathos* of these two poems that Crispus himself seems to have died just before the petition of recall could be granted and thus narrowly missed being re-united with his friend in Rome.[14]

---

[10] For example: *Aen.* 1.45 *scopulo infixit acuto* parallels line 11; *Aen.* 4. 3–5 on the virtues of Aeneas are echoed by verses 5–7. The imagery of the exile as sunken ship in *Tr.* 1.5.36 *naufragio, Tr.* 2.470 *naufraga, Tr.* 2.99–100 is picked up by verse 4; *Tr.* 2.577–778 prefigures verses 5–6; *Tr.* 1.6.12 *nulla positum cernere possit humo* is restated in verse 12. Although Vergil and Ovid remain a staple of Latin authors of all periods, up to and including such poets as Claudian and Sidonius Apollinaris, Ovid's *Tristia* and *ex Ponto* are less often cited in later literature. The conjunction of reminiscences from Vergil and from Ovid's poetry from exile, neither of which is significant in isolation, places these poems on a standing with the *Einsiedeln Eclogues*, the poems of Statius, and other late Julio-Claudian and Flavian poems and distinguishes them from poetic practice of later centuries.

[11] Also known from Martial and Juvenal, both of whom shared Seneca's high opinion of Crispus.

[12] It is not without significance that they built upon a friendship inherited from their fathers who were apparently on familiar terms.

[13] He had formerly been the husband of Domitia, sister of Nero's father, and was thus at once Nero's uncle and his step-father. In excoriating Agrippina for marrying her uncle, one often forgets that she had already married her brother-in-law.

[14] The timing of Crispus's death, which was suspiciously convenient for Agrippina's purpose, fueled speculation of complicity by her, which has largely been accepted.

Shackleton Bailey 443, Prato 53

Ablatus mihi Crispus est amicus,
pro quo, si pretium darem liceret,
nostros dividerem libenter annos
****
nunc par⟨s⟩ optima me mei reliquit,
Crispe, praesidium meum, voluptas,   5
†custos†, deliciae. nihil sine illo
laetum mens mea iam putavit esse.
consumptus male debilisque vivam
plusquam dimidium mei recessit.

My friend Crispus has been taken from me,
for whom, if I were allowed to pay such a price,
I should gladly divide my remaining years
****
As it is, the greatest part of me has deserted me,
Crispus, my protection, my pleasure,   5
†my guide†, my delight. My mind has already
decided that there can be no joy without him.
So, diminished, ill shall I live and feebly
as more than half of me has gone away.

1. am*ihi V*: amicus *Baehrens*, amici *Scaliger: fortasse* amice (=*xenie*) *ut singularis vocativus scriptus ad lectorem Graecis stelis.* 3. *post v.* 3 *unum versum excidisse suspicor.* 4. pars *Prato*: par *V.* 6. custos *scripsi*: pectus *Prato*: lusus *Francius*: decus *Wakefield*: portus *Baehrens.* 7. putavit *V*: putabit *Prato. V.* 8. iam male *V*: male *Shackleton Bailey*

    There should be little doubt that the same writer was the author of both of these poems. The epithets of Crispus in both poems are complimentary. The bittersweet tone of both is consistent, particularly in the *chiaroscuro* of moving from warm imagery to dark. In both cases Seneca, as also in his *consolationes*, cast his plight in mythological terms, first seeing himself as Ajax the

Locrian defiantly clinging to the rocks[15] and then wishing that he could share his remaining years, like Castor and Pollux. It would be wrong to push the analogy too far, identifying Seneca with the immortal Pollux.[16] Seneca himself was careful to call Crispus the *pars optima mei* and *plusquam dimidium mei* (10); this last is especially touching since it draws its inspiration from Horace's *propempticon* (*Carm.* 1.3.8) to Vergil.

This is one of only three non-elegiac poems among those collected in the *Codex vossianus*, and so the meter requires some explanation. This poem and also *Anth. Lat.* 442 and *Anth. Lat.* 458 were composed in hendecasyllables, yet while this poem is a lament the other two are diatribes against other philosophers (*Anth. Lat.* 442) and against a faithless lover (*Anth. Lat.* 458).[17] The threnody to Crispus, however, bears many similarities to the meter, especially of the choruses, in Seneca's plays in that there are no resolutions, few substitutions, and fewer elisions.[18] Each line

---

[15]This was one of Seneca's two favorite myths for representing his plight; cf. *Ag.* 528. The other frequent myth in Seneca is Hercules's constant reproach that no one, mortal or deity, was grateful that he rid the world of monsters. Although it might be objected that Ajax the Locrian was an unflattering comparison, the other two heroes who clung to rocks, Ulysses and Philoctetes, were also unsavory types in Roman literature of the Empire.

[16]Ovid writing to an unnamed friend at *Tr.* 1.3 and 1.5 intriguingly compares them to Theseus and Pirithous. Like Ajax the Locrian, this metaphor cannot be read too closely since Ovid unlike Theseus went unaccompanied into his Hell.

[17]Although discussion and documentation belong elsewhere, both of these poems by word choice, caesura and cadence are unlikely to have been by Seneca.

[18]That tragedies were performed during the Roman Empire is incontrovertible and thus the production of Seneca's tragedies seems probable; see Rosenmeyer (1993) 235–44. Anecdotes in Suetonius and Tacitus point to production, and Greek revivals (Jones 39–52) would imply Roman dramas as well. Theater construction and modification, as attested in the correspondence between Pliny and Trajan and in the physical evidence, are senseless without an audience, and *stelai* recording salaries paid to actors survive (Harrison 174). Side-stepping the issue of production, recitation was popular and animated (Goldberg 265–86) and is parodied by Persius in his first satire, and even in private one read

begins with a spondee, such as also many of the choral odes in the plays, followed by a choriamb, two iambs, and a syllable anceps. Diaeresis occurs almost uniformly after the choriamb. Likewise, octo- and decasyllabic lines in the choruses normally start with a spondee and often end with rhythms similar to *Ablatus mihi Crispus*, such as many of the lines in the first chorus of Seneca's *Hercules Furens*, particularly 125, 133, 146, 159, 182, and elsewhere. Examples are as readily to hand in the other plays.

The case for a Senecan composition of *Ablatus mihi Crispus* is very strong even without reference to *Crispe, meae vires*. Comparison with the *Agamemnon* alone, one of the three earliest of the plays,[19] should suffice. Lists of character traits are a standard feature of set speeches, such as at line 43 and elsewhere. Early in his career, Seneca seems to have distinguished between *credo* and *puto*, using the former for positive thoughts and outcomes, and the latter for negative ones. Thus *putavit* (8)[20] points to a world without joy, while at *Agamemnon* 694 the leader of the Chorus of Trojan Women sums up by saying *miseris colendos maxime superos putem* ("I would think that the gods should be especially worshiped by the distraught"), and Clytemnestra sneers at Electra's threat to kill her and Aegisthus with *et esse demens te parem nobis putas?* ("are you mad enough to think that you are a match for us?" *Ag.* 961). *Credis* would imply that Electra was equal to the task; *putas* exposes its futility. In the sticomathy between Agamemnon and Cassandra after 790, Agamemnon chides Cassandra as she stares vacantly with *credis videre te Ilium?* implying that (1) she does see

---

aloud, if the evidence of Caesar's lip reading and Jerome's silence is allowed.

[19]The three groups of plays as defined by Fitch and commonly accepted are: 1. *Agamemnon, Oedipus,* and *Phaedra*; 2. *Hercules Furens, [Hercules Oetaeus], Medea,* and *Troades*; 3. *Phoenissae* and *Thyestes*. There is also consensus that 1 and 2 are closer in date to each other than 2 is to 3.

[20]The perfect *putavit* should be retained rather than Prato's *putabit* since *consumptus* (9) makes it clear that Seneca's mind was made up; unfortunately *iam* cannot be used as testimony since it appears with verbs of all tenses in the plays.

it and (2) that she thinks it a good thing. After Agamemnon assures Cassandra that Mycenae was not Troy, Cassandra, knowledgeable that Clytemnestra is the half-sister of Helen and likewise an adulteress, replies *Ubi Helena est Troiam puto* ("Wherever there is a Helen there is a Troy," *Ag.* 795), implying that she can see prophetically that no good shall come from it.

So, too, *laetus* in the poems and plays points to a happiness which is ephemeral,[21] unfulfilled, or bound to be disappointed; *gaudium* is the norm for a true joy, although even *gaudium* can be used ironically. It is thus appropriate that the joy which is impossible without Crispus should be *laetum* (8), just as Eurybates when about to describe losses at sea on the return voyage, complained to Clytemnestra that *infaustum iubes / miscere laeto nuntium. refugit loqui mens aegra* ("you order me to mix an unsuitable message with a happy one. The mind shrinks from sad tidings," *Ag.* 416-417). Likewise, Strophius near the end of the play (*Ag.* 924) comes upon Electra crying and asks what cause is there for tears in a house which should be happy *(fletus causa quae laeta in domo est?).*

There are enough indications to presume that one or more lines are missing after line 3. *Dividerem* (3) privileges the well-known story of Castor and Pollux relieving Seneca of the obligation to retell it. Nor, following his practice in the plays, does it presume that he intended to inform the reader to what purpose he wished to put the years he proposed to apportion with Crispus. *Libenter* here and *libens,* which occurs throughout the plays, generally receive elaboration, and thus *libenter* wants either an *ut*-clause or a *qui*-clause to round out the period. Just as *annos* (3) never ends a

---

[21]*Laetum . . . diem (Her. O.* 1187) was supposed to have been his wedding day, but became his funeral instead, an inversion of the tradition of singing threnodies to a bride; see Oakely and Sinos (4 n. 5), who document this practice in Greek art and literature. Senecan distinctions in his use of near synonyms, such as *puto/credo* and *laetus/gaudium* are discussed in greater detail in the fourth chapter of my forthcoming book, *Fortunate for Two Senecas and Lucan.* What is remarkable is the consistency of these nuances from his earliest works, such as *De Ira,* through to the *Epistulae ad Lucilium.*

sentence in the plays, *nunc* (5) almost invariably starts one.[22] Further, except when governed by an imperative, *nunc* normally marks either a conclusion in which the parts are linked chronologically, or a shift in subject. One is, therefore, tempted to posit a brief *lacuna*, yielding a ten line poem. Although there are no observed patterns of length for threnodic hendecasyllables, such as there are for elegiacs, Seneca in the other poems (all of which are elegiac couplets) most often thought in two and four line units. Iambic *epitaphia* in Martial, for example, vary greatly in length as well as depth of sentiment. It is likewise observable in Martial that subjects of iambic *epitaphia* often have other poems written about them in elegiacs.

The polyptoton of *me mei* (5) is a typical feature of Seneca's and one which recalls Ovid's two collections written in exile. The device is used three times within a hundred lines in the *Hercules Furens* 99, 110, and 197, as well as *Troades* 916 and 994, *Medea* 969, and elsewhere. The repetition can be taken to be a sign of the self-absorption of the speaker, but in this poem as in Ovid *Tr.* 1.2.20 and 22 and *Tr.* 1.11.12 it seems equally also an expression of despair and desertion.

Crispe (6) is a vocative in apposition to *pars optima*, and hence *praesidium, voluptas, custos,* and *deliciae* are all also appositional vocatives. This makes more difficult any conjecture for the mutilated text at the beginning of line 6; it should be an *os/us* vocative, thereby making the choice a fourth declension noun, a third declension noun in -*os*, or a Greek loan word.[23] Prato's *pectus* has been printed by Shackleton Bailey, yet *pectus* in the plays is used more literally of a chest which is beaten (women) or one which is struck (men); it is generally absent as a term of endearment. The fourth declension plural *lusus*, suggested by Francius, would have a parallel at Martial 4.87.2. Even though Martial is one of Seneca's

---

[22]*Anth. Lat. 401 SB* line 6 is an inconvenient but interesting exception from Senecan practice.

[23]The problem with the text may go as far back as the Vandalic recensions and recensions under Justinian, and thus belong ultimately to uncial manuscripts; see Estefanía 123.

more frequent and astute imitators, the context of this poem is so different that it is of dubious value. At 4.87 *lusus* and *delicias* are cooed over an infant, while Bassa's devotion to motherhood (*pedere Bassa solet*) is questioned.

The vocative *custos* is not entirely satisfactory, but it offers the advantages of fitting the meter and the context. Seneca, like Plutarch, often thought in pairs of near synonyms, a contributor to forceful *clausulae* as well as a habit of mind. Thus in lines 6 and 7 *voluptas* and *deliciae* both speak to the pleasantness of their relationship, while *praesidium* acknowledges one in which Seneca found himself obliged to the courtesies which Crispus could extend. A kindred expression of such a relationship, which is not so formal or socially stratified as that of a *cliens* to his *patronus*, is *custos*, which would seem to speak to an aggressive protection, rather than the defensive *praesidium*.

The case for Senecan authorship, if strong, is entirely circumstantial. One thus has a responsibility to investigate the possibility of other authors and addressees. Although there are over a hundred known Crispi, and countless others unknown to history, the style of the Crispus poems is definitely that of Silver Latin. The reminiscences from Ovid plus the imitations in Martial yield twin *termini* which make it all but certain that the Crispus addressed is the consul of AD 44. A date far after his death in AD 48 is unthinkable since the widow Agrippina and the widower Claudius would surely have found his memory uncomfortable. The writer of *Ablatus mihi Crispus* was clearly conversant with *Crispus, meae vires* and well disposed towards it. He thus had to be within the circle of dissemination of Seneca's poems between AD 44 and AD 48. One presumes a very limited group since Seneca was officially *persona non grata*.[24] Echoes in structure, sense, word usage, and

---

[24]One dismisses the possibility that the latter poem could have been written in ignorance of the former. Literacy rates, particularly at the highest attainment levels, were exceptionally low in antiquity, and the existence of well-defined circles fairly guaranteed that all major literary figures knew each other. For literacy rates, see Bowman and others in Humphrey's collection of essays.

rhythm look to the same hand. Given such skill in handling a meter other than the elegiac couplet or epic hexameter, only one poet active at the time is a plausible candidate, Seneca.

The two Crispus poems are of great importance to an understanding of Seneca and a re-evaluation of his personality and position at court and for this reason their authenticity must be rigorously established and then staunchly defended. Too often Seneca is viewed too glibly as a dour Stoic or as a Stoic who preached moderation while he amassed obscene wealth. The Crispus poems, however, show a man capable of deep tenderness and even more importantly genuine gratitude.

After word. If one accepts that Seneca was the author of the five poems reproduced in this article then there might be grounds to revisit Leo's dismissal in 1878 of the *Hercules Oetaeus* as genuine.[25] The case is not without difficulties and the thesis complex enough to deserve to be examined with reservation. That said, if one triangulates preferred sources of verbal reminiscence and techniques of composition among the poems, the *Hercules Oetaeus*, and Seneca's other plays, the over-lay of patterns for these three groups would favor a surmise that the author of one was the author of all. Catullus and Tibullus, for example, find echoes in the *Hercules Oetaeus*: the chorus of Oechalian maidens at *Hercules Oetaeus* 104 enters singing *Par ille est superis*, a strong echo of Catullus 51.1, particularly strong since both Lesbia and Hercules proved disappointments.[26] Similarly, *vagus per artus errat (Her. O. 706)* and *Tu quicumque es (Her. O. 592)* look to Tibullan models.

Cadence and rhythm in the choruses of the *Hercules Oetaeus* are also remarkably similar to the plays and to *Ablatus mihi Crispus*. *Her. O.* 641 closely parallels lines 5 and 10 of *Ablatus*

---

[25]The case against Senecan authorship was best laid out by Friedrich. Rosenmeyer (1989, xvi), while voicing doubts, is unwilling to distance the play from Seneca, as is also (if less so) Sandbach 160–61.

[26]So, too, *tantum ut* is extremely rare yet occurs at Catullus 72.3 and Seneca *Hercules Oetaeus* 639; these references are owed to a discussion by Carmine Ianicelli and Luciano Stupazzini on ClassL 28 Aug 1997.

mihi Crispus, while the cadence of *Hercules Oetaeus* 1336 is equivalent to line 5. The strongest parallel is at 1344–1345 where *quis tibi exiguam tui partem reliquit* matches the rhythm, words, and sentiment of line 4.

The *Hercules Oetaeus* conforms to Seneca's distinction between *puto* and *credo*. At 1301–1303 since Hercules is trying to provoke Jupiter he reverses *crede* and *puto*. Hercules similarly reverses the two verbs sarcastically when he bemoans his paternity; compare as well *meus credetur Amphitryon pater* (1248), *credi novercam Juno* (1500), and *credi meus pater* (i.e. Juppiter, 1507). References to Orpheus and Thebes follow Seneca's normal pattern, such as, *vati credere Thracio* (1100) and *Semelenque puta* (i.e. Alcmena, 1916). One might also adduce *putant Getae* (1041). *ardere credas* (i.e. Mt. Pindus) would seem problematical except that it is contrasted almost immediately with *urere addentem putes* (i.e. Hercules, 1744); that is, it is much more likely that Pindus will burn than that Hercules will. The strongest evidence of Senecan dichotomy in his use of *credo* vs. *puto* is at 1978–1981 where Alcmena sees Hercules *ex machina*. First she says *fallor an voltus putat* but when she comes to believe she says *credo triumphis*.

The disjunction between *laetus* and *gaudium* is also observed in the *Hercules Oetaeus*, such as when Hercules put on a brave face while surmounting his funeral pyre: *laetus adeone ultimos / invasit ignes?* (1608–1609). Later on, Hercules advised his mother not to cry so as to deprive Juno of *Schadenfreude*: *Iuno cur laetum diem / te flente ducat? paelicis gaudet suae / spectare lacrimas* ("Why make Juno's day with tears? She exults to see the sadness of her rivals," *Her. O.* 1675–1677). None of this evidence is in and of itself decisive nor is its sum incontrovertible; yet, it seems full enough to point more to the master than a mimic.

BIBLIOGRAPHY

Ahl, Frederick. 1986. *Seneca: Three Tragedies*. Ithaca.
Shackleton Bailey, D. R., ed. 1982. *Anthologia Latina I: Carmina in codicibus scripta*. Leipzig.
Bowman, Alan K. 1991. "Literacy in the Roman Empire: Mass and Mode." In *Literacy in the Ancient World*, edited by John H. Humphrey, 119–31. *JRA*, Supplement 3, 1991. Ann Arbor.
Burriss, Eli Edward. 1932. *Seneca in Corsica*. New York.
Coffey, Michael and Roland Mayer, eds. 1990. *Seneca: Phaedra*. Cambridge.
Costa, C. N. D., ed. 1973. *Seneca: Medea*. Oxford.
Estefanía, Maria Dulce. 1991. "Il codice salmasiano e gli epigrammi di Seneca." In *Seneca e la cultura*, edited by Aldo Setaioli, 121–29. Perugia.
Fantham, Elaine. 1983. "*Nihil iam iura natura valent*: Incest and Fratricide in Seneca's *Phoenissae*." In *Seneca Tragicus: Essays on Senecan Drama*, edited by A. J. Boyle, 61–76. Victoria.
—, ed. 1982. *Seneca's Troades*. Princeton.
Fitch, John G. 1981. "Sense-pauses and Relative Dating in Seneca, Sophocles, and Shakespeare." *AJP* 102:289–307.
Friedrich, Wolf-Harmuth. 1954. "Sprache und Stil des *Hercules Oetaeus*." *Hermes* 82:51–84.
Goldberg, Sander M. 1996. "The Fall and Rise of Roman Tragedy." *TAPA* 126:265–86.
Griffin, Miriam T. 1976. *Seneca: A Philosopher in Politics*. Oxford.
Haase, Friedrich, ed. 1852. *L. Annaei Senecae 'Opera quae supersunt': Supplementum*. Leipzig.
Harrison, George W. M. 1994. *The Romans and Crete*. Amsterdam.
Jones, C. P. 1993. "Greek Drama in the Roman Empire." In *Theater and Society in the Classical World*, edited by Ruth Scodel, 39–52. Ann Arbor.
Leo, Friedrich, ed. 1878. *L. Annaei Senecae tragoediae*. Berlin.

Oakley, John H. and Rebecca H. Sinos. 1993. *Weddings in Ancient Athens*. Madison.
Prato, Carlo. 1964. *Gli epigrammi attribuiti a L. Anneo Seneca*. 2nd ed. Rome.
Pratt, Norman T. 1983. *Seneca's Drama*. Chapel Hill.
Riese, A. 1894. *Anthologia Latina*. Leipzig.
Rosenmeyer, Thomas G. 1993. "Seneca's *Oedipus* and Performance: the Manto scene." In *Theater and Society in the Classical World*, edited by Ruth Scodel, 235–44. Ann Arbor.
—. 1989. *Senecan Drama and Stoic Cosmology*. Berkeley.
Sandbach, F. H. 1975. *The Stoics*. London.
Segal, Charles. 1986. *Language and Desire in Seneca's Phaedra*. Princeton.
Tarrant, R. J., ed. 1985. *Seneca's Thyestes*. Atlanta.
—. ed. 1976. *Seneca: Agamemnon*. Cambridge.
Westman, Rolf. 1983. "*Fore, fore ut* und *futurum* bei Seneca." In *Studies in Classical and Modern Philology Presented to Y. M. Biese on his 80th Birthday*, edited by Y. Blomstedt, 163–69. *Annual of the Academy of Sciences*, Series B 223. Finland.
Zwierlein, Otto, ed. 1986. *L. Annaei Senecae tragoediae*. Oxford.

Wine, Women, and What?
Some Vices in Seneca's *De Ira*

Alexander MacGregor
University of Illinois at Chicago

Quodcumque sibi imperavit animus, obtinuit. Quidam ne umquam riderent consecuti sunt; vino quidam, alii venere, quidam o m n i u m o r e interdixere corporibus; alius contentus brevi somno vigiliam indefatigabilem extendit; didicerunt tenuissimis et adversis funibus currere et ingentia vixque humanis toleranda viribus onera portare et in immensam altitudinem mergi ac sine ulla respirandi vice perpeti maria (*De Ira* 2.12.4).

---

omnium ore *C*: omnium ori *P*: omni in re *vel* omnium more *dett.*; *fortasse* canore; *potius* <balineo atque> *ante* umore *supplenda*.

The mind achieves whatever it commands itself <to do>. Some persons have succeeded in their goal of never smiling; some have enjoined themselves from wine, others from sex, some from *a l l   w e t n e s s*; another, content with snatches of sleep, prolongs an untiring watch; others have learned to run along the thinnest tightropes, or carry heavy weights scarcely to be supported by human strength, or dive to unfathomed depths and endure the sea without breaking for breath.[1*]

These exempla of habits or difficulties overcome are meant to strengthen Seneca's case that *ira*, too, can be overcome by an effort

---

[*]Notes are listed at the end of the paper by special request of the author.

of the will. Clearly *omni umore* gave scribes trouble, and has resisted explanation since: a lack that this note hopes to remedy. Lipsius skirted the issue: "in metu aquae intercutis: atque hodie sunt exempla," in fear of dropsy, that is.[2] His belief does not accord with ancient practice: Celsus distinguishes various types of dropsy (3.21.1), none arising from exposure to *umor* though all are treated by restrictions on the element, wine-drinking in particular as well as sexual activity.[3] Seneca, however, does not have a single cause in mind, if *alii . . . quidam . . . alii* is any indication. His point in any case is the exercise of will power, granted that *interdixere* suggests an underlying medical reason for refraining from the three indulgences of Wine, Women, and whatever the reading *umore* may mean, or conceal.

The only other elucidation that the passage has received is Basore's unhelpful translation:[4] "others <have cut themselves off> from every kind of drink," which is flatly impossible; some fluid intake is necessary for life.[5] If Basore meant hard liquor by "drink"—an anachronism—the tricolon "wine, women, and hard liquor" would be strange indeed, with sex equivalent to sherry.

In sum, to elucidate the passage one must start from scratch. The modern cliché "Wine, Women, and Song" suggests itself at the outset as a possible parallel to Seneca's run of thought, "Wine, Women" and something. Now, Seneca says that our bodies can do without all three indulgences; but at first glance *corporibus* applies far better to Wine and Women than to Song. Still, Song certainly heightens (or leads to) the pleasures of Wine and Women; moreover, the incantatory power of Song to move or stay building-blocks or tigers suggests that ancient physiologists may at times have credited Song with physical effects that put it on a par with Wine and Women.

If Song is wanted here, an easy conjecture will provide it: *canore*. This often poetic word applies now to song that lulls (so e.g. Ovid *Met.* 5.561 and *Ars* 3.315), now that rouses to war (so Verg. *G.* 4.71; Petron. 5.19): the physical power of song in either case, which is wanted here. As for the palaeography of it, *canore* and *umore* both reduce to five minims plus *-ore* in Carolingian minuscule (with its unbowed "a" often open at the top); a scribe unfamiliar with Orpheus and the other wielders of song may well have succumbed to the attraction of *vino* and perpetrated an asseveration of thought if not of ductus.

Song appears as a debilitating vice at least twice in poetry, in Manilius and Silius Italicus, but without any hint of the idea (explicit in Seneca if *canore* is read) that song is one of the habits or indulgences that can be overcome by an effort of the will; in Manilius and Silius, song is mischievous, and irresistible to boot. Such a hostile characterization suggests that even though "Wine, Women, and Song" was not apparently an ancient cliché, at least the germ of the idea was latent for Seneca to appropriate and develop for his own purposes.

Manilius, who prides himself on the perfect novelty of a poem that attempts no less than a description of the Stoic god, lays his groundwork by disparaging virtually every other poem ever written: two of his proemia chronicle in detail the degeneration of didactic and of epic (2.1–56; 3.1–30), understandable targets given his composite genre. Then he goes out of his way to vilify tragedy and comedy too (5.459–476), as being simulations, and simulations of vice above all else.[6] He completes his sketch of the literary arts with lyric poetry. First there is a relatively benevolent characterization of the singers native to Lyra (5.324–338). They regale banqueters and "add their mellowness to wine" (*mulcebit sono Bacchum*); moreover, they are prone to humming and singing to themselves. All these traits find their place in the hostile, or satiric, descriptions of song in the Silius and Seneca discussed below. Finally, Manilius makes lyric poetry the climax of the priamel that concludes the proemium of Book 2: Men love wealth and love power, but above all else they love idleness and its best emblem, song (2.145–148):

> illa frequens (sc. *turba*) quae divitias, quae diligit aurum,
> imperia et fasces mollemque per otia luxum
> et blandis diversa sonis dulcemque per aures
> affectum, ut modico noscenda ad fata labores.

> A throng indeed prefer their wealth in gold;
> Prefer preferment, and the trappings of it:
> The Province, and the Axe that goes before.
> But, most of all, unmanly luxury
> And idleness—enlivened, to be sure,
> In divers ways once wheedling melodies
> Distill their sweet emotion in the ears.
> A modest effort that, compared to mine:
> To recognize the workings of our Fate.

The somewhat prudish Manilius does not mention sex in so many words, but he leaves no doubt what the *dulcis affectus* stirred by song will lead to. In any case, he himself renounces such distractions for his own work: "Fated was I to learn the laws of Fate" (2.149). It is curious that a poet should be such an enemy of poetry and all its works and pomps, but his hostility to lyric poetry in particular is not unparalleled; it is not so much part of the Stoic tradition as a visceral Roman reaction against things "too Greek";[7] as such, it reappears in Silius Italicus and even colors Seneca.

The moralistic Silius describes at some length how Hannibal frittered away the winter in Capua after his victory at Cannae (11.385–482). The description builds on Livy, who had listed without embellishment the six factors leading to the deterioration of his troops (23.18.12):[8] *somnus enim et vinum et epulae et scorta balineaque et otium*, a list that would seem to be set up in reverse order of occurrence, if it is in any order at all. At all events, Song is not explicitly mentioned, though it is one of the possible uses of *otium*. So also at 23.45.2 Marcellus exhorts his inferior forces by saying that the Carthaginians are wasting away (*marcere*) thanks to the dissoluteness of Capua: *vino et scortis omnibusque lustris . . . confectos*. The *lustra* are their "wallows" or "dens"—a word originally applied to animals, and appropriately transferred to degenerate and bestial human behavior.

The medley that Silius weaves out of his source has no tricolon equivalent to "Wine, Women, and Song" anywhere, but presents all six of Livy's factors in kaleidoscopic configurations, the whole presided over by a decorous and duly patriotic Venus who sends down her putti and their arrows to wound Moorish hearts, and even Hannibal himself. Here, for the first time in the story it would seem, Song puts in an appearance as a factor that can unman a hero as well as his army;[9] as noted above, Livy had not mentioned Song explicitly, only *otium*.[10]

> amplexu multoque mero somnoque virorum....
>   ... madenti
> post epulas sit grata chelys segnisque soporas
> aut nostro vigiles ducat sub numine noctes....
> Bacchi dona volunt *epulasque et carmina rursus*
> Pieria liquefacta lyra....
> mollitae flammis lymphae languentia somno
> membra fovent.[11]
>   (11.397, 407–409, 414–415, 419–420)

> With close embrace and much of wine unmixed
> And sleep for heroes....
> Now may a sodden Hannibal enjoy
> The after-dinner pleasures of the lyre,
> And then prolong the sluggard past the dawn,
> Or spend his sleepless nights beneath our thrall....
> They cry once more for Bacchus' gift, and feasts
> And songs that melt in Pierian strains....
> The waters softened in the fire caress
> Their drooping members till they fall asleep.

The last of these vignettes features the bath; the transferred *mollitae* is a nice touch, as well as Silius' play on the winter mis-en-scène (so at 411 the wings of the Cupids are *nivei*): being indoors on a cold winter night had special charms for a Roman, as at Horace *Od.* 1.9.

In any case, Hannibal will not in fact succumb to the vulgar enticements Venus had listed; his undoing, the climax of the passage, occurs at the festive board to be sure (421), but only thanks to the power of Song. Silius seems to think it the worst mark of Campanian degeneracy that they sang at table (as opposed to the dialogue appropriate to a symposium, presumably); so 428–429:

> ... variasque per artes
> scenarum certant epulas distinguere ludo. ...

> They strove with all that stagecraft can command
> To mark their banquets with a carefree air.[12]

And so Hannibal's virtue succumbs to the arts of the bard Teuthras, a perverse Demodocus who chooses the most effeminate subject possible—Orpheus (439):

> haec e multis carpsit mollissima mensae. ...

> And though he had so many themes to choose,
> He chose the most unmanly for the feast.[13]

What follows is a reprise of the Orpheus myth, largely by allusion—after Ovid, what was a poet to do?—relieved by a couple of original touches: a timid Argo refuses to let herself be launched, so Orpheus charms the sea up to her instead (469–472); when the Hebrus carries Orpheus' head down to the sea, both river-banks tumble in after to follow along (476–477). In any case, after forty verses from Teuthras, Hannibal's army would never be the same (481–482):

> ... durata virorum
> pectora Castalio frangebat carmine Teuthras.

> Their battle-hardened spirits Teuthras broke
> With song Castalian.

A deft closure: *durata* echoes the essence of Orpheus at 439, *mollissima*.

In Silius as in Livy there is no cliché, tricolon or otherwise, that summarizes the debilitating factors; Wine, Women, and Song each put in an appearance, but only as details: Silius is simply embellishing Livy's list at 23.18.12. His novel contribution consists of making Song a new factor, indeed the climactic one; still, neither he nor Manilius uses "Wine, Women, and Song" as such. They thus fail to provide the clear-cut parallel needed as evidence that Seneca could have had such a cliché in mind, if it is to be restored in the text by emending *umore* to *canore*. Indeed, had Seneca intended an equivalent of "Wine, Women, and Song" as an exhaustive priamel symbolic of all possible self-indulgence, he spoiled it by overloading a good point with extraneous details: smiling first, followed by innumerable ways to occupy *otium*. But such typical prolixity resulted from the influence of Livy's list on Seneca too, whether directly or through popular moralizing in the same vein; to be sure, Seneca is concerned not with lax military discipline but bad habits in civil society. For all of that, Livy's influence will go far towards explaining the problematic *umore*.

Seneca's tricolon, whatever its climax, was not self-contained (apart from the medical suggestion of *interdixere*); it constitutes a segment integrated into a longer sequence comparable to Livy's in overall effect. Now, every debilitating factor in Livy and Silius corresponds to something on Seneca's list, except for one: their baths are apparently absent from Seneca, nor does his elemental *umor* occur in Livy and Silius, for obvious reasons. But on examination it emerges that the one apparent mismatch is in fact a match: *umore* can refer to baths by extension, though the word itself is hardly a synonym; if baths are indeed the climactic indulgence to be overcome by sheer will power, the fact would be better attuned to Roman sensibilities than a modern cliché that cannot be paralleled.

To run through the items in Seneca, then, in the light of Silius and Livy. Their correspondence with Seneca is obvious with Wine and Women. Less obviously, the *ludi* explicitly condemned by

Manilius or Silius and implicit in Livy's *otium* correspond well enough with the men that Seneca mentions at the outset who succeed *ne umquam riderent*, and thus eschew *ludi* in favor of *seria* more appropriate to a *vir gravis*; by the same token, the Song that Silius reprobates is also subsumed under the head of Smiling (or amusement). As for the banquets in Livy and Silius, take away Seneca's Wine, Women and implied Idleness, and we are left with that mere necessity Food; Seneca's rearrangement removes any need for an explicit mention of banquets.

If we likewise view Seneca's concluding embodiments of will power—the deliberate insomniacs, tightrope-walkers, weight-lifters, and swimmers—in light of Livy's *otium* (and not e.g. Juvenal's Greekling at 3.77), then they too are virtuous to the extent that it is better to take up the tightrope than sit idle. Such had been the explicit view of Manilius as well, who sketches (with uncharacteristic approbation) several of the activities that Seneca recommends: at 5.157–173 the native of Lepus will take to juggling; more to the point, "By nights he wakes, since work outweighs mere sleep / And drills his leisure hours in divers sports" (*invigilat curis, somnos industria vincit, / otia per varios exercet dulcia lusus*, 5.172–173); at 5.416–430 some natives of the Dolphin indulge in the sort of recreational swimming possible in the *piscina* of a bath, at 431–435 others becomes professional divers (their ability to hold their breath is implied), and at 438–445 yet others do gymnastics on a spring-board; at 5.650–655 the more reputable natives of Engonasin turn to tightrope-walking.

So far, then, the correspondences are close; the one detail in Livy or Silius that is apparently missing in Seneca is the Bath. The fit would thus become perfect if *umore* were Seneca's way of referring to the climactic debilitation that everyone else calls the Bath. Not that *umor* of itself "means" bath, of course; rather, Seneca the Stoic would merely be playing his philosophy and its elements to the hilt.[14] In the *De Ira* itself, it is the Fiery temperament (out of the four *potestates* that correspond to the elements) that is by nature prone to *ira* (2.19.1). As a rule, Seneca uses *umor* for the element which we automatically and misleadingly call "water," whenever the element is not in its "watery" form as in ponds or aqueducts but diffused or suspended in droplets (so e.g. at *NQ* 1.3.12, where *umor* gives the rainbow its colors). So here; it is not Baths as such, much less potable water, that a man can do without, but the debilitating manifestations of that element. Had Seneca meant only baths, he could have said so; clearly he meant to include other examples of harmful indulgence in *umor*,[15] such as the Assyrian perfumery at Silius 11.402 and the unguents implied at Horace *Ep.* 1.2.29 (where the jeunesse dorée of Phaeacea spend their time *in cute curando*). Seneca himself decries unguents at *De Vita Beata* 7.3 (discussed below) as well as *Ep.* 83.5, 86.13[16] and 108.15 (with the famous *optimus odor est nullus*); and there were always the lethal but unavoidable damps of autumn so dear to Libitina, quite apart from other "damps" that Celsus considered a risk to health.[17] For Seneca, *umor* is understandably the element of choice for dissolution and decay, as in the third book of *Quaestiones Naturales*, where he prefers a cataclysm to end the universe, rather than the traditional *ecpyrosis*.[18]

In any case, *umor* not *aqua* would be the word to cover the whole range of the noxious manifestations, few of which are recognizably water-as-such. Since Seneca modernizes Livy's topos for his own purposes,[19] he is not visualizing the actual *lustra* in Livy (hovels that likely served as bar, bath and bordello all in one), much less poetic exaggerations such as the water or snow "softened" on a brazier in Silius,[20] but rather a proper Roman bath of his own day, complete with a *caldarium* full not of water but steam.[21]

Seneca reveals an encyclopedic knowledge of baths, despite his reservations about them. *Ep.* 86 is largely devoted to fashions in bath-houses; the austerity of Scipio's is made to point up the degeneracy of modern luxury, which among much else requires a sea-view (86.8): the ancient equivalent of a sea-side motel with its own swimming pool.[22] In *Ep.* 56.1 Seneca purports to be living upstairs from a bath-house: *supra ipsum balneum habito*.[23] This is hardly the *balneum* in one of his own villas, since he describes the noise from an assortment of perfect strangers indulging themselves in pastimes recommended at *De Ira* 2.12.4: grunting away as they lift weights, singing out loud,[24] and swimming.[25] Here there is no suggestion that any of the activities are worthwhile (they distract him from his studies, his only concern of the moment), though Seneca had seen their virtue in *De Ira* (as had Manilius); the overall tone in *Ep.* 56 is satiric, not least the pretence of cheap lodgings.[26]

Elsewhere Seneca has little good to say of the baths, hot baths in particular[27]: *in omnem vitam balneum fugimus, decoquere corpus atque exinanire sudoribus inutile simul delicatumque credidimus* (*Ep.* 108.16): "all my life I have avoided the bath, and think that it is unhelpful and indeed over-refined to stew your body in one and enfeeble it with all the sweating."[28] Seneca is not saying that the bath might cause a particular ailment (the way Lipsius seemed to take *umor*; see above n. 2) but only that the bath, along with such accoutrements as ointments and perfumery, were apparent necessities that one could train oneself to do without.

Moreover, the bath conduces to moral weakness, as do the rest of the habits that the rational *animus* tells us to overcome. Seneca (who also prides himself on not drinking wine at *Ep.* 108.16) remarks on the practice of wine-bibbing after the bath at *Ep.* 68.7 and 122.6; at *NQ* 1.16.3 it was at the baths that Hostius Quadra picked up his sexual partners;[29] *De Vita Beata* 7.3 provides an unpleasant medley of everything that went on there: *convenies ... voluptatem latitantem saepius ac tenebras captantem circa balinea ac sudatoria ... mollem, enervem, mero atque unguento madentem, pallidam aut fucatam et medicamentis pollinctam*: "around the baths and steam-rooms all too often you will encounter temptation lurking, and heading for the shadows . . . soft and effeminate and dripping with wine and unguents, their complexion either sallow or else in make-up and as life-like as a corpse."[30]

In any case, such a steam bath is full of *umor* along with unguents and much else that could be called "fluid";[31] it would as such provide the inset tricolon *vino ... venere ... omni umore* with a proper little climax of its own, since the element itself outranks its two embodiments. The wise man overcomes all three as a display of will power, in the context of the *De Ira*; but there remains the tone of medical necessity noted at the outset, which supports the contention that *umor* is not so much a synonym for "bath" as a category, diagnostic and philosophical both, that subsumes the bath as its major component. Celsus had enjoined wine, sexual activity, and the baths together as a matter of course in cases of dropsy (see below n. 3). Seneca separates the threesome for his own purposes, but his *omni umore* inadvertently echoes, or retains, the phrasing of Celsus (3.21.6: *balineum atque omnis umor alienus est*). Seneca also echoes the physician in that he is avowedly describing feats of self-control; *a fortiori*, if a man can give up indulgences like wine, sex, and the baths, he can give up *ira* as well. The physician, with no philosophical axe to grind, merely comments that the prognosis in dropsy is much better for slaves, who can be forced to follow the regimen prescribed; *inutilis libertas* (3.21.2).[32]

In sum, *omni umore* should be retained in the text, even though the conjecture *canore* has its merits (which would increase considerably if a proper parallel emerges). But, given that the phrasing of Celsus at 3.21.6 is an exact parallel to *omni umore*, the supplement <*balineo atque*> should be added before *omni umore*: not that Seneca is deliberately reproducing the phrasing of Celsus (he is composing a somewhat disorganized medley off the top of his head, after all), but as a reminiscence of the generic medical jargon that the valetudinarian Seneca must have heard from his own physicians time and again. The loss of *balineo atque* from the archetype is understandable. Postclassical scribes can hardly have regarded bathing as a pleasure that belonged with the other items listed; then, shorn of its explicit referent, *omni umore* proved susceptible to the various corruptions found in the MSS extant. In sum, the coherence and appropriateness of the tricolon disappeared with the philosophy that underpinned it; no later age would steel its nerves to renounce the enticements of "Wine, Women, and Wet."[33]

INDEX AUCTORUM:

Aeschines 1.10 (*In Tim.*).
Cornelius **Celsus**: *De Medicina* 1.3.4, 13, 34; 1.4.2; 2.7.17; 3.21.1–2, 5–6, 8, 12–13, 15–17; 3.27.1; 4.2.4; 8; 4.5.3–4; 4.12.7; 4.20.3–4; 4.27.2; 4.31.2; 5.26.34.
Horace: *Ep.* 1.2.29; *Od.* 1.9; *Sat.* 1.1.27; 1.2.27, 30–35, 77–89, 116–118; 1.4.76.
Juvenal: 2.40; 3 passim; 3.77.
Justus **Lipsius** ad Sen. *Ep.* 12 ad init.; 56.1; *De Ira* 2.12.4.
Livy: 23.18.12; 23.45.2.
Manilius: 2.1–56, 145–149; 3.1–30; 5.175–173, 324–338, 416–485, 650–655.
Mann, Thomas: *Der Tod in Venedig*.
Martial: 3.44.12.
Ovid: *Ars* 3.315; *Met.* 5.561.
Petronius: *Sat.* 5.19; 73; 91–92.
Pliny: *N.H.* 28.13.50–52; 28.14.53, 56; 29.7.14; 29.8.26.
Poe, Edgar Allan: *The Facts in the Case of M. Valdemar*.
L. Annaeus **Seneca**: *Ep.* 12 passim; 15.4; 56.1, 2, 5; 68.7; 78.8; 83.5; 86.6, 8, 10, 13; 108.6, 15–16; 122.6; *De Ira* 2.12.4; 2.19.1; *NQ* 1.2.4; 1.3.12; 1.16.3; 3.29.7; 4.2.2; 4.13.1–11; *De Vita Beata* 7.3.
Silius Italicus: 11.385–482.
Valerius Maximus: 9.1. ext.
Vergil: *G.* 4.71; 4.510.

NOTES

1. The text is that of L. D. Reynolds, ed. *Senecae Dialogi* (Oxford, 1977); translations are by this writer unless otherwise noted.

2. Ad loc. in the Elsevir edition (Amsterdam, 1672). "Dropsy" is an obsolete cover term for any systemic edema, in Latin called either *aqua intercus* or *hydrops*. Pliny recommends an entire pharmacopeia of desiccants for the condition; they would have been palliative at best, since the commoner edemas result either from subcutaneous bacterial

infiltration or from congestive heart failure. Nowhere does he suggest that "like *causes* like" (though some of his cures seem to depend on the antipathy between Fire and Water); Lipsius is apparently following a contemporary belief that excessive contact with "water," in whatever form, caused dropsy by a sort of osmosis.

3. The elemental term blurs our distinction between ingested "liquids" and external "dampness" or "humidity." Sexual activity (understandably falling under *umor*) is contraindicated during convalescence from dropsy (Celsus 3.21.17: *ubi convaluit aliquis, diu tamen alienus ei veneris usus est*); wine should be used with caution (3.21.8; 3.21.13); only occasional bathing is recommended (3.21.17). Precisely the same three indulgences are contraindicated in *gravedo* (the common cold, 4.5.3), along with sunlight: *abstinere a sole, balneo, vino, venere debemus*. Wine and bathing should be restricted in colic and diabetes (4.20.3–4; 4.27.2), abstinence from sex and wine for a year may confer immunity to arthritis (4.31.2), and sex is better without wine (1.3.34): in sum, the practices to be eschewed in Seneca's triplet (assuming that *umor* is sound and refers to all manifestations of the element) can each be contraindicated for a wide variety of medical reasons. Pliny included abstinence from wine and baths in his list of remedies "that depend on our own effort" (*ab animo hominis pendentes*, *NH* 28.14.53), a categorization reminiscent of Seneca.

4. J. W. Basore ed., *Seneca's Moral Essays* (London, Loeb Classical Library 1928), 1.193.

5. Even in the most extreme cases Celsus allows some fluid intake; see below n. 15 for details.

6. His vignette of drama is bracketed by other natives of Cepheus who help set the tone: at the outset, moralists who feign a severe mien and praise the words of Cato (their deeds go unmentioned here, but see the doings of the *tertius Cato* at Juv. 2.40); then guardians who delude themselves that they actually control their minor wards (5.449–458); finally actors who can make you believe anything (5.477–485). In sum, a medley that will reappear in Juvenal; the theme uniting the natives is a gift for simulation (*commenta* 477).

7. So in its bluntest expression the words of Cato the elder to his son: *quod bonum sit illorum litteras inspicere, non perdiscere* (Pliny *NH* 29.7.14); "to take a look at their literature is worthwhile, but not to study it."

8. Valerius Maximus 9.1 ext. gives a florid reworking of Livy doubtless representative of the popular tradition (see below n. 19 for a discussion); Livy's simple check-list is easier to work with.

9. For the Phaeaceans as the remote source for such indulgence, see M. W. Dickie, "Phaeacian Athletes," *Papers of the Liverpool Latin Seminar IV* (1983) 237–76.

10. Perhaps because Livy was only interested in the effectiveness of Hannibal's troops, while Silius focuses on the hero himself and his moral deterioration, symbolic of the army as a whole.

11. The intervening verses detail the military exercises that such peacetime carousing pre-empted. In 409 *ducat* = *producat*: Hannibal will either sleep, or stay awake, too long.

12. This Duff translates "using various arts, they sought to set off their banquets by means of stage-plays," which is incompatible with the bardic recitation that follows. Take *scenarum* with *artes*, rather, with *ludo* the opposite of *seria* as at Hor. *Sat.* 1.1.27; that is, Teuthras is using resources available to Roman mime or melodrama, which is no commendation. Trans. J. D. Duff (London and Cambridge, Loeb Classical Libary 1934), 2.133.

13. Duff translates "chose out of many, as most grateful to those who sat at meat" (see above note 12, 133). If Duff is right, and Orpheus is specially appropriate for diners as such, it must be on the grounds of his dismemberment. Silius had something else in mind: the embodiment of Song made a fitting climax to the course of degeneracy that the Carthaginians pursued after Cannae.

14. Celsus begins things with a discussion of the four elemental temperaments (1.3.13). In his day the doctrine competed with others; later "the Humours" would hold the field uncontested.

15. Fluid intake beyond a bare minimum is contraindicated at Celsus 3.21.5–6 (no water), 3.21.8 (a minimum of wine), 4.2.8, 4.5.3–4, 4.20.3–4 (only a little honeyed *mulsum*), 4.27.2; he seems to have nothing against unguents and in a few cases recommends them (possibly for the sake of the rub-down: so esp. paralysis at 3.27.1).

16. To bolster his case against excessive bathing and unguents, Seneca misquotes Horace *Sat.* 1.2.27 (*pastillos Buccillus olet* for *Rufillus*) and misunderstands it to boot as perfumery not breath fresheners. In the course of *Quaestiones Naturales* (likewise a late work, and written in some haste if its disorganization is any sign) Seneca misquotes Vergil and Ovid more than a quarter of the time (twelve misquotes out of a total of forty-four, including Tibullus ascribed to Ovid

at 4.2.2).

17. The *nimia abundantia umoris* in dropsy was obvious (Celsus 3.21.2; cf. 3.21.8, 12, 15f); so also in hydrocephalus (4.2.4) but it is not given as characteristic of diabetes (4.27.2). Despite his emphasis on reducing the imbalance of an "element," his treatments at least make sense; *contra* the more "philosophical" Pliny with his simples and antipathies.

18. See esp. *NQ* 3.29.7, where the spreading cataclysm is likened to bodily disintegration: *quemadmodum in morbum transeunt sana et ulceri vicina consentiunt*: "the way healthy tissues turn to diseased, and those adjacent to an ulceration assimilate to it," *pace* Corcoran, who renders the last "sores infect the adjacent areas" (ed. LCL, 1971) and Leitao independent of Corcoran, "as sores spread to adjacent areas" (*Materiali e Discussioni*, forthcoming). Seneca's easy equation of elemental cataclysm and individual putrefaction colors his use of *umor* in the *De Ira* passage as well, I think. See also *Ep.* 78.8 (our sense of pain is eventually deadened by *corruptus umor*) and n. 3 for Celsus. Poe's *The Facts in the Case of M. Valdemar* recalls Seneca's morbid taste: the mesmeric suspension of death is an idle curiosity as long as the elderly subject is merely desiccated; it is his near-instantaneous dissolution that excites the horror.

19. Seneca need not be drawing on Livy directly; Hannibal's fatal winter was a commonplace. Valerius Maximus 9.1 ext. represents a vulgarized tradition; his emphasis on the corruption of the hero, not to the fore in Livy, is reflected in Silius: *illa vigilantissimum ducem, illa exercitum acerrimum dapibus largis, abundanti vino, unguentorum fragrantia, Veneris usu lasciviore, ad somnum et delicias evocavit*: "Capua enticed that untiring leader, that disciplined army, into somnolence and luxury with its plenteous banquets, copious wine, the fragrance of its ointments, and much too wanton indulgence in sex." Baths would be implicit in unguents.

20. Granted that *mollitae* at 11.418 is transferred from the soldiery, the participle better fits *lymphae* if the brazier is heating not bath-water but snow. That would be the nadir of luxury; at *NQ* 4.13.1–11 Seneca castigates the trade in snow and ice, *cum emere aquam turpe sit*. Nero liked sherbet in August.

21. Also known by the misnomer "Spartan" (*Laconicum*), and to us as the "Russian steam bath."

22. Seneca's *luxuria* is a "technological advance" in American English. The one language has little feel for improvement, the other for wretched excess.

23. At an inn in Baiae, not Rome, according to Lipsius (2.190b), which is plausible since many of the letters refer to his travels in the area; but at 56.5 he writes as if subjected to the din of Rome itself (e.g. *ad Metam Sudantem*) in much the same spirit as Juvenal 3. Summers does not address the problem of the setting (London, Macmillan 1910) 234.

24. *Ep.* 56.2 *adice . . . et illum, cui vox sua in balineo placet.* Probably the modern "bathroom baritone" rather than someone reciting poetry melodramatically (though there would have been little practical difference); cf. *Ep.* 108.6, where the context ensures that *vox* means "song": dilettanti attend philosophical lectures *quemadmodum in theatrum voluptatis causa ad delectandos aures oratione vel voce vel fabulis ducimur*, and Manilius 5.336, where the native of the Lyre "Sings to himself, a comfort to his ears" if not necessarily his captive audience: *solus et ipse suas semper cantabit ad aures.* Cf. also Hor. *Sat.* 1.4.76 *suave locus voci resonat conclusus*; poetry is in question at Mart. 3.44.12 *in thermas fugio: sonas ad aurem* and Petr. 73, 91, and 92 *de balneo tamquam de theatro eiectus sum.*

25. A lighter regimen is recommended for the elderly at *Ep.* 15.4: *cursus et aliquo pondere manus motae et saltus* of various kinds. Similar dumb-bells are wielded by the girl in the famous "bikini" mosaic from Piazza Armerina.

26. Cf. *Ep.* 12, where he has been away from a suburban villa of his for so very long that seedling trees he had just now planted are gnarled and dying, and his one-time pet slave has aged even faster than he himself has. Both here and in *Ep.* 56 the "facts" subserve the moral of the piece; it would be worth investigating how often Seneca indulges in fictions for the sake of the moral. Lipsius saw *Ep.* 12 for the self-satire it is: "facete de senectute sua narrat" (2.37).

27. So also Celsus on empirical grounds in a number of conditions (2.7.17); hot baths are risky for the fatigued (1.3.4) and for those with a weak head (1.4.2). Bathing of any kind is contraindicated for paralysis (4.12.7), colic (4.20.3–4), and gangrene (5.26.34).

28. Cf. *Ep.* 86.6: *multa sudatione corpora exinanita*; at 86.10, warming to his topic, he says that a condemned slave should be sentenced to being "bathed alive" (*vivum lavari*) in bath-water *similis incendio*. His own preferences ranged from cold when young to tepid in his old age (*Ep.* 83.5). Cf. Pliny *NH* 29.8.26, who speaks of food eaten by the bather

"cooking" in the bath.

29. Seneca denounces Quadra for any number of reasons; one that has gone unremarked is the plain fact that he picked up his partners in a common bath-house. Horace had had little good to say about finding sexual partners on the open market (*Sat.* 1.2.30–35; 77–89) except that it avoids the risks of adultery; he himself recommends the judicious use of house-slaves at need (116–18), presumably the course that constituted *aurea mediocritas* in the case at hand.

30. The verb *pollingere* is normal of preparing a corpse for the pyre; Seneca seems to envision something on the order of modern mortuary cosmetics, given the details preceding, or Aschenbach's rejuvenation in *Der Tod in Venedig*. At Athens "vice in the shadows" had been addressed by a law of Solon, "who held deserted and dark places in great suspicion," that opened the *gymnasia* at dawn and shut them at dusk (Aeschines 1.10, *In Tim.*); see Thomas Scanlon, "*Gymnikê Paideia*," *CB* 74.2 (1998) 156.

31. So Seneca notes that there are haloes around the lights in a steam bath, because the air is thickened by moisture (*NQ* 1.2.4); cf. Pliny *NH* 28.13.50–52 for other *umor* in a bath.

32. Pliny makes a similar point; to his shame, L. Lucullus needed a slave to keep him to his diet: *pudenda re servo facilius parere quam sibi* (*NH* 28.14.56).

33. I am grateful to my colleagues Matthew W. Dickie and William Wycislo for their suggestions in the course of this paper.

The Dual Citizenship of the Roman Stoics

Mark Morford
University of Virginia

For Anna Lydia Motto

Stoic doctrine about citizenship began as a reaction to the political theories of Plato and Aristotle. Zeno's polis was "a group of people living in the same place and administered by law" (whereas Aristotle had defined the city as a *koinonia*, a community of citizens).[1] Zeno's community consisted of morally good (or "wise") people, men and women, who alone were capable of friendship, political association, and freedom.[2] His polis therefore did not have the class distinctions of Plato's ideal city, nor did it need the basic institutions of the Greek city—a system of education, temples, lawcourts, gymnasia, currency, and the institution of marriage. Since these institutions are imperfect and virtue is perfect, there is no need for them in a community of virtuous people.[3] In their place the god of the city, Eros, is also the god of friendship (*philia*) and freedom (*eleutheria*), the facilitator of

---

[1] *SVF* 3.329 (Long & Sedley 67J); Arist. *Pol.* 1.1 (1252a). For the continuity of Stoic political thought with Platonism see Parente (1980). Cf. Erskine 33: "Zeno's *Politeia* can be seen as a conscious rejection of Plato's *Republic*, yet . . . Plato's work could be said to have worked as a catalyst."

[2] For Zeno's *Politeia* see especially Erskine 1–42 (ch. 1); Schofield, esp. ch. 2; Baldry, with commentary on the fragments of the *Politeia*.

[3] *SVF* 1.264 (Plut. *De Stoic. Rep.* 1034b): "Zeno teaches that we should not build temples of the gods, for a temple is not worth much and is not holy"; *SVF* 1.266 (Stob. 43): "Zeno said that we should adorn cities not with statues but with the virtues of their inhabitants."

concord (*homonoia*), co-worker with the citizens in assuring the city's security (*soteria*).[4]

Though much in Zeno's *Politeia* was an embarrassment to many Stoics, his views were never formally rejected. His authority remained unquestioned throughout the history of the Stoa.[5] Cicero, however, called Zeno (*Fin.* 3.5: *SVF* 1.34) *non tam rerum inventor ... quam novorum verborum*, "not so much the creator of concepts as of new words," and Quintilian (like Cicero, a non-Stoic), said that if you were to ask a Stoic if Zeno or Cleanthes or Chrysippus were *sapientes*, he would reply:

> magnos quidem illos ac venerabiles, non tamen id, quod natura hominis summum habet, consecutos. (*Inst.* 12.1.18: *SVF* 1.44)

> They were great men, worthy of reverence, yet they did not achieve that thing which is the highest possession of human nature (*sc.*, perfect wisdom).[6]

Nevertheless, Zeno set the terms of Stoic political discourse, whatever problems his ideal doctrines caused in the practical world. The political doctrines of the Neronian Stoics are, then, part of a continuum evolving from Zeno himself. Seneca's doctrine of dual citizenship has its roots in Zeno's *Republic*.[7]

Plutarch summarizes the goal of Zeno's *Politeia* as follows:[8]

---

[4] *SVF* 1.263 (Ath. 561c), quoted by Schofield 27.

[5] So Sedley 98: "It was every bit as unthinkable for a Stoic to criticize Zeno, or to question his authority, as it was for an Epicurean to show such disrespect to Epicurus." Seneca (*Ep.* 83.9) calls Zeno *vir maximus, huius sectae fortissimae ac sanctissimae conditor*.

[6] The Stoic philosophers recognized that they were not *sapientes*, e.g., *SVF* 3.657 (Sextus Empiricus 7.432), 662 (Plut. *De Stoic. Rep.* 1048e: cf. *SVF* 3.668); see also Erskine 74.

[7] See Schofield 93–103 (ch. 4) for discussion of and solution to the problems inherent in this statement.

[8] *SVF* 1.262 (Plut. *Alex.* 329a–b). For discussion see Baldry 12–13; Schofield 104–11 (Appendix A: "Zeno and Alexander"). Immediately following the second quotation are the words (omitted in *SVF* 1.262) "and

That we may not live in separate cities or demes, each apart with separate laws, but that we might think of all men as our fellow-demesmen and citizens, and that there might be one [common] life and order, like that of a flock grazing together in a common pasture.

Plutarch continues:

Zeno wrote this fashioning it as if it were a vision (*onar*) or image (*eidolon*) of the philosopher's good government (*eunomia*) and constitution (*politeia*).

Zeno's vision is Utopia, an ideal society, "a philosophical enquiry."[9] It is not set in a particular time and place, and in abolishing the institutions of Greek cities it suggests an alternative to the Greek polis, just as it provides an alternative vision to Plato's ideal state. It is "an ideal society where all are wise, living in harmonious communities."[10] It is not modeled on a particular Greek city-state (e.g., Lycurgan Sparta), still less is it a pattern for a world-state.[11] The rigorous logic of Zeno's Utopia would indeed have embarrassed his followers, because it questioned—indeed, did away with—the institutions and principles of the communities in which they lived. Like Plato, Zeno saw existing cities as corrupt,[12]

Alexander supplied the deed (*ergon*) for Zeno's word (*logos*)," where *logos* seems to imply "system expressed in words" (translated by Schofield 104: "it was Alexander who gave effect to the theory"). For the problem of *logos* see Tarn 2.421 (answered by Schofield 106).

[9]Erskine 23: "What Zeno put forward in his *Politeia* was not a description of a world state or community . . . but a philosophical enquiry."

[10]Erskine 22.

[11]This is the thesis of Tarn 2.399–449 (Appendix 25: "Brotherhood and Unity"), esp. 399; 418 for the notion that Lycurgan Sparta was the basis of Zeno's *Politeia*. For convincing criticism of Tarn see Erskine 18–27, expanding the arguments of Baldry 6–8.

[12]*SVF* 1.226 (Diog. Laert. 7.32) for Zeno's low opinion of the *me spoudaioi*, i.e., the inhabitants of existing poleis.

but he imagined a society in which all citizens are equal and all are morally good. Such a society needs neither law nor temples, nor gymnasia and the other institutions of the Greek polis.

Zeno's theories focused on the moral gulf between cities as they actually are and communities in which Eros would achieve the goals of law, which are freedom (*eleutheria*) and happiness (*eudaimonia*) for the citizens. Law and the other institutions of the actual city-state exist because of the moral imperfections of its inhabitants. They are therefore causes of division—between law-abiding and law-breaking, rich and poor, educated and uneducated, pious and impious, citizen and non-citizen, and so on. Plutarch (*SVF* 1.262) focuses on the contrast between divisions and separation in existing cities on the one hand, and, on the other, Zeno's unified community, symbolized by the flock (*agele*). The flock grazes together and Zeno exploits the similarity of *nómos* (law) and *nomós* (pasture) to sharpen the focus on the common law or pasture (*koinos nomos*).

Zeno, therefore, shifted the definition of the city away from a community bound, but also divided, by legal, religious, political and social institutions. Since his citizens were morally good, they were linked by Virtue and motivated by Eros. Thus they achieved concord (*homonoia*), which, as we have seen, was the guarantor of the city's security. Citizens of his city, morally good and living in harmony, achieved the goals of freedom and happiness, which in existing cities were the goal of laws and institutions.

Zeno was not concerned with the size of his city, nor with the question of whether there could be more than one ideal city.[13] What distinguished his city from existing Greek poleis or Plato's ideal city was its harmonious unity (*homonoia*), based on virtue and friendship, which were energized by Eros. Thus the Greek poleis and their institutions no longer were needed in Zeno's ideal world. The individual city's institutions and laws (differing from one city to another) were replaced by the community of virtuous citizens united under universal law. By turning away from the notion of

---

[13]Baldry 8; Erskine 22.

people living in separate communities Zeno opened the way for the idea of the cosmic city, of which all good human beings are citizens. This step seems to have been taken by Chrysippus in Book 3 of his *On Nature*, "drawing out more clearly the logical consequences of Zeno's own ideas," so that his cosmic city was "the community of all rational beings who are citizens of the universe."[14]

In the third century BCE it was not practical to think of the city in these terms. The city-state was giving way, not to the world-state (as posited by Tarn) but to empires based on military power and economic wealth, each led by a monarch. A different kind of political organization would be necessary to make the cosmic city of Chrysippus even marginally relevant. This proved to be the Roman empire, whose expansion into the Greek world in the first half of the second century began the process of realizing the philosopher's ideal citizenship of the universe. There are two distinct phases in the process: the first required a doctrine that met the needs of a governing elite administering a vast area; the second required one that spoke to the needs of members of that elite, whose field of action was restricted by the imbalance of power between their class and an autocrat who controlled the military. The first phase finds its voice with Panaetius and the family of the Scipiones and their friends, the second with Seneca.

The administration of an empire by a governing elite needed both justification and encouragement, and this was provided by Panaetius. His doctrine primarily concerned duty, a necessary consideration for the Roman governing elite. His perspective is that of the senatorial class, justifying its imperial mission by appealing to the community of humankind, and encouraging its members to assume heavy responsibilities in the assurance of their place in the divinely ordered cosmos. Freedom and happiness were now to be

---

[14] Schofield 102, who discusses Chrysippus' doctrine of the cosmic city in ch. 3, 57–92. Note p. 74, quoting Philodemus *On Piety* (col. vii.12–viii.4, Henrichs): "He (Chrysippus) writes comparable things in *On Nature* ... Thus he says ... in the third [book] that the universe of the wise is one, citizenship of it being held by gods and men together."

achieved in the context of service to the wider community of humankind and the gods.

For the Roman politician the family was far more important to one's public career than was the case in Athens or Sparta. Panaetius acknowledged its significance in his hierarchy of duties.[15] The citizen's duties in his dual role as a member of a particular state and of the universal community of humankind and gods were not mutually exclusive. Instead they were an expanding series of concentric circles (an image developed later by Hierokles).[16] The traditional duties of the Roman towards the gods of the state and towards parents and family continued to be central, without detracting from the wider duties to all mankind and the gods. Thus he became truly a citizen of the cosmos.[17] The virtuous person's *oikeiosis* ("affinity" or "orientation") directed him to the proper objects of his *officium*, and his affinity could be as well towards the wider community of humankind (including peoples governed by Rome) as towards his own family and city.[18] Here is Cicero's most explicit statement of this doctrine (*Fin.* 5.65):

> in omni autem honesto ... nihil est tam illustre nec quod latius pateat quam coniunctio inter homines hominum et quasi quaedam societas et communicatio utilitatum et ipsa caritas generis humani. quae nata a primo satu, quod a procreatoribus nati diliguntur et tota domus coniugio et stirpe coniungitur, serpit sensim foras, cognationibus primum, deinde amicitiis, post vicinitatibus, tum civibus et iis quo publice socii et amici sunt, deinde totius complexu generis humani.

---

[15]See Cicero, *Off.* 1.58 and 1.60.

[16]Aul. Gell. 9.5.8, for the date of Hierokles. For the text of his *Ethike Stoicheiosis* (Berlin Papyrus 9780) see von Arnim, with valuable introduction; see also Prächter.

[17]Defined by Cicero, *N.D.* 2.154, as: *communis deorum atque hominum domus aut urbs utrorumque*, "the common home of gods and humankind or the city of both [gods and humankind]."

[18]The best introduction to Stoic *oikeiosis* is Pembroke; valuable also is Striker.

> In every good activity there is nothing brighter or more widespread than the community of human beings, and, so to speak, cooperation and sharing of benefits and, generally, love (*caritas*) of the human race. This begins at birth, because children are loved by parents, and the whole family is linked by marriage and children. It (*caritas*) gradually spreads abroad, first to relatives, then to friends, then to neighbors, then to citizens and those who are "Friends and Allies of the [Roman] People," and finally it embraces the whole human race.

This phase of the Stoic doctrine of the duties of the citizen was appropriate for an elite with a tradition of public service and the exercise of power gained through political competition. But the rise of military *principes* and the establishment of the monarchy required a change of focus. Under the principate the question of duty and its objects led to exquisite dilemmas for the Stoic. His *oikeiosis* might be towards people whose interests were incompatible with those of the state, represented by the *princeps*. So long as the *princeps* was capable of the rational pursuit of virtue his interests and those of the Stoic citizen would generally coincide. But when the *princeps* was neither rational nor virtuous then the *officium* of the Stoic towards the objects of his *oikeiosis* conflicted with his *officium* towards the *princeps*. If the conflicting *officia* could not be reconciled, then he might withdraw from active participation in the *res publica*, for Zeno had taught that the wise person will participate in politics unless there is an impediment: *accedet ad rem publicam, nisi si quid impedierit* (Sen. *De Otio* 3.2: *SVF* 1.271).[19]

This is a central issue in Senecan Stoicism. Seneca's special contribution was to reconcile Zeno's and Chrysippus' doctrine of dual citizenship to the realities of Roman public life under a morally

---

[19]For further references see Dionigi 199–201. The source of the quotation is not in the surviving fragments of Zeno's *Politeia*.

imperfect *princeps*. The individual might now achieve freedom and happiness through private activity, if he were compelled to withdraw from public life. The emphasis on activity is significant: Stoic *otium* was still *negotium*. Activity in the particular *res publica* of Rome might be precluded, but the wise person could never be prevented from activity in the *res publica* of the universe. The individual could fulfill his duty by serving all mankind. Seneca showed how the original doctrines of Zeno's *Politeia* were still applicable by reference to the dual citizenship of the wise person, by aiming at the goal of personal tranquillity (and through this achieving liberty and happiness), and, finally, by using reason to estimate (*aestimare*) the proper objects of his *oikeiosis* and so to know what was his *officium* as a citizen of the universe.

With Seneca, therefore, the doctrine of the virtuous person's dual citizenship is closely bound up with the question of political participation. Zeno had made personal liberty the criterion for participation, and he implied that an obstacle to participation also diminished individual freedom.[20] The virtuous person could not cooperate with a corrupt ruler such as Nero without compromising his liberty. His dilemma then would be whether to attempt to cooperate or to withdraw.[21]

Withdrawal from public life could appear to the *princeps* as treason. There were clear rules about senatorial duties under the principate.[22] Attendance at the meetings of the senate was a senatorial *officium*, expected, if voluntary, in the republic, but

---

[20]Besides *SVF* 1.271 (= Sen. *De Otio* 3.2), quoted above, Zeno makes the implication in his rewriting of Sophocles (*SVF* 1.219) from: "He who goes into a tyrant's presence is his slave, even if he goes [as] a free man," to: "... is not his slave, if he goes [as] a free man."

[21]Suicide does not seem to have been thought of as a primary means of withdrawal, although Seneca is rather inconsistent on this subject. See Griffin (1976) 367–88; Grisé 193–223 (ch. 7: "L'Option stoïcienne"), esp. 206–17 for Seneca. Grisé rightly says that Seneca's criterion for choosing suicide is liberty, and that reason must be the basis for such a choice.

[22]See Talbert 134–52, esp. 134–36.

compulsory under the principate.[23] Deliberately to choose not to attend was *secessio*, treasonous non-cooperation. This was the leading charge against Thrasea at his trial in 66 (Tac. *Ann.* 16.27.2). Seneca used *secessio*, however, of withdrawal into private life or retirement,[24] but in military and political contexts it had negative connotations. These are defined in Eprius' accusation of Thrasea:

> requirere se in senatu consularem, in votis sacerdotem, in iure iurando civem, nisi contra instituta et caerimonias maiorum proditorem palam et hostem Thrasea induisset. (Tac. *Ann.* 16.28.2)

> In the senate I look for an ex-consul; at the offering of vows I look for a priest; at the taking of oaths I look for a citizen—unless Thrasea has openly assumed the role of a traitor and an enemy, against the traditions and ceremonies of our ancestors.

From this perspective, withdrawal was not *in usum rei publicae*, and it was a betrayal of one's duty to the state as a citizen.

Eprius' accusations were based on the assumption that the only duty of the citizen is towards the state. To appeal to one's duty as a human being towards other human beings was (in his view) no less than treason, for one cannot hold two citizenships. Three decades later Quintilian used the Stoic Cato himself as the example of the loyal citizen participating in political life (*Inst.* 11.1.36): *hic, qui bello civili se interfecit, Cato eloquens senator fuit*, "this man, who during the civil war killed himself, was an eloquent senator."

---

[23]Cic. *Dom.* 8, for the republic. Under the principate attendance ceased to be compulsory at 60 (Sen. *De Brev. Vit.* 20.4) or 65 (Sen. Rhet. *Controv.* 1.8.4). Dio 55.3.1–3, is evidence for substantial absenteeism (cf. Dio 54.18.3).

[24]E.g. *De Otio* 1.1 and 6.4. There are twenty-one other examples of this usage of *secedere* or *secessus* (but never *secessio*) in Seneca's *Dialogi* and *Epistulae*.

He contrasted the dutiful citizen with philosophers who shirk the *officia civis* (*Inst.* 11.1.35):

> at vir civilis vereque sapiens, qui se non otiosis disputationibus, sed administrationi rei publicae dederit, a qua longissime isti, qui philosophi vocantur, recesserunt, omnia, quae ad efficiendum oratione quod proposuerit valent, libenter adhibebit, cum prius, quid honestum sit efficere, in animo suo constituerit.

> The man who is a dutiful citizen and truly wise, who gives himself not to private (*otiosis*) discussions but to the administration of the state (from which those who call themselves "philosophers" have retreated very far)—this man will willingly bring to bear everything which has the power of putting into action that which he proposes in his speech, once he has decided what is the virtuous course of action.

Thus the true citizen is the wise man who uses reason to decide on the virtuous course of action, and then willingly does all he can to further this course. Philosophers who retire into *otium* have abandoned their responsibilities as citizens of the state, and their scholarship is of no practical use. In this view the state (i.e., Rome) is the only *locus* for virtuous action; as a corollary, to maintain that one can have a primary *officium* towards one's fellow beings in the cosmos is to abandon one's *officium* as a citizen of Rome.

Seneca is inconsistent on this issue, but eventually he arrived at a viable restatement of the doctrines of dual citizenship articulated by Zeno and Chrysippus. He agreed that the first duty of the citizen was political participation, and he said that, other things being equal, it was cowardice not to serve:

> ipse te interroga . . . utrum velis vivere in macello an in castris. atqui vivere, Lucili, militare est. itaque hi qui iactantur et per operosa atque ardua sursum ac deorsum

eunt et expeditiones periculosissimas obeunt fortes viri sunt primoresque castrorum: isti quos putida quies aliis laborantibus molliter habet turturillae sunt. (*Ep.* 96.5)

Ask yourself whether you would prefer to spend your life in the market place or in the camp. And yet, Lucilius, to be alive is to be on campaign. And so those men who are restlessly active, who go up and down through laborious and difficult places, who undertake the most difficult patrols—these men are courageous soldiers and leaders in the camp. Those who spend their time in shameful inactivity while others labor are doves.

The military metaphor is fundamental in Seneca's views on the citizen's duty. The military term *statio* (Greek *taxis*) defines duty as if the citizen were a soldier assigned to a particular post.[25] Elsewhere Seneca says that the virtuous person must accept the commands of fate with military courage (*Ep.* 94.7): *omnia fortiter excipienda quae nobis mundi necessitas imperat*, "we must accept courageously all the commands that universal necessity imposes upon us." Further, he says (*Ep.* 107.9): *malus miles est qui imperatorem gemens sequitur*, "he [the person who is reluctant to follow the dictates of fate] is a bad soldier if he follows his commander groaning." Finally, Seneca returns to the metaphor of *statio* (*Ep.* 120.18):

---

[25]Pohlenz (1.324–15) shows how the metaphor was peculiar to Seneca (cf. Pohlenz 2.157). For the philosopher as soldier see Sextius (Q. Sextius Niger: *PIR* S474) at Sen. *Ep.* 59.7. He said that the wise man must deploy all his virtues like an army marching under threat of enemy attack, *quadrato agmine*. Socrates may have originated the metaphor (see Pl. *Apol.* 28d–e) but Cicero, *Sen.* 73, attributes it to Pythagoras. For the relationship of the military ethic to the virtuous life see Harnack, esp. 27–42.

ideo magnus animus conscius sibi melioris naturae dat quidem operam ut in hac statione qua positus est honeste se atque industrie gerat.

The mind that is aware of its better nature will labor to conduct itself virtuously and intelligently in this post [*statione*] in which it has been placed.

Seneca's priorities are clear. The citizen will choose to serve in his assigned post unless something prevents him, and the vocabulary of duty (*statio, status, munus, officium, mundi necessitas, imperat*) enjoins upon him the necessity of performing his assigned role in the state as if he were a citizen soldier.

How then can a more precise definition of Zeno's *nisi si quid impedierit* be reached? Seneca discusses the problem from several perspectives, which have in common their reliance on Zeno's *Politeia*. The goal of his doctrine was to allow the individual to maintain his freedom and happiness (of which tranquillity was an important component) while still fulfilling his duty as a citizen of Rome and of the universe. He shows how impediments to fulfilling the former duty, as a citizen of Rome, could not be impediments to fulfilling the latter. The virtuous person is a citizen of the universe, to whatever extent he may be hindered from participation in the *res publica* of Rome.

In *De Tranquillitate* 3.3 and 3.5 Seneca quotes Athenodorus (probably the son of Sandon) as advising a retreat into *otium* when the times became too corrupt for public activity.[26] In retirement,

---

[26]Athenodorus, son of Sandon, contributed a *bellum hypomnema* on duty, used by Cicero in the *De Officiis*: Cic. *Att.* 16.11.4, 16.14.4; cf. *Fam.* 3.7.4. He became an adviser to Augustus: see Griffin (1976) 324; Rawson 233–57, esp. 243–45. Athenodorus Kordylion, older than the son of Sandon and like him a native of Tarsus, was persuaded by Cato to live with him at Rome, where he died: Str. 14.674.14M; Plut. *Mor.* 777a and *Cato Min.* 10; D. L. 7.34.

said Athenodorus, the good citizen could still perform his *munus* towards his fellow citizens and human beings:

> ita tamen delituerit ut, ubicumque otium suum absconderit, prodesse velit singulis universisque ingenio voce consilio.

> He still will be in hiding in such a way that, wherever his secret place of retirement is, he will want to help individuals or the whole [human race] by means of his wisdom, his voice, or his advice.

But Seneca rightly criticizes Athenodorus for advocating too precipitate a retreat: one should withdraw *sensim relato gradu et salvis signis, salva militari dignitate,* "gradually, with standards uncaptured and military dignity unimpaired" (*De Tranq.* 4.1). Nor did Athenodorus sufficiently take into account the precise kinds of impediments to participation, which would allow for a partial or gradual withdrawal. Seneca's own doctrine follows:

> militare non licet: honores petat. privato vivendum est: sit orator. silentium indictum est: tacita advocatione cives iuvet. periculosum etiam ingressu forum est: in domibus, in spectaculis, in conviviis bonum contubernalem, fidelem amicum, temperantem convivam agat. officia civis amisit: hominis exerceat. ideo magno animo nos non unius urbis moenibus clusimus sed in totum orbis commercium emisimus patriamque nobis mundum professi sumus ut liceret latiorem virtuti campum dare. (*De Tranq.* 4.3–4)

> He may not serve in the army: let him run for political office. He must live as a private individual: let him be an orator. He is forbidden to speak: let him help (his fellow-) citizens by means of his silent support. Even the Forum is dangerous for him to enter: in private houses, at the public shows, at dinner parties, let him play the role of a good companion (*contubernalem*), a loyal friend, and a

moderate fellow-guest. He has lost the duties (*officia*) of a citizen: let him perform those of a human being. Therefore with a generous spirit we have not shut ourselves inside the walls of one city, but we have sent ourselves out to interact with the whole world. We have declared that the universe is our fatherland, so as to give ourselves a broader field for virtue.

Seneca defines the impediments to continued participation by dual circles of action. In the one, the room for participation becomes increasingly restricted in the context of the city of Rome; in the other the good citizen's influence widens until he acts primarily as a citizen of the community of all gods and humankind. His *oikeiosis* is towards his fellow human beings, and his *officia civis* are maintained in the universal city when he is hindered from performing the *officia civis* at Rome.[27]

Seneca thus put into a Roman context the political doctrines of Zeno and Chrysippus. In *Ep.* 55.4 he takes Servilius Vatia, a *praetorius dives* who retired from public activity under Tiberius, as an example of an *ignavus* whose retreat was self-serving and lacked the *officia hominis* of the rational good man. Vatia was hiding, not living: *at ille latere sciebat, non vivere*. The good man, by contrast, cannot separate himself from humanity and live for himself. Even in retreat he conducts the *negotium animi* and serves others. Thus Seneca combines the Stoic doctrine of dual citizenship with the traditional *officia* of the Roman senatorial class.

There are many other passages in which Seneca describes the withdrawal of the good man from public life. They contain the following common elements:

1. the use of reason to achieve the goals of virtue, freedom and happiness;

---

[27] Seneca's doctrine is consistent with his own gradual retreat from public political activity: see Tac. *Ann.* 14.53–56 and 15.60.2–4. He uses Socrates as the *exemplum* of the wise man who remains free under a tyranny at *De Tranq.* 5.1–4.

2. the military metaphor;

3. the idea that the role in life that the virtuous person chooses is a *statio*, an assigned place for the performance of one's *munus* or *officium*;

4. that *otium*, defined as withdrawal from public activity, is still *negotium*;

5. that the virtuous person's *otium* is the field for the performance of his duty as a citizen of the universe.[28]

Seneca refines his doctrine in the *De Otio*. He appears to counsel a more decisive withdrawal than in the earlier work, and to approach closer to the doctrine of Athenodorus.[29] The context of the discussion, however, is different: the theme of the *De Tranquillitate* is peace of mind, of the *De Otio* withdrawal from public activity. In the *De Otio*, then, there is greater emphasis on the benefits performed towards humankind by the individual:

> hoc nempe ab homine exigitur, ut prosit hominibus, si fieri potest, multis, si minus, paucis, si minus, proximis, si minus, sibi. nam cum se utilem ceteris efficit, commune agit negotium. (*De Otio* 3.5)

> This surely is what is demanded of a human being—that he be of use to human beings, to many if that can be achieved; to few if it be less possible; to those closest to him if it be still less possible; to himself if it be less still. For whenever he makes himself useful to others he is transacting the business of the whole community.

---

[28]For *otium* and *negotium* see André (1962), esp. 5–25 for etymology. For the connection between *otium-negotium-militia* cf. the chorus of soldiers in Ennius' *Iphigenia* (Aulus Gellius 19.10.12 = Ennius *fr.* 241–48W), and Skutsch (1953) 193–201 and (1968) 157–65.

[29]*De Otio* 8.3–4 seems to accept Athenodorus' doctrine of withdrawal, apparently contradicting the criticism in *De Tranq.* 4. The text breaks off here, as Lipsius 253 and 259, first saw. The argument may therefore be incomplete: Seneca might have gone on to resolve the contradiction.

Here again is the schema of contracting circles of action and expanding circles of *beneficia*. Again, too, the virtuous person's *oikeiosis* will be towards *bonae artes*, which will allow him to serve all mankind, *ut prosit hominibus*.

More explicitly than in the *De Tranquillitate* Seneca builds his doctrine (in the *De Otio*) on the foundation of dual citizenship:

> duas res publicas animo complectamur, alteram magnam et vere publicam qua di atque homines continentur, in qua non ad hunc angulum respicimus aut ad illum sed terminos civitatis nostrae cum sole metimur, alteram cui nos adscripserit condicio nascendi; haec aut Atheniensium erit aut Carthaginiensium aut alterius alicuius urbis quae non ad omnis pertineat homines sed ad certos. . . . huic maiori rei publicae et in otio deservire possumus, immo vero nescio an in otio melius, ut quaeramus quid sit virtus. (*De Otio* 4.1–2)

> In our mind we embrace two republics. The first is large and truly "public" and includes gods and human beings. In it we do not look at this or that corner, but we limit the boundaries of our republic with the sun. The second republic is that in which the circumstances of our birth have enrolled us. This will be Athens or Carthage or some other city which belongs not to all human beings but to a definite group. . . . This former greater republic we can serve even as private individuals—indeed, perhaps better in private so that we can enquire into the nature of Virtue.

Seneca's doctrine is consistent with Zeno's *Politeia*. In the context of the Greek polis Zeno had looked beyond the particular limitations of the city's institutions. Seneca, when the virtuous citizen is prevented from participation in the public life of the state, justifies the *statio* of *otium* by appealing to his citizenship in the community of the universe. In so doing he preserves the Stoic principles of *oikeiosis* and *officium*, while his doctrine is consistent with the traditional duties of the Roman senatorial class and with their orientation towards the family. Thus the virtuous person is truly a citizen of two republics.[30]

BIBLIOGRAPHY

André, J. M. 1989. "Sénèque: De brevitate vitae," "De Constantia sapientis," "De Tranquilitate animi," "De otio." In Haase 1724–1778.

——. 1966. *L'Otium dans la Vie Morale et Intellectuelle Romaine des Origines à l'Époque Augustéenne*. Paris.

——. 1962. *Recherches sur l'Otium Romain. Annales Littéraires de l'Université de Besançon* 52. Paris.

Arnim, H. von. 1903–1924. *Stoicorum Veterum Fragmenta*. 4 vols. Leipzig. (Repr. Dubuque, Iowa, n.d.): abbreviated as *SVF*.

——. 1906. *Hierokles, Ethische Elementarlehre. Berliner Klassikertexte* 4. Berlin.

Baldry, H. C. 1959. "Zeno's Ideal State." *JHS* 79:3–15.

Beveridge, M. J. 1974. "The Active and the Contemplative Life in the Prose Works of Seneca." Diss. University of North Carolina, Chapel Hill.

Chaumartin, F.-R. 1989. "Quarante ans de recherche sur les oeuvres philosophiques de Sénèque (Bibliographie 1945–1985)." In Haase 1545–1605.

Dionigi, I. 1983. *De Otio*. Brescia.

Erskine, A. 1990. *The Hellenistic Stoa: Political Thought and Action*. Oxford.

Griffin, M. 1997. "Philosophy, Politics and Politicians at Rome." In Griffin and Barnes 1–37.

---

[30]The virtuous *princeps*, Marcus Aurelius, used the same doctrine to encourage himself in continuing to bear the burden of public responsibilities: "My city and my fatherland is Rome, insofar as I am Antoninus. Insofar as I am a human being, the universe is my city and my fatherland" (*To Himself*, 6.44).

—. 1976. *Seneca: a Philosopher in Politics*. Oxford.
Griffin M. and J. Barnes, eds. 1997. *Philosophia Togata I: Essays on Philosophy and Roman Society*. 2nd edition. Oxford.
Grisé, Y. 1982. *Le Suicide dans la Rome Antique*. Montreal and Paris.
Haase, W., ed. 1989. *ANRW* II.36.3. Berlin.
J. Lipsius. 1615. *L. Annaei Philosophi Opera Quae Exstant Omnia*. 2nd edition. Antwerp.
Harnack, A. 1981. *Militia Christi*, translated by D. Gracie. Philadelphia. (Orig., Tübingen 1905).
Long, A. A., ed. 1971. *Problems in Stoicism*. London.
Long, A. A. and D. Sedley. 1987. *The Hellenistic Philosophers*. 2 vols. Cambridge.
Motto, A. L. 1970. *Guide to the Thought of Lucius Annaeus Seneca*. Amsterdam.
Parente, M. Isnarde. 1989. "Ierocle Stoico." In Haase 2201–26.
—. 1980. "La Politica della Stoica Antica." *Sandalion* 3:67–98.
Pembroke, S. G. 1971. "Oikeiosis." In Long 1971:113–49.
Pohlenz, M. 1959. *Die Stoa*. 2nd edition. 2 vols. Göttingen.
Prächter, K. 1901. *Hierokles der Stoiker*. Leipzig.
Rawson, E. 1997. "Roman Rulers and the Philosophic Adviser." In Griffin and Barnes 233–57.
Schofield, M. 1991. *The Stoic Idea of the City*. Cambridge.
Sedley, D. 1997. "Philosophical Allegiance in the Greco-Roman World." In Griffin and Barnes 97–119.
Skutsch, O. 1968. *Studia Enniana*. London.
—. 1953."Die ennianische Soldatenchor." *RhM* 96:193–201 (= "The Soldiers' Chorus in the *Iphigenia*," in Skutsch (1968) 157–65.
Striker, G. 1983. "The Role of *Oikeiosis* in Stoic Ethics." *Oxford Studies in Ancient Philosophy* 1:145–67.
Talbert, R. A. 1984. *The Senate of Imperial Rome*. Princeton.
Tarn, W. W. 1948. *Alexander the Great*. 2 vols. Oxford. Repr. Chicago 1981.

Imperial Rome and the Habitations of Cruelty

Hans-Friedrich Mueller
Florida State University

magistrae optimae mitissimaeque

The military power of Rome stood as a fortress against threats from without, but its citizens still faced hosts within. Lucius Annaeus Seneca, the younger, recalls a stroll taken by a contemporary, Gaius Caesar:

> Adeo inpatiens fuit differendae voluptatis, quam ingentem crudelitas eius sine dilatione poscebat, ut in xysto maternorum hortorum . . . inambulans quosdam ex illis cum matronis atque aliis senatoribus ad lucernam decollaret. (*De Ira* 3.18.4)[1]

So impatient was [Gaius Caesar] of postponing his pleasure—a pleasure so great that his cruelty demanded it without delay—that he decapitated some of his victims by

---

[1] Translations are slightly modified versions of those found in the editions of Seneca and Livy in the Loeb Classical Library. For an overview of the various methods of execution in ancient Rome, consult Latte; *Du châtiment*. Other acts of Caligulan cruelty are catalogued by Sen. *De Ira* 3.18.3–19.5 (cf. also *De Tran. An.* 14.5; *Ad Poly.* 17.5). On Seneca's access to τὸ κρυπτὸν τῆς πολιτείας, see Graeme; Gercke 282. In this essay, we share the view of Griffin (26): "the connection of Seneca's philosophy with Seneca's political life often lies, not in the realm of his own conduct, but in the problems and preoccupations he shared with his readers." We shall thus proceed on the assumption that contemporary political concerns inform Seneca's philosophical works.

lamplight, as he was strolling with some ladies and senators on the terrace of his mother's gardens.

Would such behavior have constituted an aberrant horror? Seneca recollects an excursion among his fellow citizens:

> Avarior redeo, ambitiosior, luxuriosior, immo vero crudelior et inhumanior, quia inter homines fui. Casu in meridianum spectaculum incidi, lusus expectans et sales et aliquid laxamenti . . . contra est . . . mera homicidia sunt. (*Ep.* 7.3–4)[2]

> I come home more greedy, more ambitious, more voluptuous, and even more cruel and inhuman—because I have been among human beings. By chance I attended a mid-day exhibition, expecting some fun, wit, and relaxation. . . . But it was quite the reverse. . . . It is pure murder.

One is tempted to conclude that, inasmuch as the tastes of rulers and ruled coincided so closely, one must surely deem the Rome of Seneca's day singularly happy. Seneca, the philosopher, disagreed. He diagnosed a corrosive moral and ethical flaw in the character of his contemporaries.

> Non privatim solum sed publice furimus. Homicidia conpescimus et singulas caedes: quid bella et occisarum gentium gloriosum scelus? Non avaritia, non crudelitas modum novit. (*Ep.* 95.30)

---

[2]See Baumer 118–22 for an analysis on the role the games play in the thought of Seneca as schools for transforming humans into animals; for a more sympathetic analysis, see Barton 11–81.

We are mad, not only individually, but nationally. We check homicide and isolated murders; but what of war and the much-vaunted crime of slaughtering whole peoples? There are no limits to our greed, none to our cruelty.

In this essay, we shall attempt to examine a Roman vice and character flaw, cruelty, as it was diagnosed by a thoughtful citizen of the early empire.[3] We shall then trace that vice through Roman history in the surviving work of that philosopher's older contemporary, the historian Livy.[4] This second excursion through Roman history will enable us to view the roots of what Seneca considered a contemporary danger. And, whether or not one views moral failure as an active historical agent, we shall at least, by examining the views of these two early imperial spectators, gain a contemporary perspective on the intellectual and moral climate of a crucial period in the history of Rome.

Cruelty, according to Seneca, is viciousness and savagery (*atrocitas*) in punishing (*Clem.* 2.4.1) as well as an inclination of the spirit towards harshness (*Clem.* 2.4.3).[5] Cruelty, like other

---

[3]There are some eighty-two occurrences in Seneca's major prose works of the various forms of the word for cruelty (*crudel–*); substantival, *crudelitas*; adjectival, *crudelis, crudele*; and adverbial, *crudeliter, crudelius*. See Motto 57–58 for a synoptic analysis of the role "cruelty" plays in Seneca. For a general survey of cruelty in Republican Rome, see Lintott 35–51. See also the recent collection of essays in Viljamaa et al.

[4]Livy, who was approximately fifteen when Caesar was assassinated in 44 BC, lived to see the accession of Tiberius. When Livy died in AD 17, Seneca was already in his early twenties. Seneca himself lived until AD 65, and thus in turn provides eye-witness testimony that spans the entire Julio-Claudian dynasty. Between the lives of historian and philosopher, moralists both, we thus traverse the century that irrevocably transformed Republic into Empire. See Heldmann.

[5]One notes that both Hoppe (1229 l. 13) as well as Lewis and Short (484 s. v. *crudelitas*) use quotes from Seneca as their leading definitions. In the *De clementia* cruelty is the defining quality of the tyrant as opposed to the good ruler (a figure approximated to Hellenistic kings) whose defining quality is *clementia*; see Griffin 157 for an analysis of Seneca's

vices, arises from the emotions (*Ep.* 85.10).⁶ It is thus corporeal (*Ep.* 106.6). The corporeal aspect of cruelty is of special significance in light of Seneca's basic definition, because the body is the site where cruelty almost always acts, generally punishing when no punishment is called for.⁷ The motivation for such cruel behavior is pleasure. Cruelty can include killing for the sake of killing (*Clem.* 2.4.1), for the pure pleasure of shedding human blood (*De Ira* 2.5.1). Ominously, when cruelty takes pleasure in punishment it becomes a habit (*Ep.* 108.18), in effect acting upon and changing the constitution of the perpetrator.⁸ Cruelty and pleasure in bloodshed change the human being into the wild animal (*Clem.* 1.25.1). Habitual cruelty thus begins to pass over into savagery (*Clem.* 2.4.2) or even madness when murder becomes a pleasure

definition.
⁶On the passions in Roman literature see Braund and Gill.
⁷Nevertheless, failure to punish quickly (when punishment is expected) can also be cruel (*Ben.* 2.5.3; *Clem.* 1.2.2), and even when there are grounds for punishment, one can be cruel if one punishes excessively (*Clem.* 2.4.3). For this reason, the line between what is proper and what is cruel can be a narrow one. Severity, for example, which is a virtue, can pass over into cruelty (*Clem.* 2.4.4).
⁸One recalls that a *bonus animus* is, according to Seneca, a god that inhabits human flesh (*Ep.* 31.11; see Griffin 220). The human body is thus the site where both virtues and vices reside. Both alcohol (*Ep.* 83.20–25; see Motto and Clark) and meat-eating (*Ep.* 108.18) provide pleasures, and thus provide graphic and analogous illustration of how other pleasures and emotions, including the derangements of cruelty, may act upon the body, and change an individual's constitution or predilections. The body itself is, moreover, the site upon which time, death, and fate do their cruel work. The philosopher places human cruelty, both private and public, in the context of this universal fate. Fate (variously termed *fatum, fortuna, mors*) awaits all humankind (compare Rosset, especially 17–19). Death is cruel because it abuses our bodies (*Ad Marc.* 10.6) and murders impersonally (*Ad Helv.* 15.2–6; death is, however, at least fair [*Ad Poly.* 1.4]). Seneca, eclectic as he was (see Motto), is of two opinions in the face of death. On the one hand, one should not kill oneself, just because one faces execution; why take on the job of cruelty (*Ep.* 70.8)? On the other hand, one need not continue to live if life inflicts too many cruelties (*Ep.* 78.18; see Griffin 367–88). In short, Seneca's philosophical and psychological investigations of cruelty appear firmly rooted in the body (both personal and political).

(*voluptas*, *Clem*. 1.25.2).[9] In short, cruelty is, according to Seneca, an emotion that takes possession of mind and body. It acts upon the bodies of others in punishing and killing. The act of punishing and killing without justification tends to arouse pleasure in the perpetrator. This pleasure acts in turn upon (and changes) the perpetrator's constitution and character.[10]

Cruelty, Seneca argues, can manifest itself either publicly or privately; people are capable of cruelty both as individuals and as statesmen (*Ben*. 1.10.2). The ruler's cruelty is, however, more damaging, because the ruler has a wider selection of possible victims, and, as opposed to the statesman's power to make war, the private citizen has comparatively far less scope for cruelty (*Clem*. 1.5.2).[11] Nevertheless, it is only lack of power that prevents many from being cruel (*Ep*. 42.4)—an important point: cruelty rests on unequal power.

The conduct of those with authority is thus particularly crucial.[12] Seneca outlines the scope available for cruelty in his own day when he asks Nero to interrogate himself:

---

[9] As the madness increases in severity, the afflicted takes pleasure in the number of victims killed (*Clem*. 1.26.5).

[10] When I was her student at the University of South Florida in Tampa, Dr. Motto often told us that the ancients, especially Seneca, still spoke to current issues. Indeed, a cursory glance at today's criminals reveals the clear-sightedness of Seneca's diagnosis. Rothman's many case histories demonstrate over and over again how deeply rooted, even sociopathic, cruelty is in pleasure; see also Baumeister. Modern ethicists debate the proper attitude to cruelty as well. Shklar places cruelty at the center of her moral program, the vice that must be avoided before all others. This position has evoked criticism, for example, from Jackson 11–14, who takes offense at Shklar's hierarchy of moral values, and seeks to place Christian love (he calls it "strong agapism") back in the moral center. One turns from moderns to Seneca with keener appreciation.

[11] One hopes too that the power of the state will intervene to prevent private cruelty. Seneca cites with approval the example of Augustus who prevented his friend Vedius Pollio from feeding a slave to his lampreys (*De Ira* 3.40.3). Slaves of course enjoyed almost no legal protections (Watson). On Seneca's attitude towards the institution, see Griffin 256–85.

[12] On cruelty in Seneca that focuses on the ruler see Bellincioni 37–44.

Egone ex omnibus mortalibus placui electusque sum, qui in terris deorum vice fungerer? ego vitae necisque gentibus arbiter; qualem quisque sortem statumque habeat, in mea manu positum est . . . haec tot milia gladiorum, quae pax mea comprimit, ad nutum meum stringentur; quas nationes funditus excidi . . . quibus libertatem dari . . . mea iuris dictio est. (*Clem.* 1.1.2)[13]

Have I of all mortals found favor with Heaven and been chosen to serve on earth as vicar of the gods? I am the arbiter of life and death for the nations; it rests in my power what each person's lot and state shall be . . . all those many thousands of swords which my peace restrains will be drawn at my nod; what nations shall be utterly destroyed

---

[13]Some have seen in these words praise and justification of monarchy as a system based on the will of God. Interesting in this light is the commentary of John Calvin to the *De Clementia*, written on the eve of his conversion: *Est etiam illa confessio religionis nostrae, non esse potestatem nisi a deo: et quae sunt a deo ordinatas esse. ad Rom. XIII* (Battles 30). Fears (495) agrees, remarking, however, that Seneca's "concern is *clementia*, and for this reason he does not elaborate upon the election of Nero by the gods to serve as their vice regent." This is precisely the issue. One can surely read Seneca's statement as a simple reflection of contemporary political reality couched in terms of prevailing imperial ideology (put into the mouth of the beneficiary of this ideology). Should we, however, believe that Seneca himself agreed with the statement he put in the mouth of Nero? Seneca provides too many criticisms of power to allow us to read as straightforward praise this speech from the mouth of a character, as it were, in a composition. Compare Millett 8 on the dangers of the resurgence of absolute rule in our own day: "Torture is the ultimate act of state power. In arrogating to itself the capacity to torture its citizens, the state has assumed absolute power over them." The absolute power that gives free reign to *atrocitas animi in exigendis poenis* (*Clem.* 2.4.1) is exactly the danger that Seneca addresses. The *De Clementia* is an analysis or critique, not a justification, of such power. It simply recognizes the reality of Nero's power, and hopes to come to terms with it; the piece is eminently practical. For Seneca's historical sympathies on the side of republican *libertas*, see Griffin 182–201; Rudich 13–15, 53.

... which shall receive the gift of liberty—this it is mine to decree.

Seneca also delineates rather vividly the cruel ruler:

> Sanguine humano non tantum gaudet, sed pascitur ... et suppliciis omnium aetatum crudelitatem insatiabilem exercet nec ira sed aviditate quadam saeviendi furit. (*Ben.* 7.19.8)[14]

> He not only delights in human blood, but feeds upon it ... he also exercises his insatiable cruelty in the torture of persons of all ages, and his frenzy is the result, not of anger, but of a certain delight in cruelty.

Abrogating the civil rights of fellow citizens is cruel. Cruelty, however, makes life more dangerous for the ruler because it incurs the hatred of his subjects (*Clem.* 1.8.7; 1.18.3). Cruelty in fact foments the rebellion of slaves and subjects (*Clem.* 1.26.1), and the leader who has yielded to cruelty's temptations will survive only through further crimes (*Clem.* 1.13.2). Cruelty unleashed on the body politic results in a cycle of increasing violence similar to the changes wrought on the constitution of the individual in response to the stimulations of pleasure.

Cruelty creates a society suffused with fear (*Clem.* 1.26.2; 1.7.3), and such a civilization tends, moreover, to break down because cruelty breaks down its most fundamental bonds. Human beings are able to live with one another only because their relations are regulated and because they recognize one another's common humanity in their exchanges of services. Cruelty breaches those

---

[14] Roman statesmen who are cited as examples of cruelty include Sulla (*Ben.* 5.16.3) and Julius Caesar (*Ben.* 5.16.5). One may find cruel leaders among foreigners as well including Carthaginians (*De Otio* 8.2), Parthians (*Ep.* 4.7), and Alexander (*Ep.* 94.62).

normal rules of exchange. One owes, for example, the cruel no debt of gratitude (*Ben.* 7.19.8; 6.4.3).[15] Against this danger to his own society, the strongest weapon Seneca can recommend is public odium and hatred (*Ben.* 3.17.1).[16] Given the nature of power in his day, Seneca could hardly have advised otherwise. In fact, when searching for models of conduct for those living in cruel societies, Seneca turns to slaves, showing that Romans have much to learn from those who are utterly in their power.[17] Once more we observe that unequal power lies at the heart of cruelty. All society is shot through with various chains of command or series of potential victims subject to the authority of potential offenders: slaves to masters, captives to spectators at public games, and, finally, because the gods cannot be cruel,[18] all persons of every category to the looming figure of the Roman emperor.

His older contemporary Livy will help us put Seneca's general view of cruelty into historical context.[19] In Livy cruelty is never

---

[15]For Seneca's practical advice in handling gifts from the cruel, compare *Ben.* 7.20.1–4; 2.18.6.

[16]Only the brave are especially fortunate, because they endure dangers more readily than the cruel inflict them (*Ep.* 24.5).

[17]Slaves provide noble exemplars (see, for example, *Ben.* 3.23.2–3). It is cruelty and the practice of treating human beings as if they were tools that turn slaves against their masters (*Ep.* 47.5).

[18]Despite their potential power, Seneca does not impute cruelty to the gods. In fact, the gods, according to Seneca, observe human action and desire that humans act in accordance with virtue. Those who contemplate the heavens cannot be cruel, for they know that the gods witness everything (*Ep.* 102.29). In a lighter passage, Seneca observes that the clouds are not so cruel as really to desire the animal sacrifices that are offered to them in order to avert hailstorms. Delight in blood is cruel, the clouds, on the other hand, are not cruel, because they do not, in fact, delight in blood (*NQ* 4b.6.3).

[19]There are sixty-nine occurrences in Livy's extant works of the various forms of the word for cruelty (*crudel–*); substantival, *crudelitas*; adjectival, *crudelis, crudele*; and adverbial, *crudeliter, crudelius*. The cruelest decade is the first with twenty-nine occurrences. The cruelest book is the third with twelve occurrences. The third decade checks in more gently with eighteen overt instances of cruelty. The fourth reveals fifteen instances. The remaining five books provide five instances of cruelty. Other vices frequently associated with cruelty are *superbia*, twenty times; *libido/stuprum*, eleven times; and *avaritia*, ten times.

associated with natural phenomena, gods, or non-human entities (thus conforming tacitly to Seneca's views). Cruelty is imputed only to human beings and is further restricted to men who hold some form of authority over others. Tracing the history of cruelty through the extant works of Livy reveals three broad divisions or ages of cruelty. *Crudelitas regia*, exemplified by Amulius and Lucius Tarquinius, sets the tone for the first great age when the cruelty of men who hold consular, dictatorial, decemviral or military authority is exercised against the plebs by the likes of Appius Claudius, Postumius, and Papirius. This age of internal cruelty is followed by one in which Rome faces outwards and confronts a series of cruel tyrants: Hannibal, Hieronymus, and Philip. Within this age, one Roman, Pleminius, brings the odium of cruelty upon the Romans in actions that bind him to the past, cruelty towards fellow Romans, and to the future, cruelty towards people subject to Roman authority. Towards the end of this age, Flamininus ushers in the last phase of cruelty. A series of Romans, Popilius, Licinius, Lucretius, and Hortensius abuse the people of lands newly organized under Roman hegemony. A series of embassies arrives in Rome to plead before the Senate which becomes a sort of *tribunus provinciarum* in the expanded realm.

Livy uses cruelty with some precision. In Livy cruelty is generally a code-word for the crime of a man who holds authority over other people (by *imperium*, tyranny, right of conquest, or the like), but abuses that authority to deprive his victim, under the guise of punishment, not only of property (which reveals the perpetrator's greed), but also, and more importantly, of the very integrity of the victim's person and his dependents' persons, often not only through beatings and/or physical restraint, but by methods that also reveal a perverse sexual craving in the perpetrator (we may compare Seneca's more general notion of *voluptas* in cruelty). This

---

Cruelty is expressly associated with *poenae* and *supplicia* eight times. For a closer analysis of all these terms see Moore, and Hellegouarc'h. For a survey of cruelty in Livy that sees the Stoic determinism of Panaetius projected onto the pageant of Roman history in a manner acceptable to upper class Roman ideology see Viljamaa.

potent mixture of *libido, superbia,* and *poenae exercendae* in the exemplar of cruelty leads us to some of Livy's finest rhetoric in the description of vice. We shall see the changing shape of cruelty in a changing Rome, and we shall be in a position to make some general statements regarding Livian cruelty in the light of Livy's own statements regarding vice. We shall then put this historical view of cruelty into the context of contemporary imperial Rome and the philosophical investigations of Seneca.

Crudelitas regia quickly delineates its main features in the conduct of Amulius who deprives his brother Numitor of his throne, kills the son, and restricts Rhea Silvia to the life of a Vestal Virgin, thus depriving her of her personal liberty, that is, the free use of her body (1.3.3). This idea of enslavement will prove a common feature of Livian cruelty as will violence done to family members of the principal victims. That the gods do not approve of such royal misconduct we learn from Sextus Tarquinius, youngest son of King Lucius Tarquinius, who, feigning a transfer of allegiance to the Gabii, complains of his father's cruelty, and calls the punishments that his father inflicts impious, that is, without regard for the divine order (1.53.6–9). Fathers possess a rightful authority over sons, and thus have the right to punish (*patria potestas*), but with right comes responsibility. Overstepping just punishment is cruel and *impius*.

Cruelty's attacks on the body (through imprisonment, beatings, execution, and the like) infringe on one's freedom (*libertas*).[20] After the abolition of the monarchy, the nobles were freed from the abuse that they previously had sometimes suffered under the kings whose arbitrary authority (*superbia*) had extended to punishment of their persons.[21] The nobles masked their freedom (*libertas patrum*), however, as general freedom (*libertas omnium*).[22] Hence,

---

[20] See Bruno (1966a) 248–49 on the association of *crudelitas* with *regnum* and *superbia,* and the opposition of this nexus to *libertas.*

[21] Haffter (248) calls *libertas* the opposite of *superbia*; see also Halle 195.

[22] Bruno (1966b) 114–16. For fuller discussion, see Hellegouarc'h 542–59, and Wirszubski.

the removal of absolute rule (*regnum*) did not remove attendant cruelties, because members of the nobility in their new offices of consul, decemvir, military commander, in short, as holders of lawful authority or *imperium*, were themselves subsequently in positions to abuse their new authority.

The plebeians protest. Laetorius, for example, denounces Appius Claudius (2.56.7–8). The consul, according to the tribune, will overstep his authority and physically abuse the plebs, thus becoming a butcher (*carnifex*, 2.56.8).[23] On the other hand, according to the speech of the tribune C. Terentilius Harsa, the plebs cannot act cruelly towards the nobility. They do not have legal authority over the nobility, although plebeians, for their part, are subject to the nobility's absolute authority (*immoderata, infinita potestate*) in the persons of the nobility's elected representatives, the consuls (*duos . . . dominos*) "who while free themselves and without restraint, brought to bear all the terrors of the law and all its punishments upon the plebs" (3.9.4). To protect themselves, the plebs wish to define legally the power of the consuls (3.9.5). Again, we see clearly the precondition necessary for cruelty to occur—authority without restraint. The very idea, however, that the plebs should circumscribe the legal authority of the nobility with a legal authority of its own is considered a hostile attack. When Quintus Fabius attacks Terentilius' law, he does so by telling plebeians that they have protection *from* cruelty and that anything more would be oppression (3.9.9–10).

The patricians, as we have noted, mask their dominance under the rubric *libertas omnium*. The power of the nobility is freedom, of the plebs, cruelty. When plebeians wish to try Appius Claudius after the decemvirate is abolished, they are told:

---

[23]Dionysius spells out the situation in somewhat greater detail (9.46). The plebs do not share equally in the public rights (τῶν κοινῶν ἀγαθῶν) but instead have been deprived of full freedom of their physical persons like slaves captured in war. Livy also associates cruelty with war as we shall see more clearly in later books, although even early in his history, war waged by Volsci and Aequi against the Romans (victims of unwarranted aggression) is described as *crudeli superboque* (3.9.5).

Crudelitatis odio in crudelitatem ruitis et prius paene quam
ipsi liberi sitis dominari iam in adversarios voltis. (3.53.7)

Hatred of cruelty is driving you headlong into cruelty, and
almost before you are free yourselves you are wishing to
lord it over your adversaries.

The power or legal authority to punish is clearly a necessary condition for cruelty, and the nobility cannot imagine the plebs possessing such authority without attendant cruelty.[24]

Livy gives us a clear picture of punishments that are excessive and thus cruel under the rule of the decemvirate as well as the conditions that allowed the abuses to occur: plebeians, in losing the right to appeal, lost their defense against the authority of magistrates, and were consequently punished wantonly and cruelly (*libidinose crudeliterque*, 3.36.5–7). The beatings are here associated with arbitrary, perhaps even sadistic, pleasure (*libidinose*), but are not given free of charge: "they ceased even to respect a person's body; some they scourged with rods, others they made to feel the axe; and, that their cruelty not go uncompensated, they bestowed the victim's property on his slayer" (3.37.8). Cruelty and the power to punish brings with it the power to enrich oneself, and cruelty is thus associated with greed.

Livy is especially adept at revealing the lust of the official who abuses his authority. Appius Claudius, while decemvir, covets the person of Verginia:

Ap. Claudium virginis plebeiae stuprandae libido cepit

---

[24]Livy, according to Nicolet, longs for a Ciceronian *concordia ordinum*, which longing, interestingly enough, is expressed by the more reasonable members of the nobility and which, rather than equality, idealizes a balance of power (to prevent excesses like cruelty).

.... postquam omnia pudore saepta animadverterat, ad crudelem superbamque vim animum convertit. M. Claudio clienti negotium dedit, ut virginem in servitutem adsereret neque cederet secundum libertatem postulantibus vindicias. (3.44.2–6)

Appius Claudius was seized with the desire to debauch a certain plebeian maiden. ... But finding her modesty was proof against everything, he resolved on a course of cruel and tyrannical violence. He commissioned Marcus Claudius, his client, to claim the girl as his slave, and not to yield to those who demanded her liberation.

We have now seen the stock themes of cruelty in Livy who lays comparatively greater emphasis on lust than Seneca in situations where a magistrate deprives another person of liberty (here a reduction to slavery).

Livy too, however, like Seneca,[25] distinguishes cruelty from severity. The father who kills his daughter is not cruel. Verginius only appears cruel: "he had been impelled by pity to an act of seeming cruelty" (3.50.7). We know that Verginius is saving his daughter from cruelty. What, though, would enable Verginius to appear cruel (if Livy uses the term cruelty, as we argue, with precision)? As a father, Verginius possesses authority over his daughter, and has the inherent right to punish her. Killing her, however, as a punishment would be excessive, hence cruel. On the other hand, inasmuch as he is not exercising his right to punish, but instead is preventing his daughter from being debauched, thus preserving her *pudicitia*, Verginius cannot be cruel.[26] He does not

---

[25] See above note 7.
[26] On the role of severity in the protection of *pudicitia* and the importance of *pudicitia* as a political, moral, and religious value in the early empire, see Mueller.

fulfill the necessary conditions.²⁷ It is also interesting that Livy reduces the struggle against the decemvirs to this one dramatic incident of cruelty. In this reduction, we can see also the analogous reduction of a whole nexus of concepts into the code-word cruelty, which by itself is enough to evoke tyrannical associations.²⁸

With the passing of the decemvirate, we witness cruelty next at the hands of a military tribune, Postumius, who punishes excessively and cruelly (4.50.4), and murders in a fit of rage. Not only are soldiers subject to summary justice while on campaign, but even after they have again become civilians, they can lose their personal freedom for debt. In another case, Manlius defends a centurion, and decries "the arrogance of the patricians, the cruelty of the money lenders" (6.14.3), thus suggesting an identification of the nobility with financial oppressors and cruelty with greed. Again, cruelty implies a punishment that entails the loss of personal liberty. Further oppressions include mass beatings (8.27). Lust is added to the mix when an attractive adolescent boy cannot pay his debt. The subsequent events so incense the plebs that a new birth of liberty results (*aliud initium libertatis*, 8.28.1):

> Florem aetatis eius fructum adventicium crediti ratus . . . adulescentem . . . cum ingenuitatis magis quam praesentis condicionis memorem videret, nudari iubet verberaque adferri. quibus laceratus iuvenis cum se in publicum proripuisset, libidinem crudelitatemque conquerens feneratoris. (8.28.3–5)

> Regarding the lad's youthful prime as additional compensation for the loan . . . when he saw that the youth had more regard to his honorable birth than to his present

---

²⁷Compare the case of Aulus Postumius, who, if he had killed his son as punishment, would have been guilty of cruelty: *occupaturus insignem titulum crudelitatis fuerit* (4.29.6).

²⁸One may compare the fuller account of Verginius' speech in Dionysius of Halicarnassus (11.40) where Appius' crimes run the gamut from beatings to sexual abuse of both boys and girls.

plight, he had him stripped and scourged. The boy, all mangled with the stripes, broke forth into the street, crying out upon the moneylender's lust and cruelty.

The disgusted populace forces the senate to convene, and the consuls propose legislation that "for money lent, the debtor's goods, but not his person, should be distrainable" (8.28.9). We note not only beatings and lust (customary companions of Livian cruelty), but also that liberty entails the fundamental right to one's physical person, one's body.[29]

Towards the end of Livy's first decade, we observe that cruelty plays a role in international relations as well. Camillus tells the Senate that they have the power to treat cruelly another people over whom they have legal authority by right of conquest:

> Di immortales ita vos potentes huius consilii fecerunt ut, sit Latium deinde an non sit, in vestra manu posuerint; itaque pacem vobis, quod ad Latinos attinet, parare in perpetuum vel saeviendo vel ignoscendo potestis. voltis crudeliter consulere in deditos victosque? licet delere omne Latium, vastas inde solitudines facere. (8.13.14–15)

> The immortal gods have given you such absolute control of the situation as to leave the decision in your hands whether Latium is henceforward to exist or not. You are therefore able to assure yourselves of a permanent peace, in so far as the Latins are concerned, by the exercise of either savagery or forgiveness, at your discretion. Would you adopt cruel measures against those who have surrendered or been vanquished? You may blot out all Latium, and make vast solitudes.

---

[29]Bruno (1966b, 118) notes that the plebs' struggle for liberty involved both the active ability to participate in politics and the passive "freedom from fear."

The gods have an interest in how Romans exercise the power that the gods have bestowed upon them.[30] We may note too that the power granted to Romans as a people is strikingly similar to the power of the individual emperor that Seneca outlines for Nero (*Clem.* 1.1.2).

As Rome turns outward from its internal struggles, cruelty appears most frequently in the exercise of military authority over the conquered. In Livy's usage, the rights of conquest bring responsibilities similar to the responsibilities that magistrates have in their dealings with free citizens. Abuse of that power is cruelty. Enemies of Rome, such as the Samnites, are often depicted as treating Romans cruelly. Roman response to foreign cruelty is, however, not cruel:

> In Samnio Cluviarum praesidium Romanum, quia nequiverat vi capi, obsessum fame in deditionem acceperant Samnites verberibusque foedum in modum laceratos occiderant deditos. huic infensus crudelitati Iunius, nihil antiquius oppugnatione Cluviana ratus, quo die adgressus est moenia, vi cepit atque omnes puberes interfecit. (9.31.2–3)

> In Samnium the Roman garrison at Cluviae, which had defended itself successfully against assault, was starved into submission. The Samnites, having scourged their prisoners in brutal fashion, put them to death, although they had surrendered. Incensed by this act of cruelty, Junius felt that nothing should take precedence over an attack on Cluviae. He carried the place by storm on the day he arrived before it, and slew all the grown-up males.

---

[30]Elsewhere Livy expressly states his own view that cruelty is by nature a crime both against others' legal rights and against the divine moral order (*contra ius omne et fas*, 32.21.23–25; cf. 9.36.4).

Because the Samnites had accepted the Romans into a formal state of surrender, the Samnites exercised a certain legal authority under the rights of war over the Romans.[31] Legal authority brings with it the obligation to refrain from excess. The Romans, however, are not deemed cruel when they kill all adult male Samnites. Does Livy judge Roman behavior by different moral standards? The Romans stormed the Samnite city. Because the Romans had neither requested nor received formal authority over the Samnites, the requisite preconditions for cruelty had not been established, and the execution of the Samnites by the Romans was consequently not cruel.

As Rome expands, the Roman people face a series of foreign tyrants, notable for their cruelty. Philip of Macedon is called to account before the Romans at the conference of the Aetolians by the Athenians for a crime unique in Livy's history, cruelty to the dead:

> Verum enim vero id se queri . . . adeo omnia simul divina humanaque iura polluerit ut priore populatione cum infernis deis, secunda cum superis bellum nefarium gesserit. omnia sepulcra monumentaque diruta esse in finibus suis, omnium nudatos manes, nullius ossa terra tegi. (31.30.4–5)

> But they did, however, complain that he . . . had so polluted human and divine law alike that on his first raid he had waged impious war on the gods of the world below, on his second, with the gods above. All the tombs and monuments in their land had been destroyed, the shades of all the dead left naked, no man's bones left with their covering of earth.

This cruelty certainly fits our Livian formulation. The living have authority over the remains of the dead because the dead are *ipso*

---

[31]On the rights of war, surrender, and further literature, see the studies of Seavey, Flurl, and Volkmann. See also Livy who distinguishes normal (legitimate) war damages (31.30.2–3).

facto unable to care for their own remains. Hence, the living likewise have certain responsibilities towards the dead and their earthly remains.

Other actions of Philip also illustrate Seneca's dictum that cruelty must be cruel in protecting itself from retribution (*Clem.* 1.8.7). After putting certain men to death, Philip thought it prudent to kill their children as well.[32] Moreover, as a father he murdered his own son (40.24.6–7). Compounding the cruelty of murder, we may add Philip's lust (e.g. 32.21.24–25). Philip is the exemplar of all the cruelties of the tyrant: arrogant power, lust, and physical abusiveness including murder (31.31.17).[33]

Livy's portrait of Hannibal consists of a description both of his virtues and of his vices. Cruelty is prominent:

> Has tantas viri virtutes ingentia vitia aequabant, inhumana crudelitas, perfidia plus quam Punica, nihil veri, nihil sancti, nullus deum metus, nullum ius iurandum, nulla religio. (21.4.9)

> These admirable qualities of the man were equaled by his monstrous vices: his cruelty was inhuman, his perfidy worse than Punic; he had no regard for truth, and none for sanctity, no fear of the gods, no reverence for an oath, no religious scruple.

We soon see Hannibal's cruelty in action at the capture of Saguntum: he cruelly orders all adult men put to death (21.14.3).[34] Livy does temper this charge of cruelty by adding that it may have

---

[32]This act of cruelty likewise inspired further acts of cruelty (Liv. 40.4.1–6). Compare the widow who killed her children to save them from Philip's lust (40.4.6) to Verginius. Philip bears responsibility for any cruelty.

[33]Philip does eventually repent of his many cruelties (40.54.1–2).

[34]The language (*imperium crudele . . . ut omnes puberes interficeretur*) is very similar to the language Livy used in describing the massacre of Samnite men by Roman order (*puberes interfecit*, 9.31.2–3). Nevertheless, the Roman massacre was, we may recall, not cruel.

been necessary militarily under the circumstances (21.14.4), but no such excuses are offered in Livy's description of the cruel sack of Victumulae:

> Postero die deditione facta praesidium intra moenia accepere; iussique arma tradere cum dicto paruissent, signum repente victoribus datur, ut tamquam vi captam urbem diriperent. . . . omne libidinis crudelitatisque et inhumanae superbiae editum in miseros exemplum est. (21.57.13)

> The next day they surrendered and received a garrison within their walls. Being commanded to give up their weapons they complied: whereupon a signal was suddenly given to the victors to sack the town, as if they had taken it by storm. . . . Every species of lust and cruelty and inhuman insolence was visited upon the wretched inhabitants.

Cruelty here follows the established patterns. A formal surrender had given Hannibal legal authority over the conquered as well as a concomitant responsibility to treat the conquered humanely. The contrast between formal surrender and the pardonable destruction which takes place in the heat of battle is explicit. Excessive destruction indicates sadistic pleasure (*libidinis*).[35]

Roman actions, on the other hand, are also somewhat problematic in regard to their treatment of the Iliturgi. Scipio explains the distinction between various foes. The Carthaginians, like the Romans, are fighting for glory and legitimate authority or power, *imperium*, but the Iliturgi are perpetrators of cruelty, and this,

---

[35]Although Hannibal himself is not shown in acts of cruelty with overt sexual content, he is an African, and Livy does portray the excessive sexuality of Africans in general and Numidians in particular, when Masinissa is supposedly saving Syphax' wife and Hasdrubal's daughter in Cirta from Roman cruelty (30.12.14–18). It is also interesting to note that this helps turn the accusation of cruelty against the Romans back on Masinissa.

according to Livy's Scipio, justifies the excessive anger of the Romans and the punishment they mete out. Scipio encourages his soldiers:

> Multo infestioribus animis cum eis quam cum Carthaginiensibus bellum gerendum esse; quippe cum illis prope sine ira de imperio et gloria certari, ab his perfidiae et crudelitatis et sceleris poenas expetendas. (28.19.6–8)

> They must wage war against them with more animosity than against the Carthaginians. With these it was a contest almost devoid of anger in pursuit of power and glory; from the Iliturgians they must exact the penalty for treachery and cruelty and crime.

The punishment which Scipio considers just is graphically and pathetically described by Livy:

> Inde decurrunt cum clamore in urbem iam captam ab Romanis. Tum vero apparuit ab ira et ab odio urbem oppugnatam esse. nemo capiendi vivos, nemo patentibus ad direptionem omnibus praedae memor est; trucidant inermes iuxta atque armatos, feminas pariter ac viros; usque ad infantium caedem ira crudelis pervenit. (28.30.6–7)

> Thence they dashed down with a shout into the city already captured by the Romans. It was then in truth evident that the city had been attacked out of anger and hatred. No one thought of taking men alive, no one thought of booty, although every place was open for plunder. They slaughtered the unarmed and the armed alike, women as well as men; pure anger went even so far as to slay infants.

Scipio may have justified his course, but Livy's description provides subtle indications that he disagreed. All the ingredients of real cruelty are present: quasi-formal authority (*urbem iam captam*), a deranged mental condition (*odio* and *ira*), greed (the promise of *praedae*), and the violation of persons, including noncombatants (*ad infantium caedem*).

The case against the Roman Pleminius is flagrant and unambiguous. Scipio leaves him in charge of a captured city and in command of the Roman garrison, thus giving him opportunity for double cruelty; Pleminius both violates fellow Roman soldiers subject to his military authority and he violates a population subject to the politcal authority of Rome. This example of Rome's international cruelty is reminiscent of earlier domestic violations of the plebs. Enraged (*accensus ira*), he excessively punishes military tribunes, fellow Roman citizens, whom he orders stripped and beaten (29.9.11). His cruelty was not yet content:

> Tribunos attrahi ad se iussit, laceratosque omnibus quae pati corpus ullum potest suppliciis interfecit, nec satiatus vivorum poena insepultos proiecit. simili crudelitate et in Locrensium principes est usus quos ad conquerendas iniurias ad P. Scipionem profectos audivit. (29.9.10–12)

> He ordered the tribunes to be brought before him, and had them mangled by every torture which any human body can endure and then put to death. Not satisfied with a penalty paid by the living either, he threw them out unburied. The like cruelty was used by him against leading men of the Locrians who, he learned, had gone to Publius Scipio to complain of the outrages.

Cruelty and all its attendant circumstances are spelled out again when the Locrians complain before the Senate in Rome. The wellrounded perpetrator of cruelty emerges replete with hints of perverse sexual craving (wives and children figure prominently as objects of cruel lust, 29.17.18–20). Livy's description of Pleminius' cruelty seems to recall rhetorically the crimes of the young republic as well as herald the cruel oppression of provincials to come at the hands of their Roman overlords and perhaps even, if we read Livy with Seneca in mind, the potential cruelty of the Roman emperor himself.

We shall return to this point presently; there remain other foreign tyrants in Livy's history, and one of Rome's allies was especially unfortunate. Syracuse suffered under a series of tyrants, including henchmen of Hannibal, the unheard of lusts and inhuman cruelty (*libidines novae, inhumana crudelitas*) of Hieronymus (24.5.3–6), and finally Hippocrates and Epicydes. The cruelty of these tyrants justifies Roman intervention: the Romans besiege the city not out of hatred (*odium*), but out of love (*caritatem*) in order to capture, "not the city itself, but its cruel tyrants" (25.28.7). Although we do not in the history of these foreign tyrants learn anything new about the nature of cruelty itself, we do learn that cruelty is a useful rhetorical weapon in the arsenal of Rome's imperial program.[36] An attack upon a city becomes a defense of that city.[37]

For the sake of morale, every society must impute crime to its enemies and justice to itself. Rome's wars were, according to the official Roman view, always defensive.[38] For this reason, more interesting than criminal charges against enemies are crimes confessed. Flamininus stands accused of cruelty by two different versions of history. Cato, according to Livy, claimed that Flamininus killed a Gaul (who was in the very act of calling on the

---

[36] See Liv. 33.44.8–9. After Greece's liberation from the danger of Philip, the tyrant Nabis (also called cruel) threatens the liberty of Greece; see Walsh (1996).

[37] Dunkle 13: "*Crudelitas* is a vice most closely associated with the tyrant in Roman political oratory and ... in Roman historiography of the late republic and early empire. In [a] passage of the *Ad Herennium* the adverbial forms of *crudelitas* and *superbia* together with *vis* are presented as political terms of abuse (1.8; cf. Cic. *Inv. Rhet.* 1.22). These three terms are used regularly in various combinations with a fourth, *libido*, in political invective of the late Republic to describe tyrannical behavior." See also Halle 179; Opelt, especially 165–68; and Hellegouarc'h 439–41.

[38] On Rome's defensive imperialism, see Linderski.

name of the Roman people) for the sake of a male prostitute's attention:

> Quinctius scorto "vis tu", inquit "quoniam gladiatorium spectaculum reliquisti, iam hunc Gallum morientem videre?" et cum is vixdum serio adnuisset, ad nutum scorti consulem stricto gladio, qui super caput pendebat, loquenti Gallo caput primum percussisse, deinde, fugienti fidemque populi Romani atque eorum, qui aderant, imploranti latus transfodisse. (39.42.11–12)
>
> Quinctius said to the prostitute, "Do you wish, since you missed the Gladiatorial show, to see now this Gaul dying?" And when he nodded, although not really in earnest, the consul, at the prostitute's nod, seized the sword that was hanging above his head and first struck the Gaul's head while he was speaking, and then, as the Gaul was fleeing and calling for the protection of the Roman people and of those who were present, he stabbed the Gaul through the side.

Wanton violence and illicit sexual passion are also present in the second version reported by Livy (from Valerius Antias), but the prostitute is female (39.43.1–4). Flamininus possesses a legal authority (as the agent of the Roman people upon whom the Gaul called). Punishing for the sake of pleasure and lust (*libido*), especially such excessive punishment, is cruelty. Livy, moreover, indicates that Flamininus' cruelty is, no matter whose version of events one accepts, a direct offense to the gods. Livy points out that people say table-prayers and make libations to the gods at official banquets. The sacred setting thus transforms a civil execution into a human sacrifice:

> Facinus, sive eo modo, quo censor obiecit, sive, ut Valerius tradit, commissum est, saevum atque atrox: inter pocula atque epulas, ubi libare diis dapes, ubi bene precari mos

esset, ad spectaculum scorti procacis, in sinu consulis recubantis, mactatam humanam victimam esse et cruore mensam respersam. (39.43.4)

This deed, whether it was performed in the manner for which the censor rebuked him, or as Valerius reports it, was savage and cruel: in the midst of drinking and feasting, where it is the custom to pour libations to the gods and to pray for blessings, as a spectacle for a shameless prostitute, reclining in the bosom of a consul, a human victim sacrificed and bespattering the table with his blood.

We also see in the actions of Flamininus a cruelty similar to the later cruelty of Caligula that would earn censure from Seneca.

Once Roman hegemony is established, all instances of cruelty may be connected with the Romans and their agents. Lycians (placed under Rhodian authority by Scipio) come before the Senate to complain about the cruelty of the Rhodians (41.6.8–11). Similarly, the defeated Carthaginians, who were not allowed to wage war beyond the boundaries assigned by their Roman conquerors, complain before the Senate about the arrogance, cruelty, and incursions of Masinissa (whom the Romans have given free reign, 42.23.4–5). The Senate, we learn, prefers right conduct to tyrannically cruel behavior. Livy demonstrates this in the amends that the Senate wishes to make for the cruelty of Popilius towards the Ligurians (42.8.5–6) in order that his example of cruelty not in the future become a disincentive to surrender for other peoples (42.8.7–8). The Senate further expressly prefers the clemency of Licinius and Lucretius' successor (43.4.5).[39] Cruelty is more here, however, than just bad policy. We note that plebs and nobles form one nation, one republic (*plebi patribusque*), and that a smoothly

---

[39]Similarly, Lucretius also figures in the complaint of cruelty which Micythion, crippled spokesman of the Cretans, makes before the Senate (though he complains more about Hortensius) in 43.7.8–11.

functioning Senate, like an ideal tribune, protects the rights of all against tyrannical magistrates. The constitutional government of the republic would thus appear to provide some protection from the abuses of arbitrary authority, from cruelty.

Although not infrequently deployed, cruelty is a term with very restricted application in Livy's extant works. Nevertheless, it is also, as we have had ample opportunity to observe and as others have noted, a standard term of rhetorical abuse in the description of tyrants: "The interpreter of [Livy] is thus alerted to the possibility of exaggeration and misrepresentation in order to produce conformity with a rhetorical stereotype of the tyrant."[40] Livy does indeed conform to standard rhetorical abuse; he calls tyrants, both foreign and domestic, cruel. Should we thus discount the importance of cruelty because it is a commonplace that Livy employs in a rhetorically predictable fashion? Furthermore, Livy expressly states in his preface that he plans to depict vices that should be avoided for the sake of the republic. We must thus ask ourselves whether Livy distorted history in conformance with contemporary rhetorical practice and a personal moral agenda.

Seneca, similarly trained in the rhetorical schools, provides valuable clues. Seneca enjoyed the practical experience of government and law that Livy lacked (and for which Livy is often attacked).[41] Seneca, the philosopher and statesman, thought deeply about cruelty, because cruelty was relevant to the practical problems of his times. It is very likely that Livy's use of the term cruelty was informed by an early imperial present very similar to Seneca's. The historian would naturally have made use of current concepts (or preoccupations). Could he have done otherwise? Can one escape one's own times? Accurate description, however, must certainly remain at the heart of historical narrative. We may thus rephrase our question: did Livy match words from his present with events from the past as closely as contemporary usage allowed? Scholars attack Livy because he did not know government and law

[40]Dunkle 20.
[41]Klotz 851.

sufficiently. In Livy's defense, we may counter that when Livy employed a concept that he did know (here cruelty), he used that concept with a careful precision recoverable through close reading.[42]

Livy's preface, moreover, informs his readers that he seeks consolation from the past in order to avoid contemplating the present. Once again, we may turn to Seneca for a glimpse of the present that troubled Livy as well as the future that he was struggling to divine from study of the past. The cruel kings, consuls, decemvirs, tyrants, and Roman functionaries described by Livy find their nightmarish augmentation and consummation in the unparalleled powers of Augustus and his successors. If, then, examples of vice, here cruelty (the vice *par excellence* of the tyrant) are a warning, against what is Livy warning his readers and what is he hoping that they will avoid? The *remedium* Livy feared may have been the unconstitutional dictator.[43] We have seen time and time again that cruelty results in the loss of one's control over one's own person, that is, loss of personal liberty and subjection to physical

---

[42]Ullman (53) writes that "if Aristotle had had his way history would have become a science," and we may, for our part, confess that "Aristotle's distinction between tragedy (which imitates actions to arouse emotions) and history (which states facts) was ignored by historians (25)" in general and by Livy in particular, for in his case, as Klotz (852) puts it, "die Milde des eignen Herzens lässt ihm alle Gewaltnaturen unsympathisch erscheinen." For Livy, great Romans embody virtue and villains vice. Compare Walsh (1955) 370: "[E]ach class is set forth as a stimulus and a warning," for Livy "regarded it as [his] duty to deter men from paths of vice (369)." See Liv. *praef.* 10; and, for a recent treatment of Livy's preface, Moles. In short, one might say that Livy searched for meaning in history and that he had a point of view. Livy moralized. But, then again, one does so as a matter of course as soon as one begins to narrate, because every narrative choice is at some level, a moral choice as well (see White). Whether or not one ought to look for morality in history at all, however, is irrelevant to judging Livy's use of cruelty. We must ask ourselves whether Livy used the term *crudelitas* accurately and consistently. He did. Whether or not one agrees that actions Livy labels cruel in fact constitute cruelty, careful attention to Livy's usage shows that the word only applies to situations that meet a narrow set of criteria.

[43]Woodman 132–34.

abuse at the hands of an unaccountable magistrate. Livy confesses that he brooded. His historical investigations gave him good reason to do so. His age had traded senate and tribunes for *tribunicia potestas*.

Seneca, on the other hand, contemplated the present, recalling Caligula and facing Nero. Seneca's preoccupation with imperial cruelty and its potential for catastrophe demonstrate that Livy's forebodings were not simply empty rhetorical phrases distorting the facts of history.[44] Both Livy and Seneca in fact underscore the eloquent assessment of Gibbon:

> Every barrier of the Roman constitution had been levelled ... every fence had been extirpated by the cruel hand of the Triumvir.... [T]he fate of the Roman world depended on the will of Augustus.... The conqueror was at the head of forty-four veteran legions ... habituated ... to every act of blood and violence, and passionately devoted to the house of Caesar, from whence alone they had received, and expected, the most lavish rewards. The provinces sighed for the government of a single person, who would be the master, not the accomplice, of ... petty tyrants. The people of Rome, viewing with a secret pleasure, the humiliation of the aristocracy, demanded only bread and public shows ... and suffered not the pleasing dream to be interrupted by the memory of their old tumultuous freedom.[45]

Gibbon's prose reveals, we must confess, a host of rhetorical commonplaces. *Crudelitas, superbia, vis, avaritia, voluptas*, and *libertas* all appear resurrected in English dress. Does, however, the

---

[44]Obviously there is insufficient space in this short essay to address the long contested issue of Livy's attitude towards the principate. Joyful collaborationist or embittered republican? There is a middle way. For a Livy who is thoughtful and groping towards an uneasy understanding of what has become of the republic, a Livy that would not exclude foreboding and anxiety for the future, see the perceptive article of Deininger.

[45]Gibbon 36–37.

moral judgment implicit in these lines reveal that here one deals in something other than history and fact? Responsible rhetoric seeks to apply a powerful vocabulary to an overpowering reality, an historical reality whose record is, like time itself, dependent on the arbitrary fictions of semantics and grammar (but inscribed sometimes too on the bodies of its victims).[46] Livy and Seneca chose their words with care. As they saw it, cruelty spoke both to the history and to the present reality of Rome. Indeed, cruelty lay at the heart of Roman greatness and power and it lay heavily upon the hearts of Rome's more thoughtful citizens. One could not know the future, but one consoled oneself with philosophy, with history, with religion, and with the justice of the gods. Seneca writes that Augustus was a god because he had not been cruel:

> Deum esse non tamquam iussi credimus . . . fatemur ob nullam aliam causam, quam quod contumelias quoque suas . . . nulla crudelitate exequebatur. (*Clem.* 1.10.3)

> We believe that he is a god, but not because we have been so commanded . . . this we confess for no other reason than because he did not avenge with cruelty even personal insults.

---

[46]Is an execution any less an execution if we call it "cruel"? Rather than mask historical reality, rhetoric may actually contribute to delineating it more accurately. Livy and Seneca faced reality as they saw it, and named it well, *crudelitas*. Manousos (16) quotes the perceptive comments of Robert Lowell on the characteristics of Roman literature: "[It has a] terrible frankness that isn't customary with us—corrosive attacks on the establishment, comments on politics and the decay of morals, all felt terribly strongly." Perhaps Lowell was another casualty of ancient rhetoric. Nevertheless, even if powerful rhetoric distorts, one must compare distortions even more monstrous that result from descriptive terms devoid of moralizing and emotional content. Compare, for example, Chomsky 49–51 and *passim* on official U.S. rhetoric during the Viet Nam war or Millett 48–47 on the language of NAZI death camps. Roman prose should not be branded suspect merely because moral judgments are made. If human beings sometimes act ethically (or unethically), the historian may justifiably delineate such behavior with appropriate terminology.

Seneca even dared hope against hope that Nero might in the future prove superior to this god, because Nero, as he argued, unlike Augustus, had in all the world shed never a drop of human blood (*Clem.* 1.11.3). Alas, it is a bitter thing to know the future.[47]

BIBLIOGRAPHY

Barton, C. A. 1992. *The Sorrows of the Ancient Romans.* Princeton.
Battles, F. L., and A. M. Hugo. 1969. *Calvin's Commentary on Seneca's De Clementia.* Leiden.
Baumeister, R. F. 1997. *Evil: Inside Human Cruelty and Violence.* New York.
Baumer, A. 1982. *Die Bestie Mensch: Senecas Aggressionstheorie, ihre philosophischen Vorstufen und ihre literarischen Auswirkungen.* Frankfurt am Main.
Bellincioni, M. 1984. *Potere ed etica in Seneca: Clementia e voluntas amica.* Brescia.
Braund, S. M. and C. Gill, eds. 1997. *The Passions in Roman Thought and Literature.* Cambridge.
Bruno, L. 1966a. "*Crimen Regni* e *Superbia* in Tito Livio." *GIF* 19:236–59.
—. 1966b. "*Libertas Plebis* in Tito Livio." *GIF* 19:107–30.
Chomsky, N. 1989. *Necessary Illusions: Thought Control in Democratic Societies.* Boston.
Deininger, J. 1985. "Livius und der Prinzipat." *Klio* 67:265–72.
Du châtiment dans la cité: supplices corporels et peine de mort dans le monde antique. 1984. Collection de l'École Française de Rome 79. Rome.
Dunkle, J. R. 1971. "The Rhetorical Tyrant in Roman Historiography: Sallust, Livy and Tacitus." *CW* 65:12–20.

---

[47]Institutional cruelty would grow progressively worse after Nero, and especially so after Constantine; see MacMullen.

Fears, J. R. 1975. "Nero as Vice Regent of the Gods in Seneca's *De Clementia.*" *Hermes* 103:486–96.
Flurl, W. 1969. *Deditio in fidem: Untersuchungen zu Livius und Polybios.* Augsburg.
Gercke, A. 1971 [1896]. "Senecas Abhandlungen im Rahmen der Zeitgeschichte." In *Seneca-Studien*, 282–328. Hildesheim.
Gibbon, E. 1845 [1782]. *The History of the Decline and Fall of the Roman Empire.* Vol. 1, edited by H. H. Milman. New York.
Graeme, W. C. 1965. "Seneca the Younger under Claudius." *Latomus* 24:65–69.
Griffin, M. T. 1976. *Seneca: A Philosopher in Politics.* Oxford.
Haffter, H. 1964. "Rom und römische Ideologie bei Livius." *Gymnasium* 71:236–50.
Halle, L. 1957. "A Study of Moralization in Livy." Diss. Bryn Mawr University.
Heldmann, K. 1987. "Livius über Monarchie und Freiheit und der römische Lebensaltervergleich." *WJA* 103:209–30.
Hellegouarc'h, J. 1963. *Le vocabulaire latin des relations et des partis politiques sous la République.* Paris.
Hoppe, H. 1906–1909. "*Crudelitas.*" In *Thesaurus Linguae Latinae.* Vol. 4, 1229–1232. Leipzig.
Jackson, T. P. 1992. "The Disconsolation of Theology: Irony, Cruelty, and Putting Charity First." *Journal of Religious Ethics* 20:1–35.
Klotz, A. 1926. "Livius." In *RE* 13.1:816–852.
Latte, K. 1940. "Todesstrafe. B. Rom. 3. Formen." In *RE.* Suppl. VII, 1614–1618.
Lewis, C. T. and C. Short. 1879. *A Latin Dictionary.* Oxford.
Linderski, J. 1995. "*Si vis pacem para bellum:* Concepts of Defensive Imperialism (1984)." In *Roman Questions*, 1–31. Stuttgart.
Lintott, A. W. 1968. *Violence in Republican Rome.* Oxford.
MacMullen, R. 1986. "Judicial Savagery in the Roman Empire." *Chiron* 16:147–66.
Manousos, A. 1984. "Falling Asleep over the 'Aeneid': Lowell, Freud, and the Classics." *CLS* 21:16–29.

Millett, K. 1994. *The Politics of Cruelty: An Essay on the Literature of Political Imprisonment*. New York.
Moles, J. 1993. "Livy's Preface." *PCPhS* 39:141–68.
Moore, T. J. 1989. *Artistry and Ideology: Livy's Vocabulary of Virtue*. Frankfurt am Main.
Motto, A. L. 1970. *Seneca Sourcebook: Guide to the Thought of Lucius Annaeus Seneca*. Amsterdam.
Motto, A. L., and J. R. Clark. 1993. "Seneca on Drunkenness." In *Essays on Seneca*, 155–61. Frankfurt am Main.
Mueller, H.-F. 1998. "*Vita, pudicitia, libertas*: Juno, Gender, and Religious Politics in Valerius Maximus." *TAPA* 128:221–63.
Nicolet, C. 1960. "*Consul Togatus*: Remarques sur le vocabulaire politique de Cicéron et de Tite-Live." *REL* 38:236–63.
Opelt, I. 1965. *Die lateinischen Schimpfwörter und verwandte sprachliche Erscheinungen: Eine Typologie*. Heidelberg.
Rosset, C. 1993. *Joyful Cruelty: Towards a Philosophy of the Real*. New York.
Rothman, G., M. D. 1971. *The Riddle of Cruelty*. London.
Rudich, V. 1993. *Political Dissidence under Nero*. London and New York.
Seavey, W. D. 1993. "*Ius belli*: Roman Ideology and the Rights of War." Diss. U. N. C.
Shklar, J. 1984. *Ordinary Vices*. Cambridge, Mass.
Ullman, B. L. 1942. "History and Tragedy." *TAPA* 73:25–53.
Viljamaa, T. 1992. "*Crudelitatis odio in crudelitatem ruitis*: Livy's Concept of Life and History." In *Crudelitas: The Politics of Cruelty in the Ancient and Medieval World (Proceedings of the International Conference Turku [Finland], May 1991)*, edited by Viljamaa, T., et al., 41–55. Krems.
Viljamaa, T., et al., eds. 1992. *Crudelitas: The Politics of Cruelty in the Ancient and Medieval World (Proceedings of the International Conference Turku [Finland], May 1991)*. Krems.

Volkmann, H. 1990. *Die Massenversklavungen der Einwohner eroberter Städte in der hellenistisch-römischen Zeit.* 2nd ed. rev. by G. Horsmann. Stuttgart.

Walsh, J. 1996. "Flamininus and the Propaganda of Liberation." *Historia* 45:344–63.

Walsh, P. G. 1955. "Livy's Preface and the Distortion of History." *AJP* 76:369–83.

Watson, A. 1983. "Roman Law and Romanist Ideology." *Phoenix* 37:53–65.

White, H. 1980. "The Value of Narrativity in the Representation of Reality." *Critical Inquiry* 7:5–27.

Wirszubski, C. 1950. *Libertas as a Political Idea in Rome.* Cambridge.

Woodman, A. J. 1988. *Rhetoric in Classical Historiography: Four Studies.* London.

ΜΗ ΧΕΙΡΩΝ ΠΑΤΡΟΣ: The Rising Generation in Euripides' *Heracleidae*

J. D. Noonan
University of South Florida

Euripides' *Heracleidae* is a play that once attracted rather scathing critical superlatives; Wilamowitz' comment that the play is the "least significant" of Euripides' dramas and Schmid-Stahlin's verdict that it is the "weakest" of Euripides' political plays are typical of the sorts of comments I have in mind, and such comments remain influential.[1] However, with the recent publication

---

[1] Wilamowitz-Möllendorf 343 and Schmid and Stahlin 417. Many of the aspersions cast on the play by later critics first arise in the writings of von Schlegel, whose status as philologist, philosopher, and Romantic literary figure virtually guarantees that adverse criticism of the *Heracleidae* will persist among those who can envision a better play than tradition has left us. In his *History of Classical Literature* of 1796, Schlegel already says . . . *unter diesen* (sc. seventeen canonical Euripidean tragedies) *scheinen mir die Herakliden und die Schutzgenossennin die schwächsten* (3.311); all references are to this edition. By 1808 in the *Vorlesungen über dramatischen Kunst und Literatur*, the same two plays are labeled *Gelegenheitstragödien* and they succeeded, Schlegel surmises, only as *Scmeichelei gegen die Athener* (5.126). Furthermore, all of the alleged defects of Euripides' craftsmanship that are picked over by later classicists—Makaria's disappearance from the drama after her declaration that she will accept death as a human sacrifice; the absence of discussion among other characters after her voluntary slaughter; Hyllus' absence from the play (except as reported by others); the non-reappearance of Demophon after the Argive army is driven off; the failure of the rejuvenated Iolaus to return; and the very late appearance of the arguably importunate, unsympathetic Alcmene—are first rehearsed by Schlegel (5.127). The drama that eliminated such alleged flaws would, in my view, demand more actors than the ancient contest permitted and several improbable, Romantic episodes alien to the Euripidean context and relevant only to the neo-medievalist spirituality that Schlegel wished to embrace.

of new editions and translations for both scholars and students who work in English,² the play will now undoubtedly be read and analyzed more often than it was in past decades, and readers need to be aware that there have always been at least a few scholarly critics who have found parts of the *Heracleidae* interesting or even important.³

My comments in this paper are linked with the favorable or approving criticisms of the drama, but I want to give the hostile critics their due as well. Wilamowitz, for example, argues that the *Heracleidae* fails because it lacks "economy of matter" and thus does not comprise an Aristotelian *hen* ("one thing" or "one action") with a properly articulated beginning, middle, and end.⁴ For Wilamowitz, this was mainly the fault of a *régisseur*, who cut an episode and part of a choral song from the play, missing pieces which he, Wilamowitz, could restore from fragments assigned to *Heracleidae* and from its argument.⁵ This is a dismissal of the play on a basic, yet sweeping scale. No defense of the *Heracleidae* which says only that the drama has interesting connections to political and diplomatic events at the start of the Peloponnesian

---

²Even though Diggle already provides an eminently usable new text, Ambrose (pref.) could still call the play "rather neglected" in the commentary he produced for use in the classroom. Since then Wilkins (1993) has provided the sort of scholarly commentary in English that the play deserves. Kovacs' texts (1995 and 1996) give us another edition of the Greek text accompanied by a translation into English and a set of textual observations that are interesting to compare to Diggle's text and Diggle's many critical notes on the text of the play.

³Although I do not always cite them in the text or in notes, the reader should be aware that Burnett (1976; which is, for me, the single best piece on the play), Avery, and Burian have all influenced my views about both small details and about the most general questions raised in this play. It also seems to me no accident that these three influential pieces about the *Heracleidae* were produced in the 1970s; that decade focused attention on the combination of imperialism, democracy, and the presumed superiority of elites (the few) in Western countries, especially the U.S. Political concerns then present shaped the critics' questions about the ancient drama.

⁴Wilamowitz 337.
⁵*Ibid.*, 338; 344–46.

War, or only that its treatment of Makaria's sacrifice sheds light on the Athenian attitude toward women, confronts Wilamowitz' denigration of the *Heracleidae* directly or fully, though each defense rings true and each points to an excellent segment of the drama or to a fascinating aspect of the context in which the drama was first produced. Ever since the work of Zuntz,[6] which shows that the *Heracleidae* is not taken up with the "merely occasional" epiphenomena of Athenian politics, and in works that examine the significance of Makaria's sacrifice[7] as that act fits into a repertory of images[8] from myth that is useful for Athenian social construction

---

[6] Zuntz sees the play as an expression of the political significance of private and public κέρδος, which he defines as "self-interest" (33), and of the readiness to sacrifice for the community (46–47). Zuntz also deems the play "a gem of concentrated action" (27), partly due to its "plain and lucid structure" (38). For me, public κέρδος in the play would better be defined as Athenian σωτηρία, a combination of security, prosperity, and awareness of the values sanctioned by traditional myth and religion; (cf. Burian 7–8); but the main point is that Zuntz finds in the *Heracleidae* both dramatic themes essential to the welfare of the *polis* and a readily comprehended dramatic development.

[7] Wilamowitz (343) is nearly alone in thinking that Makaria lacks interest. He argues that she holds her life so cheaply and gives it up so readily that we cannot even call such an act as hers a sacrifice. Spranger holds the equally eccentric view that events in the drama made her sacrifice unnecessary and that the report given to Alcmene in line 792 means that she, too, is alive. Schmitt (3–4; 15; 29; 44–47 and 52–56) provides the commentary on the Makaria-episode upon which what might be called the consensus about Makaria's self-sacrifice rests. This view of the majority who have written about Makaria is refined and brought up to date by Wilkins (1990).

[8] Loraux would deny that Athenian females even existed in the Athenian *imaginaire*, partly because they did not exist lexically (116–19), but this appears to ignore the fact that ἡ 'Αθηναίη, the Homeric form of the name of the goddess, had pre-empted that spot in the lexicon, nor are 'Αττικαὶ νῆες, for example, any less Athenian for being called 'Attic.' One can only surmise that Rabinowitz (62–64) finds Makaria uninteresting because her sacrifice is presented as voluntary by Euripides (R. describes this as the "illusion" of freedom) and because the men of her family, not Makaria herself, gain from the sacrifice. Pohlenz (359–60) already sees that the sacrifice of a daughter by her mother Praxithea in Euripides' fragmentary *Erechtheus* (see *frag*. 360, 22–40 [Nauck]) is closely related to the action of Makaria in the *Heracleidae* (cf. Schmitt

and propaganda, a focus on ideology has emerged as the basis of enlightened criticism of the play. This is a fruitful line of investigation into important aspects of the *Heracleidae*; still, such a path of inquiry does not automatically or necessarily lead to a defense of the drama's wholeness, unity, and intelligible structure[9]—those Aristotelian *desiderata* that Wilamowitz found lacking in this play.

32–37 and 63–69). The lost *Erechtheus* has been thrust back into discussions of Athenian images of heroic women by Connelly, who reads the Parthenon friezes as a version of this story. Art-historical questions aside, it is good to have this reminder that the Athenian *polis* needed images to mold female opinion. Connelly reminds literary scholars that the Sorbonne papyrus 2823 gives the speech of Athena to Praxithea in which the mother is ordered to make a *temenos* where her daughters (two sisters apparently joined their younger, sacrificed sibling under the terms of an oath) are buried (77) and that the role of women in sustaining the community is paramount (79). Makaria, Praxithea, and Praxithea's oath-bound daughters are perhaps manipulated by the *polis*, but not brutalized by it. In any stable and relatively free society, it seems to me, the "many," both male and female, are made to wish to conform, not forced to do so.

[9]Today the prevailing view of the text of *Heracleidae* is that only modest lacunae mar its completeness (Diggle 158); but Wilkins (1993, xxx–xxxiii) thinks that an alternate version might have existed. Lesky is one of the last to maintain that an entire episode has disappeared from the received text, but his view has had little support. It is the hypothesis prefixed to the play which is one source of doubt about the completeness of the text, but this summary of the plot is not itself free from error—its author says that a human sacrifice had to be made to Demeter, when the play clearly says that it was the daughter of Demeter (κόρῃ Δήμητρος, 408–409) who demanded a maiden of high birth (not the "most noble" maiden, as the argument puts it) as a sacrificial victim. The participle ἀποθανοῦσαν in line 14 of the hypothesis should, perhaps, be emended to ἀποθανουμένην on the grounds that the author of the hypothesis made a slip (Makaria was "about to die," not already dead, when she was praised by those who then rushed off to battle). Zuntz (129–52) gives a thorough picture of the problems associated with this and other Euripidean dramas' hypotheses; he favors the view that one author of the summaries did not have first-hand knowledge of the texts of some plays, only a "Tales from Euripides" (135–38). On the fragments supposedly attributable to this play but not found in the received text (a second source of doubt about the play's completeness), Wilkins' verdict of *non liquet* (1993, xxx) seems correct.

Perhaps the first critic to confront squarely Wilamowitz' wholesale dismissal of the *Heracleidae* was MacLean,[10] who argues quite persuasively that until the *leitmotiv* of the drama is identified, arguments for, from, or against its unity and design cannot be constructed with any assurance. It may simply be added here that arguments concerning the economy of the play are even less assured than those about its unity in the absence of an understanding of the controlling theme of the drama. If the *leitmotiv* of the play is made explicit, then, in turn, it may be possible to show that this now explicit, thematic unity has a reciprocal relationship with the ideological concerns of the drama. The title of the play is the first bit of evidence that deserves attention in the search for the *leitmotiv*; the matrix of ideas that unifies the drama is conveyed by the suffix *-idae*.[11] The *leitmotiv* of the *Heracleidae* is the notion of a generational crisis, a crisis that affects the young who are coming of age after the great hero is gone, the crisis of the *epigonoi*, the ones born too late for direct participation in legendary deeds alongside the traditional heroes. However, that same crisis, produced in this drama by the threat and then the onset of war between Argos and Athens, is also the crisis of the *gerontes*, the ones who have lived too long and cannot free themselves from notions about heroism that may be outworn, an ideology of the heroic that may not serve any state (whether Athens or Argos) which is striving for advantage or success. Through its various episodes, the *Heracleidae* shows that there is a price to be paid in suffering, no matter whether a character identifies with the

---

[10]MacLean 202–3 and 214–17. However, MacLean somewhat undercuts his own case by positing a large lacuna at or near the play's conclusion (218–19), because he is unwilling to accept the treatment of Eurystheus at the play's end. Stoessl (219–21) by contrast to MacLean, finds the final episode powerful, tragic, and in harmony with the moral concerns and the theodicy of the rest of the play. For me, Burian (1–3;15–21) analyzes the structural problem of this episode as a coda and reversal as it needs to be treated, although I cannot agree with Burian's evaluation of Eurystheus and Alcmene in the episode.

[11]See Avery 539–40; 563–65; though I cannot agree with Avery that the patronymic extends just to men at all times.

vanished heroes or with the offspring of the heroes and their diminished stature as *epigonoi*.

It is significant that the first two words of the *Heracleidae* are the temporal adverbs πάλαι ποτ(έ). They put us in mind of the past and introduce Iolaus' comment that he has realized since "some time long ago" that there are self-serving men who are useless to their neighbors or their city and others who are just to neighbors and useful to the *polis*. Only the latter truly become "men" (ἀνήρ is predicative with πέφυκ' in *Heracl.* 2 and the usage analogous to ἀνὴρ ἀγαθὸς γίγνεσθαι). The passage of time since the "time long ago" that Iolaus recalls has been deleterious to those in this play. He and Alcmene must manage the exile of Heracles' minor sons and daughters, and he imagines how others will talk about his feeble ineffectiveness: "Look, he didn't protect the children, even though he was their kinsman and they had no father" (29f). When Copreus refers to Iolaus as an "old tomb" and a "non-entity" at 165f., this confirms the old man's fear that his old age is feckless and contemptible. Why should any Athenian risk ill-repute for the sake of a relic who outlived his kinsman's heroic career and even outlasted his own physical capacity to fight against his enemies? Later in the play, when Alcmene momentarily mistakes Hyllus' man for Copreus or some other equally arrogant Argive emissary, she warns "you'll fight ignobly against an aged pair" (δυοῖν γερόντιον, 653).

Copreus, by the way, is no less scornful in his estimate of Heracles' young sons; "even when grown strong (ἡβήσαντες) they would fight weakly against Argive hoplites," he says at 167. Demophon is saluted as the son of a noble father in 116, but Theseus is as dead as Heracles, and Demophon is not about to make costly sacrifices for the sake of others, as the play later shows. In Iolaus' estimate only Makaria can vindicate a claim that she has grown from the seed of Heracles (σπέρμα . . . πέφυκας Ἡρακλεῖον, 540f.), and she herself boasts that she grew (πέφυκα) from the sort of father Heracles was (563). The repetition of the perfect tense forms of φύω (found initially in line 2) shows that she has become the ἀνήρ or "heroic figure" of the piece, to give her the title that the play confers on the one who sacrifices for others. Thus, Makaria excepted, the picture of the age groups who are rather old or rather young in the time after Heracles' death is an unflattering one.

Furthermore, the play shows that even the undoing of time's modality can bring no better result. Told by the chorus that there is no way he will regain youth once more in 707f. (οὐκ ἔστιν ὅπως / ἥβην κτήσῃ πάλιν αὖθις), Iolaus still wishes his strength were once more what it was when he destroyed Sparta (740) with Heracles. Iolaus certainly prayed νέος γενέσθαι (851), according to the report of the messenger who witnessed the old man on the battlefield. However, when Iolaus is rejuvenated and when Alcmene is given power over the defeated Eurystheus, they show that their aim is (τὸ) ἀποτείσεσθαι δίκην ἐχθρούς, to use the formulation he himself used in his invocation to Hebe and Zeus at 852f. It is never shown in the *Heracleidae* that this "paying back" of enemies has anything but a chance connection to the success of the *polis*. The vengeful killing of Eurystheus serves one aristocratic Argive *genos*, the expelled Heracleidae, for the time being, but in the long run it is to be a mark against the Argives, even those descended from Heracles' children, for they will forget Athenian magnanimity toward their forebears and invade Attica.

The rejuvenation of Iolaus (hearsay in the *Heracleidae*) shows that Euripides deliberately brought the possibility of the renewal of youthful life into the minds of his audience, and the alleged sloughing off of old age by Heracles' kinsman and comrade-at-arms only makes sense if the tragedy is about some division between or among generations. Of course, themes of generational conflict and the restoration of youth have resonance from Dionysiac religion (the god as ἐνιαυτὸς δαίμων and the bringer of renewed fertility), from comedy, from epic, from earlier tragedy, and from contemporary political rhetoric, so that it is necessary to say what specific aspects of these "generational" themes the *Heracleidae* examines.

As early as *Iliad* 1, Nestor already is reminding the Achaeans at Troy that their generation is no match for the heroes whom he had known earlier. It is at least an interesting coincidence that Nestor's brief catalogue of that earlier, better generation ("Perithoos, Dryas, Kaineus, Exadios, godlike Polyphemus, and Theseus the Aegeid, like unto the immortals," *Il.* 1.263-265) culminates in the name of Theseus and his patronymic, while in Euripides' *Heracleidae* a pair of Theseids, Demophon in particular, faces the challenge posed by Heracles' children and by their claim to protection, a claim or plea that arises partly out of their fathers' kinship and guest-friendship. To be sure, in the earliest of Athenian tragedies, the inadequacy of Xerxes, who cannot live up to the warlike standards of his allegedly insuperable father Darius, oppresses the son and is one of several factors that helps to drive him to excess and to ruin.

In other words, many changes may be rung on the theme of the incommensurable generations, but treatments such as the Homeric and Aeschylean ones just mentioned, although influential in some general sense, are only ancillary to an analysis of generational crisis as the controlling motif of the *Heracleidae*. Strauss[12] points out that in the Athens of Euripides and his audience the conflict of the generations had specific political and ideological constructions. This means, I believe, that in an innovative society (and fifth century BC Athens certainly felt both the pull of innovation and the resistance of tradition), generational conflict is both ever-present and yet always changing its specific content (as when Aristophanic fathers and sons quarrel even over their tastes in songs and musical styles). One quite specific way of imagining the generational crisis is found in the *Heracleidae*. To put this another way: the play reads political arguments about Athenian σωτηρία (the *salus populi*

---

[12]Strauss (121) calls Theseus, the Athenian national hero, the preeminent symbol of the Athenians' focus on the transition from generation to generation, because of his connections to the ephebate and to rituals of initiation. Athenians all saw themselves as Theseids, on Strauss' interpretation of Sophocles, *OC* 1066 (128). Mythical symbols are crucial to Strauss' interpretation because he stresses the ideological, constructed nature of generational conflict at the time of the Peloponnesian War; real attacks on Athenian fathers, real lawsuits against them, and real degeneracy among sons may *not* (my emphasis) have been on the increase, he wisely reminds us (144f).

that is the supreme concern of any organized society) and views about Athenian youth's "preparedness" for the defense of their *polis* into the phenomenon of the succession of generations which cannot replicate one another as they might have done in an wholly traditional society or in more traditional times.

Even stated boldly, what I call the play's *leitmotiv*—the crisis of the generations—hints at the economy the *Heracleidae* exhibits. Like the *Troades*, which stages a procession of different characters (Hecuba, Cassandra, Andromache, Helen) for whom the end of the Trojan War is itself a new crisis, the *Heracleidae* enacts the crisis of a war's beginning, and the pageant of its characters shows that each suffers because a traditional code of heroes demands what a democratic *polis* such as Athens does not necessarily produce. That missing factor is what Euripides calls *eugeneia*[13] and where it does exist (in Makaria or Alcmene) the play shows us that *eugeneia* may not necessarily be an advantage to the city-state, but only to the heroic figure and her tribe. As soon as the notion is established that the *Heracleidae* is a drama about the twin fears that democracy cannot produce heroes in its late generations and that clannish, "eugenic" heroes can sunder the state in pursuit of private or familial advantage,[14] then the unity of the drama can also be recognized.

In the rest of this piece, I want to show how new light is shed on particular parts of the play, once the whole drama is interpreted as a *contestation* (Vernant's word,[15] which means the "calling into question" of contradictory, but equally valid, moral claims) over demands made by the success-oriented democratic *polis* and private, traditional, aristocratic *eugeneia*. My reading of Vernant convinces me that the sort of "calling into question" or *contestation*

---

[13]See Avery 540–42 and Burnett (1971) 14–15 on this quality.

[14]Burnett (1971, 14) is alone in seeing that *genos* is a central problem in *Heracleidae*.

[15]Vernant (203–7) argues that myth in epinician is used to create ethical paradigms, while the use of myth in Attic tragedy is problematizing, that is, myth in tragedy is used to give form to ethical controversy by granting each contentious voice its due.

that he sees as the aim of tragedy cannot permit one value to triumph over another opposing value. There is not so much a clear message to be found in tragedy, even when tragedy borrows from political rhetoric of a decidedly partisan sort, as does the *Heracleidae*, as there is an almost irreconcilable antagonism. None of the values held in equipoise in this "calling into question" is defeasible, and we should not expect the *Heracleidae* to say which are the proper values or which are the wrong ones (praise and blame are the work of epic, history and *encomium*), but rather to show what the cost of defending values is. Of course, the cost is always suffering of some kind, and the few passages to be discussed here show that the several characters' responses to the threat and to the start of the war between Argos and Athens are all responses that entail loss of life, reputation, or identification with the city-state.

First of all, the opening of the play, in which the young sons of Heracles are gathered around Iolaus as suppliants at the altar of Zeus at Marathon, is even more important than previously acknowledged. For Euripides' Athenian audience, Marathon was not merely a toponym, but part of the name of a vanishing generation. By the early years of the Peloponnesian War many or most of the *Marathonomachai* must have been dead and the youngest veterans of that battle were octogenarians-to-be. Yet Athenians had singled out that generation as the embodiment of a heroism which had its root in the post-Cleisthenic, democratized *polis*—perfect grist for an ideological mill in the city that now imposed democracy on others, except that Marathon was a unique moment, perhaps incapable of being re-enacted by *epigonoi*. After all, men in their twenties when they fought at Marathon—the only participants likely still to be alive as the Peloponnesian War began—had every right to regard themselves as the foundational generation of what had since come to be called the Athenian democracy. Their commanders had known the tyrants; they themselves were the first products of the Cleisthenic tribes and demes.

More importantly, the generation that fought at Marathon had been succeeded by a generation that came of age around 460 BC,[16] and that intermediate generation had had a spotty military record (Thuc. 1.98–117, provides a summary). Parts of Boeotia were gained by military conquest and then lost; the same was true in the area around Megara; Aegina and Euboea could not be so fully controlled as the Athenians wished; and in the mid-440s the Athenians had concluded a less-than-satisfactory truce with the Peloponnesians, one that left Attica open to attack from many quarters (the Saronic Gulf, the isthmus of Corinth, the northwest). So Athenian memory and imagination were extremely selective when it came to a question of the political usefulness of forebears as models for the generation that was to come of age around 430 BC.

One ought to be keenly aware that when Pericles mixes praise of the Athenians who withstood the Persians in the 490s and 480s BC together with an injunction to the present generation not to leave Athens less great than it was when it was inherited by them from their ancestors, he is both obfuscating (at Thuc. 2.36.4, for example, he says that he will not dwell on events that his audience knows directly) and voicing a genuine fear. His listeners in 431 BC could still see among them, perhaps, only a few relics of the men who fought at Marathon, but these were always used to stir up patriotic emotion (at Thuc. 1.144.4–5, Pericles joins praise of the forebears who pushed back the Medes with the present worry of being inferior [λείπεσθαι] to those ancestors),[17] while the actual

---

[16]The preference for thirty-year truces, well known from Aristophanes and Thucydides, suggests that this is the approximate boundary (three every hundred years?) for a generation insofar as that idea existed in Athenian minds. Von Leyden (101) argues that elderly people (how old?) at the end of the fifth century BC (when exactly?) could have had direct knowledge of events stretching back only to the start of the Pentekontaetia, so about seventy years or two generations.

[17]Since this piece appears in a volume which is commemorative in nature, perhaps the evidence of those grey-haired German volunteers who flocked to the colors in 1914 (adduced by Pohlenz [356] commenting specifically on the mixture of emotions evoked by the arming of Iolaus)

fathers of the present Athenian generation go unmentioned for the most part by Pericles except when it is said that they handed over the Athenian ἀρχή "not without struggling" (2.36.2). Their losses, however, (in Egypt, for example, where they exacerbated Persian dislike or in smaller failures, such as Pericles' own unsuccessful siege at Oiniadai; see Thuc.1.109–10 and 111.2–3) had left their sons with real anxieties about Athens' openness to attack. So inured have we become to Thucydides' view that the growth of Athens inspired fear in the Lacedaimonians that we may well forget that Athenians had strategic nightmares themselves. An Athenian of thirty years of age (old enough to be a *taxiarch*) at Athens at the start of the Peloponnesian War would have spent some of his years hearing the bad news about Athenian military setbacks and pondering Athens' vulnerability to future attacks.[18] The spectacle of fatherless sons below the age of military usefulness who are protected by two feeble elders and are clustering at an altar at Marathon plays on a very specific fear about the young.

Furthermore, it may also be argued that the opening of the *Heracleidae* alludes to the crisis of the generations by "staging" what later became a highly political use of theatrical display during the Dionysian festival: the public presentation in the theater of the male orphans who were to be raised collectively by the *demos*.

---

may be admitted as valid. My father (b. 1909) often spoke about the memory of elderly Union soldiers whom he saw as a boy in 1919 when they joined the victory parades at the end of WWI; in fact, the Roosevelt administration organized the Final Encampment of the Grand Army of the Republic almost seventy years after the last battles of the American Civil War. Thus it is that both individuals and governments select a heroic generation for remembrance and as an image for the construction of an ideology.

[18] Of course, if Thucydides is believable, the Corinthians, too, and Archidamos himself warned the Lacedaimonians and their allies not to surrender any part of what their fathers had left them (1.71.7 and 85.1), so that the fear of falling short of "glorious ancestors" was a rhetorical commonplace in almost all Greek discourse about war in the 430s. Even after falling somewhat out of favor, Pericles continued to insist that Athenians must not fall short of their ancestors, according to Thuc. 2.62.3 (τῶν ... πατέρων μὴ χείρους ... φανῆναι).

Goldhill has written convincingly about the ideological content of this preliminary ceremony at the Greater Dionysia.[19] I simply add here that the singling out of such orphans by Pericles in the Funeral Oration (Thuc. 2.46.1, makes the final, substantive remark of this speech a promise that the city will raise the children of the dead μέχρι ἥβης) and the out-of-doors gathering of Heracles' young, male children (the female relatives are pointedly said to be inside the temple, and the adult Hyllos is twice reported to be in action somewhere "offstage" in the play) may well constitute two bits of evidence that the ritual presentation of war-orphans who were soon to become ephebes either in the theater before the plays or in some other civic setting had late-fifth century origins, although it is attested with certainty only in the fourth century. It is logical to think that such a presentation of war-orphans eligible to become military trainees might have taken place firstly within the phratries (where their then living fathers had presented them in early childhood), perhaps at the κούρειον-rite of the Apaturia, and an innovation came about when they were presented collectively to the *demos* at the Dionysia of the following spring.

A theatrical coup, indeed, if the opening of *Heracleidae* re-enacts some ceremony (either from within the phratries or from a plenary assembly) still fresh in the minds of the audience. Depending on the exact date of the production of the play,[20] this

---

[19]Goldhill (100–6) analyzes the ceremonies that preceded the plays, beginning with those known from the 460s BC down to the time of Isocrates and Aeschines, from whom we get our best information about the presentation of orphans "onstage" at the Great Dionysia. It is the presence of *xenoi* at this festival (they were arguably fewer at the Lenaia in the dead of winter) that makes this and the other ceremonies conducted before the dramas were put on such an important part of the civic discourse by which Athens communicated its power to the rest of Greece, according to Goldhill.

[20]For me, Delcourt (118) already demolishes the view that Eurystheus' prophecy at the end of *Heracleidae* is so clearly linked to Spartan invasions of Attica before 427 BC that it provides the exact *terminus ante quem* of the play's appearance, but Delcourt undercuts her own logic by arguing that the play can be dated to the time just after the sack of Plataea.

opening might even allude to the loss of Pericles (this despite the metrical mismatch of the names Heracles and Pericles) because he had so emphatically alluded to the public duty of raising the sons of deceased veterans in the speech which closed the first year of the Peloponnesian War. The whole play certainly invites speculation about the ability of the young sons of Heracles, now the wards of the doddering survivor Iolaus, to defend themselves, their native city, or their host city. Wistfully, for a moment, as if this were a sermon for initiates into Dionysian *mysteria* and not a tragedy, the drama suggests that an older generation could be revitalized, just as Iolaus is reportedly rejuvenated in the midst of battle. But the messenger who reports the wonderful appearance of Hebe and Heracles as the bestowers of a second youth on Heracles' old kinsman and companion-at-arms has the outlook of that suspicious English detective who found it easier to believe in "miracle[s] that happened twenty years ago than in one of yesterday morning." The audience doubtlessly feared that Athens had used up its miracles at Marathon sixty or more years earlier, so that as a late-born generation, it ought not to rely on miraculously rejuvenated grandsires, only on itself and, looking forward, on the children it had raised in not entirely traditional ways.

The second, very impressive part of *Heracleidae* that can be more clearly understood, if the crisis of the *epigonoi* and their elders is seen as the central problem of the drama, is the self-sacrifice of Makaria. As Schmitt[21] says, this episode is part and parcel of Euripides' examination of Athenian *Staatsbewusstsein*—we may translate this as "statist-consciousness" or "*polis*-consciousness," if "statist" sounds excessively modern. Makaria's prominence in the middle of the drama certainly shows that the willingness to surrender life itself in exchange for whatever

---

[21]For Schmitt (1–2), the first "patriotic" changes in the old legends must have come about at the time of the Persian Wars, so that Euripides' is the secondary re-fashioning of legends that originally had religious, but not preponderantly ethical, dimensions; *Staatswesen* (polity) now sometimes became the central focus of Euripidean drama, she maintains, and patriotic sacrifice is essential to the existence of the *polis*.

is defined as being more valuable than life does truly exist in the generation that lives after the heroes have vanished, but Makaria's action is prompted, we must note, by a not necessarily democratic focus on *eugeneia*. Little or nothing needs to be said about Makaria by other characters in the drama after she goes off to be slaughtered as an offering to *Korē*, because, as Pohlenz,[22] following Schmitt, puts it, Makaria's act is not a ritualized *Opfer* (other Euripidean dramas examine the theatricality and emotional impact of rituals of sacrifice and self-sacrifice),[23] but a dramatized declaration of *Opfermut*, the courage to make one's self a sacrificial victim. And her courage and altruism are discussed at some length by Demophon and Iolaus before she leaves to become a human sacrificial offering. Makaria's expressed wish to be held only by Iolaus or by other women when she has had her throat cut is as emotionally affecting as any later comment about her could be. Out of military necessity, the ideology that promoted sacrifice for the *polis* incorporated mostly male paradigms, but women had to be marshaled behind protreptic images and slogans, too. Of course, in Iolaus' own words, words that are incorporated into the title of this piece, "among many, you might find (sc. only) one not inferior to a father" (μὴ χείρων πατρός). Although Iolaus uses the masculine form *hena* in 327 for the unique "one among many" who is not inferior to a father, in this drama Makaria is clearly the one who needs to be viewed as true to a heroic standard set by the earlier generation. She must be viewed in contrast to other *epigonoi*, and especially in contrast to Demophon, who are inferior to their fathers. An interesting detail confirms that some ancient source—perhaps whichever redactor it was that altered our text by giving the name Makaria to Heracles' daughter and the name Copreus to Eurystheus' messenger—had the contrast of morally unequal generations in mind. Copreus is uniquely, as readers of

[22]Pohlenz 355.
[23]Now see Scodel on the maiden daughter as the highly valuable property of the household and the public, sometimes even sexual, display that the sacrifice of the virgin daughter may involve.

Iliad 15.641 may remember, the "inferior father of a better son," the exception who proves the rule.

To return to my argument, it is Demophon (in stark contrast to Makaria and with special irony, if Theseus was a symbol of generational transition as Strauss argues) who best shows that a democratic *polis* may well fail to produce a son who embodies the heroism of his forebears. And then, in a not-so-surprising reversal (reversal is among Euripides' techniques or tactics as early as the *Medea*) at the play's end, Alcmene shows that private, ancestral, or "eugenic" values may exalt the sufferings of heroism so greatly that they make an ideological fetish of hatred and death even to the point of being willing to destroy advantage or success for the *polis*.

To examine Demophon and Alcmene briefly as representatives of different generations, I want to look at two separate bits of speech and dialogue involving these characters. In my interpretation, these passages are at least united in that they are both free of any attempt to produce an ἔπαινος or *eulogium* of Athens (an intention often read into the play as a whole).

Lines 401–424, spoken by Demophon make explicit this son of Theseus' lack of εὐγένεια. His unwillingness to sacrifice his own daughter for a victory of the *polis* over its enemies and indeed even for the physical safety of his *polis*, is based on his desire to be and to be seen as just. This wish is noble enough, but his refusal is also based on his calculation of what the partisan or factional reactions might be, if he sacrificed some maiden of high birth. This calculation leads him to advise Iolaus to find a way in which the children of Heracles can save themselves and the land that is sheltering them, but it must be a way that does not arouse prejudice or slander against him. Such a lukewarm defender of the suppliants is not willing to risk life or even his own standing as a βασιλεύς/προστάτης (the latter word connotes a sort of factional leader in the Athenian assembly) in the eyes of the *polis* for the sake of the νόμοι that protected suppliants. Demophon falls into a no-man's land between the two sorts of men Iolaus had said (in the very first lines of the play) that he had learned to recognize over the course of a long career: the man just to his neighbors

(Demophon wants to be perceived as that sort of man) and the one who is bent on gain/success, very good to himself, and useless to his city (Demophon is, unfortunately, all this, too; neither able himself to make, nor able to compel someone else to make, a terrible sacrifice for the safety and victory of his *polis*). The notion that an entity such as a city is a kind of corporate person is a modern one, but the *Heracleidae* suggests that Athens through the son of Theseus, who is arguably its corporate embodiment, may become good at seeking advantage for itself and useless to others.

The passage that involves Alcmene, covers the last hundred lines or more of the play. In my view, far more weight has to be granted to a part of Alcmene's claim for revenge against Eurystheus than critics generally concede.[24] Crucial to seeing the strength of her claim is understanding the weakness of the responses that the squire-messenger, Eurystheus[25] and the chorus make to Alcmene from line 960 to the end of the play.

When Alcmene asks whether some νόμος prevents killing the captured Eurystheus, the messenger's answer is: it seems best to the leaders of this land. Surprisingly, this answer is rarely interpreted as the evasive or negative answer that it really is, but Alcmene understands that the squire-messenger cannot claim the authority of νόμος, merely that of the προστάτεις. She questions him further, "Isn't it a fine thing to kill ἐχθροί?" She knows full well that is, indeed, the common custom of the Greeks or of Greek aristocracies,[26] and she wonders why Hyllus put up with the

---

[24]Burnett (1971) 21–25 is the exception.

[25]Once more, only Burnett (1971, 25), properly emphasizes the emptiness of Eurystheus' smooth, but craven words.

[26]Blundell (26–59) devotes considerable attention to the notion of paying back enemies in kind, as various Greek writers express that notion in genres other than tragedy. The concept is intuitively equitable, and one reference provided by Blundell seems especially apposite here: in Thuc. 7.68.1–2 Gylippus and the other Syracusan generals encourage their troops to fight against the Athenians with special eagerness knowing that revenge against the aggressor is νομιμώτατον; in fact, to retaliate against enemies is most sweet, "as the saying goes" (τὸ λεγόμενον). Justifications of the proverbial principle can be found even in Plato and Aristotle, as Blundell shows.

decision to keep Eurystheus alive (indeed, earlier, at 938f., this messenger had said that Hyllus and Iolaus had sent Eurystheus with him to Alcmene because they knew very well that she would delight in seeing her enemy fallen into misfortune). "Should he have disobeyed this land?" is the ironic response from the squire-messenger, who understands obedience to authority—that of the προστάτεις—in the *polis* but not much else beyond that. "He should not have allowed this man to live," is Alcmene's more sure response; but the squire-messenger objects that there was nobody to do the deed. "I assert that I am somebody," says Alcmene, "I would do it." Even the blame or loss of reputation that the squire-messenger says that she will suffer for the killing of the imprisoned Eurystheus does not stop her from her vengeance. The certainty and swiftness with which she will kill Eurystheus is conveyed by the future perfect πεπράξεται.[27]

If the reader allows that Alcmene has the better of the argument here with the squire-messenger, then the approval of the chorus at the moment of her immediate departure to kill the Argive king at 1053 is not surprising. She incorporates the power of νόμος as much as or more than the brothers who are the βασιλεῖς or προστάτεις of the Athenians and her indifference to censure marks her are more deserving to be called εὐγενής than they are. The validity of her hatred is confirmed by divinely ordained caprice: the dead Eurystheus, or at least his head, will be a talisman when it is entombed at Pallene, beyond which holy place the yet-unborn descendants of Heracles (more *epigonoi* who will fall short of their ancestors) will proceed at the risk of their own ultimate defeat. If killing Eurystheus will produce an advantage for Athens, then the chorus will have no objection. Those critics who profess to be astonished by the chorus' quick acquiescence have missed the point that these subjects of Demophon wish to be shareholders in a city that pursues κέρδος, which is not to be equated with mere money-grubbing, but with safety and success—no bad things.

---

[27]See Smythe for an exact parallel.

By showing how much of *nomos* and *eugeneia* Alcmene incorporates and thus rehabilitating her insistence on retaliation, by arguing that the play lessens the stature of Demophon, and by suggesting that each of them must be interpreted in light of demands made by genealogy (the same demands as those made on the young, suppliant sons of Heracles and on his daughter Makaria), I am attempting to focus attention on a fundamental issue raised in this drama. That issue is the conflict between a *polis* organized for success and its best individuals' highest values, values which pre-date any *polis* and certainly conflict with the view of what the *prostateis* of a democratic *polis* are, as far as this drama is concerned. This is a play which deserves a higher reputation and wider readership than it has had in the past, and the central question it poses should be of interest to any democratic society (such a society must necessarily, it seems to me, pursue the advantage of the many): does the heroic excellence of the few run counter to the success of the city? If the answer can sometimes be "yes," then democracy must always beware lest some "few" attempt to pursue a heroic vision which destroys the advantage of the state. However it must equally beware lest a democratic polity produce no heroes at all after the time of its glorious founding generation, but rather only those who pursue private and public advantage, however defined. This, or something like this, seems to me to be the ultimate significance of Euripides' *Heracleidae*. And this supremely important question arises from the conflict of generations which is "staged" in the drama. This is a perennial conflict, but one viewed at Athens around the time of the start of the Peloponnesian War with the last sixty or seventy years of Athenian history and the last two Athenian generations uppermost in mind. What the rising generation, let us call them the generation of 430 BC, would achieve could only be anticipated with some dread.

BIBLIOGRAPHY

Ambrose, Z. P. 1990. *Euripides' Heraclidae*. Bryn Mawr.
Avery, H. C. 1971. "Euripides' *Heracleidai*." *AJP* 92:539–65.
Blundell, M. W. 1989. *Helping Friends And Harming Enemies*. Cambridge.
Burian, P. 1976. "Euripides' *Heracleidae*: An Interpretation." *CQ* 71:1–21.
Burnett, A. P. 1976. "Tribe, City, Custom and Decree in *Children of Heracles*." *CP* 71:4–26.
—. 1971. *Catastrophe Survived: Euripides' Plays of Mixed Reversal*. Oxford.
Connelly, J. B. 1996. "Parthenon and *Parthenoi*: a Mythological Interpretation of the Parthenon Frieze." *AJA* 100:53–80.
Delcourt, M. 1930. "Euripide et les événements de 431–424." *Serta Leodiensia*. Paris.
Diggle, J. 1984. *Euripidis Fabulae, I*. Oxford.
Fitton, J. W. 1961. "The *Suppliant Women* and the *Herakleidai* of Euripides." *Hermes* 89:430–61.
Garzya, A. 1972. *Euripides: Heracleidae*. Leipzig.
Goldhill, S. 1990. "The Great Dionysia and Civic Ideology." In *Nothing To Do With Dionysos?* edited by J. Winkler and F. Zeitlin. Princeton.
Kovacs, D. 1996. *Euripidea Altera*. Leiden.
—.1995. *Euripides: Children of Heracles; Hippolytus; Andromache; Hecuba*. Cambridge, Mass.
Lesky, A. 1977. "On the *Heraclidae* of Euripides." *YCS* 227–38.
Leyden, W. von. 1949/50. "*Spatium Historicum*." *Durham University Journal* 42:101.
Loraux, N. 1993. *The Children of Athena*, translated by C. Levine. Princeton.
MacLean, J. H. 1934. "The *Heraclidae* of Euripides." *AJP* 55:197–224.
Pohlenz, M. 1930. *Die Griechische Tragödie*. Gottingen. Repr. 1954.

Rabinowitz, N. S. 1993. *Anxiety Veiled: Euripides and the Traffic in Women*. Ithaca and London.
Schlegel, A. W. von. 1796;1808 [1962–74]. *Kritische Schriften und Briefen*, edited by E. Lohner. Stuttgart.
Schmid, O. and W. Stahlin. 1961. *Geschichte der Griechischen Literatur* 7.1.3. Munich.
Schmitt, J. 1921. *Freiwilliger Opfertod bei Euripides*. Giessen.
Scodel, R. 1996. "Δόμων ἄγαλμα: Virgin Sacrifice and Aesthetic Object." *TAPA* 126:111–28.
Smythe, H. 1920. *Greek Grammar*. Cambridge, Mass. Repr. 1956.
Spranger, J. A. 1925. "The Political Element in the *Heracleidae* of Euripides." *CQ* 19:117–28.
Strauss, B. 1993. *Fathers And Sons in Athens*. Princeton.
Stoessl, F. 1956. "Die Herakliden des Euripides." *Philologus* 100:207–34
Vernant, J.-P. 1981. *Mythe et Société en Grèce Ancienne*. Paris.
Wilamowitz-Möllendorf, U. von. 1882. "Excurse zu Euripides *Herakliden*." *Hermes* 17:337–64.
Wilkins, J. 1993. *Euripides: Heraclidae*. Oxford.
—. 1990. "The State and the Individual: Euripides' Plays of Voluntary Self-Sacrifice." In *Euripides, Women, And Sexuality*, edited by A. Powell. London and New York.
Zuntz, G. 1963. *The Political Plays of Euripides*. Manchester.

Concerning the Plane Trees in Seneca's Twelfth Epistle

Michele Valerie Ronnick
Wayne State University

In 1982 in the pages of *Classical Antiquity*, Thomas Habinek drew our attention to the image of concentric circles in paragraphs 4–9 of Seneca's twelfth epistle to his younger friend Lucilius.[1] Thereafter examining the thoughts expressed by earlier figures such as Homer and Heraclitus about circles, Habinek concluded among other things that to his knowledge there was "no other classical text which likens human life to a set of concentric circles."[2] Based upon this *argumentum ex silentio*, Habinek gave credit to Seneca for developing the trope, for "without specific evidence . . . it is impossible to deny credit for the image to Seneca."[3] Habinek then analyzed the way the image as a graphic representation of the days, months and years of a person's life fit into Seneca's interpretation of the maxim from Heraclitus that "one day is equal to all."[4] There is, however, more here that contributes to Seneca's meaning than Habinek has noticed.

The letter opens with a description of a trip Seneca makes in his maturity to a suburban villa in an unnamed location that had been in his possession for a long time. As Habinek accurately points out, this epistle "is a particularly artful treatment of the pleasures and disappointments of old age," and one whose topic was well-suited

---

[1] For other comments on this letter see Gagliardi. See also the notes made by Summers 168–75. For textual criticism see Wagenvoort; Alexander 102; and Baldwin.
[2] Habinek 66. For the influence of this image see Ronnick 8.
[3] Habinek 66.
[4] For an interpretation of this idea see Stégen.

to Seneca's own "advanced age."[5] After noticing with alarm the many marks of neglect on the grounds of his estate, Seneca comes to realize that these were due in fact to the effects of age, and not to the slothfulness of careless caretakers. He then turns to a discussion of the stages of life, which he likens to a pattern formed by a series of inscribed circles. The image is important per se in the ways explained both by Habinek, and by his predecessor Walter C. Summers. But neither scholar examined how the image fit into the larger context of the letter itself. For the circles and the plane trees are significant aspects of the philosophical message that Seneca intended his letter to convey.

Seneca has carefully crafted the prose that precedes the introduction of his image of concentric circles. The preceding paragraphs, in fact, prepare the way for it. Immediately prior to the section on circles, amid the crumbling masonry (*putria . . . saxa* 12.2.5) of his dilapidated villa, Seneca describes some plane trees that have no leaves (*nullas habent frondes*, 12.2.7).[6] They are in his eyes in need of immediate attention (*apparet . . . has platanos neglegi*, 12.2.6–7). "How knotty and dried up the branches are, how miserable and dirty are the trunks" (*quam nodosi sunt et retorridi rami, quam tristes et squalidi trunci*, 12.2.8–9). Seneca then turns with irritation to his overseer and declares with the voice of a fault-finding accuser that this would not have happened, if someone had dug around them, and if someone had watered them (*hoc non accideret, siquis has circumfoderet, si irrigaret*, 12.2.9–10). After the overseer defends himself by saying that those particular trees were old (*illas vetulas esse*, 12.2.9–10), Seneca remembers that he himself had planted them, and had seen them come into their first foliage as well (*ego illas posueram, ego illarum primum videram folium*, 12.2.12–3.1). Seneca then catches sight of a decrepit old man near the entrance (*conversus ad ianuam*

---

[5]Habinek 67.
[6]The Latin text here cited is that of Reynolds. All translations are my own.

... *iste decrepitus*, 12.3.14–15), who unbeknownst to Seneca, was as a youth Seneca's pet slave.

The thematic relationship here that underlies the beginning of Epistle Twelve is one between the cylindrical tree-trunks, the curves of the circles, and the cycles of human life. Moreover, it is apparent from the start in the opening words of the letter (*quocumque me verti, argumenta senectutis meae video*, 12.1.1). The verb *verto* is repeated as the compound verb *adverto* at the start of the fourth paragraph (*debeo hoc suburbano meo quid mihi senectus mea, quocumque adverteram*, 12.4.1), and later echoed by another compound verb *converto* that is used to describe how Seneca happens to notice the old slave (*conversus ad ianuam*). Like the rings in the woody tissue of the tree trunks, the areas of turned soil that surround their trunks, and the concentric circles of life, Seneca turns around his villa and discovers indications of his own senescence. He finally comes face-to-face with the decrepit old man, whose aged body has actually come "full circle" so to speak by turning back to its beginnings, namely its days of childhood. These aspects inscribe each other, and artfully link together the imagery set forth in the letter's initial paragraphs.

This movement of the epistle which then turns literally with its author (*conversus ad*) from the knotty old plane trees to the sight of an old man is significant. For it creates a visual connection between the old, yet still upright trees and the nearly dead old man. He is, in fact, so close to assuming the supine posture of the dead that Seneca quips sardonically that the old man's body "had been rightfully moved toward the door" (*merito ad ostium admotus*), in a jocular reference to the Roman practice of pointing the feet of a corpse in the direction of the threshold. This contrast between the vertical trees and the nearly horizontal man deftly transfers the discussion from one concerning vegetable life to one about human existence.

Seneca, then, thinking that the slave was some sort of homeless vagabond looking for a place to die, accuses his overseer of gathering up the moribund slaves of other people for burial (*quid te delectavit alienum mortuum tollere*, 12.3.3–4). At that point the old man identifies himself, and the stunned Seneca with a note of sarcasm turns his disbelief back upon the man by asking if his second childhood has started since his teeth were falling out all over again (*dentes illi cum maxime cadunt*, 12.3.10). Thus the nearly defunct body of Seneca's former favorite foreshadows the future, not only of Seneca's plane trees, but also of Seneca's own body. In a flurry of falling teeth and deciduous leaves, men and trees alike will be felled ultimately by death, and all will suffer their trunks to lie prone at some point.

It is right to give the details of the landscape in this epistle some attention. Charles Segal noted in an essay on Senecan tragedy, that Seneca "with his feeling for the emotive quality of visual scenes . . . often creates an objective correlative for . . . psychological events through images of place or landscape."[7] Furthermore "the *locus horridus* of gloomy forest or strangling trees expresses the nightmare world of fear, anxiety, and despair."[8]

Segal's observation in regard to Seneca's tragedies is also true in the case of Epistle Twelve. For Seneca has created a "landscape" of himself, past, present and future. He has used, as Segal noted, "his rhetorical technique of projecting personal emotion into a cosmic frame."[9] The framework is of course the symmetry and asymmetry between Seneca's inner world and his outer environment. As Seneca surveys his estate, suffused with the memory of what was, i.e. the constructive period of his youth and the planting of fresh, young vegetation, he is abruptly confronted with an altered picture of what is. Things seem to be the same, but they are in fact markedly different. Thus the landscape of Seneca's memory meets the landscape of his reality. Seneca's true position in terms of time does not square with the position of his soul, or with the changes yet to come with the passage of time. This scene of recognition provides an adroit transition to the next section of the letter.

[7]Segal 180.
[8]*Ibid.*
[9]*Ibid.*, 173.

Seneca begins this portion of the epistle describing the type of pleasure that is to be found in the final phase of temporal existence. He supports his thesis with examples (fruit, human beings, and wine) whose pleasures are evanescent ones, and whose seasons have just passed by. For each of these conveys the idea of ripe fullness and timely completion. Seneca tells us "every day is a unit of life" (*unus . . . dies gradus vitae est*, 12.6.5–6) and our " life as a whole holds larger circles that are inscribed with smaller circles" (*tota aetas . . . orbes habet circumductos maiores minoribus*, 12.7.1–2). These circular units make up our lives. The smallest of these is that of a day which "moves from its beginning to its own end, from sunrise to sunset" (*hic ab initio ad exitum venit ab ortu ad occasum*, 12.7.1).

This concept concerning both a beginning and an end formed by the points of a circle anticipates the next part of the epistle. For Seneca uses an allusion to an observation of Heraclitus, namely, that "in the case of a circle's circumference, beginning and end are common (*frag*. 103)," to move to a direct reference to Heraclitus.[10] Seneca tell us "that Heraclitus said that *unus . . . dies par omni est*" and then advises us that each day "must be regulated as if it ended a series, as if it filled out and completed a life" (*ordinandus est dies omnis, tamquam cogat agmen et consummet atque expleat vitam*, 12.8.2–24).[11]

In this way Seneca also brings to bear upon his argument a basic Heraclitean tenet that every "object (action/event/state of affairs)—as illustrated by a point on a circle—will appear possessed of opposite properties, depending on the perspective from which it is viewed." Thus the ground is paved so to speak for the next section of the epistle about Pacuvius' daily burial (*nullo non se die extulit*), for Pacuvius' actions are both foolishly absurd and frighteningly correct at same time. Pacuvius is facing the fact of his mortality on a daily basis. He is afraid that each day might be his last, but this does not in Seneca's eyes liberate him nor make

---

[10]Robinson 60–61.
[11]*Ibid.*, 149.

him any wiser. As Habinek notes Pacuvius is "locked inside the circle that is his life, consigned to endless, tedious repetition of the same action."[12] Seneca wants us to understand that a person's entire existence form birth to death is based on an ever widening cycle of days, and that every beginning has the potential of also being an end. Furthermore, each "diurnal ring" is perfect unto itself in its cyclical beginning and end. Each day dies its own death, and any day can be the day of our own death.

That humans can be compared to trees, to be sure, is not new to Seneca, and the falling teeth and deciduous leaves at 12.3.10 attest to this. The trope is seen in several places in the Roman literature of the early empire. Vergil's *Aeneid* provides one example. At 4.441–448, Aeneas is likened to an oak buffeted by strong Alpine winds as Dido appeals to him (*ac velut annoso validam cum robore quercum . . . Alpini Boreae nunc hinc nunc flatibus illinc eruere inter se certant*). From Lucan's epic comes the famous description of Pompey at *BC* 1.136–140. There Pompey is likened to "a tall oak tree as it clings with roots no longer strong, [and] stands by its own weight alone, throwing out bare branches into the sky and making shade, not with its leaves, but with its trunk" (*qualis quercus sublimis . . . nec iam validis radicibus haerens / pondere fixa suo est, nudosque per aera ramos / effundens trunco, non frondibus efficit umbram*).

The plane trees (Platanus orientalis) themselves as members of the plant kingdom bring with them an especial significance, for they are "one of the oldest and most cherished shade trees cultivated by man."[13] "One of the many trees that Rome had adopted from the Greek world" according to Russell Meiggs, the plane graced many public and private places.[14] A few decades after Seneca, Pliny the Younger took care to describe the plane trees that ornamented his own Tuscan villa in the sixth paragraph of his fifth epistle.

---

[12]Habinek 69.
[13]Li 57. Pages 56–83 contain details concerning the three most common species in the plane tree family, *platanus orientalis, platanus occidentalis* and *platanus x acerifolia*.
[14]Meiggs 276.

The tree's scientific name comes from the adjective πλατύς, and stems from the ample spans reached by its branches according to most sources. A botanist such as M. L. Fernald, on the other hand, maintains that the name refers to the tree's wide, hand-shaped leaves.[15] However the name platanus was actually derived, it is possible to imagine that Plato may well have been amused by the similarities between his name and that of the tree.

The tree often appeared as a scenic backdrop in the landscape of philosophical discussion.[16] Cimon was reported to have "converted the Academy from a dry and treeless place to a well-watered grove laid out with well-shaded walks." Varro mentions a young plane tree growing on the grounds of the Lyceum which according to Theophrastus had an extensive root system (*Theophrastus scribat Athenis in Lyceo, cum etiam nunc platanus novella esset, radices trium et triginta cubitorum egisse*, RR 1.37).

A passage concerning the landscape in Cicero's *De Oratore* 1.7.28, openly imitates that shared by Socrates and Phaedrus in Plato's *Phaedrus*.[17] As the speakers plan to continue their next day's discussion al fresco, Cotta asks:

> Cur non imitamur, Crasse, Socratem illum, qui est in Phaedro Platonis? Nam me haec tua plantanus admonuit, quae non minus ad opacandum hunc locum patulis est diffusa ramis, quam illa, cuius umbram secutus est Socrates, quae mihi videtur non tam 'ipsa acula,' quae describitur, quam Platonis oratione crevisse: et, quod ille durissimis pedibus fecit, ut se abiceret in herbam, atque ita illa, quae philosophi divinitus ferunt esse dicta, loqueretur, id meis pedibus certe concedi est aequius. Tum Crassus: Immo vero commodius etiam: pulvinos poposcisse, et

---

[15] Li 83.
[16] Meiggs 272.
[17] For an interpretation of the "dramatic landscape" of Greek drama see Roy 98–118.

omnes in eis sedibus, quae erant sub plantano, consedisse dicebat.¹⁸

"Why, Crassus, don't we copy Socrates as he appears in *The Phaedrus* of Plato? For your plane tree, one that casts with its wide-ranging branches as deep a shade as the one Socrates sought after, has brought this to mind, [one] which seems to me to have grown, not so much out of the description of the little stream, but out of the actual speech of Plato, and [has brought to mind] what Socrates did with his well-toughened soles when he threw himself on to the grass, and thus began the discussion that philosophers term divine. Such certainly can be more fairly granted to my feet." To which Crassus replied: "On the contrary, we'll be even more comfortable." Crassus then called for pillows according to Cotta, and they all sat down on those 'seats' which were under the plane tree.

Thus Cicero contents himself with making his speakers feel more comfortable than Socrates was under the branches of the Roman plane tree that he has transplanted from Plato's dialogue into his own. Seneca, on the other hand, uses certain details about the landscape in Epistle Twelve to emphasize a portion of Socrates' thought in the *Phaedrus* (230d).

In the Platonic dialogue, Phaedrus, after locating a shady spot outside the city under a sizable plane tree that stands near the Ilissus River, tells Socrates that Socrates seems like a stranger to the countryside. Phaedrus declares: "You don't leave the city-border, and it seems to me that you do not venture outside the walls at all" (οὕτως ἐκ τοῦ ἄστεος οὔτ' εἰς τὴν ὑπερίαν ἀποδημεῖς, οὔτ' ἔξω τείχους ἔμοιγε δοκεῖς τὸ παράπαν ἐξιέναι, 230d). Socrates defends himself by saying that he is fond of learning. "Country places and trees don't teach me anything" (Συγγίγωσκέ

---

¹⁸Wilkins 5.

μοι, ὦ ἄριστε. φιλομθὴς γάρ εἰμι· τὰ μὲν οὖν χώρια καὶ τὰ δένδρα οὐδέν μ' ἐθέλει διδάσκειν, 230d).

With Socratic irony, however, by the end of the dialogue this proves not to be true. For one of the reversals of the dialogue springs from the unexpected knowledge that the living creatures of the countryside such as nymphs, plane trees, and cicadas have things to teach human beings about the passion of love and the deepest nature of self, and that these creatures are perhaps intimations of the divine after all.

Seneca, in an artful twist, plays out his own Roman rendition of Socrates to Lucilius' Phaedrus. He has adapted the meaning of Socrates' remarks about the countryside for his own purposes. Far from the walls of the city on the grounds of his country villa, the sight of the barren, nodular branches and squalid trunks of the aged plane trees suggest the shape of his own wizened limbs and torso. For the condition of his country villa, of its inhabitants, and of its trees has a lesson to teach Seneca about his own senescence.

In Plato's *Phaedrus*, Socrates sits near the flowing river literally in the dark under the leafy plane tree discussing his thoughts about the immortality of the soul. In Cicero's *De Oratore*, the interlocutors sit on their pillows below an equally umbriferous plane tree. In Seneca's twelfth epistle, however, there is neither deep shade nor flowing water. The leafless plane trees stand in arid soil, and cast no shadow over the human characters. But the plane trees, with or without their leaves, stand as symbols in the literary landscape of each of their respective philosophers. For Plato and Cicero, the trees are verdant and healthy "umbrellas" that shelter the speakers and foster their discussion by making the locale cool and comfortable. In Seneca's case, they do not provide the utility of shade, but instead stand out as stark symbols of something all living creatures have in common, namely their mortality.

Nevertheless, Seneca is not satisfied to conclude at this point, and he spends the final portion of the letter discussing the especial nature of human mortality. For in spite of the evidence of these "anthro-arboreal" similes, no Stoic would maintain that plants and trees had souls, even if they seemed as if they did because they live and die in ways that suggest patterns of human life. They do possess, however, "growth power," (φύσις) and their seeds contain the logos of their structure.[19] Furthermore, vegetable life and even inanimate objects such as the rocks and stones that make up the walls of Seneca's villa have properties which are similar to soul, and which keep them together in a particular configuration while they are alive. This is known as "cohesion" (ἕξις). A human being in turn can cultivate the growth powers of them both. Thus the Stoic in Seneca could say about the rocks "this villa grew up between my hands" (*haec villa inter manus meas crevit*, 12.1.5–6), and about the trees "I had planted those (trees)" (*ego illas posueram*).

Human beings, on the other hand, have the ability to determine their own ends. We are unlike a plane tree, a decrepit villa, an over-ripe pear, or the last of the wine, for we can select the day of our own demise. With the words of Epicurus, Seneca tells Lucilius that suicide is a way to achieve such a self-determined end. He states that "it is wrong to live under constraint, but there is no need to live under constraint . . . let us thank God that no one can be held in life" (*malum est in necessitate vivere sed in necessitate vivere necessitas nulla est . . . agamus deo gratias quod nemo in vita teneri potest*). Thus Seneca has inverted certain elements of the landscape seen in traditional philosophical treatments by Plato and Cicero to underscore his thoughts in Epistle Twelve on human mortality and free-will.

BIBLIOGRAPHY

Alexander, W. B. 1917. "Notes on Seneca's Letters." *CQ* 11:102.
Arnold, E. Vernon. 1911. *Roman Stoicism*. New York. Repr. 1971.
Baldwin, B. 1993. "Seneca, Ep.12.5." *Gymnasium* 100:251–53.
Burnet, J., ed. 1973. *Plato, Platonis Opera*. Oxford.
Gagliardi, Paolo. 1988. "Lingua e stile nell'epistola 12 di Seneca." *Vichiana* 17:163–73.

---

[19] Arnold 188–89.

Habinek, Thomas. 1982. "Seneca's Circles: *Ep.* 12.6–9." *ClAnt* 1:66–69.

Li, Hui-Lin. 1963. *The Origin and Cultivation of Shade and Ornamental Trees.* Philadelphia.

Meiggs, Russell. 1982. *Trees and Timber in the Ancient Mediterranean World.* Oxford.

Reynolds, L. D., ed. 1965. *L. Annaei Senecae ad Lucilium Epistulae Morales.* Oxford.

Robinson, T. M., ed. 1987. *Heraclitus, Fragments.* Toronto.

Ronnick, Michele Valerie. 1996. "Seneca's *Epistle* 12 and Emerson's 'Circles'." *Emerson Society Papers* 7:8.

Roy, Jim. 1996. "The Countryside in Classical Greek Drama and Isolated Farms in Dramatic Landscapes." In *Human Landscape in Classical Antiquity*, edited by Graham Shipley and John Salmon, 98–118. London.

Segal, Charles. 1983. "Boundary Violation and the Landscape of Self in Senecan Tragedy." *A & A* 29:172–87.

Stégen, Guillaume. 1972. "Unus dies par omni est." *Latomus* 31:829–32.

Summers, Walter C. 1910. *Select Letters of Seneca.* London.

Wagenvoort, H. 1916. "*Quaestiunculae Annaeanae.*" *Mnemosyne* 44:150–52.

Wilkins, A. S., ed. 1963. *Cicero, De Oratore, Books I and II.* Oxford.

Elephants, Pompey, and the Reports of Popular Displeasure in 55 BC

Jo-Ann Shelton
University of California, Santa Barbara

In the late summer of 55 BC, residents of Rome celebrated the inauguration of the first permanent stone theater in their city. Construction of the theater had been commissioned by Gnaeus Pompeius Magnus, the powerful military leader and politician who was serving his second consulship in that year. For the inauguration, Pompey had ordered lavish dramatic spectacles in the new theater, and animal killings (*venationes*) in the circus. We have five ancient accounts of these *venationes*, ranging in date from 55 BC to about AD 200. Three of the authors report that the spectators were distressed by the suffering of the elephants who were being killed on the final day of these events. For modern readers, this record of humane sentiment is a comforting note in an otherwise bleak history of Romans abusing animals for entertainment because it seems to indicate that the Roman enthusiasm for watching the infliction of pain and death was, on some occasions at least, tempered by compassion for the victims. However, there are no other reports of spectator sympathy for arena animals on any other occasion. We cannot, therefore, from this one record, draw any conclusions about the frequency of compassionate responses by Roman audiences; but we may be intrigued about why this one display of public distress at Pompey's *venationes* engaged the interest of both contemporary and later writers. In this paper, I want to examine the significance which the events of that day may have had both for those who attended and for those who recorded them. I believe that the ancient reports tell us more about a tradition of anti-Pompeian commentary than about humane sentiment among the Roman public.

Pompey had ordered the production of the *venationes* to enhance the pleasure which he expected the Roman people to experience at the opening of his theater. To finance the construction of the theater, Pompey used the booty from his successful eastern military campaigns, for which he celebrated a dazzling triumph in 61 BC. The idea of building the theater had come to him while he was visiting Mytilene on his return from these campaigns (62 BC), and was delighted to hear his exploits glorified in the theater there. His theater was to be similar in design, but larger and grander (Plu. *Pomp.* 42.4). *Triumphatores* had traditionally used war booty to provide benefits for the inhabitants of Rome and thus enable them to savor the victories achieved by their army. The most common benefits were public entertainments, banquets, and distributions of money or gifts, but *triumphatores* also underwrote the building of religious structures.[1] Pompey's theater was, of course, a structure intended for secular use, but to comply with tradition, he also commissioned the design of a temple dedicated to Venus Victrix, Venus the Victorious, a deity who had helped ensure military victory for the Romans. The temple was built at the top of the theater auditorium, whose rows of seating thus appeared to be grand steps leading up to the temple.[2] According to Tertullian, in order to avoid condemnation Pompey called his building not a theater, but a temple of Venus under which there were tiers of seats for spectacles: *non theatrum, sed Veneris templum nuncupavit, cui subiecimus, inquit, gradus spectaculorum* (*De Spect.* 10.5). Most people, however, knew that the real purpose of the construction was to provide a permanent site for people to assemble for the dramatic spectacles (*ludi scaenici*) which the state produced several times a year as part of its public entertainments.

The construction of the theater had undoubtedly been controversial, at least among the senatorial class. Tacitus reports

---

[1] Veyne (235–36) discusses the benefactions of *triumphatores*.
[2] The design of Pompey's theater-temple is reported by Suetonius, *Claud.* 21, and Aulus Gellius 10.1.7. Pliny (*NH* 8.7.20) identifies Venus Victrix as the deity. For the conjunction of theaters and temples, see Hanson.

that Pompey was censured by his elders (*Ann.* 14.20). Cicero's opposition may perhaps be judged from his silence. Nowhere does he comment on the progress of the construction; by contrast, the basilica project of Aemilius Paullus is among the news of Rome which Cicero reports to Atticus in a letter of 54 BC (*Att.* 4.16.8). The idea of a permanent entertainment site had long troubled members of the senatorial class, so much so that previous attempts to build one had been scuttled. In 154 BC, for example, work had begun on a theater, but in 151 the Senate decided to tear down the project because it was "useless and harmful to public morals."[3] Moral decay was not, however, the only or even the main reason for the senatorial opposition to a permanent theater. A more compelling reason was a fear that gatherings of lower-class people—who were considered irrational and unpredictable—in the emotionally charged atmosphere of entertainments posed a considerable threat to public order. (There was, of course, a connection made between the notion of moral decay and the notion of acting against senatorial control, the latter being perceived as a manifestation of the former.) Nonetheless, state sponsored entertainments had originated early in Rome's history as thanksgiving celebrations offered to the gods in return for their support in military campaigns or in ending epidemics or famines. The religious element of these events made their production obligatory; any lapse might result in the loss of divine protection. Moreover, by the late republican period, public entertainments had become a key ingredient of the Roman political process because politicians recognized that they could use these popular events to influence the opinions of urban crowds.[4] The production of the

---

[3] Livy *Ep.* 48: *inutile et nociturum publicis moribus*; see also Val. Max. 2.4.2. On the theater as a threat to public morality, see also Tac. *Ann.* 14.20.

[4] See Hopkins 14–20. On the considerable direct influence of the urban plebs on the outcome of elections and the assignment of provinces and military commands, and the need for aristocratic politicians therefore to curry favor with the plebs, see Vanderbroeck 163–64; Yakobson (1992) and (1995); and Morstein-Marx. These studies contradict Veyne's assertion (259–61) that popular favor was a *reflection* of political glory

events was one of the duties of the aediles, and funding came from the state treasury. However, aediles with aspirations for higher political office were willing to add a supplement to the production budget from their own private funds in order to provide more extravagant spectacles and thus ingratiate themselves with voters. In a passage lamenting the waste of private money on public entertainments, Cicero writes that it had become a custom in Rome to demand sumptuousness from aediles (*Off.* 2.16.57).[5]

He himself had produced three sets of entertainments (*ludi*) during his aedileship of 69 because he knew that they delighted people (*delectant homines ludi, Mur.* 40). Plutarch reports that Caesar, recognizing the political value of expenditure, spent lavishly on spectacles and banquets during his aedileship of 65 BC and obliterated ("flooded out") his predecessors' reputations for generosity (*Caes.* 5. 8–9; cf. Suet. *Jul.* 10.1). In addition, politically ambitious individuals and families frequently sponsored special (one-time) entertainments entirely with private funds, allegedly to honor past deeds or deceased family members, but in reality to keep their name before the public and win political support for future campaigns.[6] In 65 BC, for example, Caesar produced a very expensive gladiatorial show to commemorate his father, who had been dead twenty years (Dio 37.8.1). The urban masses, for their part, used their presence at spectacles as an opportunity to demonstrate loudly and clearly their opinions about the politicians and their policies. In the rigidly stratified society of ancient Rome, where a small number of people possessed most of the wealth and power, opportunities for free expression by the lower classes were

rather than a means to attain it, and that the euergetism of the Roman oligarchy was based primarily on a desire "to be loved by the plebs."

[5] In *Pro Milone* 35, Cicero states that Milo used up three patrimonies to charm the masses with spectacles. Livy (7.2.13), comparing the humble origins of *ludi scaenici* to the opulent productions of his own time, claims that in his day even wealthy kingdoms could scarcely support the "insanity."

[6] Vanderbroeck (18–19) maintains that, because social status was not hereditary, members of the Roman upper class constantly had "to demonstrate their serviceability to the *res publica.*"

rare. However, the relaxed atmosphere of the spectacles, and perhaps the safety which the lower classes felt in their assembled numbers, created situations where the crowd displayed its approval or disapproval with no apparent restraint. The upper class, in turn, tolerated these activities as legitimate expressions of popular will. Thus the entertainment sites served important functions for both the upper and lower classes, but functions which were in a sense contradictory because the rulers, in order to gain and retain control of the state, needed to yield control, albeit temporarily, to the masses. Popular approbation and condemnation were carefully noted by upper class politicians. In his discussion of how popular expression at public spectacles in Rome was valued as the "verdict" of the entire nation, Bell writes: "When the crowd shouted, its noise was usually read without nuance as a single unanimous force."[7]

In *Ad Atticum* 2.19 (59 BC), Cicero comments that popular opinion (*populi sensus*) about Pompey could best be discerned at a theater and at spectacles.[8] He then gives two examples. At a gladiatorial show, Pompey and his allies were insulted with hisses. And at a theatrical show, the audience asked an actor to repeat again and again the line *nostra miseria tu es magnus*, "to our misfortune, you are great." (*Magnus*, "great," was understood as a pun on Pompey's cognomen.) Then to the applause of the entire audience, the actor continued with this line: *eandem virtutem istam veniet tempus cum graviter gemes*, "a time will come when you will sorely lament this very strength of yours." In *Pro Sestio* 55–59, Cicero recounts a situation at a theater in 57 BC. The Senate had just passed a resolution to recall him from exile and, according to Cicero, the people were delighted. When the senators appeared soon afterward in the theater, they were greeted with applause by the spectators. But when Cicero's arch enemy Clodius arrived, the people lashed out at him with curses and rude gestures. The activity on stage was often less important than the activity in the seating

[7]Bell 21.
[8]Cf. *Sest.* 50 (106): *Etenim tribus locis significari maxime de re publica populi romani iudicium ac voluntas potest: contione, comitiis ludorum gladiatorumque consessu.*

area. Morstein-Marx, discussing the process of canvassing for votes, writes that the "supplication" of the populace "can usefully be regarded as a performance before the audience of the Roman People, which observed and judged its aspiring leaders go through their parts and delivered its verdict at the *comitia*."[9] At *ludi*, politicians faced an audience eager to announce its verdict immediately and vociferously, and just as eager to observe how the politicians would respond, that is, how they would "act." In *In Pisonem* 65, which Cicero delivered shortly before the inauguration of Pompey's theater, he taunts Piso.

> Fac huius odii tanti ac tam universi periculum—si audes. Instant post hominum memoriam apparatissimi magnificentissimique ludi, quales non modo numquam fuerunt, sed ne quo modo fieri quidem posthac possint possum ullo pacto suspicari. Da te populo. Committe ludis. Sibilum metuis? . . . Ne acclametur times?

> Take this test of the great and universal hatred against you—if you dare. The most lavish and magnificent games in the memory of mankind are about to take place, games the likes of which not only have never before taken place, but also I cannot at all believe can ever in the future take place. Entrust yourself to the people. Venture into the games. Are you afraid of hisses? . . . Do you fear that you will not be applauded?

What is difficult for us to ascertain now is how spontaneous the crowd's responses were, that is, to what extent the opinions of the lower class were actually shaped by the upper class, and to what degree politicians manipulated the crowds to produce a favorable response for themselves, or an unfavorable one for their opponents. In *Pro Sestio* 54 (115), Cicero admits that paid agitators were

---

[9]Morstein-Marx (forthcoming).

sometimes planted in the audience to stir up the spectators.[10] During the political instability of the late republican period, the custom of free expression at entertainment sites posed two threats to the senatorial class. On the one hand, it seemed to confer too much power on the volatile lower classes, who might slip out of control; on the other hand, it created opportunities for unscrupulous politicians to manipulate the collective behavior of the audience for their own purposes. In either case, the competition for popular favor endangered traditional political institutions.

Pompey's plan for a permanent theater appears to have been a bid for the popular favor which he thought would elevate him above his senatorial colleagues and secure for him enduring supreme power in the Roman state. Consider his position at this time.[11] He had earned a reputation as Rome's most capable military leader. His quest for *gloria* had begun at an early age. In 81 BC, when he was only twenty-five years old and had never held a magistracy, he was granted an extraordinary *imperium* to eradicate Marian forces in Africa (Plut. *Pomp.* 11.1). He completed this assignment so successfully that his jubilant troops hailed him as Magnus ("Great"), an epithet which he continued to use as a cognomen (Plut. *Pomp.* 13.5). Even more remarkably, he was awarded a triumph, becoming the first *eques* to enjoy the privilege (Plut. *Pomp.* 14; Cic. *Man.* 61). Plutarch notes that Pompey's youth and his non-senatorial status contributed greatly to his popularity

---

[10]Cicero's claim that the responses the agitators provoked were weak and easily distinguished from honest ones can be viewed with some skepticism because his purpose in this passage is to establish that the responses of the audience were spontaneous. Plutarch (*Pomp.* 48.7) offers a vivid description of Clodius and his chorus of anti-Pompeians at Milo's trial in 56 BC. Vanderbroeck (61–62 and 143–44) discusses claqueurs at spectacles, trials and assemblies.

[11]Pompey's career is examined by van Ooteghem; Gelzer; Rawson; Gruen; Leach; Seager; Greenhalgh (1980) and (1981). The portrait which emerges from these studies is one of irreconcilable features, of a man who wanted to work within the system, but yet to dominate it, to be accepted by his senatorial colleagues, but yet to be preeminent, to support the constitution, but yet to have it bent again and again to allow him extraordinary power.

among the masses (Plut. *Pomp.* 14.6). He celebrated his second triumph in 71, for his victories in Spain against Sertorius (Plut. *Pomp.* 22.1). As Gruen notes, "the stunning rise to power and authority of Pompey the Great constituted the single most important political fact of the 60s."[12] After his consulship in 70 BC, with Crassus as his colleague, he was again granted two extraordinary *imperia*, the first in 67 BC (*lex Gabinia*), against Mediterranean pirates (Plut. *Pomp.* 25 and 26; Cic. *Man.* 44 ; Dio 36.23–37). "An immediate consequence of Pompey's appointment was a substantial fall in grain prices, to the unrestrained joy of the populace."[13] The second *imperium*, in 66 BC (*lex Manilia*), was against Mithridates, king of Pontus in Asia Minor (Plut. *Pomp.* 30; Cic. *Man.* 5 and 70; Dio 36.43 and 44). Once again Pompey proved that he was a brilliant general and, in his settlement of the eastern territories, a skillful strategist. His third triumph, celebrated in 61 BC, was an extravagant affair. "The event was a consummate piece of propaganda, meticulously stage-managed to record indelibly in the imaginations of the Roman audience an image of Pompey's power and majesty."[14] So numerous were Pompey's achievements that, even though the triumph occupied two days, there was still not time to exhibit displays of all of them. Pompey boasted that he had extended the boundaries of the Roman empire to the ends of the earth, had substantially increased the tax revenues coming into Rome from its imperial territories, and was now also bringing in an enormous amount of booty (Diod. 40.4.1; Plut. *Pomp.* 45.3). Plutarch states that this event was so unusual because Pompey was celebrating his third triumph over a third continent; the first honored his victory in Africa, the second, Europe (Spain), and now the third, Asia (Minor), so that he seemed to have brought the whole world into his three triumphs (Plut. *Pomp.* 45). Pompey was only about forty-five years old at this time and he reminded some of

---

[12]Gruen 268.
[13]*Ibid.*, 436.
[14]Beacham 157. Primary sources for the triumph are Plutarch, *Pomp.* 45; Vell. Pat. 2.40.3 and 5; Flor. 2.13.9.

Alexander the Great. Writing about 150 years after the event and therefore with the wisdom of hindsight, Plutarch declares:

ὡς ὠνητό γ' ἂν ἐνταῦθα τοῦ βίου παυσάμενος, ἄχρι οὗ τὴν Ἀλεξάνδρου τύχην ἔσχεν· ὁ δὲ ἐπέκεινα χρόνος αὐτῷ τὰς μὲν εὐτυχίας ἤνεγκεν ἐπιφθόνους, ἀνηκέστους δὲ τὰς δυστυχίας.

How Pompey would have benefited if his life had ended at this point when he enjoyed the good fortune of Alexander. For the time which followed brought him only successes that made him liable to envy, and failures that could not be remedied. (*Pomp.* 46.1)

Whether it was envy or a fear of Pompey's ambition which motivated his fellow senators, they blocked several of his projects, and he found that the support he had carefully assembled was eroding. Therefore in 60 BC he formed a political alliance with Caesar and Crassus and, with their combined resources, they were able to force their will upon the state. The cost of their strong-arm tactics was, however, unpopularity with both the senatorial and lower classes. Reference has been made above to the occasion in 59 when audiences at theatrical and gladiatorial spectacles expressed their disapproval (*Att.* 2.19.2–3).[15] In another letter to Atticus (2.21), written about the same time, Cicero states:

Cum diu occulte suspirasset, postea iam gemere, ad extremum vero loqui omnes et clamare coeperunt. Itaque

---

[15]Seager (94–95) contends that Pompey was the prime target of popular criticism because the public saw him "as the senior partner and chief beneficiary of the coalition, and so assigned the greatest responsibility to him. But it also reflects the opposition's knowledge that of the three Pompeius was by temperament by far the most concerned about public opinion."

ille amicus noster insolens infamiae, semper in laude versatus, circumfluens gloria, deformatus corpore, fractus animo, quo se conferat, nescit.

Although the common people had sighed for a long time in secret, now at last they all began to groan, and finally to speak out and to shout. Therefore that friend of ours, Pompey, unaccustomed to unpopularity, always surrounded by praise, overflowing with glory, now disfigured in body and broken in spirit, does not know what to do with himself.

In the years between 60 and 55, Pompey, the man whom Sallust described as "moderate about all other things except unrestricted power" (*modestus ad alia omnia nisi dominationem*, H. 2.17 in *OCT*), suffered several humiliating defeats in the courts, assemblies and Senate house.[16] Nonetheless in 57 BC he was granted (despite Clodius' vigorous opposition) a five-year appointment to oversee the vital grain supply, at a time when food shortages had provoked a riot in a theater and attacks on the Senate (Cic. *Att.* 4.1.6, *Dom.* 5–14; Dio 39.9.2). Pompey engaged in his commission so zealously that he filled the markets with an abundance of grain, a feat which surely garnered the approval of the fickle urban populace (Plut. *Pomp.* 49.4, 50. 1 and 2). The *triumviri* renewed their alliance in 56 and agreed to secure the election of Pompey and Crassus as consuls for 55. To accomplish this goal, they used obstruction and violence, first to delay the date of the election and then to intimidate opposing candidates and hostile voters (Plut. *Pomp.* 52. 1 and 2, *Crass.* 15, *Cat.* 41; Dio 39.31). Once elected, Pompey and Crassus pushed through legislation granting themselves extraordinary provincial commands for a five year period, Crassus in Syria, Pompey in the two Spains and Africa (*lex Trebonia*: Plut. *Pomp.* 52.3, *Cat.* 43, *Caes.* 28; Dio 39.33–36, and Vell. Pat. 2.48.1, mention only the

---

[16]Gruen (111) itemizes Pompey's long "string of frustrations."

Spains). Their apparent contempt for traditional institutions angered and frightened many people, some of whom angrily pelted statues of Pompey after a heated Senate debate (Plut. *Cat.* 43). While Crassus made preparations to travel to Syria, Pompey assigned his provinces to legates so that he could remain closely involved in political developments in Rome. Their triumvirate colleague, Caesar, was still in Gaul, accumulating military glory and booty; his successes threatened to overshadow Pompey's reputation.[17] It is against the background of these events that we must view Pompey's construction of a permanent entertainment venue.

In addition to the theater and temple, the building complex included a meeting place for the Senate, with a highly visible statue of Pompey (at the foot of which Caesar was assassinated in 44: Plut. *Caes.* 66; Cic. *Div.* 2.9.23), and a large park which was open to the public and adorned with a beautiful colonnade (Ov. *Ars* 1.67, 3.387; Prop. 2.32.11–12, 4.8.75) and a display of statues and paintings (Plin. *NH* 35.59, 114, 126, 132).[18] Beacham aptly comments that Pompey had built for himself a "continuous triumph."[19] The temple of Venus Victrix, the statue of Pompey in the assembly room, and the displays in the park were perpetual reminders of his outstanding contributions to the Roman state. However, Pompey wanted more than esteem for his past exploits in war. He also wanted to convert his military glory into unassailable political authority by securing durable support from the masses.[20] Greenhalgh notes that Pompey had built "a palace of entertainment

---

[17]Plut. *Pomp.* 50. Wiseman (12) discusses the competition at Rome for *gloria*, which could be had only at the expense of others, and therefore drew *invidia*. He uses Pompey as an example of "that competitive instinct, that urge to be first and greatest" (7). See also Hopkins (107–16) on competition in Roman political life.

[18]Tacitus (*Ann.* 13.54.3) writes that, in Nero's time, visitors to Rome were taken to Pompey's theater to be shown the greatness of Rome.

[19]Beacham 158.

[20]Pompey was hoping for the impossible. Because it was so bribed by aristocratic munificence, "the urban plebs (or parts of it) . . . was notoriously faithless" (Yakobson [1992] 51).

which would associate his name permanently with pleasure and detract from the glory of whoever happened to put on a show there."[21]

His theater was designed to gather the Roman people together for pleasurable activities during which they would happily express their gratitude and even love for him.[22] The inauguration in 55 was particularly important to Pompey's political efforts, and he therefore spared no expense for the entertainments. Consider Cicero's description of the preparations in the passage from *In Pisonem* quoted above (also *Off.* 2.16.57; and Asc. 1). The plays were selected and staged so as to remind the spectators of Pompey's military successes. In the *Clytemnestra*, for example, a string of 600 mules crossed the stage carrying the booty which the dramatic character Agamemnon had seized at Troy (Cic. *Fam.* 7.1.2).[23] Undoubtedly the Roman audience was prompted to recall Pompey's own magnificent triumphal procession of 61, and his willingness to use his war spoils to build the very theater in which they were now enjoying themselves. The crowd's applause was the satisfying response he had counted on. Of course, he expected this exhilarating situation to be repeated many times, over many years, but later writers describe this moment as a high point of his life, never again matched. Lucan, for example, records the story that on the eve of the fateful battle of Pharsalus (48 BC), Pompey dreamed of his theater:

---

[21]Greenhalgh (1980) 175.

[22]Vanderbroeck (163) remarks: "The foremost reason for a politician to seek support among the lower citizenry was that it was the only *legitimate* alternative to work his will if agreement among the elite proved impossible." The importance which Pompey placed on displays of approbation in his theater would seem to argue against Vanderbroeck's opinion that collective behavior in the theater and the circus tended to be anti-*popularis* (77–80, 143–44).

[23]Six years later, shortly before the battle of Pharsalus, L. Domitius Ahenobarbus and many others, complaining that Pompey wanted the power of a monarch, derisively called him Agamemnon and king of kings (Plut. *Pomp.* 67.3, *Caes.* 41.2; App. *BC* 2.67).

Nam Pompeiani visus sibi sede theatri
innumeram effigiem Romanae cernere plebis
attollique suum laetis ad sidera nomen
vocibus et plausu cuneos certare sonantes.

(7.7–12)[24]

He dreamed that he was seated at his own theater, and
saw a countless throng of Roman people, and heard his
name being raised to the stars by their happy voices,
and the resounding tiers competing in applause.

The story is also recorded by Plutarch, who adds that Pompey dreamed that he was decorating the temple of Venus Victrix with war booty. Plutarch then remarks that the dream could be interpreted as a bad omen because Caesar was a descendant of Venus (*Pomp.* 68.2, also *Caes.* 42.1; and App. *BC* 2.68).[25] In the summer of 55 BC, however, with the crowd's applause ringing in his ears and providing what Bell terms "the validating power of popular judgement"[26] Pompey must have believed that his plan was successful.

Among the inaugural events was an exhibition of animal killings (*venationes*), held in the circus and designed to produce an even more enthusiastic show of crowd support.[27] The Circus Maximus held perhaps ten times more spectators than the new

---

[24]At 1.131–133, Lucan characterizes Pompey thus: *Famaeque petitor / multa dare in vulgus, totus popularibus auris / impelli, plausuque sui gaudere theatri.*

[25]"Venus Victrix" was the war cry of Caesar's troops at Pharsalus; Pompey's war cry was "Invincible Hercules" (App. *BC* 2.76). Just before the battle of Pharsalus, Caesar vowed a temple to his ancestor, Venus (App. *BC* 2.102). Vanderbroeck (33) astutely observes that, on the eve of this decisive battle, whose victor would emerge as the ruler of Rome, Pompey dreamed not that he was a monarch, but that he had *dignitas* within Roman society.

[26]Bell 18.

[27]Plass (43) observes that "spectators were as important as the show itself, since their attendance in great numbers at a public event *was* the show in a political and social sense."

theater,[28] and *venationes* excited crowds even more than stage entertainments (*ludi scaenici*). The word *venatio* means "hunt," but several different types of events were included in the category of entertainment *venationes*: the display of performing animals, animals killing other animals, and animals being killed by people.[29] Like all entertainments in which animals are victimized, disabled and destroyed by humans, *venationes* appealed because they proved that humans could indeed gain control over the savage and menacing elements of their environment. Although we have no written record of *venationes* before 186 BC, the torture and killing of animals as a public spectacle had a long history in Rome.[30] Ville maintains that urban *venationes* developed in the third century BC and were directly linked to Rome's experiences with Carthage, with hunting practices in north Africa and with the importation of African animals to Italy.[31] However, they probably had an older, indigenous, and agricultural beginning, although the development of some of the events was undoubtedly influenced by the practices of real hunts. In rural areas, people killed animals which threatened their survival by preying on livestock or consuming food plants. And several times a year, the agricultural community gathered together to re-enact and celebrate its divinely-assisted efforts to eradicate species which steal human food. For example, rabbits were killed every year at the state-sponsored spectacles (*ludi*) held in April to honor the goddess Flora, and at the annual festival of Ceres, also in April, foxes were set on fire (Ov. *Fast.* 4.681–682,

---

[28]Pliny (*NH* 36.115) reports that the theater held 40,000 people, but a figure of less than 20,000 is more probable (Beacham 160). The Circus Maximus held at least 250,000 spectators.

[29]Animals were also used to kill humans; such events (which the Romans also found entertaining) were considered executions of criminals (*damnationes ad bestias*), not *venationes*. See Coleman (1990).

[30]Livy (39.22.2) first uses the word *venationes* to define a spectacle when reporting a slaughter of lions and leopards in 186 BC, but he does not state that this was the first occurrence of such spectacles.

[31]Ville 51–56. On the history of *venationes*, see also Auguet (81–84); Hopkins (11–12); Wiedemann (55–67). D. G. Kyle, *Spectacles of Death in Ancient Rome*, London and New York, 1998, did not reach me in time to be used in this paper.

5.371–372; Mart. 8.67). In urban areas, very few people had personal experience with hunting or the damage to their food supply caused by species like rabbits and foxes, but the *venationes* in arenas allowed them to participate as spectators in the process of pest control, and without risk of injury. The symbolic dimensions of the publicly-witnessed destruction of pest species made the events appealing. The *venationes* provided reassurance that the orderly and rational civilization which the Romans had created could confront a hostile, chaotic, irrational, and therefore dangerous Nature, and subdue it.[32] There were no moral constraints about tormenting and causing pain to the animals because they were "enemies." In fact, their suffering was the penalty they paid for threatening humans (even as human criminals were executed in arenas by very painful methods, such as being attacked by animals). As the Romans expanded their imperial territory during the republican period, they imported to Italy animals from the most remote regions of their empire, and beyond. Now the slaughter of exotic and fierce animals, while still symbolizing human domination over Nature, also signified Roman military and political control over the rest of the world. The capture and long distance transport of these animals entailed enormous expense, considerable danger and careful planning. Thus the apparent ease with which the Romans brought the animals to their city, and the frequency with which they then destroyed them, offered proof that their state was powerful and prosperous, and could afford the costs of bringing pleasure to the urban masses, a pleasure which was in some sense a reward for their superiority to the rest of the world.[33] In addition,

---

[32]Beagon (153–56) contends that Pliny and many of his fellow Romans believed that Nature is a theater that provides spectacles for mankind. Coleman (1996, 68), discussing spectacles where one (non-human) species killed another, observes that the Romans "set up Nature to stage a self-destructing spectacle of combat: the ultimate manifestation of the domination of empire."

[33]Plass (18), writing about various violent spectacles at Rome, states that "the original simple expenditure of physical energy was transposed into conspicuous consumption of public resources measured by both blood and money and carrying the symbolic meaning which frequently

the animals were viewed as representatives of the regions from which they had been imported, and the slaughter of lions from Africa, for example, dramatically symbolized the triumph of the Roman military in bloody battles with fierce, but ultimately inferior human Africans. *Venationes* thus allowed spectators to participate in the process of imposing Roman justice on a barbarian world. The gathering together of the Roman people was an important element of these spectacles because it reaffirmed their existence as a community, united by their responsibility to impose order on the rest of the world and by their right to enjoy the success of their state's military expansion and ventures. The gratification of the popular desire to see the victimization of exotic species was one method for men of wealth and political ambition to advance their careers. Because *venationes* were so expensive and troublesome to produce, they offered proof to voters that the producer (*editor*) was generous, attentive to popular wishes, had the important military and political connections needed to obtain animals from foreign lands, and was thus worthy of election to a position of great power and prestige. In the late republican period, competition was intense to eclipse the *venationes* produced by one's political rivals and predecessors. One familiar story is that of Caelius' pestering of Cicero, then governor of Cilicia (51–50 BC), in order to obtain leopards from that province to display during his year as aedile (Cic. *Att.* 6.1.21, and 2.11, and *Fam.* 8.2.2, 8.4.5, 8.6.5, 8.8.10, and 8.9.3).

To celebrate the inauguration of his theater, Pompey arranged for the exhibition of several hundred lions (Plut. *Pomp.* 52.4; Plin. *NH* 8.20.53) and leopards (Plin. *NH* 8.24.64), baboons and a rare lynx (Plin. *NH* 8.28.70), and, perhaps for the first time in the circus, a rhinoceros (Plin. *NH* 8.29.71).[34] But the grand finale was the

---

accompanies consumption."

[34]In 46 BC, Caesar exhibited a giraffe for the first time. Coleman (1996, 62) discusses the exhibition of exotic animals as a demonstration of one's control over foreign territory and one's possession of powerful foreign allies. "Pompey's rhinoceros made a statement about his power base; and when Caesar capped it with his giraffe, he may have been

slaughter of about twenty elephants. Elephants were a crowd-pleaser for several reasons. As the largest land mammal, they were—and still are—an impressive sight. In addition, they had been used as war machines by Rome's enemies, and the humiliation of elephants could be interpreted as the humiliation of human opponents. Roman soldiers first encountered elephants during Pyrrhus's invasion of Italy (Flor. 1.13.8).[35] In 275 BC, Manius Curius Dentatus gave inhabitants of Rome their first view of elephants when he displayed in his triumph some which he had captured from Pyrrhus (Plin. *NH* 8.6.16). In 251 BC, during the First Punic War, L. Caecilius Metellus brought back to Rome Carthaginian elephants captured in Sicily. Pliny reports that they were displayed in his triumphal procession and then either prodded through the Circus "in order to increase the contempt for them" (*ut contemptus eorum incresceret*) or killed with javelins (*NH* 7.43.139; 8.6.17). Thereafter, Metellus' descendants adopted the elephant as a family emblem and placed representations on coins which they minted.[36] Elephants were also prominently displayed on Carthaginian coins as a symbol of that city's military strength.[37] Some might argue that they symbolized Carthaginian cruelty because at the end of the war, Hamilcar used elephants to trample to death rebellious mercenaries (Polyb. 1.82.2). In the Second Punic War, Hannibal used war elephants in Italy,[38] but, in 202 BC, the Carthaginians and their elephants were defeated on African soil by P. Cornelius Scipio, who then transported some of the elephants to

---

assisted by Cleopatra." (Dio 43.23.1, records the appearance of a giraffe.) See also Jennison (30, 51–59).

[35]Florus, in the second century AD, writes that the Romans would have won a battle at Heraclea in 280 BC, but Pyrrhus' elephants charged and frightened the Roman horses, and "turned the battle into a spectacle" (*converso in spectaculum bello*). His comment provides evidence of how, for Romans of the imperial period, staged battles were more real than actual battles.

[36]For the numismatic evidence, see Scullard 274 n.90; also Toynbee 53.

[37]Scullard 170–73 and 275 n.92.

[38]Livy 23.13.7; for numismatic evidence, see Toynbee 36.

Rome for his triumph (Zonar. 9.14). "This must have been a moment of tremendous feeling for the Romans: Hannibal, who had defied them for so long and had come so near to overwhelming them, was at last humbled, and the elephants in the procession must have reminded them that the war had been completed in Africa and by the man who came to be called Africanus."[39]

During the second century BC, the Romans themselves used elephants in battle, and in 167 BC, L. Aemilius Paullus, after his victory against Perseus at Pydna, had army deserters trampled to death by elephants (Val. Max. 2.7.14). About this time, the Senate voted a resolution forbidding the importation of African animals into Rome, perhaps because of the inherent dangers, but the resolution was repealed, or at least amended, when a tribune appealed to the popular assembly to allow African animals for use in the circus (Plin. *NH* 8.24.64).[40] The action of the assembly may be an indication of how popular *venationes* were with the urban masses. And the display of elephants continued to be an attraction in the first century BC. Pliny, for example, reports that elephants fought in the circus in 99 and 79 BC; on the latter occasion at least, the audience was treated to the novelty of matches in which elephants fought bulls.[41]

Pompey, like those famous generals who had preceded him in victories over African nations, capitalized on the symbolic significance of elephants. In 81 BC, after his conquest over the Marians[42] and their African allies, Pompey spent several days

---

[39]Scullard 170.

[40]Ville 54–55 discusses the problems of assigning a date to this legislation.

[41]Plin. *NH* 8.7.19; Ville (89) addresses the confusion about the meaning of *pugnasse* in Pliny's accounts here and in 8.6.17 (mentioned above).

[42]The Marians were led by Cn. Domitius Ahenobarbus, descendant (perhaps grandson) of Cn. Domitius Ahenobarbus who in 121 BC used elephants in his successful battles against Gallic tribes and then, to celebrate this victory, rode through the province on an elephant (Suet. *Nero* 2; Flor. 1.37). The younger Cn. Domitius may be the brother of the L. Domitius who called Pompey "Agamemnon"; see above n.23; and, on the family connections, Seager 10 n.25.

hunting lions and elephants because, he declared, the wild animals of Africa must not be left without experiencing the strength and courage of the Romans (Plut. *Pomp.* 12.5). He also shipped to Rome some of the elephants he had captured from the African kings and planned to enter the city triumphantly in a chariot drawn by four elephants, perhaps to prompt a comparison between himself (he was now only twenty-five years old) and Alexander the Great.[43] His plan was thwarted by the narrowness of the city gates and he was forced to use horses (Plin. *NH* 8.2.4; Plut. *Pomp.* 14.4). Twenty-five years later, during his second consulship, Pompey coerced legislation which assigned to him the provinces of Africa and the two Spains, and he inaugurated his theater complex with lavish *venationes*. He undoubtedly hoped that the elephant killings which he commissioned for the circus would remind the Roman populace of his past glorious achievements in Africa and presage similar successes for the future. The slaughter of elephants was intended to validate Pompey's claim to supreme authority and to demonstrate that, with him as their leader, Romans could feel confident in their domination of both the physical and political worlds.

That must certainly have been Pompey's intention: to amuse the spectators and to bring them the pleasure which comes from knowing that you are a superior race and will, with excellent leadership, remain superior. Elephants possessed several attributes which made them ideal representatives of the victims of Roman ascendancy. They were, like many of the people the Romans had subjugated, strange-looking. In addition, their enormous size and strength conveyed an impression of almost invincible power—"almost," because the Romans had, of course, vanquished military forces, particularly those of Hannibal and other Africans,

---

[43]Toynbee (39) describes a coin from Cyrene depicting Alexander in a chariot drawn by four elephants, an allusion to his return from India; he also discusses the Hellenistic practice of associating Dionysus and Alexander with elephant-drawn chariots (see also Plin. *NH* 8.2.4), and contends that Pompey's plan was probably a "conscious imitation of the Hellenistic practice." Rawson (28) characterizes Pompey's behavior as "willful and hubristic conduct."

which employed elephants. The harnessing of an elephant to a chariot both demonstrated a real subjugation of the natural world and also symbolized the subjugation of people living in territories inhabited by elephants. Elephants displayed in arena combats represented the most intimidating of Rome's human opponents, and yet, because elephants are bulky and have large floppy ears, long flexible trunks, and a lumbering gait, they can appear comical. What a perfect combination of qualities for the amusement and edification of the Roman mob—a situation in which the *editor* not only symbolically recreates the harrowing battles against Rome's most formidable enemies, but also presents an opponent which can be so easily ridiculed.[44] Thus a spectacle which begins as a terrifying re-enactment of war ends as a farce, and the audience is reassured that an apparently formidable enemy was, in the end, not just inferior, but absurdly inferior.

Our earliest report on Pompey's *venationes* is a skillfully-crafted eye-witness account by Cicero, who was describing the inauguration events in a letter to Marcus Marius (*Fam.* 7.1), who had been unable to travel to Rome for the festivities, probably because of illness. Cicero wrote to console him on missing events which he (Cicero) had earlier predicted would be "the most lavish and magnificent games in the memory of mankind" (*Pis.* 65, cited above).[45] To mitigate Marius's disappointment, Cicero tells him that he was, in fact, fortunate to have been absent because the entertainments were tedious. Wiedemann rightly reminds us that Cicero's purpose in writing the letter is consolation; however this is not the only reason why the Roman politician "marshals every possible argument to suggest that the games were a failure."[46] Cicero writes of the *ludi scaenici* that they were very elaborate (*apparatissimi*), but not to Marius's tastes (*non tui stomachi*). And he even suggests that the emphasis on grand spectacle ruined any

---

[44]Metellus' elephants, in a passage cited above, were prodded to increase the audience's contempt for them.

[45]In the penultimate sentence of the letter, Cicero reminds Marius that he had requested a letter describing Pompey's spectacles.

[46]Wiedemann 140.

possibility of true amusement: *apparatus spectatio tollebat omnem hilaritatem*. To reinforce his point that extravagance can actually detract from the enjoyment of men with good taste, he asks: *Quid enim delectationis habent sexcenti muli in* Clytaemnestra? *aut in* Equo Troiano *craterarum tria milia*? "What pleasure is there in 600 mules in the *Clytemnestra*, or in 3000 wine bowls in the *Trojan Horse*?" He then modifies his point by saying that such excesses won the admiration of the crowd (*popularem admirationem*), although they would have given no pleasure (*delectatio)* to Marius.[47] The underlying message is that Pompey successfully catered only to the tastes of the rabble, which could be won over by lavish spectacles.[48] Of course, that was precisely the group which Pompey was hoping to win over.

After a brief dismissive mention of some athletic competitions, Cicero describes the *venationes* in the same scornful tone.

> Reliquae sunt venationes binae per dies quinque, magnificae, nemo negat; sed quae potest homini esse polito delectatio, cum aut homo imbellicus a valentissima bestia laniatur aut praeclara bestia venabulo transverberatur? Quae tamen, si videnda sunt, saepe vidisti; neque nos, qui haec spectamus, quicquam novi vidimus. Extremus elephantorum dies fuit. In quo admiratio magna vulgi atque turbae, delectatio nulla exstitit; quin etiam misericordia quaedam consecutast atque opinio eius modi, esse quandam illi beluae cum genere humano societatem.

---

[47] It is worth noting that the word *delectatio* appears seven times in this letter, a fact which persuades me that the main theme of the letter is "pleasure." Cicero begins it by consoling Marius for having been absent during Pompey's entertainments (pleasure lost), and then ends it by consoling himself (*me consolor*) with the thought of Marius' future visit (pleasure anticipated). The central portion of the letter dwells on different definitions of pleasure and on Pompey's failure to provide the populace with pleasure.

[48] There is a similar message in *Off.* 2.16. 56 and 57.

The last events to report are the animal spectacles, two a day for five days. They were magnificent. No one denies that. But what pleasure can there be for a man of refined tastes when either a feeble human being is mangled by a very strong animal, or a beautiful animal is pierced by a spear? In any case, even if these things are worth seeing, you've seen them many times. I, who was among the spectators, saw nothing new. The final day was the day of the elephants. On that day, the mob and crowd experienced great wonder, but no pleasure. In fact, a certain compassion arose, and an opinion of this sort, that this huge animal has a certain kinship with the human race.

Cicero's grudging admission that the *venationes* were *magnificae* (a statement which corresponds to the earlier use of *apparatissimi*) tells us that the *venationes*, like the *ludi scaenici*, were produced on a grand scale, and that Pompey seemed, by the usual criteria, to have successfully performed the role of generous *editor*. But Cicero immediately undercuts this compliment by commenting that a man of refined tastes (*homini polito*) could not find pleasure (*delectatio*) in the mutilation of either a man or a beast. Again a comment in this section seems to correspond to an earlier phrase (*non tui stomachi*). Yet Cicero offers a different explanation for why the *venationes*, as opposed to the *ludi scaenici*, were distasteful to men of refinement like himself and Marius. Although Cicero did not find *ludi scaenici* generally to be distasteful, he judged those commissioned for Pompey's celebration to be of a mediocre quality which even an abundance of "special effects" could not mask. In his comment about *venationes*, however, he suggests that they were always and generally distasteful because witnessing physical injury, however lavish the production, does not bring pleasure to a man like himself. He also mentions that the animal spectacles offered nothing new, a serious flaw certainly in a period when politicians were eager to satisfy audience demands for novel stimulations. Cicero next describes the crowd's response to the slaughter of elephants: there was *admiratio*, but not *delectatio*. The conjunction of the words *admiratio* and *delectatio* occurs also in the description of the *ludi scaenici*, but there Cicero draws a contrast between the undiscriminating admiration of the crowd and the lack of pleasure for men like Marius and himself. Here he implies that even the crowd felt no pleasure, despite its admiration for the scale of the event. It is interesting to note how Cicero both focuses and expands his disparagement of Pompey's *venationes*. Whereas he previously remarked that the hypothetical mutilation of any beast (general category) was not pleasing to refined men (small number), he now observes that the actual mutilation of elephants (specific category) did not please the common crowd (large number). For Cicero, the real novelty during the many days of entertainment, the event most worth reporting, was the audience's anomalous response to the killing of the elephants. The role expected of spectators was: 1) to enjoy (and express gratitude to the *editor* for) the torment and slaughter of animals which they perceived i) as dangerous and hostile both in the wild (nature) and in battle (culture), and ii) as symbols of Rome's enemies; and 2) to participate as witnesses to a recreation of Pompey's victories in Africa. As Coleman notes, in her discussion of events in which humans were executed, spectators were expected to identify with those who were implementing justice, rather than with those criminals being dispatched. If the sympathies of the audience were transferred to the "objects" being displayed, the *editor* would find himself alienated.[49] For Pompey to achieve his goal of bringing pleasure to the populace, the spectators had either to objectify or to demonize the elephants. But an extraordinary situation occurred. As Cicero relates, there arose among the spectators a certain compassion (*misericordia*). Although Cicero makes no explicit comment that the widely-anticipated *venationes* were a failure, the reader's final impression of this report must be that they failed. In four days of expensive

---

[49] Coleman (1990) 58. She cites Pompey's elephants as evidence for her statements.

combats, Pompey offered nothing new. On the fifth and final day, he provided grand spectacle, but not pleasure. In fact, in a most startling and embarrassing inversion of his design, he produced the opposite of pleasure. For the spectators, the elephant slaughter provoked pity, and thus discomfort and dis-pleasure. We might ask what consolation Marius would derive most from this account: the satisfaction of having missed tedious spectacles, or the satisfaction of knowing that Pompey had failed, at least partially, to win the adoration of the crowd?

One other element of Cicero's report deserves scrutiny: his explanation for the discomfort of the audience. He tells us that the spectators pitied the elephants and held the opinion that a certain closeness or kinship (*societas*) existed between humans and elephants. For a few moments in the Roman circus, the crowd denied the rigid distinction between humans and animals, a construction which is so critical for human justifications of our exploitation of other animals. In those brief moments when the spectators recognized that the elephants were not alien, they could no longer ignore their pain, and therefore could no longer experience pleasure. But Cicero's phrasing is curious because the extension of kinship is an element of Stoic theories of justice, and is thus perhaps a surprising sentiment for a spontaneous mob expression.[50] Perhaps the crowd commented only that the elephants seemed human-like in their response to distress, and the educated Cicero recorded their comments as a philosophical statement. Or perhaps the crowd actually did express a philosophical position that elephants *are* close or akin to us and that their mistreatment therefore constitutes a denial of justice.

A second report on Pompey's elephants is given by Pliny the Elder in a compilation of stories about elephants (*NH* 8. 20–21).

---

[50] Among Stoic philosophers, kinship, that is, a feeling of mutual belonging, was the foundation of justice, but the Stoics excluded animals from considerations of justice, or moral rights, by arguing that animals lacked rationality and thus the ability to participate in our circle of kinship. See Sorabji 122–24; also Motto 178 (6b).

Although written about a hundred years after the event, it provides considerably more detail than Cicero's account.

> Pompei quoque altero consulatu, dedicatione templi Veneris Victricis, viginti pugnavere in circo aut, ut quidam tradunt, XVII, Gaetulis ex adverso iaculantibus, mirabili unius dimicatione, qui pedibus confossis repsit genibus in catervas, abrepta scuta iaciens in sublime, quae decidentia voluptati spectantibus erant in orbem circumacta, velut arte non furore beluae iacerentur. Magnum et in altero miraculum fuit uno ictu occiso; pilum etenim sub oculo adactum in vitalia capitis venerat. Universi eruptionem temptavere, non sine vexatione populi, circumdatis claustris ferreis. (Qua de causa Caesar dictator postea simile spectaculum editurus euripis harenam circumdedit, quos Nero princeps sustulit equiti loca addens.) Sed Pompeiani missa fugae spe misericordiam vulgi inenarrabili habitu quaerentes supplicavere quadam sese lamentatione complorantes, tanto populi dolore ut oblitus imperatoris ac munificentiae honori suo exquisitae flens universus consurgeret dirasque Pompeio quas ille mox luit imprecaretur.

> In the second consulship of Pompey, during the inauguration of the temple of Venus Victrix, twenty (elephants) or, as some have reported, seventeen fought in the circus against Gaetulian men armed with javelins. The battle waged by one elephant was remarkable. When its feet had been pierced through, it crawled on its knees against its human opponents, snatched their shields, and threw them in the air. The spectators experienced pleasure when the shields, as they fell to the ground, made a loop, as if thrown by design, not by the rage of the huge animal. There was also a wondrous sight when another elephant was killed by a single blow, for the javelin thrust under its eye had reached the vital parts of its head. All the elephants

together attempted to break out from the iron barricades which surrounded them, and this caused anxiety among the people. (Therefore, at a later date, when Caesar the dictator was planning a similar spectacle, he surrounded the arena with trenches which the emperor Nero later removed to add seats for the equestrian class.) But Pompey's elephants, when they had lost hope of escape, sought the compassion of the crowd and supplicated it with an indescribable gesture and bewailed their fate with a kind of lamentation. There resulted so much grief among the people that they forgot the generosity lavished in their honor by General Pompey and, bursting into tears, all arose together and invoked curses on Pompey for which he soon paid the penalty.

Pliny's use of the phrase *ut quidam tradunt* informs us that the story of Pompey's elephants had attracted the attention of several earlier writers. From Pliny we learn that the spectators had initially experienced pleasure (*voluptas*) in watching a wounded elephant's attempts to defend itself, paid no heed to its suffering, and been delighted when it crawled on its knees toward its tormentors and flung their shields into the air—delighted because they construed the animal's desperate actions as the clever tricks of a trained performer. In the imperial period, the spectacle of trained elephants performing tricks was not uncommon at Rome. We have accounts, for example, of elephants kneeling, walking on tightropes, and hurling weapons through the air.[51] Such comic movements may also have been displayed in the republican period. At Pompey's *venationes*, however, the wounded elephant was not a performer; it was fighting for its life, yet the audience did not make a

---

[51]Sen. *Ep.* 85.41; Dio 61.17; Plin. *NH* 8.2 and 3 (4–6). Perhaps the most poignant, if least credible story is of an elephant who was slow to learn and therefore frequently whipped. He was discovered one night to be practicing his tricks all alone in the moonlight (Plin. *NH* 8.3.6; Plut. *De Soll. An.* [12] 968c).

distinction, perhaps because to do so would have meant denying themselves pleasure. The elephant amused the spectators because it presented an incongruous display of a clumsy animal mimicking the actions of a skillful human.[52] Another source of wonderment which Pliny reports was the sight of an elephant killed by a single javelin skillfully thrust through its eye. Again, the fate of the elephant was of no concern, as the audience focused on the accuracy with which the human "hunter" hit his "target." Plass argues persuasively that public brutality was accepted as entertainment at Rome as long as there was an underlying "reassuring sense of order"; pleasure ends when "violence threatens to become seriously disturbing."[53] At Pompey's spectacle, the sense of order was destroyed when the elephants stampeded. Certainly the potential for danger was one of the attractions of these events, which re-enacted both human battles against Nature, and Roman battles against bellicose humans. However, the spectators did not expect to encounter imminent danger to their own life and limbs. The fear they experienced was vicarious, as they watched other humans (*bestiarii* and *venatores*) engaged in combat with animals. When the elephants stampeded, the fear of the spectators became real and personal, and it displaced the pleasurable sensation which arose from the vicarious fear. This, in itself, would constitute a failure for Pompey. But a more startling situation followed: the frustrated and tormented elephants seemed to surrender and beg for mercy.[54] In

---

[52]Pliny (*NH* 8.2.4) and Aelian (*NA* 2.11) both record an amusing spectacle of elephants trained to mimic dancing humans and to act like well-mannered humans at a dinner party.

[53]Plass 21.

[54]Martial (*Spect.* 17) describes a scene at the opening of the Colosseum in AD 80, where an elephant, who has just engaged in a battle with a bull, appears to supplicate the emperor. Pliny's account is remarkably similar in some respects to a story told by Tacitus (*Ann.* 3.22 and 23) about an event which occurred in AD 20. Aemilia Lepida was on trial, accused by Quirinus of fraud, adultery, and poisoning. On the days of the *ludi* which interrupted her trial, she went to Pompey's theater. There, with wailing and lamentation, she called on her ancestors and on Pompey himself, whose buildings and statues were visible, and she moved the audience to such sympathy that it wept and shouted curses at Quirinus.

this re-enactment of war, the enemy admitted defeat and sought clemency. Now an elephant which kneeled was a suppliant, not an entertainer. The spectators' emotions were in turmoil because the elephants were no longer amusing, because their movements reminded the audience of their pain. The indistinct line between laughter and sorrow had been crossed. Unlike Cicero, Pliny offers no philosophical basis for the spectators' distress. They simply responded on an emotional level to what they perceived to be a human-like appeal for pity, even as they had earlier responded with delight to a human-like juggling act. But pity is not a pleasurable experience, and the disappointed crowd, contrary to Pompey's plan to buy popular favor through his generosity, forgot his generosity, became angry at the *editor* and invoked upon Pompey curses for which he soon paid the penalty. The remark about curses is a reference to the fact that Pompey's fortunes declined within a short period and, seven years later, he was defeated in battle by Caesar (who was careful not to allow an elephant stampede at *his* spectacle in 46 BC!) and killed while fleeing to Egypt. Pliny's report invites us to make associations, first, between the killing of African elephants (and African men: Gaetulians) in Rome and the killing of a Roman general off the coast of Africa, and, second, between public dissatisfaction with Pompey in 55 BC, and his failures in subsequent years.

A third account of the *venationes* is found in Dio Cassius (39.38). Writing about two hundred and fifty years after the event, Dio first states that the inauguration events included musical and athletic competitions in the theater, and, in the circus, horse races and the slaughter of many wild animals of all kinds.

λέοντές τε γὰρ πεντακόσιοι ἐν πέντε ἡμέραις ἀναλώθησαν, καὶ ἐλέφαντες ὀκτωκαίδεκα πρὸς ὁπλίτας ἐμαχέσαντο. καὶ αὐτῶν οἱ μὲν παραχρῆμα ἀπέθανον, οἱ δὲ οὐ πολλῷ ὕστερον. ἠλεήθησαν γάρ τινες ὑπὸ τοῦ δήμου παρὰ τὴν τοῦ Πομπηίου γνώμην, ἐπειδὴ τραυματισθέντες τῆς μάχης ἐπαύσαντο, καὶ περιιόντες τάς τε προβοσκίδας ἐς τὸν οὐρανὸν ἀνέτεινον καὶ ὠλοφύροντο οὕτως ὥστε καὶ λόγον παρασχεῖν ὅτι οὐκ ἄλλως ἐκ συντυχίας αὐτὸ ἐποίησαν, ἀλλὰ τούς τε ὅρκους οἷς πιστεύσαντες ἐκ τῆς Λιβύης ἐπεπεραίωντο ἐπιβοώμενοι καὶ τὸ δαιμόνιον πρὸς τιμωρίαν σφῶν ἐπικαλούμενοι. λέγεται γὰρ ὅτι οὐ πρότερον τῶν νεῶν ἐπέβησαν πρὶν πίστιν παρὰ τῶν ἀγόντων σφᾶς ἔνορκον λαβεῖν, ἦ μὴν μηδὲν κακὸν πείσεσθαι.

Five hundred lions were destroyed in five days, and eighteen elephants fought against heavily armed men. Some of the elephants died on the spot, but others died a little later. For, in contradiction to Pompey's plan, some were pitied by the people when, having been wounded, they stopped fighting and walked around and stretched their trunks toward heaven. And they lamented in such a way that they even caused talk that they were not acting in this manner by chance, but were crying out against those oaths in which they had trusted when they journeyed from Libya. And they were calling on the gods to avenge them. For the story is that the elephants did not embark on the ships until they received a sworn oath from their handlers that they would suffer no harm.

A few lines later (39.39.1), Dio reports that Pompey pleased the populace to no small degree with his spectacles, but he displeased them very much in the matter of the arrangements which he and Crassus made for military campaigns in their provinces.

Like Pliny, Dio provides the information that the *venationes* of 55 BC attracted the interest of several writers ("the story is"). Dio does not mention a stampede, but he describes in some detail the unusual behavior, recorded by Pliny only as *inenarrabili*, "indescribable," which converted the experience of the spectators from pleasure to distress. However in Dio's report, the wounded elephants do not appear to beg for clemency, but rather to present a claim for justice. They "argue" that their handlers had violated sworn oaths that they would not be harmed. If Dio's reader assumes that the handlers were themselves African, then their behavior matches the stereotype which Romans had, since the Punic Wars, of perfidious Africans. However, if the handlers were Roman (and there is no way of knowing their nationality), then there is surely an irony in the Roman treachery toward these natives of Africa. As in the earlier accounts of Cicero and Pliny, the spectators in Dio's account came to the circus for enjoyment, but were placed in a situation which caused them discomfort because it forced them to see the elephants as acting like injured humans and therefore deserving moral consideration. In fact, the elephants' lament of a breach of contract was effectively a request for moral consideration. I earlier mentioned that Cicero's account of the crowd response could be viewed in the context of Stoic theories of justice. Dio's account should be compared with Epicurean theories. For Epicureans, the foundation of justice was contract formation. Epicurus himself had excluded animals from considerations of justice, or moral rights, on the grounds that they lacked rationality and were thus unable to enter into contracts with us.[55] Dio, however, suggests that the crowd at Pompey's games believed that the elephants *had* entered into a contract and therefore had been treated unjustly when the contract was violated. The spectators in Dio's report thus use a philosophic basis different from Cicero's to protest the mistreatment of the elephants, but we again have an account of a Roman crowd framing its protest in philosophic terms. Dio's story may be an accurate record of events, or it may be a record on to which he or his sources embroidered an explanation for the elephants' actions, an explanation derived in part from the philosophical schools and in part from the "scientific" lore about elephants. Pliny, for example, in a passage unrelated to Pompey's spectacles, reports that elephants are known to refuse to board ships until their handlers swear an oath that they (the elephants)

---

[55]Sorabji 162–63.

will return.⁵⁶

Dio's concluding statement, that the events which celebrated the opening of Pompey's theater gave the Roman masses no small pleasure, does not contradict Cicero, who grudgingly admitted that most of the events pleased the masses. However, Dio's telling of the event more clearly isolates the crowd response to the elephant slaughter and thus stresses its anomalousness.

Our fourth account of the *venationes* was written by Plutarch (*Pomp.* 52.4) about one hundred and fifty years after their occurrence. We might expect that Plutarch, who elsewhere reveals an interest in the moral status of animals,⁵⁷ would report a demonstration of human compassion, but there is no mention. His entire account of Pompey's spectacles is quite brief, and is introduced by the statement that Crassus (Pompey's colleague in the consulship of 55) went to his province at the end of his term.

> Πομπήϊος δὲ τὸ θέατρον ἀναδείξας ἀγῶνας ἦγε γυμνικοὺς καὶ μουσικοὺς ἐπὶ τῇ καθιερώσει, καὶ θηρῶν ἁμίλλας ἐν οἷς πεντακόσιοι λέοντες ἀνῃρέθησαν, ἐπὶ πᾶσι δὲ τὴν ἐλεφαντομαχίαν, ἐκπληκτικώτατον θέαμα, παρέσχεν.
>
> But Pompey dedicated his theater and presented athletic and musical competitions at the inauguration, and provided combats of wild animals in which 500 lions were destroyed, and finally the elephant battle, a most astounding and terrifying spectacle.⁵⁸

---

⁵⁶Pliny (*NH* 8.1.3) uses this information as evidence that elephants understand the significance of religious practices (such as swearing an oath). On the difficulty of moving elephants on to water vehicles, see O'Bryhim.

⁵⁷Plutarch's work includes: *De Sollertia Animalium* (On the Cleverness of Animals), *Bruta Animalia Ratione Uti* (Animals are Rational), and *De Esu Carnium* (On Eating Meat).

⁵⁸I have used both "astounding" and "terrifying" to translate the Greek word ἐκπληκτικώτατον because Plutarch gives us no precise indication of whether the spectacle caused astonishment or terror.

The following sentence informs us that Pompey was admired for these things and regarded with affection, but regarded no less with ill-will because he assigned his provinces and armies to legates so that he could remain in Italy with his wife.[59] Thus the description of the spectacles is framed by statements which present a contrast between the actions of Crassus and Pompey; the description itself, moreover, serves to build a positive portrait of Pompey ("admired") which is immediately opposed by a negative portrait ("not admired"). If Plutarch seems to ignore an instance of audience displeasure, it may be because the information would compromise his rhetorical design. Thus we learn from him only that the elephant battle was a very astounding or terrifying spectacle, with no explanation of why. His comment that the inauguration events won admiration and affection for Pompey does not preclude his knowing of audience displeasure at the final event. Dio, for example, was able to report both that the audience pitied the elephants and that it gained no small pleasure from the events overall. He was also able to create the same "admired - not admired" dichotomy as Plutarch. Ultimately we gain from Plutarch's description of the inaugural events a quite different impression than from Cicero's; the former persuades us that they achieved their purpose (i.e. won popular favor for Pompey), while the latter persuades us that the elephant spectacle ruined Pompey's plans.

Our fifth account is provided by Seneca the Younger in his philosophic essay *De Brevitate Vitae* (13.6–7), written about a hundred years after the event. His purpose is not to provide a historical record, but to engage his reader in a consideration of philosophic issues. One of Seneca's topics in this essay is that men waste their time on frivolous pursuits such as ball games, sunbathing, and treating unimportant subjects as significant. (Did he have a premonition of modern Classical scholarship on elephants?) As examples of useless data, Seneca lists the information that Dentatus was the first to have elephants in his triumphal

---

[59]*his wife*: Julia, the daughter of Julius Caesar, Pompey's colleague in the triumvirate and, later, opponent in the civil war.

procession, that Sulla was the first to give a spectacle with unleashed lions, and that Metellus was the only Roman to have one hundred and twenty elephants walk in his triumphal procession. Seneca was particularly opposed to preserving a record of Pompey's elephant fight and thus honoring it as a noteworthy achievement because he believed that the publicity might provoke other men to emulate it.

> Num et Pompeium primum in circo elephantorum duodeviginti pugnam edidisse, commissis more proeli innoxiis[60] hominibus, ad ullam rem bonam pertinet? Princeps civitatis et inter antiquos principes, ut fama tradidit, bonitatis eximiae memorabile putavit spectaculi genus novo more perdere homines. Depugnant? Parum est. Lancinantur? Parum est. Ingenti mole animalium exterantur. Satius erat ista in oblivionem ire, ne quis postea potens disceret invideretque rei minime humanae. O quantum caliginis mentibus nostris obicit magna felicitas! Ille se supra rerum naturam esse tunc credidit, cum tot miserorum hominum catervas sub alio caelo natis beluis obiceret, cum bellum inter tam disparia animalia committeret, cum in conspectu populi Romani multum sanguinis funderet, mox plus ipsum fundere coacturus. At idem postea Alexandrina perfidia deceptus ultimo mancipio transfodiendum se praebuit, tum demum intellecta inani iactatione cognominis sui.

> Is it relevant to any good purpose that Pompey was the first to produce in the circus a fight of eighteen elephants

---

[60]*innoxiis*: I follow the Oxford edition of L. D. Reynolds. One manuscript reads *noxiis* which is inappropriate in this context where concern is expressed for the lives of the men. In *Ep.* 7.5, Seneca sanctions the arena executions of criminals: *Quia occidit ille, meruit ut hoc pateretur. Cf.* Seneca's use of *noxii* in *Ep.* 70.27.

against innocent men drawn up in battle formation?[61] The leading citizen in the state and a man of exceptional goodness among ancient leaders, as the report goes, thought that destroying men in a novel fashion was a memorable kind of entertainment. "Fight? That's not enough. Be torn to bits? That's not enough. Let them be crushed by the massive weight of the animals." It would have been better for this story to pass into oblivion, lest some powerful individual learn and emulate this very inhuman deed. What a thick fog great good fortune puts in our minds! Pompey believed that he was above the natural order of things at the time when he cast so many groups of wretched men before monstrous beasts born under a foreign sky, when he arranged a war between beings so unequal, when he caused a huge amount of blood to be shed before the eyes of the Roman people, and would soon force the people themselves to shed even more blood.[62] But later this same man was deceived by Alexandrian treachery and exposed himself to be stabbed through and through by the lowliest slave.[63] Then finally he understood the hollow boast of his name.[64]

Seneca strays from his main topic (the inappropriate interest in insignificant data) to raise several other topics dear to his heart. First, he deplores the fact that Pompey was so uncaring of human life that he put men in a situation which proved fatal. The words

---

[61]The first elephant fights in the circus had occurred decades earlier (see above). Seneca does not specify in what respect Pompey was "first."

[62]Seneca is referring to the civil war which broke out in 49 BC.

[63]After his defeat by Caesar's forces at Pharsalus in 48 BC, Pompey sailed to Egypt. The Egyptians did not want him to come ashore. They sent a small boat out to meet his ship, as if to help him land. When Pompey entered the small boat, they stabbed him.

[64]*his name*: a reference to the cognomen Magnus (Great) which Pompey received for his swift and decisive victories in Africa in the late 80s (see above).

ingenti mole animalium exterantur ("let them be crushed by the massive weight of the animals") may be a reference to the stampede reported by Pliny. It is not surprising that Seneca fails to mention any spectator compassion for the elephants. As a Stoic, he would have thought that sympathy for animals was misplaced (see above n.50). Seneca's second point is that Pompey was blinded ("fogged") by his good fortune and wrongly believed that he was invulnerable to failure and that he could work outside the laws of Nature, by bringing humans and animals together in a bloody circus combat, for example. Seneca's discussion highlights several ironic correspondences: Pompey produced both an unnatural arena event and an unnatural civil war; he was unmerciful at the spectacle and was subsequently denied mercy by the Egyptians; he received his cognomen Magnus for his defeat of the Africans, but was subsequently killed by them; he was once at the pinnacle of power, but died ignominiously. Pliny's account correlated Pompey's downfall with his inability to please the crowd. Seneca, who makes no mention of the crowd's reactions, correlates Pompey's downfall with his failure to understand his place in the universe and to realize that the most exalted man may share the fate of the lowliest.

The five extant accounts of the elephant slaughter differ in tone, purpose, and details. The authors may, moreover, have "contaminated" their reports by enhancing them with material from other stories about elephants, or even about humans (see, for example, above n.54). Nonetheless we can derive from the accounts a narrative outline. *Pompey's lavish expenditure on the entertainments for the inauguration of his theater achieved its goal, that is, the urban masses were pleased by them. Nonetheless, one surprising mishap did occur. On the final day, the behavior of the elephants failed to amuse the spectators who, quite contrary to expectation, pitied the animals.* This unanticipated conclusion to the extravagant and otherwise well-received spectacles was recorded by Cicero and other writers who became sources for later authors. There is no doubt that the story became well known—too well known according to Seneca, who wished that it would pass into oblivion (although ironically he helped to preserve it). But what was it about the *venationes* that engaged the interest of Pompey's contemporaries? Since the tormenting of elephants had been a circus event as early as 251 BC, it is difficult to believe that Roman spectators in the late republican period had never before observed the actions of terrified and wounded elephants. The trumpeting, raised trunks and massing together, described by Pliny and Dio, are common behaviors for elephants in distress. Nor, given the long history at Rome of public slaughter, is it probable, as Seneca suggests, that this particular event was unusually cruel. It even seems unlikely that no Roman spectator had ever before expressed sympathy for the victims of arena violence. If there was anything anomalous about this event it was that so many spectators felt pity and voiced displeasure. And yet if the spectators were truly annoyed at Pompey, their annoyance was certainly not construed by other politicians as a permanent conversion to the opinion that the abuse of elephants was inherently wrong. In 46 BC, just nine years after Pompey's spectacles and two years after his death, Caesar, the victor of Pharsalus, commissioned a spectacle of at least forty elephants in the circus (where protective trenches were constructed), with no recorded whisper of audience displeasure.[65] What then was the significance of Pompey's *venationes*? The answer lies in part in the fears of Pompey's peers and competitors. For members of the senatorial class, who were uneasy about his powerful position in the Roman state and anxious about the additional popular support which would accrue to him from a permanent theater and grandiose spectacles (whose

---

[65]Plin. *NH* 8.22; App. *BC* 2.102; Dio 43.23.3; Suet. *Jul.* 39.3. The elephant spectacle was one event in the entertainments which accompanied Caesar's triumph. On one evening during the celebrations, Caesar was escorted through the streets by elephants carrying lighted torches in their trunks: Suet. *Jul.* 37.2; Dio 43.22.1. Caesar was celebrating several victories, including the decisive defeat of the Pompeian forces in Africa in 46 BC. The Pompeian forces, led by Q. Caecilius Metellus (whose adoptive family displayed the elephant as an emblem; see above), employed elephants in the final battle, but the animals panicked and, in fleeing, trampled their own men; *BAfr.* 83–86; Dio 43.8.1–2.

"themes" were designed to remind the audience of Pompey's *gloria*), the public expression of dis-pleasure, the reversal of expectation, was a gratifying incident. However inconsequential the moments of audience discomfort may actually have been in comparison to the several days of pleasure which Pompey's other events produced, men like Cicero were relieved to see that Pompey's bid for popular favor was not an unqualified success; and they were therefore also eager to publicize this incident. Pompey's detractors could moreover easily magnify the story, put a "spin" on it, and record for posterity that, in the end, in the final verdict, the people had rejected Pompey's ostentatious attempt to buy their approval. The man whom Cicero had described as being "unaccustomed to unpopularity"[66] had failed to please the *populus*. The embarrassing elephant incident had several symbolic features which could also be exploited. The declaration of compassion for the elephants was startling because the audience seemed to be denying the boundary between human and animal, civilization and nature, order and chaos which such spectacles were designed to reaffirm. Moreover, the sympathy for African animals could be construed as a rejection of the military achievements by which Pompey had earned his powerful position in the state. In a symbolic sense, Pompey had, with his elephant spectacle, produced a repudiation and nullification of the Roman domination of the world which he wanted to celebrate. The failure of the event was so convenient for his critics that I want to go way out on the limb of speculation and suggest that it is even possible that the protests were instigated, or at least encouraged and amplified, by anti-Pompeian agitators in the audience. We know that such orchestrations did occur at public events, but the evidence for an orchestrated protest on this occasion is admittedly very slim. Two elements in our accounts might provide evidence; first, Pliny's report that the spectators arose "all together," *universus*,[67] and

---

[66] *Att.* 2.21 (quoted above); cf. Plut. *Pomp.* 49.1.
[67] Pliny's description may, however, be influenced by protests at the circus in his own (early imperial) time.

second, Cicero's and Dio's implication that the spectators expressed their compassion in terms of a philosophic belief that the elephants had been denied justice. We can imagine that Pompey's critics may have sat, disappointed, through several frustrating days of entertainments when the crowd's adulation of Pompey was unshakable; but, on the final day (their last chance to rain on his parade), when they heard some isolated murmurs of compassion for the elephants, they may have rejoiced, seized the opportunity, and fanned the individual protests into a collective behavior, even providing some rather sophisticated reasons for the emotional outbursts. Of course, if the complaints about the spectacle arose without prompting and spread spontaneously, the event was even more newsworthy. In any case, Cicero's letter offers evidence of how and why the story of the incident was publicized and preserved by Pompey's contemporaries.

Decades and centuries later, the story still attracted interest, but for different reasons. After Pompey's ignominious death, Romans reflected on how a man who had conquered so many nations and reached the pinnacle of power could fall to such a low point, and they wondered whether his fate could have been predicted and whether it provided any lessons. In the conjecturing about when and why his fortunes had begun to decline, the report of events at the inauguration of his theater seemed to supply satisfying answers: the fall began at the very moment Pompey reached the pinnacle, and it originated with his attempt to secure permanent popular approbation. He heard applause in the theater, and then curses in the circus. He pleased the spectators, then displeased them. This simplistic interpretation of Pompey's career gives the Roman populace a starring role in the making and breaking of its leaders, and serves perhaps to warn other aspirants to power that the will—and the pleasure—of the people must not be ignored. This shaping of the story was undoubtedly influenced by the development during the imperial period of "dialogues" between the emperor and the people at entertainment venues. "Long after *contiones* and *comitia* had disappeared, the people continued to express their hopes, fears, and resentments freely and often forcibly at the public shows. No emperor was able to curb this 'theatri licentia' and many had to bow before it, in matters large and small."[68] Seneca discovered other lessons in the story of Pompey's *venationes*. For him, the elephant spectacle offered moral enlightenment about the foolishness of considering oneself above the laws of Nature, and Pompey became an *exemplum* of the destructiveness of self-ignorance and hubris. The man who claimed he had imposed order on the world had no real understanding of order. The story recorded by Pompey's contemporaries also offered succeeding generations the easily recognized coincidences which hindsight can interpret as omens (and the Romans loved omens). Pompey had conquered Africa, killed Africans, and chosen the elephant as a symbol of his victory. But in the circus, when he was again killing Africans, the elephants ominously won the support of the Roman people. Then Pompey was killed off the coast of Africa, and his forces were defeated in Africa when their own elephants (treacherously?) trampled them. The incident in the circus in 55 BC seemed to foreshadow Pompey's pathetic end.

Thus a public expression of sympathy for elephants was exploited both by Pompey's contemporaries and also by later writers to serve several different purposes. An investigation of why and how the incident was recorded can increase our understanding of the significance of popular protests in Roman society. Unfortunately, it can tell us little about compassion among the Roman people.

* I wish to express my gratitude to Anna Lydia Motto and John R. Clark for their many and valuable contributions to the scholarship on Seneca the Younger. Their critical insights have helped us all to appreciate the work of this fascinating Roman.

** This article is dedicated to Tyk, an African elephant who was shot to death on August 20, 1994, while trying to escape the torment of the circus.

---

[68]Cameron 160.

BIBLIOGRAPHY

Auguet, R. 1972. *Cruelty and Civilization: The Roman Games.* London.
Beacham, R. C. 1995. *The Roman Theatre and Its Audience.* London.
Beagon, M. 1992. *Roman Nature: The Thought of Pliny the Elder.* Oxford.
Bell, A. J. E. 1997. "Cicero and the Spectacle of Power." *JRS* 87:1–22.
Cameron, A. 1976. *Circus Factions. Blues and Greens at Rome and Byzantium.* Oxford.
Coleman, K. M. 1996. "Ptolemy Philadelphus and the Roman Amphitheater." In *Roman Theater and Society*, edited by W. J. Slater, 49–68. Ann Arbor.
—. 1990. "Fatal Charades: Roman Executions Staged as Mythological Enactments." *JRS* 80:44–73.
Gelzer, M. 1959. *Pompeius.* 2nd edition. Munich.
Greenhalgh, P. 1981. *Pompey, the Republican Prince.* London.
—. 1980. *Pompey, the Roman Alexander.* London.
Gruen, E. S. 1974. *The Last Generation of the Roman Republic.* Berkeley and Los Angeles.
Hanson, J. A. 1959. *Roman Theater-Temples.* Princeton.
Hopkins, K. 1983. *Death and Renewal.* Cambridge.
Jennison, G. 1937. *Animals for Show and Pleasure in Ancient Rome.* Manchester.
Leach, J. 1978. *Pompey the Great.* London.
Morstein-Marx, R. "Publicity, Popularity and Patronage in the *Commentariolum Petitionis*." Forthcoming in *ClAnt*.
Motto, A. L. 1970. *Guide to the Thought of Lucius Annaeus Seneca.* Amsterdam.
O'Bryhim, S. 1991. "Hannibal's Elephants and the Crossing of the Rhone." *CQ* 41:121–25.
Ooteghem, J. van. 1954. *Pompée le Grand. Bâtisseur d'empire.* Brussels.
Plass, P. 1995. *The Game of Death in Ancient Rome.* Madison.

Rawson, E. 1978. *The Politics of Friendship: Pompey and Cicero*. Sydney.
Scullard, H. H. 1974. *The Elephant in the Greek and Roman World*. Ithaca, N.Y.
Seager, R. 1979. *Pompey. A Political Biography*. Berkeley and Los Angeles.
Sorabji, R. 1993. *Animal Minds and Human Morals*. Ithaca, N.Y.
Toynbee, J. M. C. 1973. *Animals in Roman Life and Art*. Ithaca, New York.
Vanderbroeck, P. J. J. 1987. *Popular Leadership and Collective Behavior in the Late Roman Republic (ca. 80–50 BC)*. Amsterdam.
Veyne, P. 1990. *Bread and Circuses*, translated by B. Pearce. Harmondsworth.
Ville, G. 1981. *La Gladiature en Occident des origines à la mort de Domitien*. Rome.
Wiedemann, T. 1992. *Emperors and Gladiators*. London.
Wiseman, T. P. 1985. "Competition and Co-operation." In *Roman Political Life, 90 BC – AD 69*, edited by T. P. Wiseman, 3–19. Exeter.
Yakobson, A. 1995. "Secret Ballot and Its Effects in the Late Roman Republic." *Hermes* 123:426–42.
—. 1992. "*Petitio et largitio*: Popular Participation in the Centuriate Assembly in the Late Republic." *JRS* 82:32–52.

Roman Religion: Fragments and Further Questions

W. Jeffrey Tatum
Florida State University

In his *De Superstitione*, Seneca attacked the civic religion of the Romans and the sacraments of the Jews; he paused from his disparagement of the latter's pointless practices just long enough to pay them the following backhanded compliment:

> Illi tamen causas ritus sui noverunt; maior pars populi facit quod cur faciat ignorat. (August. *C.D.* 6.11)

> They [viz. the Jews], however, know the origins and meanings of their own rituals. The greater part of the Roman people performs rituals without knowing why it does what it does.

The wise man, Seneca says elsewhere in his treatise, performs public rituals because the laws require them, not because they are pleasing to the gods (August. *C.D.* 6.10: *tamquam legibus iussa, non tamquam diis grata*). The point, though familiar, remains an intriguing one, at once sociological and philosophical—and, from Augustine's perspective, theological and therefore religious. But the question must arise, has the Christian saint entirely misappropriated this *aperçu* by the Stoic moralist? By this I do not refer to Augustine's shifty avoidance of the fact that Seneca's philosophizing was unlikely to have proved any less hostile to certain tenets of the new faith than it had been to the old idolatries, but rather: was Augustine right, in terms of a proper appreciation of Roman religion, to consider Seneca's *De Superstitione*, with its obvious emphasis on correctness of belief (at the very least on the correct interpretation of the meaning of ritual practice), to be a valid religious discourse in the first place?[1] Or is this yet another, if very early, instance of the imposition of Christianizing assumptions on the analysis of pagan Rome?

It was not so long ago that Augustine's entire representation of Roman religion (or Seneca's, for that matter) was regarded as essentially sound (hence paganism's vulnerability to Christianity). To Warde Fowler, Roman religion had, by the second century BC, "become meaningless ... the outward form of the cults may be maintained in such particulars as most closely concern the public life of the community; but as a religious system expressing human experience we have had done with these things."[2] Kurt Latte, in his once standard handbook, made the following, similar observation: "für die Oberschicht hatte die römischen Religion in letzen Jahrhundert der Republik jede Kraft verloren."[3] Such views no longer prevail. Classicists have learned to recognize the perils of their Christianizing assumptions about the nature of religion and of religion's purposes. "If we wish to compare our culture with foreign peoples," wrote Cicero in his *De Natura Deorum*, "we will discover that in other respects we are no better and sometimes even inferior; however, with respect to religion (*religio*), by which I mean the worship of gods, we are superior by far" (2.8). Cicero here translates *religio* as *cultus deorum*, that is, as ritual worship, and scholars have been correct to stress the importance of the punctilious performance of ritual in the all important maintenance of the *pax deorum*. We have by now been taught by Clifford Geertz to appreciate, in spite of our Protestant inclinations, how powerful a religious experience ritual is. And, whereas in the case of civic religion we have always recognized, with the ancients, how enormously ritual contributes to what Bagehot called the "dignified

---

[1] Augustine and Seneca in this passage: Bardy and Comebès 108. An interesting and, its title notwithstanding, rather general study is D'Angers. The *De Superstitione* was evidently a dialogue; see Griffin 413.
[2] Warde Fowler 353.
[3] Latte 287.

parts" of the constitution, we can now view the role of ritual in civic religion as something very different from sheer pageantry.[4]

And so handbooks change. The new orthodoxy finds its canonical form in Mary Beard's important contribution to the authoritative pages of the *Cambridge Ancient History*:

> Roman religion had its centre in politics, military activity and public life. The gods of the Roman state, in co-operation with its political leaders, ensured Rome's safety, prosperity and victory in war; while, on the part of men, the proper fulfilment of ritual and cult obligations ensured the gods' continuing support of the city. Religion was not principally concerned with private morality, ethics or the conduct of the individual Roman citizen.[5]

This unquestionably represents a salutary advancement on the strictures of Warde Fowler. The centrality of ritual is emphasized appropriately, and, elsewhere in the article, the alien quality of Roman religion is acknowledged, all in remarkable and commendable contrast to the approach of the handbooks of earlier generations. Clearly, classicists have learned much from anthropologists of religion. But have we learned enough? Our sources for the study of Roman religion are fairly abundant, but are they adequate to allow us to recuperate in any satisfactory sense the complete nature of the Roman religious experience? If they are not, ought we to be, at the very least, somewhat less dogmatic in our modern formulations of precisely what it is that Roman religion was about? It is the purpose of this paper to review some of these questions as they concern religion in the Roman Republic. If, in the end, there are a few definitive answers, I may still hope that the

[4] A complete bibliography is uncalled for here. Among the most important recent work is: Linderski; Rawson; Beard and North; Price; Liebeschuetz.

[5] Crook, *et al.* 729.

inquiry will gratify, just a little, the woman who introduced me to Latin and to the world of the Romans.[6]

Central aspects of the current conceptualization of Roman religion are made clear in the above citation from the *Cambridge Ancient History*: religion is understood to be equivalent to *religio*, especially to state cult, to the extent that questions of belief, of personal satisfaction, and of personal morality tend to be excluded from discussion. Furthermore, purist concentration on Roman public cult has led some (though not the author of the *CAH* article) to cast the philosophizing of Cicero and others into outer darkness, far removed from the honest confines of the traditional practices and lore that constituted "genuine" Roman religion (though it is generally conceded that philosophical texts may contain material relevant for antiquarian purposes).[7] Now there can be no resisting the observation that, once philosophy is excised, the weight of our evidence, such as it is, favors such a summary. But it is perhaps not a useless exercise to revisit the quality of our evidence.

A high proportion of our material evidence pertains to the public cults, unsurprisingly. And our literary evidence, it must always be stressed, when it is not poetical in nature, tends to cluster about political episodes, so, once again, its reference to civic religion is predictable enough. Classicists seem always condemned to tread warily the path of circular argumentation, and the civic and elite bias of our sources has not gone unnoticed.[8] But, in the study of religion, we must recognize our sources for what they are: not authoritative texts but cultural informants. Informants are obviously vital to students of religion, but they are far from unproblematic, and here we could learn much by continuing to

---

[6]Too late for me to take into consideration here, I have acquired D. Feeney, *Literature and Religion at Rome: Cultures, Contexts, and Beliefs*, Cambridge, 1998, which explores, along fascinating and promising lines (if not persuasive in every particular) several of the issues dealt with in this paper.

[7]It is probably true, as is maintained by Brunt, that the religious sensibilities of *most* Romans were unaffected by the philosophizing of the late Republic; philosophy's effect on the elite must remain quite another matter, however.

[8]See the recent essay by North.

consult the work of anthropological colleagues who engage in the study of living religious traditions. It is not that informants can "get it wrong"—in a certain sense, they *cannot* get it wrong, which means that every reference to ritual and to the gods by any source deriving from the Republic remains relevant to our attempt to grasp their religious expectations. Nevertheless, in limited supply, informants can provide a set of perspectives so inadequate that it results in a seriously skewed comprehension of a religion, one that emerges quite at odds with the totality of the evidence, once that totality becomes more accessible. For instance, the discrepancies between the ordinary practices of ordinary Buddhists, in South and in East Asia, and the concerns elaborated in the writings of Buddhist scholars and sages of philosophic bent have at times led occidental academics to banish the former from the category of Buddhism altogether, in spite of sheer logic.[9] Fortunately, this biased line can be isolated (and corrected) through the observation of living practitioners. By contrast, the impediments to our ever getting a grasp of paganism "on the ground," as it were, are formidable and very likely insuperable. We do find hints. Cicero insisted that no educated person believed fables of punishment after death (*Tusc.* 1.10–11). What of uneducated persons? Again, Cicero tells us that only the vulgar practiced divination by lots at the temple of Fortuna at Praeneste (*Div.* 2.86–87). Why did they persist when their betters left off? Elite Greeks and Romans agreed in deeming ordinary people "crude, untaught yokels to whom it is not even granted to understand citizen affairs, much less to discuss matters pertaining to the gods" (Min. Fel. 12.7), a premise that reveals how limited the value of elite informants can be, for certain purposes in any case. Clearly, one vital dimension of religion for a large segment of the population was participation in *collegia* and in other cults associated with the neighborhood (however defined), such as the worship of the *lares compitales*, activities in which ordinary Romans could take part as something other than mere observers.[10] Elite indifference to these practices (except as sources

---

[9] Lopez 6–18 and 259–63.
[10] On *collegia*, see Linderski 165–223; Ausbüttel.

of political menace or support) has left us without satisfactory guides for interpreting their fairly abundant archaeological traces. And the question must arise of the elites' competence to understand (and to explain to us) the meaning of these activities for their participants. Seneca may well have been right when he asserted that at rituals the greater part of the people have no notion of what they are doing, but I do not like having to take his word for it, and, if the Romans were anything at all like the vast majorities of peoples studied by anthropologists, in a very real sense Seneca was wrong. Whether they are regarded as meaningful or meaningless, rituals tend to prompt a response in those who enact them, and it is unclear why the Romans should have been singularly numb. Even if we limit our sights to civic religion, we must take care not simply to follow the verdict of the elites ancient and modern that public religion is essentially a form of crowd control. We must at least consider the possibility that our elite sources have, on the subject of religion as in so many others, ignored a world of attitudes and experiences that are not rendered unimportant simply because they went unrecorded.

That Romans of the elite classes suffered keen anxieties over ritual correctness is well known.[11] Yet, for all their apprehension, Roman aristocrats were taught to control their worries, lest they be accused of unmanly superstition.[12] This gendering of religious practice and decorum invites further interest. When Cicero, banished by his enemy, wrote to Terentia that *neque di, quos tu castissime coluisti, neque homines, quibus ego semper servivi, nobis gratiam rettulerunt* (*Fam.* 14.4.1: "neither the gods, whom you have worshiped so spotlessly, nor men, whom I have always served, have shown us gratitude"), it is difficult to conclude that he refers primarily to her participation in public rites, like those of the *Bona Dea*, which were *pro populo*, or to the maintenance of familial *sacra*, for which men were ultimately responsible (and in any case Cicero and Terentia belonged to different *familiae*); instead, he must be thinking of her personal worship of the gods,

[11] Morgan 30–31.
[12] See, for example, Cic. *Dom.* 103–5.

whatever form that took, be it public or private.¹³ That impression receives possible confirmation in another letter to Terentia written years later, in which Cicero reported to his wife that his morbid anxiety had been relieved during the previous night when he vomited bile:

> statim ita sum levatus ut mihi deus aliquis medicinam fecisse videatur. cui quidem tu deo, quem ad modum soles, pie et caste satis facies. (*Fam.* 14.7.1)
>
> I was so immediately relieved that it seemed to me that a god must have doctored me. So do please pay our debt to this god, with piety and purity, as is your habit.

Terentia's activities were obviously regarded by Cicero as commendable, because they were dedicated, in Cicero's mind at least, to the well-being of himself and his family. Did such a division of ritual labor continue into the lower classes? One also wonders whether fretful religiosity carried class connotations as well: when Cicero distinguished *religio* from *supersitio* in *De Natura Deorum* (2.71), he derived the latter from the distasteful habit of those persons "who spent whole days in prayer and sacrifice to ensure that their children should outlive them." Whoever these persons were, they were not devoting their days to rituals designed principally to support the *res publica* in its political or military endeavors; instead, they were seeking the gods' help in very personal matters. The same can be said for the countless Romans who turned to the gods in their quest for personal health. Much, though not by any means all, of this evidence comes from the imperial period, by which time, in the view of MacMullen, "the chief business of religion, it might be said, was to make the sick well."¹⁴ None of this need seriously undermine the centrality of civic religion to men like Cicero. But, in view of the many other strands of religious activity that we can glimpse even in the

---

¹³During his censorship, the elder Cato held L. Veturius responsible for the neglect of his family's *sacra*; see Gell. 6.22.3.

¹⁴MacMullen 49. See also Blagg 211–20; Comella.

politically oriented writings of the elite, it is patent that we must take pains not to allow our surviving informants to constitute *the* Roman religious mentality or to set incontrovertible parameters for what constitutes Roman religion.

Even within the elite we can detect conflicting perspectives. Let us consider the much examined contest between Caesar and Bibulus over the efficacy of the latter's resort to long-distance and non-stop *obnuntiatio* in 59 BC.[15] In order to block Caesar's legislation in that year, Bibulus turned to the process whereby, after announcing that he would spend the night before an assembly examining the sky for untoward omens, he might dissolve that assembly for that day by announcing his observation of such omens to the presiding magistrate at the next day's assembly. Violence and the threat of violence prevented Bibulus from making his announcement, in response to which he took refuge in his house and posted edicts indicating that he was watching the heavens. The assemblies proceeded with their business nevertheless, and the legislation to which Bibulus objected was passed. But, for years afterwards, it was unclear to many Romans whether Caesar's legislation was valid or not. It was certainly felt by everyone to be vulnerable to religious objection, as rival politicians exasperated themselves upon one another on this very issue. In the past, this controversy was introduced as evidence of the disintegration of Roman religion. More recently, the sheer energy with which the conflict was fought out has been viewed (correctly) as a clear indication of the continuing vitality of civic religion, of its relevance to political life, and of the extent to which the changing circumstances of Roman political life (in this case the introduction of urban violence) could transform or complicate religious anxieties. And such recent approaches are all to the good. But let us take a further look at this matter, remembering as we do how the current view tends to limit Roman religiosity to punctilious ritual performance and tends to eliminate matters of belief and personal morality from the mix.

[15]Cic. *Fam.* 1.9.7; Vell. 2.44.5; Suet. *Iul.* 20.1; Plut. *Pomp.* 48; *Caes.* 14; Dio 38. 6.1–5.

Obnuntiatio came to the fore in the year 59 BC. In the teeth of senatorial opposition—and the opposition of his colleague—Caesar turned to the people to carry his first agrarian law. Bibulus attempted to block Caesar's legislation through *obnuntiatio*, but was forcibly expelled from the forum: the *fasces* were shattered and the consul himself was bathed in filth. Thereafter Bibulus retired to his house, where he spent the remainder of the year searching the heavens—exercising his right to *obnuntiatio* through edicts, as Suetonius (*Iul.* 20.1) puts it. He did not, however, announce the results of his observation (*spectio*) personally; instead, he sent lictors to do so, or at least this is the conclusion to be drawn from Dio's admittedly clouded account. The consul was imitated in his continual *obnuntiatio* by three tribunes (Dio 38.6.1–5).

Now it has long been recognized that, in order to be valid from a narrowly technical standpoint, the bad omen perceived through *spectio* must be announced in person.[16] The mere declaration by an appropriately empowered official that he intended to observe the heavens (*de caelo servasse*), while ordinarily sufficient to persuade a tribune or magistrate not to waste his time gathering an assembly only to have it dismissed because of *obnuntiatio*, was not per se a binding restriction: since the possibility, however slender, of a fruitless *spectio* had to be assumed, a determined or a rigidly scrupulous official might convene his assembly in any event. Hence the requirement to report the omen on the spot and in person.[17] So far the ineluctable logic of augural law. But the undeniable distinction between *de caelo servasse* and actual *obnuntiatio* must have been less clear to most Romans, even of the senatorial order, than it was to those learned in the augural discipline. After all, the conflict between Caesar and Bibulus, in which Bibulus' rights as a consul were denied even while augural law was technically observed, as well as Bibulus' recourse to non-stop *spectio*, were unprecedented—and owing to the long-standing tradition of

---

[16]This point has been long recognized if not long appreciated: see Valeton 82–83 and 101–2; Linderski 73–74. The same conclusion was arrived at independently by Lintott 144–45.

[17]Valeton 103.

respecting an announcement *de caelo servasse* there existed an equally undeniable body of opinion to the effect that it was *nefas* to hold an assembly while the heavens were being observed. Cicero, in the aftermath of his return from exile, insisted that the *libri reconditi* of the augurs forbade holding an assembly when an announcement *de caelo servasse* has been made (*Dom.* 39), and in a sensational *contio* conducted during his tribunate by P. Clodius Pulcher, the augurs, questioned as to the effect of Caesar's legislation passed despite Bibulus' *spectio*, answered that the consul's acts, though passed into law, were vitiated (Cic. *Har.* 48: *vitio lata esse*).[18] Bibulus' edicts unmistakably made a powerful, if technically misleading, impression on his contemporaries. In view of the tremendous stir caused by Caesar's neglect of his colleague's edicts—which went on for more than a year—as well as the pronouncements of the augurs (even granting that these were made unofficially and *in contione* and so were not formal *responsa* of the college), one can only conclude that the augural rules governing *obnuntiatio* were imperfectly understood by most senators, a conclusion that obtains even if the misunderstanding was willful on the part of some.

Even among the elite, then, what constituted punctilious performance of ritual could be a contested affair. It was by no means a simple service: more than one opinion, more than one voice could be raised and could be raised legitimately. Everyone reacted to the same religious controversy, but, obviously enough, different groups invested different significance to different components of a consul's ritual consultation of omens. If we do not wish to return to the old idea that it was all an empty show, then we must conclude that different Romans had different *beliefs* about the meaning of *obnuntiatio*. Or, if the word belief must be deemed unacceptable in its connotations, we must conclude that radically different expectations prevailed concerning which elements of the procedure mattered most. It is the scholar's job to sort out these issues, but it cannot be a sound procedure to attempt to determine which party

[18]Cf. Schol. Bob. 146 (St); Dio 38.13.5 (both admittedly likely to be derived from Cicero). On the nature of the *libri reconditi* mentioned by Cicero see Linderski 496–523.

was wrong and which was right even in terms of Roman religion: for a time, both views kept a vital existence. Modern scholars are right to relate this controversy to the political and social perturbations of the period. Each side sought to sustain the traditional meaning of *obnuntiatio* in what seemed a very untraditional context. In addition, and this is where morality slips in, it is hard to escape the idea that the ritual expectations of Bibulus' supporters were influenced by their disapproval of Caesar's violent political methods, which were certainly contrary to *mos maiorum* and hence immoral.

The recognition of expectations that differ among various individuals and groups, especially in response to changing contexts and new personal purposes, hardly constitutes a return to the Christianization of Roman religion. On the contrary, it is exactly what contemporary anthropological research, especially feminist anthropological research, into traditional societies has succeeded in demonstrating. Such studies frequently address the manifold complications that come into view when scholars deviate from an academic point of view based solely or largely on the expectations and practices of the dominant group. When examined from more than one perspective, something which obviously can be done more easily when the culture under study is a living one, cultural structures which must be described as traditional and even conservative can be shown nevertheless to be sites for considerable creativity and contest, for groups and for individuals alike, a fuller account that often requires a reconsideration even of the dominant group's own ideology.[19] The experience of these differences, over time, establishes new interpretations of the most traditional religious practices, "new senses of meaningfulness—or meaninglessness."[20] Rituals are hardly "out there" and determinative. They are cultural forms that are constantly recreated for and by individuals as well as communities: "the tension between discovering new meanings that are already there and shaping new meanings, is what allows for a sense of empowerment in subjects

[19]Watkins 218.
[20]Ortner 128.

whose agency is reproducing hierarchies even as they are creating the spaces for new forms of relationship."[21] Nothing can be ruled out as a factor in the dynamic of traditional ritual: "the multiple contingent nature of structures and social events, and the distance between subjects and cultural forms create a locus where human agency—the struggle over meaning—can take place."[22] The controversy over *obnuntiatio* in 59 BC (and subsequently), though confined to the elite, represents a struggle over meaning within the traditional parameters of Roman religiosity—under circumstances that were perceived by many to be far from traditional.

What place, if any, is there for us to consider Roman morality and Roman beliefs and expectations in the study of Roman religion? Let us agree that such matters were not objects of ultimate concern. Still, that hardly relegates them to irrelevance. Consider the case of Cicero's house on the Palatine, which was confiscated and at least partially destroyed when the orator was exiled by Clodius in 58 BC.[23] Part of Cicero's property was consecrated to Libertas, in association with a shrine to this goddess that was constructed by Clodius to commemorate the occasion of the orator's banishment. Consequently, when Cicero was restored to citizenship in 57 BC, the restoration of his Palatine property was blocked by Clodius' assertion that there was a religious impediment. Only the senate could adjudicate this matter, and for expert guidance that body turned to the college of pontiffs, which heard arguments on both sides. Although Clodius' speech does not survive, it is clear from Cicero's response, the *De Domo Sua*, that the former tribune stressed the inescapable claims of punctilious ritual performance: *dedicatio magnam . . . habet religionem* (*Dom.* 127: "a consecration establishes a strong ritual restraint"). Cicero countered by adducing three arguments. First, he insisted that Pinarius, the youthful pontifex who had overseen the dedication, must have made mistakes (*Dom.* 134–35, 139–41). Second, he maintained that Clodius' dedication had violated the *Lex Papiria*,

---

[21]Mahoney and Yngvessor 62–63.
[22]Watkins 219–20.
[23]For narrative and sources see Mitchell 158–60.

an ancient law regulating dedications.²⁴ And, finally, he attacked Clodius' immorality: Clodius, averred Cicero, was in the habit of manipulating religious institutions for his own personal purposes; furthermore, and more to the point, the man was so objectionable that his ritual acts must perforce be vitiated: "is it possible for a single word of religion to drop or fall from such a mouth?" (*Dom.* 104). Cicero makes the point that there must be a connection between the character and intentions of a celebrant and the efficacy of his ritual actions:

> equidem sic accepi, pontifices, in religionibus suscipiendis caput esse interpretari quae voluntas deorum immortalium esse videatur; nec est ulla erga deos pietas nisi sit honesta de numine eorum ac mente opinio, ut expeti nihil ab iis quod sit iniustum atque inhonestum arbitrere. (*Dom.* 107)

> I have always understood that, where religious obligations are undertaken, the chief thing is to interpret the will of the immortal gods; nor is piety towards the gods anything but a sound belief regarding their will and purpose, a judgment, that is to say, that the gods seek nothing that is unjust or immoral.²⁵

Now it will hardly do to dismiss this passage as mere philosophizing.²⁶ This was, for Cicero, an important speech dealing with a hotly contested religious issue and delivered in public before the college of pontiffs. The orator was hardly looking for ornamentations simply to adorn and to protract his speech. And, in any case, elite Romans were at this time beginning to think about their religious actions by means of the vehicle of (Greek) philosophizing, a serious enterprise that ought to be reckoned a genuine part of Roman (or, better, some Romans') religious

---

²⁴See Tatum (1993a).
²⁵Translation by Nisbet (160).
²⁶Jocelyn 92.

sensibilities.[27] In the end, Cicero was persuasive, since the pontiffs later ruled that Clodius' shrine to Libertas could be removed from its site without compromising any ritual restriction (*sine religione*). Admittedly, it appears that Cicero's claim based on the *Lex Papiria* was in the event the most influential element in his argument. But that should not distract us from his other points and the degree to which he elected to elaborate them. The fact that Cicero could expect to be persuasive by introducing moralizing arguments of a type that tended to rate the character of a ritual participant above the efficacy strictly of his actions makes it clear that he did not expect such an attitude to be alien or unacceptable to his contemporaries.[28]

It remains impossible for us to penetrate the mental experience of Roman ritual, to determine what facets meant what to different Romans. The examples cited above should suffice to show that different Romans, even within the elite, invested different aspects of certain ritual acts with different degrees of meaningfulness. The extent of such variation and its significance must continue to elude us, especially if we expand our interests to include the lower classes, who are regularly dismissed by the elite, as we have seen already, as credulous and unthinking. And, while modern analogies may spring to the scholar's mind suggesting that the ancient elite must, on this score, have gotten it right, it is sobering to be reminded that matters can be less straightforward.

Let us once more turn to a living tradition. One of the most fascinating rituals in Buddhism is the consecration of an image of the Buddha.[29] In Sri Lanka, a statue of the Buddha is consecrated by painting in its eyes, in a remarkable and complex ceremony called *netra pratisthapanaya utsavaya* ("festival of setting the eyes"). This festival combines recitations from the Pali canon, rituals to placate numerous divinities, and self-conscious allusion to the moment of the Buddha's enlightenment. The actual setting of the eyes is regarded as a dangerous action and consequently is

[27]See the very important article of Beard.
[28]See Liebeschuetz 53; Tatum (1993b).
[29]Fundamental is Gombrich. For recent discussion, with ample bibliography, see Swearer.

surrounded by multiple ritual forms that are intended to protect performers (the painting in itself is so dangerous that it is not observed by all and sundry, though the antecedents and aftermath are open to all). Of interest to us is the question of what participants in this ceremony believe is actually happening. It is a principle of Buddhism that it is a religion whose founder was a man who is now deceased: he is not a living god. Yet, if it is true that the consecration of a Buddhist image "indicates that the statue is being brought to life," what does that imply about generally held beliefs concerning the present condition of the Buddha?[30] It is far from a simple issue, predictably; rationalist explanations exist, and, in Sri Lanka, groups tend to form estimations of other groups' beliefs on the basis of status and on assumptions that conform with premises we have encountered already among the Roman elite.[31] Yet, with a broader inquiry, the pattern of ritual expectations can be shown to vary in unexpected ways. For instance, when asked what she thought actually took place during the eye setting ceremony, a Buddhist lay nun responded with conviction and conciseness: "nothing." Yet lay nuns in Sri Lanka are hardly conspicuous for their erudition, either theological or secular, and this nun was not among the exceptions.[32] This example makes quite clear how difficult it is to predict the expectations of religious participants at varying social levels. Prejudices held by elites ancient or modern are too easily persuasive in the absence of relevant data.

If we can accept the importance of philosophical discourse to our comprehension of Roman religiosity, we can see that matters of opinion, of belief, mattered to some. Cicero's *De Natura Deorum* should suffice to make it clear that for some among the elite there was, or could be, a vital relationship between knowledge and practice. This is unquestionably a central concern of Lucretius' *De Rerum Natura*, in which the poet attacks not merely those constructions of ritual and mythology that can be described as relatively simple or naive, but rather, as Monica Gale has demonstrated, also criticizes contemporary intellectual and

---

[30] Gombrich 24.
[31] *Ibid.*, 31.
[32] On lay nuns in Sri Lanka, see Bartholomeusz.

philosophical adaptations of myth and practice.[33] Lucretius, for one, would have approved of St. Augustine's approach, encountered at the commencement of this essay, to understanding Roman religion. Furthermore, Lucretius shared his and Seneca's disapproval of traditional Roman religious practices (though of course for different reasons). But Lucretius, too, remains a specimen of the elite. One cannot but wonder how profane, which is to say, how diverse, were the opinions of the many?

The difficulties should now be obvious enough. The accomplishment of the modern generation of specialists in Roman religion is nothing short of monumental: they have succeeded in jettisoning the Christianizing baggage that was so much of the freight of past investigations. Ritual *was* central, and powerful, and meaningful. But two matters must yet be dealt with. The first is philosophy. Does the modern scholar ignore this form of religious discourse, a discourse that certainly informs any cross-cultural conception of religion, simply because it falls outside the strict confines of *religio*? At the same time, can we study *religio* and *philosophia* without blurring our proper focus on *Roman* sensibilities? I for one believe that we can, and that we should. The other issue has to do with anthropology. Classics has benefitted enormously from its willingness to exploit the insights of anthropological studies of religion. But why stop? Current research in living religious traditions reveals that, as always, religious practices, when scrutinized, display ever greater complexities. Classicists will never enjoy the abundantly variegated data of their anthropological colleagues, which is why they should continue to discover what can be learned from relevant modern studies. At the same time, students of Rome must avoid the temptation to deploy—without qualification—modern constructions of contemporary religious phenomena. Anthropology offers us illuminating and suggestive analogies, not actual evidence for Roman experiences. But the sensitive application of anthropological learning is, for the classicist, a practice as

---

[33]Gale 85–98.

traditional as, say, the scholarship of Dodds. It is a scholarly tradition worth sustaining.

BIBLIOGRAPHY

Ausbüttel, F. M. 1982. *Untersuchungen zu den Vereinen im Westen des römischen Reiches*. Kallmünz.
Bardy, G. and G. Comebès. 1981. *Oeuvres de Saint Augustin: La Cité de Dieu, livres VI–X*. Bourges.
Bartholomeusz, T. J. 1994. *Women Under the Bo Tree. Buddhist Nuns in Sri Lanka*. Cambridge.
Beard, M. 1986. "Cicero and Divination: the Formation of a Latin Discourse." *JRS* 76:33–46.
Beard, M. and J. North, eds. 1990. *Pagan Priests. Religion and Power in the Ancient World*. London.
Blagg, T. F. C. 1986. "The Cult and Sanctuary of Diana Nemorensis." In *Pagan Gods and Shrines of the Roman Empire*, edited by M. Henig and A. King, 211–20. Oxford.
Brunt, P. A. 1989. "Philosophy and Religion in the Late Republic." In *Philosophia Togata I: Essays on Philosophy and Roman Society*, edited by M. Griffin and J. Barnes, 174–98. Oxford.
Comella, A. 1981. "Complessi votivi in Italia in epoca medio- e tardo-repubblicana." *MEFRA* 93:717–803.
Crook, J. A., A. Lintott and E. Rawson, eds. 1994. *The Cambridge Ancient History*. Vol. 9. 2nd edition. Cambridge.
D'Angers, J.-E. 1956. "Réfutation et utilisation augustiniennes de Sénèque et du Stoïcisme dans L'homme criminel (1644) et L'homme chrétien (1648) de l'oratorien J.-F. Senault." *Revue des Études Augustiniennes* 2:471–503.
Gale, M. 1994. *Myth and Poetry in Lucretius*. Cambridge.
Gombrich, R. 1966. "The Consecration of a Buddhist Image." *The Journal of Asian Studies* 26:23–36.
Griffin, M. 1976. *Seneca. A Philosopher in Politics*. Oxford.
Jocelyn, H. D. 1996. "The Roman Nobility and the Religion of the Republican State." *JRH* 4:89–104.

Latte, K. 1960. *Römische Religionsgeschichte*. Munich.
Liebeschuetz, J. H. W. G. 1979. *Continuity and Change in Roman Religion*. Oxford.
Linderski, J. 1997. *Roman Questions*. Stuttgart.
Lintott, A. W. 1968. *Violence in Republican Rome*. Oxford.
Lopez, D. S. Jr., ed. 1995. *Curators of the Buddha: the Study of Buddhism under Colonialism*. Chicago.
MacMullen, R. 1981. *Paganism in the Roman Empire*. New Haven.
Mahoney, M. A. and B. Yngvessor. 1992. "The Construction of Subjectivity and the Paradox of Resistance: Reintegrating Feminist Anthropology and Psychology." *Signs* 18:44–73.
Mitchell, T. N. 1991. *Cicero, the Senior Statesman*. New Haven.
Morgan, M. G. 1990. "Politics, Religion and the Games in Rome, 200–150 B.C." *Philologus* 134:30–31.
Nisbet, R. G. 1979. *M. Tulli Ciceronis De Doma Sua ad Pontifices Oratio*. Oxford.
North, J. A. 1995. "Religion and Rusticity." In *Urban Society in Roman Italy*, edited by T. Cornell and K. Lomas, 135–50. New York.
Ortner, S. B. 1989. *High Religion: A Cultural and Political History of Sherpa Buddhism*. Princeton.
Price, S. 1984. *Rituals and Power. The Roman Imperial Cult in Asia Minor*. Cambridge.
Rawson, E. 1991. *Roman Culture and Society*. Oxford.
Swearer, D. K. 1995. "Hypostasizing the Buddha: Buddha Image Consecration in Northern Thailand." *History of Religions* 34:263–80.
Tatum, W. J. 1993a. "The *Lex Papiria de Dedicationibus*." *CP* 88:319–28.
—. 1993b. "Ritual and Personal Morality in Roman Religion." *SyllClass* 4:13–20.
Valeton, I. M. J. 1891. "De iure obnuntiandi comitiis et conciliis." *Mnemosyne* 19:75–113; 229–70.
Warde Fowler, W. W. 1911. *The Religious Experience of the Roman People*. London.

Watkins, J. C. 1996. *Spirited Women. Gender, Religion and Cultural Identity in the Nepal Himalaya*. New York.

Seneca and the Empire of Signs

Daniel R. White
Florida Atlantic University
Honors College

It is not a matter of emancipating truth from every system of power (which would be a chimera, for truth is already power), but of detaching the power of truth from the forms of hegemony, social, economic, and cultural, within which it operates at the present time.[1]

The tragedy of the Caesars . . . was, in a word, the tragedy of men who, being required to play the part of gods, descended to that of beasts. . . . This we have tried to describe as the classical ideology of power.[2]

. . . how absurd it is to try to contest our society without ever conceiving the very limits of the language by which (instrumental relation) we claim to contest it: it is trying to destroy the wolf by lodging comfortably in its gullet.[3]

Seneca was a philosopher who was confronted with an abuse of power as significant, if not as extensive, as any in European history. In the principate of Nero, whose murderous tenor was set at the beginning *per dolum Agrippinae*, as Tacitus describes the machinations of the death of Junius Silanus, Seneca along with Burrus had the dubious distinction of being *rectores imperatoriae*

---

[1] Foucault 75.
[2] Cochrane 129. Cochrane (113) defines the classical ideology of power, more precisely, as "the deification of imperial virtue" combined with "its inevitable corollary, the deification of imperial fortune."
[3] Barthes 8.

iuventae. In this joint capacity, they shared a concord rare in the society of power, Tacitus says, the latter with his military concerns and austerity of character, the former "with his teachings in eloquence and his virtuous civility" (*praeceptis eloquentiae et comitate honesta*), helping one another to keep the emperor's perilous youth, if it disdained virtue, within the bounds of permissible licentiousness (*Ann.* 13.2).[4] It is on this meeting of learning and ethical restraint with wanton power that I wish to focus, for it resonates not only through the streets of the classical city, but also throughout the European tradition. It is, furthermore, the intellectual foundations of Roman Imperial dominion—what Cochrane calls the "classical ideology of power"—that I wish to highlight, for these Seneca invokes and "deconstructs" not to envision, as Cochrane does, the victory of Augustine's *civitas dei* at the end of historical time, but rather to detach the power of truth from forms of hegemony justified by metaphysics. More specifically, he was unwilling to accept the thesis that a visibly corrupt *imperium* is based on God's will. Seneca articulated his refusal by contesting the language of power's ideology so as to destroy the wolf by lodging, though not quite so comfortably, in its gullet.

Seneca's *De Providentia*, addressed to Lucilius, begins with the question: "Why some misfortunes befall good men, though Providence exists." This is an inquiry that might well concern the tutor of Nero and his friends, but its scope is far broader. Seneca's answer to the question, furthermore, offers a new twist on an old problem, as it echoes the faith of Socrates in Plato's *Apology* (30c9–d1): "I do not believe it is divinely ordained that harm be done to a better man by a worse one" (my translation). That conviction was tested in the Greek polis as it was in the Roman cosmopolis but it remained a mainstay of classical metaphysics, one that was originally set by Parmenides of Elea. The imagery that Seneca employs in the *De Providentia*, interestingly, both connects his argument with and distinguishes it from the views of good, evil

---

[4] I have provided Loeb translations, with my emendations, throughout.

and the human condition offered by that visionary Presocratic as by Plato. For all three invoke the same vehicle for the ascent of the soul—the chariot—but Seneca turns the metaphor, and the argument, in a new direction.

Built into the thought of Parmenides and Plato is the idea that ethics, ontology, and epistemology are inseparable, that the good is an invariant reality that can be known indubitably by the human mind. The good is, furthermore, the ἔσχατον or "end" of the human journey, that toward which the intellect aspires through φιλοσοφία, "the love of wisdom." This idea is implicit in Seneca's question, above, for when it is challenged a philosophical problem arises: is ethical conduct worthwhile if it is not founded in reality? Does it do any good to pursue ideals if the universe itself is constituted either through chance or, worse, through evil? In times of political corruption, this question becomes all the more vital, since, to all appearances, the pursuit of good might seem futile—even absurd. Those cousins of the Stoics, the Cynics, clearly prefigured this sentiment, Diogenes by residing in his tub. One late modern response to political adversity, the Theatre of the Absurd, both prefigures postmodern incredulity at metanarratives and offers critical insight into Seneca's skepticism. Martin Esslin defined absurdity as the "sense that the certitudes and unshakable basic assumptions of former ages have been swept away, that they have been tested and found wanting, that they have been discredited as cheap and somewhat childish illusions." He goes on to cite Camus' pronouncement, from *The Myth of Sisyphus*, "'This divorce between man and his life, the actor and his setting, truly constitutes the feeling of absurdity.'" He notes that the term means "out of harmony" and includes Ionesco's assertion that "'Absurd is that which is devoid of purpose.'"[5] Like Camus' Sisyphus, Seneca struggled to implement a humane ethic in a setting that precluded his success. Clearly out of harmony with the ethos of Nero, he nevertheless exercised his powers as a writer to counter the weight of oppression. It is no doubt anachronistic to define him as

[5]Esslin 23.

an "absurdist" per se, but, as Arrowsmith argued regarding Euripides, the Theatre of the Absurd provides a useful modern analog for some elements of his work.[6]

Esslin goes on to mark the difference between the dramatist and the philosopher: the one *presenting* the idea of absurdity, the other talking *about* it.[7] Seneca, of course, did both. The sense of the absurd expressed in Seneca's dramas, especially *Medea*, has been aptly described by Motto and Clark:

> ... even Seneca's minor characters are thoroughly infected by agitation and mutability. His *dramatis personae* literally dwell in an atmosphere of blight. We might even go so far as to say that Seneca has thoroughly deheroicized the mythic and theatrical worlds, and that he has, with a series of giant steps, taken us significantly forward toward the modern drama of the absurd.[8]

His philosophical reflections on the subject are also worth considering, for these do not so much express the absurd as transform absurdity into creativity. The result is what might now be called a *postclassical* ethic. I use the term "postclassical" in a sense parallel to that in which Lyotard has used "postmodern": to refer to an incredulity regarding the metanarratives[9]—one that

---

[6]"Consider this statement: 'As our knowledge becomes increasingly divorced from real life, our culture no longer contains ourselves (or contains an insignificant part of ourselves) and forms a social context in which we are not "integrated." The problem thus becomes that of again reconciling our culture with our life, by making our culture a living culture once more . . .' That happens to be Ionesco on Artaud, but it could just as well be Euripides' description of the nature and purpose of his own theater" (Arrowsmith 20). It could also just as well be Seneca on the need to reconcile classical culture, with its narrative of a triumphant humanity, with the reality of corruption under Nero.

[7]Esslin 25.

[8]Motto and Clark (1988) 212.

[9]Lyotard xxiv: "I will use the term *modern* to designate any science that legitmates itself by reference to a metadiscourse . . . making an explicit appeal to a grand narrative." The idea of consensus among

"deheroicizes" "the mythical and theatrical worlds" as well as the philosophical verities—that have shaped classical as well as modern civilization. What distinguishes Seneca's struggle in the *De Providentia* is that he grapples with the absurd embodied in the paradox expressed by the question (4.8.1–2): "Why does god afflict the best people with ill health or sorrow or other misfortunes?" The question in itself was not new, but its political context had shifted, so that now the persona of the emperor had entered the stage to stand in for god. In this tragicomic theatre of power, it is little wonder that we should hear Senecan laughter intoned with irony and paradox.

As Motto and Clark also argue, this question brings into focus the history of Stoic and Cynic fascination with *paradoxa*, described by Cicero in his *Paradoxa Stoicorum*.[10] But the *De Providentia* has an intriguing logic that distinguishes it in the corpus (4.8.9–10): "We are seen by god as worthy for the purpose of discovering how much human nature can suffer" (*digni visi sumus deo in quibus experiretur quantum humana natura posset pati*). In other words, on the face of it, Seneca is embracing the contradiction: evils are good. Why are they good? Because they are part of god's "experiment" (*experiretur*) to see how much difficulty we can take. But why should god want to conduct such an investigation? It could be that the deity tests human nature so as to bring out the *virtus* that invests adversity with meaning. But what if god intends, as Seneca

---

rational minds, for example, is legitimated by "the Enlightenment narrative, in which the hero of knowledge works toward a good ethico-political end—universal peace." He goes on to argue, "if the metanarrative implying a philosophy of history is used to legitimate knowledge, questions are raised concerning the validity of the institutions governing the social bond: these must be legitimated as well. Thus justice is consigned to the grand narrative in the same way as truth. . . . I define *postmodern* as incredulity toward metanarratives" (xxiv). I am arguing, *mutatis mutandis*, that Seneca's incredulity toward the legitimacy of imperial power is turned, in the *De Providentia*, into a scepticism toward the grand narrative, stemming from Virgil through Cicero and Plato, that the classical city is the endpoint of a heroic rise toward a human order ruled by *iustitia*: this incredulity I call *postclassical*.

[10]See Motto and Clark (1993a).

seems to imply in the *De Providentia*, that his preeminent creature fail? This unsettling question suggests that god is not good, at least for us. But it also suggests that the Parmenidean-Platonic idea of a justice intrinsic to the world order—the metaphysical foundation of the classical Politeia —has been appropriated for dubious political ends.[11]

I would like to consider two of Seneca's answers to the question of affliction. The first is that this testing makes us stronger or more resilient (*Prov.* 4): "to put the calamities and terrors of mortal life under the yoke is the defining characteristic of the great man" (*calamitates terroresque mortalium sub iugum mittere proprium magni viri est*, 4.6.3), for *calamitas* is "virtue's occasion" (*virtutis occasio*). *Virtus* here clearly means "virtue" and "capacity"—the ability to negotiate moral adversity and, as Seneca's metaphors indicate, "to stay on course." "You come to understand a pilot in a storm, a soldier in battle" (*gubernatorem in tempestate, in acie militem intellegas*, 4.5.5).[12] This idea of virtue as realized in the

---

[11]Cochrane (98) argues that the idea of justice functions, for classical idealism, as a principle of integration for all rational beings as for the polis. The logic of the classical ideology of power is to identify universal justice with the particular ends of the state. In seeking to know and implement the principle of justice, Cochrane argues, the idealist acts like Prometheus or Adam: "In other words, what he does is to treat knowledge not as a means to 'wisdom' but as a source of 'power.'" This is an illusory quest, however, leading to failure, for he has only substituted his own version of cosmic order for one that presumably exists independently. "His problem is thus to give currency to this counterfeit cosmic order by persuading or compelling men to accept it as genuine. The effort to do so constitutes the history of 'politics' in classical antiquity."

[12]Boyle (39) offers a more conventional picture of Seneca's use of paradox, situating it within mainstream Stoic doctrine. Referring to the final act of Seneca's *Agamemnon*, where "paradox ensues," Boyle says: "History's moral order entails human responsibility for history's crimes, even as it precludes it. . . . Clytemnestra and Aegisthus are 'morally' responsible and guilty. But in reality they determine nothing. Both intention and character in *Agamemnon*'s world, as in orthodox Stoicism, are as much the determined products of history, as the events to which they give rise." See Boyle 222 n.24, as well as Long 173–99, and Sandbach 101–3. Also see Motto and Clark (1993a) 65–67 on Seneca's use of Stoic and Cynic paradoxes. My argument takes a different tack from either of

steersperson—the Latin *gubernator* or Greek κυβερ-
νήτης—leads, in Seneca's dialogue, to the metaphor of the chariot as the vehicle of the soul in its ascent, and to his disagreement with Parmenidean and Platonic metaphysics. But before leaving this metaphor, he invokes the second answer to his question regarding the goodness of evils:

> Quid est boni viri? Praebere se fato. Grande solacium est cum universo rapi; quicquid est quod nos sic vivere, sic mori iussit, eadem necessitate et deos alligat. Irrevocabilis humana pariter ac divina cursus vehit. Ille ipse omnium conditor et rector scripsit quidem fata, sed sequitur; semper paret, semel iussit.
>
> What is the quality of a good man? To present himself to fate. Great solace it is to be swept along with the universe; whatever it is that commands us so to live, so to die, by the same necessity it also binds the gods. An irrevocable course equally impels things human and divine. The architect and regulator of all things himself has indeed written the fates, but he follows them; he obeys always, he commanded once. (*Prov.* 5.8–9)

God, who is in the business of testing human goodness by the imposition of evils, is subject to the same conditions as humanity. This is an interesting move, argumentatively, and warrants close scrutiny, particularly in regard to the metaphors of the steersperson and the charioteer. It is also, no doubt, a veiled satire of the divine persona made manifest in of all places the emperor Nero. Before attending to Seneca's metaphors, however, let's turn to those of

---

these accounts, focusing on the value of paradox itself in human adaptation. As Arnold (151) points out, "In proportion as the doctrines of any school [of Stoicism] win general recognition, its paradoxes tend to find ready acceptance, and may ultimately become truisms." He goes on to cite Seneca, *Stoica paradoxa, quorum nullum esse falsum nec tam mirabile quam prima facie videtur, adprobabo* (*Ep.* 87.1).

Parmenides and Plato, for accompanying them is the metaphysical tradition of classical antiquity.

The Cybernetics of Being: the Route of Parmenides.

The mares that carry me, as far as impulse might reach,
Were taking me, when they brought and placed me upon
    the much-speaking route
Of the goddess, that carries everywhere unscathed the man
    who knows;
Thereon was I carried, for thereon the much-guided mares
    were carrying me,
Straining to pull the chariot, and maidens were leading the
    way. (Parmenides *frag.* 1.1–5)

So begins a chariot ride that ascends toward a destination that is absolute and invariant: τὸ ἐόν (being). This endpoint of the Parmenidean journey, a philosophical articulation of the quest of Odysseus,[13] provides the ἔσχατον not only of the classical polis as it would be understood by Plato in the *Republic,* but also for the cosmopolis that would be constructed at the end of Aeneas' journey, as Jove puts it, *his ego nec metas rerum nec tempora pono: / imperium sine fine dedi (Aen.* 1.278–279). The journey of the Parmenidean narrator, the Kouros, is impelled to rise by the power of θυμός, "impulse" or "spirit."[14] It also moves along the πολύφημον "much-speaking" or, in more contemporary terms, "polyvocal" route of the δαίμων (ὁδὸν . . . δαίμονος), which is to carry the "one who knows" (εἰδότα φῶτα) through the gates of Night and Day, as the fragment continues, the keys to which are held by "much-avenging Justice" (Δίκη πολύποινος, Parmenides, *frag.* 1.14), to an ultimate destination. The goddess (θεά) tells the youth, next, that he is welcome because it is not "ill fortune" (μοῖρα κακή, line 26) that has sent him on this route, "but right

---

[13]See Mourelatos for a detailed discussion of this theme. All translations of Parmenides are by Gallop.

[14]"Impulse" is Gallop's translation.

and justice" (ἀλλὰ θέμις τε δίκη τε, line 28) to learn "all things" (πάντα), "both the unshaken heart of persuasive truth" (ἀληθείης εὐπειθέος ἀτρεμὲς ἦτορ) and the "beliefs of common men" (βροτῶν δόξας) to learn "how the things that seem are required genuinely to be, permeating all things completely" (lines 29–32). This requirement that all things have a subsistent being is fulfilled in the ultimate vision given the youth by the goddess. After directing him to the path of Persuasion, "that [*it*] *is*, and that [*it*] *cannot not be,*" and away from the other, "that [*it*] *is not* and that [*it*] *needs must not be,*" as unintelligible (*frag.* 2), she says that there is a "single story of the route remaining: that it is" which has the following attributes. It is "whole, single-limbed, steadfast, and complete; / Nor was [it] once, nor will [it] be, since [it] is, now all together" (*frag.* 8.1–5). This not only signals the development of a rationalist ontology, "the first hypothetic-deductive theory of the world," as Popper remarks,[15] but also lays the cornerstone of the classical metaphysics: that ultimate being, whether it be a Platonic Idea or Aristotelian Final Cause, is ethical, good, an exemplar toward which all beings, particularly we humans, aspire. For "it," "what-is" (ἐόν), is held in place by the Justice (Δίκη, 8.14). These fragments have been exhaustively analyzed by philosophers,[16] but what I wish to emphasize is the image of what will become the philosophical intellect ascending via chariot toward a being that is an exemplar of value, particularly of justice. It is this *iustitia* stemming from the Greeks that is, in Cicero's view, the guiding light of all virtues:

> Nam cum sic hominis natura generata sit ut habeat quiddam ingenitum quasi civile atque populare, quod Graeci politikon vocant, quidquid aget quaeque virtus, id a communitate et ea quam exposui caritate ac societate humana non abhorrebit, vicissimque iustitia, ut ipsa fundet se usu in ceteras virtutes, sic illas expetet. (*Fin.* 5.66)

---

[15]Popper 143.
[16]See Gallop's select bibliography.

> For since the nature of humanity has been so begotten that it possesses a certain civic and popular temperament, which the Greeks call "political," whatever each virtue produces, it will not be inconsistent with the community and the human concern and society I have put forth; justice, in turn, as by practice it pours itself into other virtues, so will it require them.

The civic and popular temperament bequeathed by the idealized Greek polis, said by Parmenides to order the cosmos itself, is now considered by Cicero to be inherent in human nature.

But what happens when the Ciceronian confidence in human justice breaks down? Was that idea taken to its limit in Cochrane's classical ideology of power, in which the imperial persona embodied the just order of things? If Justice is the virtue that supposedly suffuses all of the others, giving them practical value in public life, when it collapses, so it goes for the rest of *res publica*. In Seneca's heritage, stemming from Plato through Cicero and Virgil, the polis, the *communitas, urbs,* is the design that guides the artistry of statecraft. It is the mold into which just actions are poured to build the human project. So the collapse of δίκη—not only the reality which may never have existed but also the ideal—spreads like a tremor shaking the *civitas hominis*. That the cracks in the foundations of the classical city would inspire its transcendental reconstruction as Augustine's *civitas dei* is an indicator, as Cochrane argues, that the belief in the perfectability of the city of man was exhausted. But Seneca's thinking is situated in the interim, amidst the increasingly apparent demise of one order and the rise of a new. This is in part what makes him so interesting for European descendants in the era of postmodernity: a time of incredulity and decline for the West itself, the great imperial civilization whose colonies have now all rebelled and whose children write critical tomes on the theme of "postcoloniality." Seneca embodies the ambivalence that comes with the need to construct values when the foundations of all value are cracking. He rides a chariot of the human spirit, at whose reins is not Parmenides or Plato or the emperor Augustus, but, to shift the metaphor as Seneca does, a κυβερνήτης or *gubernator* far less trustworthy. It is no wonder, then, that this Stoic has a taste for irony and, more particularly, paradox, for he clearly sees the collapse of the *iustitia* that has given coherence to classical culture, yet he must also have the wherewithal to *teach* a ruler who is both at the helm of civilization and, as becomes increasingly apparent from AD 59, mad.

Seneca's eclectic style mixes Stoic doctrines with anecdote and personal experience, often enhanced by vivid metaphor, like that of the chariot, and paradox, like god's gift of suffering, typically to make some extended moral "point." All of this is appropriate to the activity of what Derrida, following Lévi-Strauss, has called the *bricoleur*: one who, in the absence of a coherent framework, takes up cultural material, *bricolage*, at hand and works it into a meaningful design.[17] Seneca qualifies well as a philosophical and literary *bricoleur* who adapts the classical tradition to the situation at hand. Creating a style that is as postclassical as Derrida's is postmodern, he has little use for "consistency." For, as the *De Providentia* makes clear, he does not believe that the metanarrative of divine justice that animated and guided classical civilization is fully intact: it has been controverted by what Cochrane calls the classical ideology of power focused in the imperial persona. Yet that does not mean he cannot temper the madness, as he did from AD 55 to 59, and reflect meaningfully on the paradoxes of what might best be described as the divine "double bind" afterwards. The double bind is a paradox generated when an injunction at one level of abstraction is contradicted at another level and an individual is, on yet another level, prevented from commenting openly on the contradiction. Its originator, anthropologist Gregory Bateson, applied the notion to the aetiology of schizophrenia.[18] He argued

---

[17]Derrida (1978).

[18]Bateson 201–78. Recent psychiatric research has established a significant genetic component in schizophrenia. However, interpersonal factors may still play an important role. As Sass (396) argues, at the close

that the parents of a person who exhibits schizophrenic patterns of communication typically proffer just such paradoxical signals to their child. So the father or mother might say, "I love you," verbally, and communicate "I hate you," by his/her facial expression, but prevent the child from commenting on this incoherence by threatening his well-being if he speaks out. The child is thus left to wield the fragments of the familial communication system as best he can in a manner that is dubbed by the rational outside community, especially by psychiatry, as "schizophrenic." When this kind of communication characterizes not only the family but also the society, the result is what Jameson speaks of as a cultural variety of schizophrenia.[19] It seems to have been apparent to Seneca that, with Nero as *pater patriae*, there was increasingly a radical discontinuity between the stated ideals of classical culture, epitomized by the assumption of imperial power, "I am the embodiment of justice," and the actual behavior of the emperor. Furthermore, one's ability to comment on and so temper the contradiction between ideal and action was increasingly attenuated and then cut off altogether. It is little wonder that Seneca would thus go on to challenge the credentials of the *divum pater atque hominum rex, Juppiter*, who grants dominion to humankind, just as Jupiter grants it to Dido (at least temporarily), "Oh queen, to whom Jupiter has given the right to build a new city and to bridle the arrogant tribes with justice" (*o regina, novam cui condere Juppiter urbem / iustitiaque dedit gentis frenare superbas, Aen.* 1.522–523). In terms of the classical ideology of power, Jupiter grants temporary power to Dido but ultimately will hand it over to the Roman emperors. Seneca is, of course, not afflicted with

---

of his "critique of neurobiological reductionism . . . the salient symptoms of some schizophrenic patients could be, in large part, direct manifestations of underlying brain dysfunctions, whereas those of other schizophrenics might be composed largely of psychological reactions of various kinds"; see his appendix, 374–97, for a review of the relevant research.

[19]Jameson 27.

madness, but like his postmodern heirs, he must learn to live in its midst.

Madness at the Reins: Plato. Socrates is also a student of madness, as Plato depicts him in the *Phaedrus*, but it is the possession of the mind by a higher power, so contradictory to human sense as to seem divine. Perhaps it is this inspired madness that provides the alternative vision to the cultural schizophrenia experienced by Seneca, and the following passages may serve as a visionary intertext for the shattered image of numinous omnipotence surmounting Nero's throne. Madness as vision yields to madness as terror; combined they generate a paradox yielding a distinctive Senecan picture of humanity, divinity and history. Under his stylus, at least momentarily, a new course opens for the chariot of the soul. For Seneca uses the oscillating polarities of paradox itself as the dynamic mechanism of human adaptation to adversity.[20]

Socrates has just been taking issue with Lysias's view (*Phdr.* 230E ff.) that love is madness, that the lover is not to be courted, and that one should prefer as a partner one who is not in love to one who is. After first giving Lysias's position its due (238C–241D), Socrates is now compelled by his δαίμων not to depart before he atones for his defamation of the god Eros, just as Stesichorus, who was blinded for slandering Helen, recanted his offense. Indeed, Socrates says he must "purify himself" through a kind of palinode confessing (243A2–B1), "This tale is not true," so that he, like Stesichorus, might recover his sight. The thesis that one possessed by love should be rejected as evil is not only recanted, but the possession by Eros is also considered divine (242E2–3) : "If Eros is, just as he is in fact, a god or a divine thing, in no way would he be evil."[21] This is exactly the thesis with which Seneca must deal when his ruling divinity turns out to be just that—κακός—and so to invest humanity with a dubious gift: one requiring another palinode

---

[20]See Motto and Clark (1993) for the function of paradox in Seneca; also see my discussion of cybernetics, below.
[21]Translations from Plato's *Phaedrus* are Hackforth's, modified.

that turns the classical tradition, at least for the deliberative moment of the *De Providentia*, toward a new heading. For the κυβερνήτης of this voyage is not Plato but, it seems, that master of paradox Heraclitus whose philosophy of "flux," and, more importantly, "contradiction" was subordinated to the stable and coherent Forms of Plato to create the mainstays of classical order. Is the pre-Socratic visionary reawakened here, at an appropriate historical moment, in Seneca's *De Providentia*?[22]

Socrates' palinode invokes a "backward turning" (παλίν-τροπον), as in Heraclitus' enigmatic pronouncement: "They do not comprehend how a thing agrees at variance with itself; it is an attunement turning back on itself, like that of the bow and the lyre" (*frag.* 71, Kahn trans., 65). A more literal rendering of the key phrase, ὅκως διαφερόμενον ἑωυτῷ ὁμολογέει, is "how a thing differing agrees with itself," or perhaps better, "how a thing *by* differing agrees with itself." This last translation is very close to one of the central concepts of the science of cybernetics. As Gregory Bateson explains: "Information, in a technical sense, is that which *excludes* certain alternatives. The machine with a governor does not elect the steady state; it *prevents* itself from staying in any alternative state; and in all such cybernetic systems, corrective action is brought about by *difference*. In the jargon of the engineers, the system is 'error activated.' The difference between some present state and some 'preferred' state activates the

---

[22]The influence of Democritus is regularly noted by Seneca, but the contributions of Heracliteanism and Cynicism are also significant. See Owen 4 n.2, for a view of Heraclitus as asserting a philosophy of contradiction rejected as a false path by Parmenides; in "Zeno and the Mathematicians," Owen points out that "Heraclitus and Empedocles were of almost equal importance for the Stoics: between Heraclides' four books on Heraclitus and Cleanthes' four on the same subject it is unlikely that the Stoic Zeno took no hand in the exegesis" (47 n.6). The two articles appear in Owen (3–26, 45–61, respectively). Atherton (365) argues that the Stoics attempted to move into a clearer statement of the ambiguities of Heraclitus' philosophy than were expressed in the philosopher's enigmatic style. Arnold (35ff.) argues that especially the Heraclitean doctrine of physical flux was fundamental to the development of Stoicism. For the importance of the Cynics, especially as critics, see Arnold 48ff.

corrective response."²³ That is, the cybernetic system corrects itself by differing; it brings itself into agreement with some preferred state by responding to differences from that state. In Heraclitean terms, it agrees with itself by differing. This kind of system works by means of contradiction, or more precisely paradox: by erring it corrects itself. As the Latin root of "error" in *errare* suggests, the word means to "wander off course," as a ship must vary around the mean of its trajectory in an "S" motion in order to stay on course or a tightrope walker must sway back and forth across the mean of the rope's line in order to stay balanced; this is how one steers, functions as a κυβερνήτης or *gubernator*. If the ship, for example, turns left it must be counter-steered right and if right left, oscillating around the plotted course. By differing from the course the steering mechanism agrees with it. Cybernetic systems may be designed to provide guidance for a system in forward motion, like the ship or tightrope walker, but they are often designed, like a thermostat, to maintain a system in steady state.²⁴ Heraclitus prefers the latter kind of model, but similar principles are operative in both designs.

As Bateson points out, the logical behavior of the paradox immanent in a cybernetic system is analogous to that of Epimenides' paradox of the liar (Cic. *Acad.* 2.29.93):²⁵ "When a man says 'I lie,' does he lie or not? If he lies, he speaks the truth; if he speaks the truth, he lies" (*si te mentiri dicis idque verum dicis, mentiris an verum dicis?*). Bateson considers this paradox in regard to the cybernetics of play; the logic of the statement "This is play" is: "These actions in which we now engage do not mean what they would mean if they were serious."²⁶ I take Seneca's paradox of

---

²³Bateson 381

²⁴See Wilden (368–77) on morphostatic versus morphogenic cybernetic models.

²⁵Bateson 184.

²⁶More precisely, if awkwardly, to quote Bateson: "These actions, in which we now engage, do not denote what would be denoted by those actions which these actions denote" (180). The sense of comic irony, with a logic similar to that of play, animating many of Seneca's writings, may be related to his employment of paradox, as well. See Motto and Clark

adversity in *De Providentia* to be both a parody of the classical ideology of power—if Nero says, "I am god," then if he's telling the truth he's lying and if he's lying he's telling the truth—and a celebration of paradox in its own right as an expression of the human condition. So Seneca quotes Demetrius's words, addressed to the immortal gods (*di immortales*) as an appropriate retort to a prevaricating god *(Prov.* 5.5–6):

> Vultis spiritum? quidni? nullam moram faciam, quo minus recipiatis quod dedistis. A volente feretis quicquid petieritis. Quid ergo est? Maluissem offerre quam tradere.
>
> Do you wish my life? Why not? I shall make no protest toward your taking back what you have given. Willingly you shall have whatever you ask of me. What therefore is my complaint? I would have preferred to offer than to relinquish.

This speech could as well have been addressed by Seneca to Nero, or by mankind to a corrupt god. In any case, the passage dramatizes the paradox of power that is both unjust and absolute, an apt characterization of the political order under which Seneca lived. Notice, furthermore, that like Nietzsche Seneca emphasizes volition (*a volente*) as the key to reconciling the paradox, not by avoiding it or subordinating it to a coherent order, but by embracing it *willingly*.

But the oscillating way of paradox is *not* the course that the history of mainstream Western philosophy was to take; its heading was set by Platonic and Parmenidean metaphysics and by a rational pilot, for being is "apprehended by intellect, the soul's only steersperson" (*Phdr.* 247C7–8). This pilot steers in terms of an ethical ontology based on the premise that reality is ultimately intelligible and just and, correlatively, that god is not evil; hence the divine does not err or vary from itself.

(1993b) 181–87, and Bateson 184.

The Christian problem of evil follows from this, for if God is omnipotent and good, how could evil exist? Answer: to *avoid* paradox, one must deny the existence of evil. Augustine would make this point at length in the *Confessions*: what exists is good, he argues, and evil is only a privation of the good (cf. Plato's reference to evils as the "opposites" of goods, in the discussion of *Phaedrus* below); it does not exist in its own right (*Confessions* 7.5.11; 8. 9). From the Good descends a hierarchy of being, whose descending levels are marked by ontological, epistemic and ethical privations, just as in Plato's Divided Line (*Rep.* 6).

Between Plato and Augustine stands Seneca, confronted with a divinity that was not so beneficent, and so he put a touchy question to the tradition: what if god is good *and* evil and so has given the gift of suffering to humankind? The Christian God incarnate, who willingly takes back the sins and sufferings of the world from humankind, is not far beyond this image, but Seneca offers a different answer.[27] His answer is not pessimistic or

---

[27]Motto and Clark (1993a, 76) cite Christian poets as a parallel, including John Donne's verse, "for I, / Except You enthrall me, never shall be free, / Nor ever chaste, except You ravish me," pointing out that in Seneca, as in the Christian tradition, "fallen man must somehow be miraculously ravished by God and God's grace if he is to be saved." Witness Bernini's sculpture, *St. Teresa in Ecstasy*. A similar sense of tortured rapture as he oscillates between the polarities of good and evil invades Augustine (*Confessions* 8).

The articulation of Christian doctrine in the Greek language, as Jaeger (6) has argued, indelibly marked the new religion with Hellenism: "With the Greek language a whole world of concepts, categories of thought, inherited metaphors, and subtle connotations of meaning enters Christian thought." Cochrane (399–400) has a similar view of the influence of the Latin language and Roman, as well as Greek, culture on Christianity. "Augustinianism emerges not as a conglomerate of indiscriminate borrowings, but as a mature philosophy which seeks to do justice to all aspects of experience, in particular to overcome the apparent discrepancy between the demands of order and those of process; i.e., between the so-called Apolline and Dionysiac elements in life. It thus provides the basis for a synthesis which . . . meets the legitimate aspiration of Classicism for a principle of order, while . . . it discloses worlds to which Classicism, from the limitations of its outlook, remains inevitably blind." If I am right, Seneca's postclassicism in the *De Providentia* builds on yet breaks from

faithfully optimistic but, in contemporary terms, cybernetic: the good of human beings is measured exactly by the quantity, and I daresay the quality, of evil dispensed to them; they are tested by the errant course of adversity and their moral worth is measured by their ability to adapt, keep their balance, and stay on course. But this course is new and dynamic, set not by the Platonic metaphysics of the past or the Augustinian faith of the future, but rather by the differential play of *truth and error, good and evil*. This paradox reduces the classical ideology of power—the presumption that absolute good is embodied in the head of state—to absurdity. The *reductio* in turn yields the incredulity toward the metanarrative of Roman imperial destiny that marks a postclassical sensibility.

Plato, like Parmenides and Seneca, follows the course of the soul's ascent in a metaphorical chariot, a creatively transformed vehicle of his own.[28] The "form of the soul" (τῆς ἰδέας αὐτῆς), Socrates says, "should be likened to the joining of powers in a winged team and charioteer." Appropriately for our theme, he goes on to say that the horses and charioteers of the gods are all "good and from the good" (*Phdr.* 246A6–7), but that those of other beings are less fortunate. In the case of human beings, the charioteer drives a pair of horses, the one being "good and beautiful and from these kinds of things," the other being "the opposite and from opposite things" (246B2–3*)*. Hence "charioteersmanship (ἡνιόχησις) is by necessity difficult and troublesome in our case," Socrates goes on to say (246B4–6). Seneca could not have agreed more, particularly when the human chariot becomes elevated to the level of the divine,

---

the narrative of classicism, to offer a vision paradoxically embracing Apollo and Dionysus in a spirit perhaps less Augustinian than Nietzschean. See my discussion of Nietzsche below.

[28]There is significant debate over where Plato got his celestial chariot and, for example, Hackforth (76–77) is skeptical that he appropriated it from Parmenides; I'm assuming that he did. For, whatever the specific qualities of the chariot, I take the *destination* of the ascent to be at least characteristically Parmenidean: that "place beyond the heavens," which is a "colorless and shapeless and touchless being that truly exists" (*Phdr.* 247C 6–7); cf. Parmenides, *frag.* 8.35–41, where spatial location and color are denied to "what is" (τὸ ἐόν).

as in the case of the Emperor, so that the all-too-human joining of good and its opposite cannot be transcended through ascent. Indeed, the *Gubernator* of the cosmos, as of the cosmopolis, is here driving a split team. Overall this is a position more worthy of Nietzsche than of Seneca, at least as he is typically read, but the text of *De Providentia* at least[29] suggests that the Stoic may have been contemplating a postclassical alternative just as Nietzsche asserted a post-Christian one, both prefiguring the cybernetics of the postmodern.

Seneca and the Daemonology of late Classicism. Seneca's chariot surely flies with a split team. Yet it is precisely this split that leads him to the historic moment of this essay, where he becomes the voice of classicism's *daimon* offering a valuable moment of *dubitatio* in the face of the literally incredible Roman imperial idea that *man is a god* or the equally odd Christian converse, that *god is a man*.[30] For his essay challenges the presupposition that it is possible to have good without evil, not in some bland relativism, but rather in a cybernetic ensemble in which they are the irreducible requirements of human aspiration. "What is the mark of a good man? To present himself to fate," Seneca says (*Prov.* 5.8). Like Nietzsche's Zarathustra, the good man chooses a precipitous path (*Prov.* 5.9): "A level course will not be for him; it is proper that he

---

[29]See Motto and Clark (1993a) 65–77, for a discussion of parallel instances of this paradox in Seneca's other writings.

[30]The association of man with god is, as Arnold (248) points out, the assumption of the "kingdom of the soul" in Stoicism, the ruling part of which is the "principate": "The principate, as it is of divine origin, and destined . . . to be reabsorbed in the deity, may rightly be called god: it is a god making its settlement and home in a human body. . . . As however the deity is not conceived in human form, and is not subject to human weaknesses, there comes a point at which . . . we part company with the divine." Seneca was confronted with a political order in which the principate itself had departed company with the divine, while still claiming its authority. His comments on the kingdom of the soul are apt: *rex noster est animus: hoc incolumi cetera manent in officio, parent, obtemperant; cum ille paullum vacillavit, simul dubitant. Ubi vero impotens, cupidus, delicatus est, fit tyrannus; tunc eum excipiunt adfectus impotentes* (*Ep.* 114, 24; cited in Arnold 239).

should go upwards and downwards, be tossed about and guide his craft amidst disorder." This last phrase, *fluctuetur ac navigium in turbido regat*, is particularly interesting in cybernetic terms, for it suggests the relationship between information and entropy in thermodynamics, as in the trajectory set by Maxwell's Demon.

Physicist Clerk Maxwell asked us to imagine

> ... a being whose faculties are so sharpened that he can follow every molecule in his course, and would be able to do what is at present impossible to us. ... Let us suppose that a vessel is divided into two portions A and B by a division in which there is a small hole, and that a being *who can see the individual molecules* opens and closes this hole, so as to allow only the swifter molecules to pass from A to B and only the slower ones to pass from B to A. He will, thus, without expenditure of work raise the temperature of B and lower that of A, in contradiction to the second law of thermodynamics.[31]

This imaginary being Maxwell called a Demon, based on the Greek δαίμων, because by its sorting activity it constrained the degradation of order into chaos, thereby maintaining the dynamic equilibrium of any thermodynamic system. Thus the Demon is the κυβερνήτης of thermodynamics, selecting the system's preferred order, say the room temperature selected by a thermostat. Just as Socrates' internal spirit prevented him from doing what is evil, so Maxwell's Demon prevents the decrease of order toward chaos. Both entities operate, as does Bateson's cybernetic intelligence, by constraining deviation from a preferred state or course. This is the basic cybernetic model of "mind."[32]

---

[31]Maxwell (1871), quoted in Szilard 32.

[32]The cybernetic model of mind defines "ideas" in terms of "differences," say that between zero and one in computation. Bateson explains (459): "I suggest to you, now, that the word 'idea', in its most elementary sense, is synonymous with 'difference.'" Mentation thus becomes describable as the transmission of differences in "circuits," for

Maxwell's analysis led Leo Szilard to publish a critique entitled, significantly, "On the Decrease of Entropy in a Thermodynamic System by the Intervention of Intelligent Beings."[33] Picture Seneca attempting "with his teachings in eloquence and his virtuous civility" to intervene in Nero's increasingly chaotic, even incendiary, handling of the orderly ideals of Roman classicism. Szilard's investigation was "to find the conditions which apparently allow the construction of a perpetual-motion machine . . . if one permits an intelligent being to intervene in a thermodynamic system."[34] He argued that this reduction of entropy and so the apparent establishment of perpetual motion in a mechanical system required "a sort of memory faculty, manifested by a system where measurements occur, that might cause a permanent decrease of entropy and thus a violation of the Second

example, in neural networks or in the communicative pathways used by a particular individual or by a culture. "Consider a man and a tree and an axe," Bateson continues. "We observe that the axe flies through the air and makes certain sorts of gashes in a pre-existing cut in the side of a tree. If now we want to explain this set of phenomena, we shall be concerned with differences in the cut face of the tree, differences in the retina of the man, differences in his central nervous system, differences in his efferent neural messages, differences in the behavior of his muscles, differences in how the axe flies, to the differences which the axe then makes on the face of the tree. Our explanation (for certain purposes) will go round and round that circuit. In principle, if you want to explain anything in human behavior, you are always dealing with total circuits, completed circuits. This is the elementary cybernetic thought" (464–65). Following Jung, Bateson defines the realm of differences as "creatura." All of creatura, he argues, is constituted by the differentiating activity of thermodynamic mentation, say by Maxwell's Demon, ranging from the most elementary living systems like cells, to human bodies and minds, to ecosystems. Cybernetic models run by trial and error, oscillating between the polarities of logical paradox as they simulate purposive activity by "goal-seeking." Thus they utilize the contradictory states that are excluded by coherent logical systems. In light of this kind of model, the use of paradox as a form of intellectual adaptation to adversity, by Seneca or Nietzsche or Foucault, takes on an interesting new significance. See Bateson (279–308) for a detailed explanation of the employment of cybernetics in the psychology, anthropology and evolutionary biology.

[33]See Szilard.
[34]Szilard 301.

Law of Thermodynamics, were it not for the fact that the measurements themselves are necessarily accompanied by a production of entropy." In other words, the production of order by the sorting activity of the Demon is exactly matched by its production of disorder, so a perpetual motion machine is impossible and the Second Law is not contravened. The Demon must use energy and hence increase entropy exactly proportionate to the reduction of entropy it has achieved by sorting the molecules.

This is all a rather technical way of saying that the selective activity of *mind* or, as Socrates' δαίμων suggests, *conscience*, in constraining disorder, its selection of a preferred state as "good" over one that is not-preferred as "evil," is itself necessarily subject to the same thermodynamic processes, the interplay of order and disorder, which it attempts to constrain. Therefore, mind must either transcend nature, as Plato's Forms and Parmenides' Being do, if it is to produce inviolate good, or it must itself be part of nature and subject to its ambivalent processes of order paired with chaos. This is the "split team," a good steed matched with a bad, that the human soul's charioteer must drive in Plato's *Phaedrus*. Seneca, raising the stakes to a higher level, wagers that God too must drive a split team, so that we are faced with an irretrievably split world. And yet, his philosopher, like Nietzsche's *Übermensch*, aspires to the task, choosing the dynamic course as the only one worthy of the human spirit.

Nietzsche, indeed, seems to agree with Seneca on the affinity between man and god, exactly in their sharing the ambivalent conditions wrought by the interplay of order and chaos:

> In man, *creature* and *creator* are united: in man there is matter, fragment, excess, clay, mud, madness, chaos; but in man there is also creator, sculptor, the hardness of the hammer, the divine spectator and the seventh day—do you understand this antithesis?[35]

---

[35]Nietzsche (1989) sec. 225.

But this is not a call to pessimism in Nietzsche any more than it is in Seneca. Quite to the contrary, both choose the precipitous path as a measure of human greatness:

> Not the height but the abyss (*Abhang*) is awesome (*furchtbar*). That abyss where the glance plunges *down* (*hinunter*) and the hand reaches *up* (*hinauf*). There the heart is dizzied before its double will. Alas, friends, can you guess what is my heart's double will?
>
> This is *my* abyss and my danger, that my glance plunges into the height and that my hand would grasp and steady itself—on the Deep!
>
> My will clamps itself (*klammert sich*) to man, with fetters I bind myself to man, because I am swept up toward the overman (*hinaufreisst zum Übermenschen*): for that way my other will wants to go.
>
> And *therefore* I live blind among (*unter*) men as if I did not know them: that my hand does not wholly lose its belief in what is firm.[36]

Here Nietzsche pictures the human "course" cybernetically, as the dynamic interplay between chaos and order, entropy and information, good and evil, that generates the adaptive flexibility of life. Just like a tightrope walker, he balances between the abyss and the peak, between the overman and man. Yet paradoxically, just as in Seneca, we find in Nietzsche's imagery that what is solid is actually the Abyss—"that my hand would grasp and steady itself—on the Deep!" Again like the tightrope walker who treads above the abyss, Nietzsche actually steadies himself on the chasm below, and so keeps his balance. Zarathustra, like the Seneca of *De Providentia, fluctuetur ac navigium in turbido regat*: he chooses to be tossed by the waves and to steer his craft in a storm. This is the

---

[36]*Zarathustra* II, "On Human Prudence," Kaufmann's translation, modified. Thanks to my colleague, Gert Hellerich, University of Bremen, for his insightful help in the translation of Nietzsche.

measure of humanity. Hence, Seneca's "generous youth," resonating with Parmenides' Kouros at the dawn of the Western Odyssey and with Zarathustra at its twilight, chooses the chariot ride into tumultuous skies:

> Iunge datos currus! His quibus deterreri me putas incitor.
> Libet illic stare ubi ipse Sol trepidat.
>
> Harness the chariot given! I am inspired by the very things you think deter me. It pleases me to stand there where the Sun himself quakes.

Upon which Seneca comments,

> Humilis et inertis est tuta sectari; per alta virtus it.
>
> It is the part of the lowly and the idle to choose what is safe; virtue goes for the heights. (*Prov.* 5.9)

It is to these heights that Seneca takes language as he contests his society, in the *De Providentia*, testing the limits of the classical ideology of power through a series of paradoxes inverting traditional values, and then transcending them. Thus later in his essay, as Motto and Clark point out, humanity is expanded to a new level: "And, in the most striking inversion of them all, the seemingly-suffering good man is ultimately perceived to be the superhero who transcends God Himself in his powers."[37] So the deity pronounces, "Bear misfortunes with strength. In this you may excel god" (*ferte fortiter. Hoc est quo deum antecedatis*, *Prov.* 6.6).

The Empire of Signs: Cybernetics Old and New. Picture the activity of Maxwell's Demon as steering the machinery of thermodynamics along the differential course of signification. This is an engine for the production of signs. Hence Bateson says,

---

[37]Motto and Clark (1993a) 81.

regarding the flow of ideas in a cybernetic intelligence, "what we mean by information—the elementary unit of information—is a *difference which makes a difference*, and it is able to make a difference because the neural pathways along which it travels and is continually transformed are themselves provided with energy."[38] Derrida's comments in *De la grammatologie* are, as communication theorist Anthony Wilden argues, "remarkably consonant with Bateson's": "The (pure) trace is *différance* . . . *Différance* is therefore the formation of form. . . . The trace is the *différance* which opens up the world of appearance [*l'apparaître*] and signification."[39] The tracing of signs through the process of differentiation is ultimately the *daemonic* activity that creates communicative structures from cells and organisms to human languages, personae and the cultural formations they produce. The Roman Empire is no exception and, amidst its language of self-formation, a hybrid of the Greek and Latin traditions, Seneca plied his trade as a philosopher in residence for the emperor. In that capacity he found himself confronted with the classical ideology of power made flesh, and explored the implications of that through the strategic use of paradox. In so doing he tried to show that the metanarrative of the classical tradition stemming from Plato had found its *reductio ad absurdum* in the policies of Nero. He also opened the way toward a philosophical tradition as divergent from that of Parmenides and Plato as it was from that of Augustine to come. By applying the paradoxical twists of the Stoic tradition to the biggest target of all—God—he created a new dimension of human creativity that would not be fully realized until Nietzsche's Madman made his famous proclamation, "God is dead."[40] With the shattering of that great Idol comes, in time, the fall of its dominion. Hence Seneca's incredulity at the divinity of imperial power may well be viewed as "postclassical" just as Nietzsche's incredulity at the twin deities of Christendom and modernity—God and

---

[38]Bateson 459.
[39]Derrida (1967) 91–95; cited in and translated by Wilden 399.
[40]Nietzsche (1974) sec.125.

Progress—is now taken to herald the postmodern. It is extraordinary that both Seneca and Nietzsche seemed to intuit that the paradoxical form of their critique would be the very syntax of the cybernetic technology that will characterize the next millennium. In a spirit of skeptical and paradoxical playfulness, both Seneca and Nietzsche fashion powerful spirits but not empires. As Derrida says of his key idea, "Not only is there no kingdom of *différance,* but *différance* instigates the subversion of every kingdom."[41] From the perspective of Barthes or Derrida or Foucault or Bateson, it is the production of *signs* in the Mode of Information[42] that yields the very "software" of imperialism. This gives a new meaning to the old adage embodied by Seneca and reborn in our time: the pen is mightier than the sword. For ideas build and ideas deconstruct every empire of signs.

BIBLIOGRAPHY

Arnold, E. Vernon. 1958. *Roman Stoicism.* New York.

Arrowsmith, William. 1968. "Euripides Theater of Ideas." In *Euripides: a Collection of Critical Essays,* edited by Erich Segal. 13–33. Englewood Cliffs, NJ.

Atherton, Catherine. 1993. *The Stoics on Ambiguity.* Cambridge.

Bateson, Gregory. 1987. *Steps to an Ecology of Mind.* Northvale, NJ.

Barthes, Roland. 1982. *Empire of Signs,* translated by Richard Howard. New York.

Boyle, A. J. 1987. *Tragic Seneca.* New York.

Cochrane, Charles Norris. 1972. *Christianity and Classical Culture.* Oxford.

Derrida, Jacques. 1982. "*Différance.*" *Margins of Philosophy,* translated by Alan Bass. Chicago.

---

[41]Derrida (1982) 22.
[42]See Poster, ch. 1.

—. 1978. "Structure, Sign and Play in the Discourse of the Human Sciences." In *Writing and Difference*, edited and translated by Alan Bass, 278–300. Chicago.
—. 1967. *De la grammatologie*. Paris.
Esslin, Martin. 1973. *The Theatre of the Absurd*. New York.
Foucault, Michel. 1984. "Truth and Power." In *Foucault Reader*, edited by Paul Rabinow, 51–75. New York.
Hadas, Moses. 1968. *The Stoic Philosophy of Seneca*. New York.
Jaeger, Werner. 1965. *Early Christianity and Greek Paideia*. Cambridge, MA.
Jameson, Fredric. 1991. *Postmodernism or the Cultural Logic of Late Capitalism*. Durham.
Kahn, Charles H. 1979. *The Art and Thought of Heraclitus*. Cambridge.
Long, A. A. 1971. *Problems in Stoicism*. London.
Lyotard, Jean François. 1984. *The Postmodern Condition: A Report on Knowledge*. Minneapolis
Motto, Anna Lydia and John R. Clark. 1993a. "Seneca and the Paradox of Adversity." In *Essays on Seneca. Studien zur klassischen Philologie 79*, 65–86. Franfurt am Main.
—. 1993b. "Seneca and Ulysses." In *Essays on Seneca*, 181–88.
—. 1988. *Senecan Tragedy*. Amsterdam.
Mourelatos, Alexander. 1970. *The Route of Parmenides*. New Haven and London.
Nietzsche, Friedrich. 1989. *Beyond Good and Evil*, translated by Walter Kaufmann. New York.
—. 1974. *The Gay Science*, translated by W. Kaufmann. New York.
—. n. d. *Thus Spoke Zarathustra*, translated by W. Kaufmann. New York.
Owen, G. E. L. 1986. *Logic, Science and Dialectic,* edited by Martha Nussbaum. Ithaca.
Parmenides. 1984. *Fragments,* edited and translated by David Gallop. Toronto.
Plato. 1972. *Phaedrus*, translated by R. Hackforth. Cambridge.

Popper, Karl. 1970. "Back to the Presocratics." In *Studies in Presocratic Philosophy*, vol. 1, edited by David J. Furley and R. E. Allen, 130–53. New York.
Poster, Mark. *The Mode of Information*. 1990. Chicago.
Sandbach, F. H. 1975. *The Stoics*. New York.
Sass, Louis A. 1992. *Madness and Modernism*. New York.
Szilard, Leo. 1972. "On the Decrease of Entropy in a Thermodynamic System by the Intervention of Intelligent Beings." Translation of *Über die Entropieverminderung in einem thermodynamischen System bei Eingriffen intelligenter Wesen, Zeitschrift für Physik*, 1929, 53, 840–856. German text 103–19; English translation reprinted from *Behavioural Science*, vol. 9, no. 4 (1964), in *The Collected Works of Leo Szilard: Scientific Papers*. Edited by B. T. Feld and G. W. Szilard. 120–33. Cambridge, MA.
Wilden, Anthony. 1980. *System and Structure: Essays in Communication and Exchange*. London.

Seneca's Second Exile: Seneca and the Romantics

William E. Wycislo
University of Illinois at Chicago

For historians of the period, Seneca's exile on the island of Corsica, an eight year interruption in his chequered political career, is a familiar episode.[1] As he himself reports, Seneca was exiled for violating the *Lex Julia de adulteriis*; he was tried in the Senate, convicted, and would have been executed if the emperor Claudius had not intervened on his behalf.[2] However sketchy the details and uncertain the facts of his banishment, Seneca's political life at Rome was interrupted late in 41 and does not resume again until the Senate recalled him in 49. Despite his enforced absence from the Roman political arena, Seneca's exile, hiatus though it certainly was in his statecraft, is noteworthy for his contribution to many of the Stoic philosophical views with which he has become identified. The *De Ira*, Seneca's lengthy analysis and censure of anger, was almost certainly the product of his exile years and complete by the time of his return to Rome.[3] A psychological study of anger in three books, the work is *sui generis* when compared with Seneca's other

---

[1] I would like to thank Professors A. P. MacGregor and Harry White for their advice and gracious assistance.
[2] Griffin (1974, 9–11) presents a brief account of the circumstances of Seneca's exile; a much more comprehensive chronicle is her 1976 text (59–63). Berger (352 and 553) is a useful source for the Roman law on adultery. *Cons. Polyb.* 13. 2 provides Seneca's own account.
[3] Griffin (1974, 398) reviews the scholarship on the dating of the *De Ira*, concluding that it must have been completed by 52 at the very latest. It is still a subject of contention whether the work was completed prior to Seneca's exile.

dialogues: its examination of a single vice not only summarizes the Stoic philosopher's thoughts on anger, it concisely represents Seneca's doctrine on the passions overall.

The moral philosophy that Seneca promotes in the *De Ira*, an orthodox Stoic rejection of the passions as sources of guidance in human conduct, is strikingly at variance with the dominant ethical philosophies of the past two centuries, a circumstance of intellectual history which accounts for a second—and far more damaging—exile.[4] Although evidence of familiarity with Seneca's teachings and acknowledgments of casual acquaintance with his ideas are commonplace until the eighteenth century, the philosopher's influence has waned since then for a host of reasons, including a depreciation of Stoicism as part of a more general dismissal of ethical systems which originate in antiquity.[5] Stoicism, however, and Seneca by virtue of an eminence which derives from his prolific literary output, have become anathema for modern moralists: as the most radical of ancient philosophies in its insistence on the primacy of reason, the Stoics discourage reliance on the very passions that modern moralists enthusiastically encourage. Seneca counsels distrust of the passions as vigorously as the European Romantics and their modern counterparts recommend them. For this reason, Seneca may well be the most anti-modern of ancient moralists, a claim considerably more injurious to his reputation than the perennial disparagements of his literary or political critics who made their debut, so the sources tell us, early in his career.[6] Seneca's exile from the modern world is

---

[4]MacIntyre (22–75) offers an insightful historical overview of the modern problems of moral discourse and its sources in the Enlightenment.

[5]Ross concludes that there is little evidence for any substantive influence of Seneca's thought (as opposed to Stoicism in general) on subsequent philosophical systems and notes the "diminishing influence of ancient philosophy in general." Gummere traces the acquaintance with Seneca's thought through the centuries, but his conclusion that Seneca's message still lives ignores the consequences of the Enlightenment and Romanticism.

[6]Suet. *Cal.* 53. 2., Quint. 10.1.125–31, and Tac. *Ann.* 13.3 furnish early criticisms of Seneca's style.

nothing less than a loss of moral authority, and "stoic," once a complimentary reference to bravery, virtue, and heroism, has become the unflattering equivalent of repression, insincerity, and insensitivity.

Various factors contribute to the disparagement of Seneca's worth as a moralist, his second, "modern" exile, and the etymological transition whereby "stoic" acquires a largely pejorative sense. A philosopher's fall from popular grace or the disfavor of a school of thought can of itself be attributable to the usual vagaries of intellectual fashion; but the disfavor has been a continuous circumstance for two centuries in Seneca's case, a dismissal best understood as an episode in a larger historical narrative which begins during the eighteenth century.[7] European Romanticism, in its philosophical aspects, signals a radical departure from the most fundamental moral presuppositions to which philosophers had subscribed since antiquity.[8] As advocates of self-expression and subjective judgment on moral issues, the Romantics repudiated the notion that universal or objective standards of conduct exist. The rebel, the outlaw, and the misfit assume heroic stature in the writings of the Romantics by reason of their very deviance and Promethean individuality.[9] The defiant and remorseless fugitive from the agonizing moral tyranny of inherited measures of virtue and vice is to be praised not blamed. In short, the Romantics extol the outcast who revels in moral individualism (however opprobrious) and expel the sage who proclaims a universal criterion of moral excellence.

---

[7]MacIntyre (35–48) examines the historical shift during the Enlightenment; Humphries (195–210) traces the origin of the assault on reason to Hume and others. Berlin (175–237) offers a perceptive analysis of the change in moral sensibilities which the Romantic Age occasions.

[8]Schenk (xiii–xviii) contains Isaiah Berlin's preface on the Romantics. Cf. Berlin 175–237, a much more elaborate overview of the problem.

[9]Schenk (xvii) includes Berlin's fitting description: ". . . the popular image of the artist in his garret, wild-eyed, wild-haired, poor, solitary, mocked-at; but independent, free, spiritually superior to his Philistine tormentors."

The Romantic quest for all that was different, odd, and exceptional, the only exception being virtue as traditionally defined, is as profound a revolution of moral sensibilities as the Newtonian revolution in scientific understanding; at least one feature of the Romantic revolt is an inevitable challenge to any scientific claims of objectivity and an attendant protest against the social conditions resulting from scientific progress.[10] In similar fashion, the moral reversal that Romanticism occasions is a sweeping and radical displacement of the received moral wisdom of antiquity, especially that of Seneca and the Stoics: the ideals of passionate self-expression and subjective judgment must, by an inexorable logic and by psychological necessity, displace any moral philosophy of self-control and distrust of the passions. Moreover, Seneca must not only typify the quintessential modern heretic, but the Stoic *sapiens* must become a symbol of psychological deformity. Had Seneca actually been guilty of the adulterous affair with Julia Livilla which allegedly prompted his exile, the Romantics would have applauded him as approvingly as they had acclaimed Goethe's Werther.[11] The philosopher's current disfavor follows, once again, from a charge of immorality, but for the more grievous offense against an enduring Romantic reverence for the requirements of the heart.

Perhaps no other work of Seneca's furnishes so complete and compelling a refutation of the ethic later venerated by the Romantics as the *De Ira*, if only because his analysis of the

---

[10]Whitehead (75–94) examines the Romantic reaction to the advances of science, particularly among the English Romantics. Gross and Levitt (20–21, 105 and 223) is a much more recent and comprehensive study of a quasi-Romantic opposition to science. Gross and Levitt cite the Romantic origins of the Postmodern hostility to science: "What is really being asserted is that there is a 'modern' science, linked to 'phallocentric' thought and the mechanisms of capitalist-racist-patriarchal domination—in other words, the science that William Blake, in an earlier era, decried as 'single vision and Newton's sleep.' By contrast, there is supposed to be an embryonic 'postmodern' science that points to the overthrow of the old order."

[11]Goethe (vii–xi) provides a brief discussion of the social influences of Goethe's character on German youth.

dynamics of a single passion, anger, is applicable to the passions in general. Addressed to his brother Novatus in response to a request for guidance on how anger might be mitigated, Seneca devotes the better part of the first two books to describing and defining anger, as well as disputing its value and utility, before replying to his brother's request with practical counsel. Although Seneca constructs a convincing case against the exhaustive claims of his imaginary interlocutor that anger is at times justified on moral grounds, his arguments are adorned with considerable rhetorical embellishment. Historical examples abound, as do extended passages detailing the calamitous personal and social consequences of anger usually portrayed as hideous and grotesque. However varied and unconventional in style, several standard Stoic themes recur in the *De Ira* that underscore the intense opposition between Seneca's moral philosophy and the Romantic *Weltanschauung*. To begin with, Seneca's treatment of anger frequently turns to a general denunciation of the passions on moral as well as psychological grounds. Likewise, anger is opposed on aesthetic grounds: vice is vividly described as loathsome and monstrous. Finally, Seneca identifies the notion of liberty with personal control of the passions rather than individual or political liberty.

Early in the *De Ira*, Seneca combines his condemnation of anger with a more comprehensive and characteristically Stoic discussion of the passions, particularly the psychological connection between the passions and reason. His initial observations emphasize the subtle hazards the passions pose.

> Primum facilius est excludere perniciosa quam regere et non admittere quam admissa moderari; nam cum se in possessione posuerunt, potentiora rectore sunt nec recidi se minuive patiuntur. (*De Ira* 1.7.2)[12]

---

[12]The text of the *De Ira* followed throughout is that of Reynolds. The translation is an adaptation of the translation provided by Basore.

> First, it is easier to exclude destructive passions than to rule them, and to deny them admission than, after they have been admitted, to control them; for once they have established themselves in possession, they are stronger than their ruler and do not allow themselves to be restrained or diminished.

Once the passions arise, they intensify and become progressively more difficult to subdue, acquiring a terrible momentum of their own. At this stage, reason easily cedes to the passions:

> Deinde ratio ipsa, cui freni traduntur, tam diu potens est quam diu diducta est ab adfectibus; si miscuit se illis et inquinavit, non potest continere quos summovere potuisset. Commota enim semel et excussa mens sic servit quo inpellitur. (*De Ira* 1.7.3)

> Secondly, reason itself, to whom the reins are handed over, is in control only so long as it has been kept apart from the passions; if it has mingled and polluted itself with them, it cannot restrain emotions which it could have removed earlier. For once the mind has been disturbed and agitated, it serves that by which it is coerced.

Here, as elsewhere in the *De Ira*, Seneca recognizes that without constant vigilance reason proceeds on behalf of the passions and arrives at conclusions which are little more than rationalizations for the passions. Furthermore, he concludes that granting the passions authority deforms the conscience, a condition the Romantics take as the norm.[13] An astute observer of the human spirit well in advance of Rousseau, Seneca likewise knew that *la raison prend à*

---

[13]Benda decries the rationalization of the passions and the accompanying distortion of conscience which has occurred among intellectuals since the Romantic Age.

la longue le pli que le coeur lui donne, but he also understood the consequences of denying reason the possibility of autonomy.[14]

Reason relinquishes its sovereignty only if it proceeds at the behest of the passions and is unable to arrive at conclusions that permit an opposite course of action. According to Seneca, the passions triumph after they have been acknowledged and accorded legitimacy, a condition he describes in some detail.

> ... difficilis ad salutem recursus est, quoniam nihil rationis est ubi semel adfectus inductus est iusque illi aliquod voluntate nostra datum est: faciet de cetero quantum volet, non quantum permiseris. (*De Ira* 1.8.1–2)

> ... the return to mental health is difficult, since, as soon as passion has been introduced and some authority has been voluntarily granted to it, no semblance of reason remains: as for the rest, it will do as it chooses, not what you allow it.

> Neque enim sepositus est animus et extrinsecus speculatur adfectus, ut illos non patiatur ultra quam oportet procedere, sed in adfectum ipse mutatur ideoque non potest utilem illam vim et salutarem proditam iam infirmatamque revocare. (*De Ira* 1.8.2)

> For the mind is not separate and does not examine the passions from outside, so that it does not allow them to advance further than is proper, but it is itself changed into the passion and is, therefore, unable to recover its useful and saving force once it has been surrendered and weakened.

---

[14]Schenk (4) includes the quote from Rousseau's "letter to Franquière (1769)" as an example of the author's allegiance to "the supremacy of the heart."

Passion assumes a forceful independence and authority which nullify the attempts of reason to consider otherwise. According to Seneca, the decision to authorize the claims of the passions is now irreversible: thought, volition and passion itself combine on behalf of the passions and whatever outcome follows from their expression. If the passions regularly overwhelm any competing moral judgments which may result from reason alone, vice—defined as the habitual indulgence of the passions—becomes habitual.

Moreover, Seneca surveys the predictable personal and social turmoil that follow for those who choose to gratify the passions as a matter of course. Anger, the passion in question, easily serves as a representative case. As with other passions, its course most often depends on whatever circumstance will satisfy it, or on the influence of other passions, such as pity or fear.

> Iram saepe misericordia retro egit; habet enim non solidum robur sed vanam tumorem violentisque principiis utitur, non aliter quam qui a terra venti surgunt et fluminibus paludibusque concepti sine pertinacia vehementes sunt: incipit magno impetu, deinde deficit ante tempus fatigata. ... (*De Ira* 1.17.4–5)

> Pity often forces anger back; for it has no enduring strength but an empty swelling, and makes use of violent beginnings; no different than winds that arise from the earth, born of rivers and marshes, they are forceful without tenacity. Anger begins with a great onslaught, then fails prematurely in exhaustion. ...

In an earlier passage, Seneca had remarked that passion often subsides only when another passion arises and supersedes it.

> "Quid ergo? non aliquando in ira quoque et dimittunt incolumes intactosque quos oderunt et a nocendo abstinent?" Facient: quando? Cum adfectus repercussit

adfectum et aut metus aut cupiditas aliquid inpetravit. Non rationis tunc beneficio quievit, sed adfectuum infida et mala pace. (*De Ira* 1.8.7)

"What then? Don't people sometimes while angry also let others off safe and unharmed and refrain from injuring them?" They do; but when? When passion has beaten back passion and either fear or desire has acquired something. Then it has not ceased because of reason, but because of the untrustworthy and evil agreement of the passions.

The transient and fitful nature of the passions that Seneca recounts, unlike the predictable and steadfast character of reason, guarantees moral uncertainty and capricious judgment as well. Dependent as they are on their own energy and inspiration, the passions incline toward excess or deficiency in general; in the case of anger, they produce conduct marked now by an erratic harshness, now by indulgence.[15] Only one fixed and reliable principle emerges from Seneca's account of the passions: everyone judges their own passions appropriate.[16] The belief in the radical moral autonomy of the individual subject, an ethos the Stoics considered the hallmark of vice, was the standard the European Romantics would eventually embrace.

Seneca's conviction that the passions readily subvert reason, an opinion commonly expressed by many moralists from antiquity on, acquired a fatalistic acceptance during the Enlightenment; but for the Romantics the celebration of the passions, no longer an

---

[15]Cf. *De Ira* 1.17.5–7. Here Seneca presents the portrait of the judge who dispenses judgment based on the erratic intensity of momentary passion. Cf. *Apocolocyntosis* 10 and 12, where Seneca describes the arbitrary rulings of Claudius. The part played by excess or deficiency is, of course, central to Aristotle's treatment of virtue and vice in the *Nicomachean Ethics*.

[16]Greenwald supports the view of Seneca that each judges their own passion appropriate and that everyone has the mind of a monarch, but from the evidence of modern psychological research.

occasion for caution, becomes a *cause célèbre*.[17] Blake, Shelley and Wordsworth in England, Fichte, Schelling and Schopenhauer in Germany, Delacroix, Doré and Géricault in France—the roster of Romantic poets, philosophers and artists—proclaim a new artistic and moral creed. Reason, Plato's charioteer in the *Phaedrus* (246a–248e), must follow where the passions lead, its traditional authority and independence a fiction and a denial of the inherent honesty of the passions. Even forthright admission of the self-deception inevitable in moral reasoning, the opinion of many Enlightenment skeptics, fails to satisfy the Romantic expectation of an unqualified allegiance to the heart.[18] More importantly, the Romantic preference for the passions is not only a disavowal of the Stoic moral ideal, but an actual reversal of that ideal: the Stoic virtues become undesirable and the vices appealing; Stoic evil becomes the Romantic good.

However exacting and extreme a standard of moral excellence, Stoic virtue demanded as assiduous an effort as Aristotelian magnanimity or the ethical ideals of other philosophical systems; similarly, some philosophers still hold that reason and restraint are necessary ingredients for moral progress, and Stoicism is no anomaly in this respect. So also, the considerable ease with which the passions corrupt reason, by no means an original insight of the Stoics, is a literary commonplace which dates to Homer. An exalted measure of moral excellence and the pursuit of it assume an unremitting struggle between the mind and the heart; it also assumes a repeated failure of the will as a typical though regrettable feature of the human condition until the Romantics. The hypocrisy, which LaRochefoucauld calls the homage vice pays to virtue, is

[17]Humphries (194–216) furnishes the background for the influence of Enlightenment thought on the emergence of Romanticism. The importance of Hume's emphasis on the passions as primary determinants in moral activity cannot be underestimated, and provides the foundation for the more radical moral philosophies of the German idealists.

[18]Schenk (3–45) extensively surveys the Romantic reaction to the Enlightenment.

only conceivable on the condition that virtue remains an ideal.[19] Blake, whose poetry and paradoxes embody the Romantic spirit, denounces moral hypocrisies which only a civilization with strict models of virtue permits.[20] A golden age or a paradise populated by Stoic sages offer unlikely escapes from the moral dilemmas La Rochefoucauld and Blake pose, but the flight from virtue itself is the likelier outcome in Seneca's system. The Romantics could not embrace the truthfulness of personal expression as a liberation from hypocrisies of the past without dismissing the conventional wisdom that the heart is an unreliable counselor. The passions had been partly attractive in Seneca's view precisely because they were effortless; they were equally attractive, however, because they produce the immediacy of pleasure which also belongs to the arts.

Seneca had to address this attractiveness if he was to successfully counter its common allure. Nonetheless, a common criticism of the *De Ira* regularly rests on a failure to appreciate that Seneca's objective (the alleviation of anger) requires a synthesis of artistry and argument, a strategy which allows the philosopher to enlist the devices and assume the role of the poet.[21] Recognizing the persuasive power of poetic technique to effect moral reform, Seneca repeatedly deviates from the stylized debate with his interlocutor in order to present repulsive descriptions of the face, character and consequences of anger and cruelty. It is with a vivid representation of the physical signs of anger in the opening chapter of the *De Ira* that Seneca introduces anger as aesthetically repulsive, and (hence) to be avoided in the moral realm.

---

[19] LaRochefoucauld, *Maxims* 218.

[20] Blake (in Woodring, 558–59) contains some of his most acerbic remarks on the paradoxes inherent in a society possessing standards of virtue: e.g., "Prisons are built with stones of Law, Brothels with bricks of Religion."

[21] Wright (39) makes the criticism that rhetorical effect interferes with the flow of the writing and that unity of structure suffers as a consequence.

Ut scias autem non esse sanos quos ira possedit, ipsum illorum habitum intuere; nam ut furentium certa indicia sunt audax et minax vultus, tristis frons, torva facies, citatus gradus, inquietae manus, color versus, crebra et vehementius acta suspira, ita irascentium eadem signa sunt: flagrant ac micant oculi, multus ore toto rubor exaestuante ab imis praecordiis sanguine, labra quatiuntur, dentes comprimuntur, horrent ac surriguntur capilli, spiritus coactus ac stridens, articulorum se ipsos torquentium sonus, gemitus mugitusque et parum explanatis vocibus sermo praeruptus et conplosae saepius manus et pulsata humus pedibus et totum concitatum corpus magnasque irae minas agens, foeda visu et horrenda facies depravantium se atque intumescentium—nescias utrum magis detestabile vitium sit an deforme. (*De Ira* 1.1.3–5)

To know that those whom anger possesses are not sane, notice how they look. For as the signs of madness are evident—a bold and threatening expression, a sullen look, a twisted face, a quickened pace, trembling hands, a changed complexion, fast and heavy breathing—so also are the marks of those who are angry: the eyes flash and blaze, the entire face turns red with blood surging from the depths of the heart, the lips tremble, the teeth grind, the hair bristles and stands on end, the breathing is forced and strident; there is noise of the limbs twisting themselves, the groaning and bellowing and unintelligible outbursts and frequent pounding of the hands and stamping the feet on the ground and a completely agitated body making raging threats, ugly to behold—the hideous appearance of those twisted and swollen with anger—you cannot know whether this vice is more reprehensible or disgusting.

After so exhaustive and forceful an account of the physiological manifestations of anger, Seneca concludes his portrait with an adjective that appropriately summarizes the passage—*deforme*: above all, anger is ugly or misshapen. The immediate connection Seneca sustains between vice and ugliness is noteworthy for various reasons. Occurring in the initial chapter of the dialogue, the passage establishes the tone of the *De Ira* and suggests that Seneca's approach will not only be philosophical, but literary. Similarly, the literary features of the *De Ira* underscore the importance of Seneca's belief in the ethical function of literature as a valuable complement to the rigors of systematic argument. Furthermore, and most significantly, Seneca's artistic aim implicitly affirms the role of pleasure as a unifying feature of morality and the arts. Seneca knew that the vices are pleasurable; he also knew that diminishing their aesthetic appeal might contribute toward their elimination in practice. As a consequence, and unsurprisingly, Seneca's literary digressions consistently emphasize the aesthetics of anger, a technique which is necessary to complement a line of reasoning that relies on definitions of anger and cruelty as sources of pleasure.

The definition of anger that Seneca proposes highlights its desirability, the chief attribute that distinguishes his definition from that of his *adversarius*.

> "Ut scias," inquit, "non esse iram poenae cupiditatem, infirmissimi saepe potentissimis irascuntur nec poenam concupiscunt quam non sperant." Primum diximus cupiditatem esse poenae exigendae, non facultatem; concupiscunt autem homines et quae non possunt. (*De Ira* 1.3.2)

> "So you may know," he said, "that anger is not the desire for punishment, the weakest are often angry with the most powerful and do not desire punishment which they have no hope of realizing." In the first place, I said it is the desire for exacting punishment, not the ability; moreover, men desire even what they are incapable of.

Rather than choose a more neutral term, Seneca retains *cupiditas*, the term that his *adversarius* had assigned to anger. Although allegedly borrowed from Posidonius' definition of anger, *cupiditas* nonetheless conveys a sense of longing or desire associated with pleasure, as does *voluptas*, another term Seneca uses in connection with anger.[22]

> Poena laedit: bono ergo poena non convenit, ob hoc nec ira, quia poena irae convenit. Si vir bonus poena non gaudet, non gaudebit ne eo quidem adfectu cui poena voluptati est. (*De Ira* 1.6.5)

> Punishment injures; punishment is therefore neither consistent with the good, nor, for this reason, is anger, because punishment is consistent with anger. If the good man does not rejoice in punishment, he will not rejoice in that passion for which punishment is pleasurable.

Sensual delight, *voluptas*, an expression that can equally well characterize an aesthetic response, applies also to a defective moral sensibility in Seneca's judgment. If anger is the urge to demand punishment, the satisfaction which accompanies its expression and corresponds to the aesthetic response is the pleasure of revenge.

Although Seneca does not include the words *ultio* or *ulciscor* in his working definition of anger, they do occur with regularity as virtual synonyms for its expression in practice. Whereas revenge involves an element of satisfaction, pleasure is an accidental component; cruelty, however, is far more vicious, and Seneca notes that pleasure is its salient feature.

> Origo huius mali ab ira est, quae ubi frequenti exercitatione ex satietate in oblivionem clementiae venit et omne foedus humanum eiecit animo, novissime in crudelitatem transit.

---

[22]Griffin (1974, 168) briefly mentions the possible influence of Posidonius on Seneca, as does Basore (112).

> Rident itaque gaudentque et voluptate multa perfruuntur plurimumque ab iratorum vultu absunt, per otium saevi. (*De Ira* 2.5.3)

> The origin of this evil is from anger, and it happens with frequent practice and satisfaction in forgetfulness of mercy and has discarded every human bond from the mind until, finally, it becomes cruelty. And so they laugh and rejoice and revel with great pleasure and, because of their leisurely savagery, are very different in appearance from those who are angry.

Cruelty verging on sadism was the natural and inevitable consequence of habitual anger for Seneca, the transition from the latter to the former requiring only repeated expression and satisfaction. The aesthetic appeal of cruelty becomes an end in itself, as the subsequent anecdote plainly reveals.

> Hannibalem aiunt dixisse, cum fossam sanguine humano plenam vidisset, "o formosum spectaculum!" Quanto pulchrius illi visum esset, si flumen aliquod lacumque conplesset! Quid mirum si hoc maxime spectaculo caperis, innatus sanguini et ab infante caedibus admotus? (*De Ira* 2.5.4)

> They say that Hannibal said "what a magnificent sight!" after he saw a trench brimming with human blood. How much more beautiful it would have seemed to him if it had filled some river or lake! Why is it amazing if you take the greatest enjoyment from such a sight, born to bloodshed and moved by slaughter from infancy?

Keats could call a thing of beauty a joy forever, thus expressing the optimistic though naive Romantic faith in the innocent aesthetic that Seneca realized was a dangerous doctrine: one may cultivate and acquire an appreciation of beauty, after all, that includes the beauty of bloodshed.[23] The brief anecdote Seneca recalls is the portrait of an artist; Hannibal is no less the connoisseur than Keats.[24]

The inseparable connection between morality and art means that every artist is also a moralist whose power to please requires a choice of subjects: either portray virtue as noble and vice as reprehensible—the formula recommended by Aristotle, Horace and Longinus—or, *mutatis mutandis*, portray virtue as invariably defective and vice as spontaneous, sincere and acceptable, the model promoted by the Romantics.[25] Shelley's announcement that "poets are the unacknowledged legislators of the world" is no idle claim; it is a candid admission of the poet's function as a moralist, a role Shelley himself performs according to a new morality and a novel aesthetic: by absolving the sincere and well-intentioned Prometheus he also exonerates the god of another name—Lucifer, the carrier of fire.[26] Hume's observation that beauty is in the eye of the beholder explains the charm of Shelley's Prometheus and accounts for the aesthetic fancy of Seneca's Hannibal as well—the one a hero of the poet's imagination, the other a villain of the philosopher's reality.[27] In either case, Hume's aesthetic of

---

[23]*Endymion* 1.1.

[24]The anecdote demonstrates that art and morality are inextricably related, a notion denied by those who subscribe to the doctrine known as aestheticism. *The Princeton Encyclopedia of Poetry and Poetics* attributes the origin of the phrase *l'art pour l'art* to Cousin in his 1818 lectures on *Le Vrai, le Beau, et le Bien*. It is employed in connection with the widely held Romantic belief "that art should not be judged by moral, political, or other nonaesthetic standards."

[25]*Philosophies of Art and Beauty* (3–138) contains generous selections on aesthetics from the works of Plato and Aristotle. The moral function of art is assumed by both. *The Princeton Encyclopedia of Poetry and Poetics* (7) mentions Gautier and Baudelaire as early proponents of the modern view that utility is not germane to art (contra Hor. *Ars P.* 343).

[26]Woodring (488–513) contains Shelley's remark and general aesthetic views in "A Defense of Poetry." Abrams (299–307) discusses Shelley's aims in characterizing Prometheus in *Prometheus Unbound*.

[27]Hume 299–300, 364, 547n., 576, 584, 590 and 608, are the relevant passages on Hume's philosophy of art.

relativity, a standard the Romantics would later embellish and refine, is as much an exaltation of pleasure as it is a definition of the beautiful; even the basest forms of human conduct produce pleasures of great intensity.

Although the Romantics grant autonomy to the arts, insisting that ethical and artistic matters are independent concerns, the pleasures that accompany the expression of the passions and the enjoyment of the arts imply an interdependence. The contention that beauty is solely a matter of personal taste not coincidentally resembles the argument that the expression of the passions is the supreme indication of moral probity: the stated ideals of truthfulness and sincerity in ethics and love of beauty in the arts conceal the ideals of personal pleasure, satisfaction, and fulfillment. But the alleged autonomy of art as a separate realm collapses because the Romantics reduce both artistic and moral issues to questions of taste, which is little more than a euphemism for what Wordsworth calls "the grand elementary principle of pleasure."[28] The Keatsian ideals of beauty as truth and truth as beauty disguise a sovereignty of pleasure that allows the coarsest forms of expression and behavior both.[29] By Stoic standards the Romantics would rank as voluptuaries those who pander to bad morals and poor taste. Seneca may portray Hannibal and Atreus as models to avoid; Byron's Manfred and Cain, however, are models to emulate, as is Goethe's Werther, whose fictional suicide for the cause of unrequited Romantic love inspired countless imitators among the German youth of the time.[30]

It was inevitable that such complimentary portrayals of misfits and moral iconoclasts in Romantic literature and art would have implications of a social and political nature that extend beyond the realm of individual taste. As Seneca and his philosophical

---

[28]Woodring (59) includes Wordsworth's comment in his "Preface to the Lyrical Ballads." Trilling (73–106) discusses the quote as part of a general analysis of the role of pleasure in literature during the nineteenth century.
[29]Keats, "Ode on a Grecian Urn" 49.
[30]Goethe vii–xi.

predecessors understood, art and morals affect fashion in politics as well. Some of Seneca's most memorable passages in the *De Ira* are detailed catalogues of the ruinous effects of collective passion, the first of which appears immediately after his description of the physiognomy of anger.

> Videbis caedes ac venena et reorum mutuas sordes et urbium clades et totarum exitia gentium et principum sub civili hasta capita venalia et subiectas tectis faces nec intra moenia coercitos ignes sed ingentia spatia regionum hostili flamma relucentia. Aspice nobilissimarum civitatum fundamenta vix notabilia: has ira deiecit. Aspice solitudines per multa milia sine habitatore desertas: has ira exhausit. (*De Ira* 1.2.1–2)

> You will see bloodshed and poisoning and base accusations of defendants, the slaughter of cities and genocide and the heads of leaders up for auction, torched houses and cities in flames and enormous spaces of territory blazing with hostile fire. Behold the scarcely traceable foundations of the most eminent cities: anger destroyed them. Behold wastelands empty for thousands of miles: anger emptied them.

If, as Wordsworth maintains, "all good poetry is the spontaneous overflow of powerful feelings," the destruction Seneca describes is the political poetry of savagery and slaughter, the social expression of an agitated fury that most easily finds its artistic outlet in music, the supreme Romantic art form.[31] The turbulence and frenzy of the passions to be heard in the driving phrases of Beethoven's *avante-garde* symphonies reproduce the spirit of revolution in which violence is beautiful and beauty violent.

---

[31] Woodring 52. Schenk (201–32) comments on the importance of music as a form of quasi-religious redemption for the Romantics.

From the *Sturm und Drang* symphonies of Haydn to the overtures and preludes of Wagner's operas, the music of the age simulates the ecstasies and agonies of passions which obtained political expression in the ideal of revolution, the *res novae* so alien to the Roman spirit and the Stoic temper.[32] The Romantics repeatedly characterize themselves as revolutionaries and proclaim their moral, aesthetic and political attitudes as a revolt against reason, conventional morality, and classical standards of beauty, but above all, a revolt against the real or imputed despotism of the past.

> Bliss was it in that dawn to be alive,
> But to be young was very heaven! O times,
> In which the meagre, stale, forbidding ways
> Of custom, law, and statute, took at once
> The attraction of a country in romance!.[33]

Thus does Wordsworth rhapsodize a rebellion of the heart that transmutes morality and the arts into matters of taste and imparts an instinctive authority to the passions, an authority unable to admit any restraint and a defiance of all authority but its own. The revolt that begins as a departure from tradition and glamorizes the French Revolution must end in a predictable disillusionment: ". . . the

---

[32]Schenk (8–14) surveys, for example, the Romantic fervor and subsequent disillusion regarding the French Revolution. Camus (47–54) discusses "the rebel" as a Romantic hero. Although Camus examines rebellion in a larger historical context, it is clear from his analysis that the idea of revolution *per se* has acquired greater acceptance since the Romantics. Benda arrives at similar conclusions. Cf. Berlin 207–37. Arendt provides a detailed and thorough analysis and contrast of revolutionary movements since the French and American revolutions. She concludes that revolution is a distinctively modern political phenomenon.

[33]Wordsworth, *The Prelude* 11.108–112. Wordsworth's early enthusiasm seems almost a deliberate contrast with Cicero's "*O tempora! O mores!*" in the *First Catalinarian*, an audacious affirmation of the *res novae* Cicero deplores.

Revolution is like Saturn," muses Georg Büchner's Danton, "it devours its own children."[34]

The "guillotine Romanticism" of which Camille speaks in *Danton's Death* aptly identifies revolution as a form of aesthetic as well as political chic, an opportunity for the riotous mob to participate in the pleasures of cruelty and share the tyranny and aesthetic sensibility of an elitist like Seneca's Hannibal.[35] Disorderly, primitive, and savage, revolution defines the Romantic spirit and represents the refusal to honor all moral, artistic, and political values but its own. This grand cause to which the Romantics pay homage merely dispenses the tyrant's prerogative to the individual; *liberté*, an ideal as ostensibly noble and innocent as the Romantic ideals of truth and beauty, disguises the more ignoble aim of pleasure for the sake of pleasure that Seneca links with moral depravity. In the final decades of the nineteenth century Nietzsche was to observe yet another fatal flaw in the Romantic preoccupation with revolutionary agendas: those who most vehemently subscribe to the view that morality and the arts are matters of taste cannot accept a relativism less than absolute: respect for individuality and the expression of the passions are little more than pretexts for the will to power. Seneca had regarded such a drive as the servitude, in fact, which enslaves those who must control others as a substitute for control of their own passions.[36]

The reign of terror to which Seneca takes objection does not issue from moral conviction or cultural tradition, much less from oppressive political regimes. Political metaphors abound in Seneca's analysis of the passions, but he applies the vocabulary of tyranny to the passions.

---

[34]Büchner 19.
[35]*Ibid.*, 4.
[36]Nietzsche (1966, 61) comments that the demands of the revolutionary are "unconditional," a desire for tyranny on the part of the revolutionary, and the pose of an aristocratic morality. Lasch (25–29) describes the elitist nature of the current revolt against convention, which Nietzsche had observed in his own day.

> Non potest hic animus fidele otium capere, quatiatur necesse est fluctueturque, qui malis suis tutus est, qui fortis esse nisi irascitur non potest, industrius nisi cupit, quietus nisi timet: in tyrannide illi vivendum est in alicuius adfectus venienti servitutem. (*De Ira* 1.10.2)

> The mind cannot obtain reliable comfort here; one must waver and vacillate if they rely on their weaknesses, if they cannot be brave without being angry, industrious without being greedy, and calm without being fearful: one who becomes the slave of any passion must live in tyranny.

Passion is not only the tyrant of the tyrant, but also of the Romantic rebel who assigns blame for his own dissatisfactions on a host of external forces, from culture and convention to class disparity. The Romantic esteem of the passions, one of the many Romantic principles at variance with the Classical tradition, encourages the very tyranny of which Seneca speaks, a despotism which Burke noticed at the heart of the French revolution and which Nietzsche would later term *ressentiment*, recognizing that a clash of ideas all too often cloaks a conflict of wills: hatred is the mask of envy, and those who resent authority wish to be dictators themselves.[37] Seneca tersely summarizes the problem and places revolutions and revolutionaries in their psychological context.

> Inviolatos nos etiam inimicis iudicamus esse debere; regis quisque intra se animum habet, ut licentiam sibi dari velit, in se nolit. (*De Ira* 2.31.3)

> We decide that we should be unharmed even by our enemies; each one is a king in his own mind, so that he

---

[37]Woodring (7–11) contains some of Burke's observations. Nietzsche (1969, 121–25) describes *ressentiment* as the envy which underlies the political hatred of the revolutionary.

wants the benefit of a freedom he is unwilling to reciprocate.

Perhaps no other word so definitively exposes the anarchy of the tyrant or the revolutionary as *licentia*, which Seneca uses to present the paradox of a freedom which is necessarily as coercive as it is permissive.[38] Neither the *libertas* of the Roman Republic nor the *libertas* of the Stoic *sapiens*, the *licentia* which Seneca describes more closely approximates the *liberté* of revolution and the Romantics, a freedom whose very expression must also subjugate. The liberty the Romantics extol camouflages a willfulness that results in the social conflict Seneca depicts in the *De Ira*, a contumacy strikingly similar to the will to power that Nietzsche detects in personal and social discord.[39] The Romantic ideal, freedom of expression, is an emperor's reality and a revolutionary's fantasy; its opposite, the *libertas* of the Stoics, relied on the Classical notion that virtue requires an arduous and vigilant personal struggle to depose passion, the would-be tyrant within us all. Seneca's second exile implies the lost influence and authority of Stoic *libertas* as a moral ideal and a cultural commonplace. Passion becomes virtuous for the moral outlaw, the rebellious artist and the revolutionary alike, but Prometheus, whom Camus calls "the model of contemporary man," Shelley's Prometheus, the bringer of fire, remains Milton's Lucifer as well, defiantly claiming evil as his good.[40]

---

[38] Arendt (115–40) notes the licentiousness inherent in the revolutionary rhetoric on freedom, particularly modern revolutionary discourse based on the French model.
[39] Nietzsche (1967).
[40] Camus (1968) 138.

BIBLIOGRAPHY

Abrams, M. H. 1971. *Natural Supernaturalism: Tradition and Revolution in Romantic Literature*. New York.

Arendt, Hannah. 1963. *On Revolution*. London and New York.

Benda, Julien. 1928. *The Treason of the Clerks*, translated by Richard Aldington. New York and London.

Berger, Adolf. 1953. *Encyclopedic Dictionary of Roman Law*. Philadelphia.

Berlin, Isaiah. 1990. *The Crooked Timber of Humanity*, edited by Henry Hardy. New York.

Büchner, Georg. 1963. *Complete Plays and Prose*, translated by Carl Richard Mueller. New York.

Camus, Albert. 1968. *Lyrical and Critical Essays*, translated by Ellen Conroy Kennedy and edited by Philip Thody. New York.

—. 1956. *The Rebel*, translated by Anthony Bower with a foreword by Sir Herbert Read. New York.

Goethe, Johann Wolfgang von. 1962. *The Sorrows of Young Werther and Selected Writings*, translated by Catherine Hutter with a foreword by Hermann J. Weigand. New York and Scarborough, Ontario.

Greenwald, Anthony G. 1980. "The Totalitarian Ego: Fabrication and Revision of Personal History." *American Psychologist* 35: 603–618.

Griffin, Miriam T. 1974. "*Imago vitae suae.*" In *Seneca*, edited by C. D. N. Costa, 9–11. London.

—. 1976. *Seneca: A Philosopher in Politics*. Oxford.

Gross, Paul R. and Norman Levitt. 1994. *Higher Superstition: The Academic Left and its Quarrels with Science*. Baltimore and London.

Gummere, R. M. 1922. *Seneca the Philosopher and his Modern Message*. Boston.

Hume, David. 1897. *A Treatise of Human Nature*, edited by L. A. Selby-Bigge. Oxford; reprint of the original edition in three volumes.

Humphries, A. R. 1963. *The Augustan World: Society, Thought, and Letters in Eighteenth-Century England*. New York and Evanston, Illinois.

Lasch, Christopher. 1995. *The Revolt of the Elites and the Betrayal of Democracy*. New York and London.

MacIntyre, Alasdair. 1981. *After Virtue*. Notre Dame, Indiana.

Nietzsche, Friedrich. 1969. *On the Genealogy of Morals* and *Ecce Homo*, translated by Walter Kaufmann and R. J. Hollingdale and edited with a commentary by Walter Kaufmann. New York.

—. 1967. *The Will to Power*, translated by Walter Kaufmann and R. J. Hollingdale and edited with a commentary by Walter Kaufmann. New York.

—. 1966. *Beyond Good and Evil*, translated with a commentary by Walter Kaufmann. New York.

Philosophies of Art and Beauty: Selected Readings in Aesthetics from Plato to Heidegger, edited by Albert Hofstadter and Richard Kuhns. 1964. New York.

Princeton Encyclopedia of Poetry and Poetics. 1972. Edited by Alex Preminger and T. V. F. Brogan. Princeton. S.v. "Aestheticism," by F. P. W. McDowell.

Reynolds, L. D. 1977. *L. Annaei Senecae: Dialogorum Libri Duodecim*. Oxford.

Ross, G. M. 1974. "Seneca's Philosophical Influence." In *Seneca*, edited by C. D. N. Costa, 116–65. London.

Schenk, H. G. 1966. *The Mind of the European Romantics*. New York.

Seneca: Moral Essays I. 1985. Edited and translated by John W. Basore. Cambridge, Massachusetts and London.

Trilling, Lionel. 1963. "The Fate of Pleasure: Wordsworth to Dostoevsky." In *Romanticism Reconsidered*, edited with a foreword by Northrup Frye, 73–106. New York and London.

Whitehead, A. N. 1925. *Science and the Modern World*. New York.

Woodring, Carl R. 1961. *Prose of the Romantic Period*. Boston.

Wright, J. R. G. 1974. "Form and Content in the Moral Essays." In *Seneca*, edited by C. D. N. Costa, 39–69. London.